Strategic Comn
in a Global Cris

This edited volume makes a unique and timely contribution by exploring in depth the topic of strategic communication and COVID-19 from a global perspective. It is widely agreed that effective and timely communication and leadership are crucial to the successful management of any pandemic. With the ongoing and possibly long-lasting impact COVID-19 has had on many aspects of communication and multiple sectors of our societies, it is critical to explore the role of strategic communication in change management during the COVID-19 pandemic and beyond. This book addresses such a need and is thoroughly grounded in rich empirical evidence gained through a global study of COVID-19 communication experiences and strategies.

In the second half of 2020, a transnational team of senior researchers conducted research to investigate COVID-19 communications (COM-COVID-19) in different countries, representing Europe, Africa, Latin America, North America, South America, and Asia. The results presented in this book provide a compelling, current picture of the COVID-19 pandemic and strategic communication globally. Chapters individually explore the national and regional experiences and discuss relevant successes and failures of pandemic communication and specific learning from the 2020–2021 crises. By emphasising the discussion on key communication channels, sources of information, facts and concerns as related to the COVID-19 pandemic, the editors call for actions to develop effective strategies within unique national contexts, which can shed light on global expectations on necessary public health responses and communication.

This book is written for scholars, educators and professionals in communication, public relations, strategic communication and corporate communication. It is also appropriate to use this book as a supplementary text for advanced undergraduate and graduate courses on relevant courses.

Ralph Tench is professor of Communication and director of research for Leeds Business School, Leeds Beckett University in the UK, and past president (2017–2020) of the European Public Relations Research and Education Association (EUPRERA). Professor Tench's research involves national and international funded projects from the private sector, the EU, public health and research councils.

Juan Meng, PhD, is the Head of the Department of Advertising and Public Relations at the University of Georgia, USA. She serves on the national advisory board of the Plank Center for Leadership in Public Relations and the Institute for Public Relations (IPR) ELEVATE. Her research specialisation includes public relations leadership, leadership development, women and leadership in PR, and global communication.

Ángeles Moreno, outgoing President of EUPRERA is a scholar at the high-performance Group of Advanced Studies on Communication (GEAC) at the University Rey Juan Carlos, with extensive experience and leadership on transnational and awarded research projects. She is included in a prominent position in the national ranking of researchers with about 27 books, 16 chapters and more than 55 academic journal papers.

Routledge New Directions in PR & Communication Research

Edited by Kevin Moloney

Current academic thinking about public relations (PR) and related communication is a lively, expanding marketplace of ideas and many scholars believe that it's time for its radical approach to be deepened. Routledge New Directions in PR & Communication Research is the forum of choice for this new thinking. Its key strength is its remit, publishing critical and challenging responses to continuities and fractures in contemporary PR thinking and practice, tracking its spread into new geographies and political economies. It questions its contested role in market-orientated, capitalist, liberal democracies around the world, and examines its invasion of all media spaces, old, new, and as yet unenvisaged.

The New Directions series has already published and commissioned diverse original work on topics such as:

- PR's influence on Israeli and Palestinian nation-building
- PR's origins in the history of ideas
- a Jungian approach to PR ethics and professionalism
- global perspectives on PR professional practice
- PR as an everyday language for everyone
- PR as emotional labor
- PR as communication in conflicted societies, and
- PR's relationships to cooperation, justice, and paradox.

We actively invite new contributions and offer academics a welcoming place for the publication of their analyses of a universal, persuasive mindset that lives comfortably in old and new media around the world.

Strategic Communication in a Global Crisis
National and International Responses to the COVID-19 Pandemic
Edited by Ralph Tench, Juan Meng and Ángeles Moreno

For more information about this series, please visit: www.routledge.com/Routledge-New-Directions-in-PR – Communication-Research/book-series/RNDPRCR

Strategic Communication in a Global Crisis

National and International Responses to the COVID-19 Pandemic

Edited by Ralph Tench, Juan Meng and Ángeles Moreno

Routledge
Taylor & Francis Group
LONDON AND NEW YORK

First published 2023
by Routledge
4 Park Square, Milton Park, Abingdon, Oxon OX14 4RN

and by Routledge
605 Third Avenue, New York, NY 10158

Routledge is an imprint of the Taylor & Francis Group, an informa business

British Library Cataloguing-in-Publication Data
A catalogue record for this book is available from the British Library

Library of Congress Cataloging-in-Publication Data
A catalog record for this book has been requested

ISBN: 978-1-032-02695-4 (hbk)
ISBN: 978-1-032-02696-1 (pbk)
ISBN: 978-1-003-18466-9 (ebk)

DOI: 10.4324/9781003184669

Typeset in Bembo
by Apex CoVantage, LLC

We dedicate this book to our families, whose love and care supported us navigating these unprecedented times together.

Contents

Figures

Infographics

Tables

Contributors

Ezinne Chioma Abaneme is an assistant lecturer in the Department of Mass Communication at Alex Ekwueme Federal University Ndufu-Alike, Ikwo. She specialises in public relations and advertising, health communication, development communication and new media (online journalism). https://orcid.org/0000-0003-0748-838X

Karen Cristina Kraemer Abreu is a PhD at Language Sciences University of Southern Santa Catarina, a member of the research group Convergence and Journalism, Federal University of Ouro Preto and a professor in the Department of Communication Science at the Federal University of Santa Maria. https://orcid.org/0000-0002-2882-8171

İnanç Alikılıç is an assistant professor at Malatya Turgut Özal University, Turkey. His research interests include communication research, research methodology and social media analysis. He has administrative positions at his university, including faculty vice dean and career development centre director. https://orcid.org/0000-0001-9079-8420

Özlem Alikılıç is an associate professor of public relations at Yaşar University, Turkey, and she has taught courses in public relations, corporate social responsibility, social media and crisis communication. She has contributed to many books and her articles have been published in most major international journals in her field. https://orcid.org/0000-0001-6311-2622

Alejandro Álvarez-Nobell is a PhD in Strategic Communication, a professor and researcher at the University of Malaga (Spain) and the National University of Córdoba (Argentina), and director of the Latin American Communication Monitor (EUPRERA). https://orcid.org/0000-0003-1384-3544

Anca Anton is senior lecturer of public relations and marketing at the University of Bucharest, Romania. Her research interests cover digital and strategic communication, organizational communication and public and civic diplomacy. She has published in *Styles of Communication* and *Romanian Journal of Journalism and Communication*. https://orcid.org/0000-0003-0201-197X

Andréia Silveira Athaydes has a PhD in Organizational Communication (UMA/Spain) and a master's degree in Management and Strategic Marketing (UCES/Argentina). Athaydes is a professor at Faculdades Integradas de Taquara/Brazil, the chairman of the Review Committee of Conferp's Public Relations Code of Ethics and the coordinator of the Brazil chapter of *Latin American Communication Monitor*. https://orcid.org/0000-0001-9911-0442

Mark Badham, PhD, is a senior lecturer in Corporate Communication at Jyväskylä University School of Business & Economics, Finland. His research focusses on news media roles in mass communication processes, digital crisis communication, social media engagement, relationship management and organizational legitimacy. https://orcid.org/0000-0003-4521-5294

Mari Bandzeladze is an associate professor and has been engaged in academic work for more than 10 years. She also provides expert consulting services for several private research companies, individuals and non-governmental and business organizations. She has 15 years of experience in marketing and sociological research planning, managing and analysing. https://orcid.org/0000-0003-0089-6065

Leli Bibilashvili works as an associate professor and is head of Journalism and Mass Communications at the University of Georgia, in Tbilisi (since 2014). She has many years of experience in both academia and the industry. She has authored several publications in the field of strategic communications. https://orcid.org/0000-0002-6586-8957

Marcus Vinicius de Jesus Bomfim is a Master in Communication Sciences, University of São Paulo, professor of the Public Relations Course at Fundação Escola de Comércio Álvares Penteado, and a member of CiteLab – Research Laboratory in Science, Innovation, Technology and Education (UFF). https://orcid.org/0000-0003-4340-3515

Gemma Bridge, PhD, is an independent transdisciplinary researcher based in Leeds, UK. She has held research officer and fellow roles at Leeds Beckett University, Queen Mary University of London and the University of Leeds. Her current work spans the fields of communication, public and oral health, food security and active travel. https://orcid.org/0000-0001-7441-9849

Sung In Choi is a doctoral student at Grady College of Journalism and Mass Communication, University of Georgia, USA. She is a member of the Crisis Communication Coalition's Crisis Research Group and lab manager of the Brain, Body, and Media lab. https://orcid.org/0000-0002-9208-6758

Camelia Cmeciu is a professor of public relations at the University of Bucharest, Romania. Her research interests cover organisational communication, risk and crisis communication, digital activism and social semiotics. She has published in *Public Relations Review*, *Comunicar* and *Global Health Promotion*. https://orcid.org/0000-0002-5533-8274

Elanor Colleoni, PhD is currently assistant professor of Corporate Reputation at University IULM in Milan, Italy. Her work lies at the intersection of corporate reputation, organizational legitimacy, corporate social responsibility and business ethics. Her research has been published in leading management and communication journals, such as *Academy of Management Review, Business & Society* and *Journal of Communication*, among others. https://orcid.org/0001–7176–0638

Cristina Fuentes-Lara is a professor of Communication at the Group of Advanced Studies on Communication at Rey Juan Carlos University, Madrid, Spain. Fuentes-Lara has published numerous journal articles of the first quartiles. Her lines of research are gender and communication management. https://orcid.org/0000-0003-3198-7701

Ebru Gökaliler is an associate professor at Yaşar University, Turkey. She teaches many courses on advertising and brand communication. She continues to publish national and international articles and book chapters. Her research interests include brand communication, advertising and consumer behaviour. https://orcid.org/0000-0002-4134-8447

Gisela Gonçalves holds a PhD in Communication Sciences (2010). She is a professor at the University of Beira Interior (Covilhã, Portugal) and coordinates the master's degree program in Strategic Communication. Her research focusses on ethics, public relations theories and government communication. https://orcid.org/0000-0001-7001-3622

Aloysius Chukwuebuka Ifeanyichukwu is a lecturer in the Department of Mass Communication, Madonna University Okija, Nigeria. His research interests are in the areas of Public Relations, New Media, African Communication Systems and Development Communication. https://orcid.org/0000-0003-0953-0254

Øyvind Ihlen, PhD, is a professor in the Department of Media and Communication, University of Oslo, and co-director of POLKOM – Centre for the Study of Political Communication. He currently leads two large projects on COVID-19, funded by the Norwegian Research Council. https://orcid.org/0000-0002-5001-3796

Yan Jin, PhD, is Georgia Athletic Association Professor at Grady College of Journalism and Mass Communication, University of Georgia, USA. She is associate director of the Center for Health & Risk Communication and co-founder of Crisis Communication Think Tank at the University of Georgia. https://orcid.org/0000-0003-4228-5529

Natia Kaladze serves as Dean of the School of Social Sciences at The University of Georgia, Georgia and is founder of the www.mediaeducation.ge platform. She was Project Coordinator and Scientific Editor for the translation of *Television Field Reporting and Production: Visual Guidebook for Storytelling* and *Mass*

Communication. She is the author of several publications in the field of strategic communications. https://orcid.org/0000-0002-3014-4369

Juan-Carlos Molleda is a PhD in Communication. He is Edwin L. Artzt Dean and Professor at the School of Journalism and Communication of the University of Oregon, USA, and the director of the Latin American Communication Monitor (EUPRERA). https://orcid.org/0000-0002-6095-2906

Grazia Murtarelli, PhD, is assistant professor of Corporate Communication at IULM University in Milan, Italy. Her research focusses on the analysis of online scenario and, more specifically, on the following issues: social media–based relationship management, online dialogue strategies, digital visual engagement processes and social media measurement and evaluation. She is a public relations student and the Early Career Representative for the International Communication Association. https://orcid.org/0000-0002-6602-8503

Cristina Navarro is an associate professor of communication at Gulf University for Science and Technology, Kuwait. Her research interests include online public relations, social media communication, professionalism leadership, and competencies, knowledge and skills. https://orcid.org/0000-0003-0522-4428

Anamaria Nicola is a senior lecturer at the University of Bucharest, Romania. Her research focusses on emotions in the media and digital consumption of news. She has published in *Romanian Journal of Journalism and Communication* and *Ethical Space*. https://orcid.org/0000-0002-1299-2348

Chinedu Jude Nwasum is a lecturer in the Department of Mass Communication, Faculty of Social Sciences, Alex Ekwueme Federal University Ndufu Alike, Nigeria. His research interests are Public Relations, Crisis Communication, Strategic Communication, Social Media, Health Communication and Political Communication. https://orcid.org/0000-0002-8455-2827

Mirko Olivieri is a doctoral candidate in Communication, Markets and Society at the Department of Business, Law, Economics and Consumer Behaviour of IULM University, Milan, Italy. His research interests lie in the fields of marketing communication and corporate communication, with a focus on digital channels management. https://orcid.org/0002-5787-6295

Valeriano Piñeiro-Naval holds a PhD in Audiovisual Communication, Technological Revolution and Cultural Change (2015). He is an assistant professor at the University of Salamanca, Spain. His research focusses on cultural heritage and tourism in the digital society and meta-research on communication. https://orcid.org/0000-0001-9521-3364

Bryan H. Reber is the Professor Emeritus in the Department of Advertising and Public Relations at the University of Georgia, USA. His research is in crisis communication and public relations theory, practice, and pedagogy. https://orcid.org/0000-0002-9160-1471

Stefania Romenti, PhD, is associate professor of Strategic Communication and Public Relations at IULM University, Milan, Italy. She is director of the Executive Master in Corporate Public Relations and an adjunct professor at IE Business School. She is founder and director of the Research Centre in Strategic Communication and president-elect of EUPRERA. Her research focusses on strategic communication, corporate reputation, stakeholder management and engagement, dialogue, social media, measurement and evaluation. https://orcid.org/0000-0002-1971-3540

Sónia de Sá holds a PhD in Communication Sciences (2017). She is a guest professor at the University of Beira Interior (Covilhã, Portugal). Her research focusses on strategic communication, gender and television. https://orcid.org/0000-0002-0964-3630

Ana María Suárez-Monsalve holds a PhD in Communication. She is a professor at the University of Medellín, Colombia, and a researcher of the Latin American Communication Monitor (EUPRERA). https://orcid.org/0000-0001-7399-3929

Ruoyu Sun, MA, is a doctoral candidate in the School of Communication at the University of Miami, USA. Her primary research interest focusses on corporate communication strategies in social media. Her interest areas also include corporate socio-political activism and internal communication. https://orcid.org/0000-0002-5395-513X

Chiara Valentini, PhD, is a professor of Corporate Communication at Jyväskylä University School of Business & Economics, Finland. She is the author of numerous peer-reviewed publications and books in the areas of strategic public relations, government communication and crisis communication in the digital environment. Dr. Valentini serves as reviewer and editorial board member of several international journals and is active with several professional organizations. https://orcid.org/0000-0003-0752-9639

Zhao Wang, MA, is an associate professor of advertising at Shanghai Normal University, China. Besides teaching, she has also provided innovative consulting service for companies in China. Her research interests focus on consumer behaviours when reacting to subtle cultures. https://orcid.org/0000-0001-5614-9451

Tong Xie, PhD, received his doctoral degree at the Grady College of Journalism and Mass Communication, University of Georgia, USA. He is a research associate at the Chinese Academy of Social Sciences in Guangxi. His research focusses on corporate social responsibility and issues management. https://orcid.org/:0000-0003-4648-3581

Foreword

The classic book *Frankenstein*, written two centuries ago by English author Mary Shelley, bears an eerie descriptive of our pandemic world today. 'Nothing is so painful to the human mind as a great and sudden change', Shelley wrote. Well, say hello to our COVID-19 world, 'a great and sudden change' accompanied by waves of pain jolting minds and lives worldwide through lockdowns, quarantines, closed borders, travel restrictions, shuttered shops and restaurants, overcrowded hospitals, empty theaters and opera houses and family gatherings and education programs made virtual. Pain is evident in the mounting frustrations, protests and sometimes violent confrontations over lockdowns, masks and vaccine mandates depicted in media coverage which, depending on the politics of media ownership, sometimes weaves disinformation and misinformation into its health messaging.

The most painful bottom line of this dramatic change totaled more than 6.32 million deaths and more than 539 million confirmed COVID cases globally by June 2022, midway through its third year. In this painful and uncertain world, accurate and trusted communications become even more vital. It's paramount to know which sources people turn to for accurate information about COVID and how to best deal with this disease and its seemingly unending variants. A related issue is how to determine the best ways to disseminate urgent messages to the public. Who manages and interprets scientific data and information about this virus for the population? What's their level of trustworthiness? And what happens if those interpretations conflict across borders, or within individual countries, based on differing individual religious, political and scientific beliefs? Does 'fake news' riddle communications and affect healthcare decisions? How can we as individuals, organizations and nations learn from and survive this great change?

This new book, *Strategic Communication in a Global Crisis*, helps answer such questions. It provides rich empirical evidence and insights into our dramatically changed world. It's a BIG book in several senses in its thorough examination of strategic communications *in*, *around* and *about* the pandemic environment. First, it's a deep, probing look into a huge strategic communications laboratory, if you will, where we may discover answers to help us deal with future global challenges in a more effective, trusting and expedient manner to reduce the pain and conflict associated with such challenges.

Second, it's a BIG book in the breadth and scope of its transnational investigations: 40 senior public relations and communication scholars from 16 countries on five continents investigated strategic communication issues, tactics and outcomes re: COVID in their nations. Collectively, these national 'pictures' provide a larger global portrait of the disease and related strategic communication issues, successes and problems. This research is also timely, appearing just as COVID variants emerge, spread and problematise our hoped-for 'return to normal'. The world, as a chorus of many voices, speaks to us in this book.

Third, the book is BIG in its in-depth investigations, as reflected in the many subtopics explored, such as media channels and platforms for delivering health information, media consumption patterns, trust behaviours, sources of information and their trustworthiness, the relative significance of various government communications, message retention and behavioural change, among others. In this manner, the research also conveys unique country and cultural insights.

Overall, the book provides a body of knowledge about the pluses, minuses and unknowns of strategic communications during the ongoing COVID pandemic. The crucial and practical knowledge gained in this research is vital today and likely will be even more so in our collective future. The book is most worthy of our exploration, reflection, discussion and learned application in the present moment. The fervent hope is that this body of knowledge will help improve strategic communications at all levels so that any future 'great and sudden change' will not produce such pain, uncertainty and suffering as experienced with COVID-19.

I highly recommend this important book for scholars, government health services personnel, and community, organizational and media leaders. The project was conceived, led, produced and brought to market by three acclaimed public relations scholars and researchers: Dr. Ralph Tench, Professor of Communication and Director of Research for Leeds Business School, Leeds Beckett University in the U.K.; Juan Meng, Ph.D., Associate Professor of PR at the University of Georgia in the US; and Ángeles Moreno, Ph.D, Professor at Rey Juan Carlos University in Spain. Sincere thanks to these scholars for bringing this great work to life.

Bruce K. Berger, Ph.D.
Professor Emeritus, University of Alabama
Founding Director, The Plank Center for
Leadership in Public Relations
Former CCO, Whirlpool Corporation

Preface

This book has emerged from a time of enforced social, political and economic transformation and change as the world travels through the COVID-19 pandemic. It is in this context of a worldwide pandemic that we came together as researchers inspired to gather global voices and research understanding about how strategic communication is being used in response to the COVID-19 crisis. The outcome is this edited book that makes a unique and timely contribution by exploring in depth the topic of strategic communication and the COVID-19 pandemic from a global perspective. The book is thoroughly grounded in rich empirical evidence gained through a transnational team of senior researchers representing Europe, North America, South America, Asia and Africa, making it one of the largest studies conducted in the field on the topic of strategic communication and COVID-19. By emphasising the diverse voices and communication strategies used by each investigated country when coping with the COVID-19 crisis, the book provides a current and compelling picture of global practice on strategic communication during and beyond the pandemic.

Most scholars and practitioners will agree that effective and timely communication and leadership are crucial to the successful management of any pandemic. With the ongoing and possibly long-lasting impact of COVID-19 on many aspects of communication and multiple sectors of our societies, it is critical to explore the role of strategic communication in change management during the COVID pandemic and beyond. This book addresses such a need. It is thoroughly grounded in rich empirical evidence gained through a global study of COVID-19 communication experiences and strategies.

In the second half of 2020, a transnational team of senior researchers conducted research to investigate COVID-19 communications (COM-COVID-19) in different countries, representing Europe, Africa, Latin America, North America, South America and Asia. Results presented in this edited book provide a compelling, current picture of the COVID-19 pandemic and strategic communication globally.

Questions discussed in the book and in different chapters include but are not restricted to:

- How successful have communications campaigns around public health messages been? What impact have they had on the public's behaviour?

What learning can be drawn from the successes and failures of the communications strategies used during the COVID-19 outbreak?

- How are the roles of different agencies with public health responsibilities understood by the public? Does the public view messages from some agencies as more credible than others? How should this shape future public health messaging?
- How well have public health messages been conveyed to different groups, including people with visible or invisible disabilities, those with the host nation language as an additional language and marginalised groups who have limited access to health information and medical resources? What are the most effective strategies for ensuring public health messaging reaches all members of society equally?
- What are the most effective ways to disseminate urgent messages to the public? What role could early warning systems and emergency notification systems have in the future?
- What impact has the COVID-19 outbreak had on the public perception of research, science and scientists? How can public understanding of research and science be built for potential future public health emergencies?
- What are the most effective strategies for updating public health messaging in the presence of new evidence? How does changing public health messaging affect likelihood to follow guidance?
- What are the most effective strategies for communicating scientific uncertainty in emergencies? How do different approaches to communicating uncertainty affect people's likelihood to follow guidance?
- What role has 'fake news' had on people's likelihood to follow guidance during the COVID-19 outbreak? What are the most effective strategies for ensuring government communications are not undermined by mis- or disinformation?

Chapters included in this collection therefore explore the national and regional experiences and discuss relevant successes and failures of pandemic communication and specific learning from the 2020–2022 crisis. In addition to the rich content and consistent writing style presented in each contributed chapter, one key feature associated with most contributed chapters of the book is the infographic presented at the end of the chapter to summarise and highlight the key findings and practical implications. Through this special feature, every effort has been made to make the content of this edited volume substantive, understandable, practical and visually engaging.

Given its sharp topic focus, wealth of empirical data and the relevance of the topic to today's strategic communication practice, this edited volume is suitable for different audiences globally. The book will provide insight and interest for scholars, educators and professionals in strategic communication, both leaders and emerging leaders, men and women, and national and international businesses. This book is appropriate for graduate and advanced undergraduate students in international public relations, communication management and strategic communication. It is also intended to advance international communication and cross-cultural research to facilitate critical thinking on public health responses and global communication. It can also be used outside academia by public health and governmental institutions and entities to aid in developing effective strategic communication amid uncertainty in any public health and safety crises.

Acknowledgements

The editors would like to specifically thank all of the researchers included in this book who took up the challenge of researching and contributing to this project as we were all in the eye of an unprecedented storm and simultaneously re-engineering our university delivery and adjusting our private lives. We also want to acknowledge the support and work of the copyediting and production team at Routledge for their very capable work during the production phase. They deserve special thanks for their support of this book, and their belief that the community of public relations and strategic communication practitioners and scholars worldwide will embrace our efforts.

Although the book focusses on the strategic health communication efforts of different counties and regions around the world, we would particularly like to acknowledge the public's responses to these messages and the impressive way we all as citizens reacted with collective responsibility. Finally – when talking about a health pandemic – a debt of gratitude is offered to all those healthcare professionals worldwide who have so diligently put themselves forward to help society as a whole.

A very special acknowledgement goes to our families. From the inception of the research idea in 2020 to the present, this book would not have been possible without their support and encouragement.

Part I

Introduction

1 A world turned upside down

Ralph Tench, Juan Meng and Ángeles Moreno

The early years of the 2020s will be remembered worldwide in modern history as a period of seismic social, political and economic turbulence, all triggered by a singular healthcare calamity. The 2020s began with an unprecedented threat to the equilibrium of human existence posed by the Coronavirus disease (COVID-19) pandemic, precipitating unforeseen disruptions to life and ways of living across the whole planet. And yet, was that disruption truly unforeseen? During the previous decades there were other infectious diseases and health emergencies, like the 2002 SARS-CoV, the 2009 H1N1 influenza, the MERS-CoV, the Ebola virus and the Zika virus, all of them highly contagious and with pernicious effects on human health.

Moreover, virologists have foreseen that a global health crisis could be produced by one of these viruses with the capacity for rapid transmission, causing serious, damaging effects to human health and ultimately perilous to life. Scientists also anticipated the ripples and impact of such a scenario beyond the health emergency itself. They even planned ahead for the disruption that such a health crisis would bring for governments and civil authorities. It was anticipated that national institutions would have to take decisions that transcended citizens' health, because they would bring knock-on effects for international mobility, commerce and global economic activities, and for the credibility of political authorities and institutions.

Scientists had predicted all this and gamed the outcomes, but the world was still not prepared to face the health emergency that one of these pandemics could truly reap, nor to accurately predict the chain of effects that could result from a crisis of such magnitude.

During the emergence of the COVID-19 crisis, societies were forced to deal with multiple paradoxes that impacted emerging debates about complex issues that necessitated urgent decisions such as nationalism versus globalisation, consumerism versus sustainability, control versus democracy and technology versus interpersonal relations.

Regarding the role of communication, a decade before the COVID-19 pandemic the World Health Organization (WHO) Review Committee had already placed risk communication at the same level as technical skills when assessing the essential capabilities required to tackle a pandemic (WHO 2018), but it was clear

DOI: 10.4324/9781003184669-2

that institutions were not prepared to face such a challenge. The COVID pandemic has emphasised the critical value and importance of communications. In a scenario where our survival depends on changing our behaviours, communication was indispensable to face the crisis and minimise the potential damage to our societies.

Some fundamental principles of effective communication management were anticipated (Tench *et al.* 2017) before the COVID-19 crisis started in 2020, but they seem to have been exacerbated and accelerated during the pandemic. Three of these macro themes have been evidenced in the COVID-19 experience.

Firstly, the awareness and recognition of the importance of *globalization* has increased. Whether we like it or not, we live in a global world and everything we do, every action we take affects people living in other parts of the world. Even if we don't travel, other places and cultures affect us as touchpoints through the food we consume, the products we buy and potentially through the people we meet. Globalization was here before COVID-19, but the recent experiences during the pandemic have underscored the bigger risks of this social model and its consequences, such as the marginalisation and polarisation of certain groups with nation-states during the past century.

Second, the process of *mediatisation* (the saturation of the media in society and people's lives) has been accelerated. As Deuze *et al.* state (2012) we don't live anymore with the media and instead live in the media. The ongoing pandemic has transformed how we all live and work. Technology has proven to be a domestic and employment life raft during the crisis. We are all using technology so much more in our leisure, to access critical news and information as well as to facilitate our personal and work-based communication.

Recent research underlined the exponential rise of media use during the pandemic lockdowns. We underline the concept of use instead of consumption, to reflect the active and multichannel use of media, with the presence of new gatekeepers that make it difficult for authorities to centralise messages and avoid the extreme proliferation of misinformation and fake news. We all now exist in a media-driven world which has accelerated and supported our acceptance during the crisis the 'new normal' practices of maintaining virtual relations with relatives and friends, working remotely and doing our school and university learning online.

Third, the process of *datafication* has also been accelerated. As citizens in our countries, we have experienced something unfamiliar to most of us: the nightly tally of data and statistics about COVID-19. This has included the infection rates, the admission numbers to hospitals and then the heart breaking nightly totals of people who have died from the disease. As the COVID pandemic progressed, the statistics focused more heavily on information related to vaccines, treatment, tests and the breakthrough infections as the Omicron variant emerged. This process became naturalised for many of us. We got used to accessing online news updates, watching TV or listening to the radio while these figures were disseminated nightly, as if we were monitoring the financial performance of a company or country against other national and international measures. To illuminate the data further, many of us have become adept at reading and interpreting data and graphs on infection and transmission rates detailing R rates and the percentages of the population in different counties who are vaccinated and unvaccinated, or who have caught the disease. We have worked with websites and interactive maps, as well as apps and monitoring mechanisms to not only track our personal health records and statistics but our movements and the proximity to others who may have been exposed to the virus. Much of the data we consume is managed and manipulated using big data analysis and machine learning.

From these big changes in our access to detailed information about COVID-19, our ability to go for a walk, travel or gain access to the more basic services has been dependent on the management and interpretation of this data. This has all promoted debates about privacy and allegations of civil liberty infringements in the form of 'Big Brother' spying through the technology we access on a daily basis from our phones and domestic devices with corporations like Amazon or Apple, as well as the software platforms we have fully integrated into our lives as we work and socialise such as through videoconferencing systems.

So, we face increased information to manage and a heightened sense of uncertainty in our daily lives which raises questions as to whether we have the agility and psychological systems to manage these expanding sources of information in an informed and reflective way.

We can say with confidence we have never lived through a global health crisis that has involved citizens to such a high degree with an appetite for instant, precise, accurate and reliable information. Similarly, it is the first time a simultaneous worldwide health crisis has depended so heavily on the behaviour of each citizen and they in turn are reliant on the information they process from government authorities and other institutional stakeholders. However, the effectiveness of communication has also been demonstrated to require levels of trust that have been eroded over many years by some groups in relation to institutions such as the media and figures of authority in society, with political leaders in particular suffering from diminished trust.

One scientific upside is that the pandemic has presented one of the biggest strategic communication laboratories, with all countries – to different degrees – being affected and exercising modes of health communication that researchers have had the opportunity to explore, evaluate and benchmark against strategic communication and crisis theories. The outcome of preliminary studies and the debates in this book suggest there is still much more to learn.

Background of the global project

At a very early stage of the COVID pandemic the European Public Relations Education and Research Association (EUPRERA) took a step to lead scientific and professional initiatives. This began in early 2020, during the first few months of the pandemic, when the virus was being detected outside China and a rapid growth of infection cases was seen in Europe. While coping with this situation, EUPRERA initiated a research project named COM-COVID to monitor the institutional communication and the responses of the public in the three European countries (the UK, Italy and Spain) that were the most severely affected. The original COM-COVID project grew as other researchers from different nations began researching in their regions. The COM-COVID initiative became a EUPRERA network that expanded quickly with 28 members joining from 18 countries. The network produced cross-cultural research and brought together scholars from Europe, North and Latin America, Asia and Africa, and 15 of these research teams and their findings are included in this book.

During the first two years of the pandemic members researched the topic with comparative data in different regions and also from diverse perspectives. Findings from the network produced both academic and wider social and practise-based knowledge transfer. Five academic journal papers and more than 25 academic presentations have been made so far, as well as discussions and influence on practitioner networks and debates. In addition, this global research network inspired the *Statement on COVID-19 Communication* initiated by EUPRERA. By applying the scientific knowledge acquired through the research network, EUPRERA decided to put together the main associations in the field and take a lead in influencing how communication was being managed in relation to the pandemic. A statement was developed to strengthen the value of the public relations profession and practitioners' expertise and knowledge in managing crises and health emergences. Fifteen professional and academic international associations, such as the EACD (European Association of Communication Directors), the Global Alliance for Public Relations and Communication Management, the Institute for Public Relations and the International Public Relations Association, with direct connections to over 200,000 communication practitioners worldwide endorsed the statement. Many of the practitioners work in the non-profit and public sectors, and the statement resulted in recognition and support from the World Health Organization through a mention on the organization's webpage.

The *Statement on COVID-19 Communication* underlined that more than ever, simply informing the public about the pandemic has been inadequate. The capacity to relay the timely and correct information quickly and clearly on different media platforms is essential to managing a public health emergency in an unbounded media landscape. In contrast, unclear and dishonest information can exacerbate the opportunities for miscommunication, in addition leading to the dissemination of 'fake news', conspiracy theories and the spread of resistant attitudes and behaviour that can compromise societies' ability to control the virus. Misleading messages and contradictory comments from leaders and institutions compromise trust, which can in turn hamper a successful collective response.

As the statement concluded, we know that timely, accurate and transparent professional communication can save lives. Public relations practitioners are key to managing a pandemic as they can facilitate and maintain relations and mutual understanding between institutions and the public (Bled Manifesto,

Van Ruler and Verčič 2002). During public health emergencies, such as the COVID pandemic, a well-coordinated and efficient communications strategy helps stakeholders to define risks, identify hazards, assess weaknesses, and promote community resilience, thereby increasing capacity to cope. Professional strategic communicators can guide the public on how to interpret information, risk, personal involvement and the actions they need to take.

Significance of this book

If public relations practitioners play a fundamental role in leading strategic communication in pivotal moments such as the COVID pandemic, one of the main questions that will need to be re-addressed is the significance of strategic communication in public health crises and emergencies when society at large is viewing and experiencing the unprecedented changes and uncertainty that have occurred as the virus intrudes on and interrupts our daily life. That is the underlying yet fundamental assumption that guided the development of the book. Chapters collected in this edited volume document a number of accomplishments:

First, the project integrates public relations theories, public health research and strategic communication practice on a topic that has affected and will continue affecting almost every single aspect of human life. Thus, it provides timely case studies and empirical investigations to reflect the evolving phases of the pandemic.

Second, the integration of various factors related to strategic communication in this project presents the nature of interdisciplinary research in our field. Although the main topic is rooted in COVID itself, the book investigates a wide range of subtopics that help advance our knowledge in strategic communication, including media platforms to obtain information, media consumption behaviours, sources of information, trust behaviours, public health message retention, knowledge conversion and application as related to behaviour change and the significance of governmental communication for individual and public life.

Third, the project itself has a strong global vision, including empirical investigations into the practice of COVID-19 communication on five continents (i.e., Africa, Asia, Europe, North America, and South America) with a group of 40 seminal scholars and contributors representing 16 countries, including Argentina, Brazil, China, Denmark, Finland, Georgia, Italy, Nigeria, Norway, Portugal, Romania, Spain, Sweden, Turkey, the United Kingdom, and the United States. Such a scope has marked this book as a first global and international investigation of the COVID-19 pandemic and strategic communication. The diverse geographic representation of the book will also enable knowledge published in this book to be widely distributed to a global audience, within and beyond the communication-related fields.

Fourth, to echo the global vision of this book, the contributing chapters in this edited volume do not only provide state-of-the-art research that examines COVID-19 communication and its impacts, they are also tailored to reflect the uniqueness in the COVID-19 coping situations which are detailed to each specific country and culture. Although the idea of building the COM-COVID network provided the overarching research theme and mission, the data, the sample, the questionnaire adaptation, findings and implications vary from country to country depending on the phases of the pandemic when each study was actually launched in the field by the specific research team of that country. Overall, the broad and diverse, yet unique points of view and results presented in the collected chapters provide a comprehensive picture to aid in understanding the role of strategic communication in building resilience during the pandemic.

Lastly, this edited volume provides practical insights to support strategic communication thinking and practice in the future. Each chapter in Parts II and III incorporates a visually engaging and expressive infographic based on solid empirical research data which aims to bridge the knowledge gap between social science research on the pandemic and its practical implications. The infographics, designed and developed by each contributing research team, also correspond to the important research questions and key trends and findings presented in their chapter. We believe there is a strong need to provide engaging visual communication information in today's digital communication environment to advance the meaning of strategic communication research in a topic like communication experiences during COVID-19 pandemic.

In summary, we are convinced that the intensity of scientific research conducted during the COVID pandemic has provided a corpus of knowledge that can help to improve communication practice in future scenarios. If we understand the main concepts and factors involved in the central role that strategic communication plays in the management of future pandemics, health emergencies and crisis, we will improve our capacity as societies to face the challenges and avoid the domino effect of subsequent crises.

Outline of the book

The book is structured in four sections and demonstrates a diversity of findings and debates in three directions: the subjects (of the communication processes), the places (geographical diversity) and the time, through longitudinal analysis and interpretations.

Apart from the introduction chapter as the first section, the second section of this edited volume attempts to address how communication practitioners in Europe, North America, Latin America and Africa adapted their communication practice and strategies to manage the changes caused by the pandemic. It provides a broad review of COVID-19 communication within the context of professional communication.

In chapter 2, Valentini, Ihlen and Tench build a strong argument that trust is an essential coping mechanism people use when they lack sufficient information or expertise to make an objective decision when coping with novel infectious diseases such as COVID-19. The discussion of trust is illustrated at the micro, meso and macro levels by illustrative examples from Europe in the context of the COVID-19 pandemic.

The next chapter in this section, by Meng, Reber and Xie, focusses on communication practitioners in North America and how they adapt their role as a facilitator of effective communication on issues related to the pandemic. Communication professionals acknowledge the significant impact of the pandemic on their daily practice but also address that they use various sources for COVID-19 information in order to develop effective adapting strategies in the changing working environment.

In their chapter on strategic communication challenges in times of COVID-19, Álvarez-Nobell, Molleda, Moreno, and Suárez-Monsalve provide a timely update of treating the pandemic as an opportunity to strengthen healthcare policies in Latin America with more systemic and comprehensive approaches. It provides the evidence, tensions and discussions resulting from the exploration of the practices carried out by strategic communication professionals in Latin America during the pandemic.

Although these three chapters have very different points of departure and emphasis, they all present the experiences from the perspectives of communication practitioners in different regions and countries. We hope the three chapters in Part II will convince the reader that strategic communication is a topic that needs urgent attention, not only in a critical moment such as the pandemic, but it actually is in high demand in communication practice when multiple changes such as technology, digitisation, working environment, organizational structure, information seeking and public policies, among others, are taking place simultaneously.

Part III, 'Global perspectives on COVID-19 communication', provides a diverse view of the COVID-19 communication practice in 16 countries. The chapters in this section are grouped by geographic region to better guide readers.

In chapter 5, Meng, Sun, Xie and Wang investigate the Chinese government's efforts, channels and policies to measure and contain the transmission of the disease while communicating COVID-19 information. Since China was the first country that reported a cluster of cases of pneumonia back to December 2019, the government used a strictly enforced top-down policy and national surveillance system to curb COVID-19 transmission. Their research highlights the importance of three triangles – the most used mobile messaging apps, the most trusted information channels and the most trusted sources of information – in COVID-19 communication in today's China when the media landscape is rapidly evolving.

The sub-section of Southern Europe includes three chapters. In chapter 6, Colleoni, Olivieri, Romenti and Murtarelli uncover the impact of corporate social responsibility (CSR) initiatives during the pandemic among millennials in Italy. Drawing on empirical data, the authors found that strategic communication through CSR initiatives helped build responsible strategies in gaining social support, promoting appropriate social behaviour, promoting community values and informing citizens.

In chapter 7, Gonçalves, Piñeiro-Naval and Sá explore how media consumption by the Portuguese influences their perception of (mis)information, including the awareness of self-protective messages. Starting with an overview of the COVID-19 pandemic in Portugal, the authors reflect upon the theoretical-practical implications of the data obtained during the second wave of the disease in Portugal.

In chapter 8, Navarro, Moreno and Fuentes-Lara examine the reactive approach of the Spanish government in providing COVID-19 information, which was questioned by health experts, professional organizations, political parties and civil society. Their findings confirm that the choice of medium does not only influence the public's sense-making of the crisis but also moderates their acceptance of crisis messages and trust in the authorities.

The next sub-section includes three chapters reflecting the region of Northern Europe. In chapter 9, Tench and Bridge explore the most used channels for information receipt and searching, the most credible sources of information, the types of messages received and remembered, and the effectiveness of the messages during the UK's initial and third national lockdowns. The authors find a synchronous use of multiple media and platforms in line with channel complementarity theory and supporting research that suggests there is an increase in media consumption during emergencies such as the COVID-19 pandemic.

In chapter 10, Valentini and Badham compare the two contrasting COVID-19 management approaches adopted by the Finnish and Swedish governments. The authors find the two approaches shaped the way the Finnish and Swedish governments communicated COVID-19 messages as well as the way people perceived their government's handling of the pandemic and their subsequent behavioural responses.

In chapter 11, Ihlen, Johansson, and Blach-Ørsten examine the three so-called high-trust societies – Denmark, Norway and Sweden – and the ways strategic communication has been used there during the pandemic. The authors present the notion of the Nordic model and argue how the model might have helped lay the groundwork for social trust, which in turn serves as a reservoir for strategic crisis communication.

The sub-section of South America shares insights from two countries: Argentina and Brazil. In chapter 12, Álvarez-Nobell argues that Argentina represents a paradigmatic case. With a left-wing populist government, it was the first country to apply restrictions on mobility in the region. The survey findings revealed that television, social media (Twitter) and online newspapers are key sources of information and that media selection has an impact on the direction of the pandemic. In chapter 13, Athaydes, Abreu and Bomfim present the Brazilian case by integrating the theory of channel complementarity and the infodemic scenario as an influencing factor for the search for complementary and reliable information channels. Their investigation identifies the level of reliability in the sources and the main messages of the federal government about the pandemic, as well as the most used communication channels for COVID-19 information.

The sub-section of North America focusses on COVID-19 communication in the United States. In chapter 14, from the perspective of the planned behaviour theory, Choi, Jin and Badham examine factors influencing Americans' preventive behaviours, including their COVID-19 vaccination intentions, in response to the US government's strategic communication about COVID-19 guidelines.

The sub-section of East and South East Europe includes three chapters. In chapter 15, Kaladze, Bibilashvili and Bandzeladze assess the efficacy of crisis communication management and tools in building COVID-19 awareness during the pandemic by the government of Georgia. The authors find the public health campaign led by the government was perceived as timely in terms of information dissemination but not at the level of preventive measures.

In chapter 16, Cmeciu, Anton and Nicola investigate the Romanian respondents' health-information-seeking behaviour and their evaluation of the government communication during the COVID-19 pandemic. More uniquely, the authors test the potential association between information-seeking behaviour with socio-demographic categories and anxiety levels.

In chapter 17, Alikılıç, Gökaliler and Alikılıç explore the role of communication by the Turkish government during the COVID-19 crisis and how it has affected the information seeking behaviours of the public. The authors describe the Turkish public as sceptical about the pandemic news received from the government compared to other channels. Although the perception regarding the withholding of reality by the government is high, the Turkish public rely more on health professionals for accurate information.

Our last contributing chapter, chapter 18, shares an African perspective of COVID-19 communication. Nwasum, Abaneme and Ifeanyichukwu evaluate public perception of government communication during the second wave of the pandemic in Nigeria. The authors find an overwhelming number of respondents felt that the government communication was unclear and insufficient, which generated social alarm and distrust. The chapter concludes with insights on how to improve the effectiveness of government communication in future health crises.

Finally, our conclusion chapter summarises some common themes emerging from the international project, as well as addressing some limitations embedded in the method and research design in global and international research. We also discuss the implications for strategic communication practice, education and future research. We hope the organisation of this book into four parts, each centring on different perspectives and various geographic regions, provides a useful lens on organising this vast yet evolving pandemic. Despite the scope of this book, we do not pretend for a moment that it is comprehensive or covers all aspects in strategic communication and the COVID-19 pandemic. However, by providing a wide range of investigation of strategic health communication in different countries, from different perspectives and during different phases of the pandemic, we believe this edited volume offers a useful starting point for scholars, practitioners, governmental officials and public health experts to integrate effective communication strategies, channels, sources and platforms into their own research and practice.

References

Deuze, M., Blank, P., and Speers, L. (2012). A life lived in media. *Digital Humanities Quarterly*, 6(1). http://www.digitalhumanities.org/dhq/vol/6/1/000110/000110.html.

Tench, R., Verčič, D., Zerfass, A., Verhoeven, P., and Moreno, A. (2017). *Communication Excellence: How to Develop, Manage and Lead Exceptional Communications.* London: Palgrave Macmillan. ISBN: 978-3-319-48860-8

Van Ruler, B., and Verčič, D. (2002, July). The Bled Manifesto on public relations. Prepared for BledCom 2002. In *9th International Public Relations Research Symposium, in conjunction with the European Public Relations Education and Research Association*, Lake Bled, Slovenia, pp. 4–7.

WHO (2018). Statement on the 1st meeting of the IHR Emergency Committee regarding the Ebola outbreak in 2018. Available from: https://www.who.int/news/item/18-05-2018-statement-on-the-1st-meeting-of-the-ihr-emergency-committee-regarding-the-ebola-outbreak-in-2018 [Accessed 21 June 2022].

Part II

Observations and responses from communication professionals around the world

2 A question of trust

Exploring trust concepts, experiences and early observations from Europe

Chiara Valentini, Øyvind Ihlen and Ralph Tench

Introduction

The COVID-19 situation in Europe has been complex, with some countries hit hard and others less affected. At the time of writing, the UK, Italy and Spain have had, respectively, 152,725; 127,680; and 80,934 COVID-related deaths (Coronavirus [COVID-19] in the UK 2021a, European Centre for Disease Prevention and Control 2021a). The figures for Norway and Finland were 794 and 974, respectively. Huge regional differences have also been noted in vaccination uptake. The UK (Coronavirus [COVID-19] in the UK 2021b) and Iceland had covered with one dose 86 and 88% of adults above 18, respectively, while the figure for Bulgaria was 16.3%(European Centre for Disease Prevention and Control 2021b). On a whole, several surveys show how citizens have been dissatisfied with the handling of the pandemic (e.g., Eurofound 2021). In many countries trust has plummeted during the period, including trust in institutions and national governments. This chapter addresses this issue. Although the focus is on Europe, we maintain that much of the theorising also applies to other contexts as well.

In times of global crises, such as those that originate from novel infectious diseases, people lack the knowledge of how to understand, cope and deal with them. Because of potentially life-threatening situations caused by these diseases, people will start seeking information to increase their knowledge on the matter and improve the quality of their decisions. Not all information is equally credible. Why, then, do people gauge some sources of information as more credible than others? Research shows that it all depends on one key factor: trust. Trust is an essential coping mechanism people use when they lack sufficient information or expertise to make an objective decision such as following health recommendations (Siegrist and Cvetkovich 2000). Thus trust influences people's behaviours in crises (Fancourt *et al.* 2020).

Trust is not to be confused with trustworthiness (Hardin 1996, 2002). Trustworthiness can induce trust. The former involves a moral dimension, whereas the latter does not. Trustworthiness of actors is often described as the trustor's perception of the ability, integrity and benevolence of the trustee (Mayer *et al.* 1995) and is evaluated in terms of intentions – honest, genuine intentions to

DOI: 10.4324/9781003184669-4

signpost the path to trustworthiness. The notion of 'encapsulated interest' has been proposed to describe the expectation of the trustor (Hardin 2002). The trustor believes that the trustee has some kind of reason to act in the best interest of the trustor. The trustee will, for instance, value their relationship. This, then, is highly context-dependent.

In health crises, it has been repeatedly shown that trust in the source of risk information highly influences people's willingness to follow public health rules and guidelines, which are particularly important to control infection spread and mortality (Bargain and Aminjonov 2020). A source is trusted when it is perceived to have appropriate knowledge and expertise to provide correct and accurate information and when it is considered as trustworthy, which practically translates to when people perceive as honest the source's intentions to supply correct information (Lucassen and Schraagen 2012). In times of pandemics, for instance, doctors are often perceived to have the best knowledge and expertise regarding an infectious disease and are trustworthy sources because they normally have no commercial interest or personal interest to recommend specific preventive behaviours. This has been demonstrated across Europe in the use of scientific advisors to create credibility and support for the regular messaging from politicians (European Commission 2020; Farjam *et al.* 2021)

The key word 'trust' frequently turns up in European media coverage of the COVID-19 pandemic, not least in reports about trust surveys, as well as in academic publications (see, e.g., Devine *et al.* 2021; Goldstein and Wiedemann 2021; Offerdal *et al.* 2021). As a concept, however, it is frequently poorly defined and many different understandings exist. This chapter seeks first to clarify the concept of trust and the mechanisms as well as the outcomes it produces. As trust is attributable to relationships at all levels of society, within and among social groups, this chapter structures the discussion of trust focussing on the micro, meso and macro levels and offers some illustrative examples of its relevance within the context of the COVID-19 pandemic.

Trust defined

Trust is perhaps one of the most studied concepts in the humanities and social sciences. Interestingly, despite the large number of papers and books about trust, Li's (2011) editorial for the launch issue of the *Journal of Trust Research* argued that at that point there was a persistent lack of consensus about trust, which does make the field interesting to navigate and interpret. To frame the discussion we can see Lane's (1998) argument that trust is a social phenomenon to be studied at interpersonal, interorganizational and systemic levels. Most conceptions of personal trust share three basic assumptions: there will be a degree of interdependence between trustor and trustee; trust provides a way to cope with risk and uncertainty in exchange relationships; and the expectation that there will not be an abuse of the vulnerability resulting from the acceptance of risk in the relationship (Colledge *et al.* 2014). Trust is also something to be given or placed, it may be placed in a person (micro), an organization/institution (meso), and the broader structures that affect roles, organizations and the like (macro), such as codes of conduct, industry bodies, relevant law and broader societal norms (Colledge *et al.* 2014). The mechanisms by which trust influences people's attitudes and behaviours are multifaceted and sometimes indirect, meaning trust can be given to a person if one believes this person is trustworthy because others in one's inner circle endorse them as giving or eliciting trust. This is a sort of 'trust spillover effect'.

Studies of trust in strategic communication have explored the phenomenon at six levels: individual (i.e., personal); institutional (i.e., organizational); financial (i.e., market); political (i.e., government); societal (i.e., public); and relational (i.e., specific relationships) (Valentini 2021). There is a plethora of trust definitions underlying different features, attributes and outcomes, but most of them depict it as a state, belief or positive expectation (Rousseau *et al.* 1998). Trust is often associated with individuals, yet depersonalised and abstract forms of trust exist too, such as institutional trust and societal trust. A common definition of trust points to how the notion involves two roles, a trustor and a trustee, and the willingness of the former to take risk based on expectations tied to the latter: '*the willingness of a party to be vulnerable to the actions of another party based on the expectation that the other will perform a particular action important to the trustor, irrespective of the ability to monitor or control that other party*' [italics in original] (Mayer *et al.* 1995, p. 712). Trust involves recognition of an assumed risk, thus setting the notion apart from confidence where no alternative course of action is considered in a particular situation (Luhmann 2000). Put differently, through trust, citizens place a bet on 'the future contingent actions of others' (Sztompka 1999, p. 25). There is a possibility for disappointment. Because of this, trust is also related to evaluation of the trustees' past performance which leads to confidence or lack of confidence, and in turn cooperation or lack of cooperation. Confidence can be 'defined as the belief based on past experience or evidence that certain future events will occur as expected' (Siegrist and Zingg 2014, p. 25).

In most situations, trust presumes reciprocity between the parties, and this is learned only through regular, honest and cooperative behaviours among individuals (Fukuyama 1995; Putnam 2001). Societal trust, for example, is a type of trust where this notion of reciprocity among individuals cooperating according to shared norms in a specific community is fundamental. In these societies, citizens trust each other, and have confidence that individuals and organizations will behave according to shared norms. Furthermore, this type of trust can be learned through direct experiences and during the process of socialisation of individuals with community norms, reciprocity and cooperative behaviours.

Trust can occur at different levels and with different intensities; that is, it can be conceptualised dichotomously (one either trusts or distrusts) or in a more graded fashion (one trusts or distrusts to a degree) (Levi and Stoker 2000). Previous research shows that trust is a multi-layered concept applicable to different types of subjects, objects and processes. So, trust can be ascribed to information, channels, institutions and undefined members too. Literature suggests that there

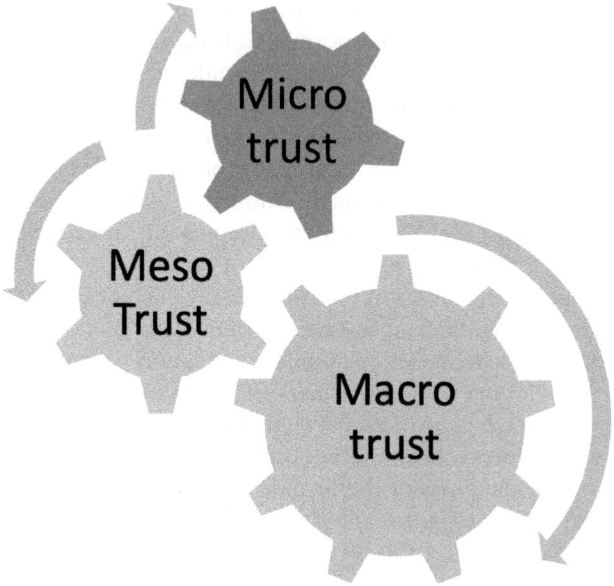

Figure 2.1 Three levels of trust

Source: Authors

is a casual relationship between these different forms of trust and that each sustains the next level. Specifically, trust in information is highly influenced by the trust in the source, and the latter is influenced by trust in the medium or channel of communication, and next to society at large (Lucassen and Schraagen 2012).

In the next section we explore specifically three levels of trust that research shows play an important role in the management of risk situations. The three levels are illustrated in Figure 2.1 and correspond to micro, meso and macro level forms of trust.

Micro: interpersonal trust

The most basic form of trust is that occurring between two individuals, a trustor and trustee. This type of trust is known as interpersonal trust and has been described as *horizontal trust*. McAllister (1995) makes a distinction between cognitive and affective foundations of interpersonal trust. The cognition-based trust relates to evidence of trustworthiness, whereas the affective foundation of trust is based on emotions. Similarly, Valentini (2021) identified two macro forms while reviewing literature on trust; these are *trust as action* and *trust as a condition* (Valentini 2021). When trust is conceived as an action, it refers to an individual's rational assessment of the trustor's behaviour. It is a rational assessment in that the trustee is involved in a cognitive appraisal of certain qualities or attributes of the trustor and the costs versus the benefits obtained in offering confidence. In the second form, trust as a condition, trust is grounded in emotional bonds between trustor and trustee. Here trust has an affective orientation and is characterised by a psychological predisposition, or willingness to be open, vulnerable and confident (Valentini 2021). Dispositional trust, also known as predisposition to trust, is an example of trust as a condition, since this type of trust is a person's psychological predisposition and refers to a personality trait, an attitude that affects an individual's likelihood to trust another person. This form of trust is influenced by salient values, such as honesty, integrity, goodwill, benevolence and familiarity (Valentini 2020). For some, family relationships early in life can influence trust formation (Uslaner 2002), however some of the exposed values can also be learned outside the family context. As a matter of fact, institutions such as schools, churches and the like play a big role in nourishing these values at an individual level and they can thus influence a person's salient values and his/her propensity to trust.

Predisposition to trust is a clear antecedent for developing interpersonal trust, but even in individuals with no dispositional trust, interpersonal trust can develop. Typically, trust is built gradually as a result of previous positive experiences with the trustee, or simply through a 'trust spilling over' effect; that is, when a person trusts another based on the positive experience with the trustee of individuals from his/her own group. In risk and crisis situations this can be trust in how you can turn to other citizens for help. The impact of trust on people's adherence to what they are informed to do is also higher among those with a higher dispositional trust (Lucassen and Schraagen 2011). Communities with high dispositional trust show generally higher levels of interpersonal trust, meaning they have confidence that a fellow citizen will act according to shared norms. Widespread levels of interpersonal trust also reinforce institutional trust, which manifests with trust in relevant groupings during a health crisis or pandemic such as public authorities, government, politicians and so on. These two contribute to the formation and maintenance of societal trust, that is, trust in generalised others (Robinson and Jackson 2001). High levels of societal trust can be a crucial asset in dealing with crises, thus providing the grounds for societal resilience. Therefore, some scholars (Devine *et al.* 2021) suggest that in countries with high levels of interpersonal trust, governments have managed the disease through emphasis on individual responsibility of citizens, based on mutual trust between citizens and the state, rather than imposing more restrictive measures. Furthermore, empirical evidence on the COVID-19 pandemic and trust from 23 countries worldwide shows that the more people endorsed moral principles of fairness and care (vs. loyalty and authority), which are core in trust, the more they were inclined to report trust in science, which, in turn, statistically predicted prescribed and discretionary behavioural intentions (Pagliaro *et al.* 2021).

Meso: trust in organizations and institutions

At the meso level, the trustee is an organization or institution. The benefits of trust within organizational settings are numerous; for example, trust has been shown to impact cooperative behaviours, organizational citizenship behaviours, organizational commitment and employee loyalty (Kramer and Tyler 1996; Paliszkiewicz 2011). It also affects investment decisions (Lorenz 1988; Baldvinsdottir *et al.* 2011) and supports economic exchanges (Arrow 1974) and the negotiation of conflicts (Kelman 2005). Trust is mentioned as a key component for risk responses and can amplify or accentuate public risk responses (e.g., Earle and Cvetkovich 1995; Renn 1998). Various forms of trust based on organizations and institutions have been studied. Of particular interest in the context of pandemics are two forms: categorization-based trust and role-based trust. Categorisation-based trust occurs when confidence is based on the premises of a shared membership in a social or organizational category. Here trust is thus depersonalised, not related to a specific individual. According to Brewer (1996), this type of trust defines 'the boundaries of low-risk interpersonal trust that bypasses the need for personal knowledge and the costs of negotiating reciprocity' when interacting with other members of that category (p. 356).

Further, through categorisation-based trust people ascribe positive values such as honesty, cooperativeness and trustworthiness to other in-group members (Brewer 1996), thus reinforcing the perception of trust. An example of categorisation-based trust is medical doctors. Individuals do not need to have an interpersonal relationship with a medical doctor to trust he/she will perform the best treatment. Knowing that doctors belong to a specific professional category with a particular code of conduct is a sufficient mechanism to offer confidence. Literature also indicates that high levels of categorisation-based trust among individuals in a community enhance societal trust (Muethel and Bond 2013; Roumeliotou and Rontos 2009; Williams 2001). That said, there are challenges to this form of trust and particularly to some professions and professional groups. The real issue is that many professions are untrusted by the general population, and this is of specific relevance to advisors from the field of communications as there is a decline for those in business-related professions which includes communicators (Nuremberg Institute for Market Decisions 2019).

The other form of trust that is highly relevant in an organizational context is role-based trust. As with categorisation-based trust, this is a form of presumptive trust since trust is depersonalised. Trust is granted on the basis of knowing that a person occupies a particular role in an organization, rather than knowing the person's capabilities, dispositions, motives and intentions. The assumption here is that if someone holds a specific role in an organization, he/she must be capable of carrying out the tasks and will fulfil the expectations related to his/her role (Barber 1983). Essentially, this type of trust reduces the risks related to knowing the trustee, as a trustor can adopt a sort of presumptive trust based upon knowledge of role relations, even in the absence of personalised knowledge or history of prior interaction. The police as a type of institution is an illustrative example of this form of trust. People trust police officers and by extension the institution of the police, based on the presumption that those working in the police have the competencies to fulfil the police duties since they occupy a specific role in this institution.

Recent studies on pandemics and institutional trust show that where there is a high level of trust in the institutions that are in charge of the health crisis there are higher levels of compliance with recommendations (Han *et al.* 2020; Olsen and Hjorth 2020) and lower mortality rates (Oksanen *et al.* 2020). A positive evaluation of the competence of authorities, perceived accuracy and honesty and a general benign view of government agencies can increase compliance with recommendations in risk and crisis situations (Prati *et al.* 2011). Interestingly, when there is an absence of trust in conjunction with low self-concern regarding the virus, trust in government significantly reduced compliance among Italians and French (Lalot *et al.* 2020). High levels of institutional trust may have unintended consequences too. People can trust the authorities to the extent that they underestimate the risks and do not take the necessary action (Wong and Jensen 2020), or underestimate the consequences of a pandemic (Wollebæk *et al.* 2020). Yet, recent research on COVID-19 seems to indicate an increased 'rally-round-the-flag' effect due to the pandemic, with trust in political institutions and actors increasing to varying degrees in many national contexts (Jennings 2020). Looking at this phenomenon in the specific context of Europe it is interesting to consider one of the key decisions taken by governments across the continent during the pandemic, which was the lockdown of citizens in their homes, away from public places as well as their places of work. According to Bol *et al.* (2021) the implementation of lockdown measures has been shown to increase trust in government in European countries. Clearly one of the key outcomes of trust that has relevance during global pandemics is its effects on voluntary deference, which is essentially an individual's acceptance and compliance with decisions without consciously questioning the authority's intentions. As such, trust has been repeatedly found to reinforce voluntary deference, which in turn helps authorities in focussing on the management of a crisis without having to continuously explain and justify their actions and their management capabilities (Kramer 1999).

Furthermore, by enhancing voluntary deference, trust influences people's attitude towards contested and conflictual issues and makes individuals more likely to accept any outcome (Tyler 1994). Yet, a healthy level of trust towards authorities, allowing for some criticism, has been considered essential to avoid the situation whereby voluntary deference turns into public blindness towards political actors' misbehaving.

Importantly, trust is negotiated. It is not something that is constant or a feeling that an organization or institution can decide that their stakeholders will share. Through language, the communicator attempts to trigger 'the audience's projection of authority and trustworthiness' onto him- or herself (Baumlin and Baumlin 1994, p. 99). Yet, people tend to question the trustworthiness of authorities when they have a social relationship with them (Kramer and Tyler 1995). So, to gain or reinforce trustworthiness, authorities need to demonstrate competence, virtue and goodwill towards individuals (McCroskey and Teven

1999). Furthermore, transparency is frequently mentioned as key for building trust, particularly in situations characterised by uncertainty, for instance regarding possible side effects (van der Bles *et al.* 2020), and is often considered a core principle of public sector communications (Canel and Luoma-aho 2020).

Public health authorities are advised to engage in 'expectation management' concerning priorities, to express cautious optimism and to let trusted local healthcare personnel administer the vaccine (Warren and Lofstedt 2021). Active communication of transparency and an expert position independent of political needs is recommended (Offerdal *et al.* 2021). Furthermore, a trusted expert position can be preserved by cultivating a position within a larger institutional field of experts and (social) media networks of expertise (Kjeldsen *et al.* in press).

Macro: trust in society

At the macro level, trust is often referred to as public or societal trust. This trust can vary country by country and among members of different cultural groups (Zaheer and Zaheer 2006). Societal trust is essentially a combination of three forms of trust: dispositional trust (Robinson and Jackson 2001), rule-based trust – that is, a generalised confidence in the rules of a society as a result of socialisation into the structure of rules (March and Olsen 1989) – and categorisation-based trust (Kramer 1999). Different studies have pointed out the benefits generated from widespread societal trust for communities, organizations and individuals as well as for economic, political and social purposes. Societal trust is typically seen as a form of social capital (Coleman 1990; Field 2002; Putnam 2001) and portrayed as an asset for society. Social capital often describes the resources of a community and the degree of shared values and trust within it which, for instance, facilitates collective action. Looking explicitly in Europe, in the Nordic countries, the levels of trust and social capital have been described as the Nordic Gold (Rothstein and Holmberg 2020) (see the chapters in this book on the Nordic countries). Country-level indicators of social capital can be in fact measured by the degree to which people within a country demonstrate general trust in others and trust their structure of rules (Bjornskov 2010; Knack and Keefer 1997). Societal trust has been found to be an important predictor for international business performance (Muethel and Bond 2013). It has been shown to have explicit health, safety and environmental consequences – and is a precondition for citizens to feel safe and secure (Spadaro *et al.* 2020). Norms of trust and the belief in the solidarity of others are what helps society avoid the tragedy of the commons (Rothstein 2000).

Trust is also seen as a social mechanism that reduces complexity and uncertainty (Luhmann 1979, 1993; Renn 2008). Without trust, societies would be characterised by chaos and paralysing fears (Luhmann 1979; Valentini and Kruckeberg 2011). In this sense, trust can help develop solidarity in society and reinforce social order (Misztal 1996). When thinking about global pandemics, such as COVID-19, the level of uncertainty was high among the general population in Europe and across the world. For many months, it was not clear when, where and how the disease originated and not much was known about how to cure it. Governments and international organizations across the globe had to change their strategy and recommendations for reducing the spread of this new infectious disease as more knowledge about it emerged. Many countries faced challenging public health situations, and without public trust, many societies would have ended up in total chaos. While differences in the management of the pandemic are visible, as studies from different countries and regions in this book demonstrate, some were more successful than others. Despite the differences, with time a general public trust was established in most countries and this has helped authorities and international organizations to avoid total paralysis.

Yet, societal trust does not come from nowhere. Through their communication actions, strategic communicators can promote solidarity, a sense of trust, and generally reinforce those values that underlie a trusting society, and by doing so they can strengthen the diverse systems interactions and help them function (Heath 2018; Valentini and Kruckeberg 2011). During pandemics certain roles, such as that of the strategic communicator, can be critical to mediate between the different stakeholders (subjects of trust) and the focal organization (object of trust) (Bentele 1994). But why is it important to foster societal trust? As Putnam (1993) observed, 'The greater the level of trust within a community, the greater the likelihood of cooperation. And cooperation itself breeds trust' (p. 171). High levels of trust are indicative of resilient societies that can 'resist, absorb, accommodate to and recover from the effects of a hazard in a timely and efficient manner, including through the preservation and restoration of its essential basic structures and functions' (United Nations Office of Disaster Risk Reduction [UNISDR] 2009, p. 24).

Communication has a huge role to play to help foster resilience (Norris *et al.* 2008). Longstaff and Yang (2008) studied health pandemic crisis situations and highlighted that a society is more likely to recover from the disaster if it has access to trusted information and is subsequently more resilient. Societal trust predicts the extent to which citizens will trust that others will act according to the norms and rules of the society, and subsequently this will affect the citizens' own behaviours. Putting it differently, if social distancing and wearing a mask have become a social norm during the COVID-19 pandemic, citizens of a community with high public trust are most likely going to conform to these preventive norms without government imposition and will trust others to do the same. A study on Swedish citizens' level of interpersonal trust during the first year of the COVID-19 pandemic shows that not only do citizens demonstrate their trust but the coronavirus crisis has even increased trust in other people, meaning Swedes have increased their dispositional trust, which is one important component of societal trust (Esaiasson *et al.* 2021).

An example of trust at the macro level is also trust in the body of science as a collective or institution in society. Descriptions of a 'post-truth society' are floated (e.g., Block 2018; Mcintyre 2018; Waisbord 2018), frequently

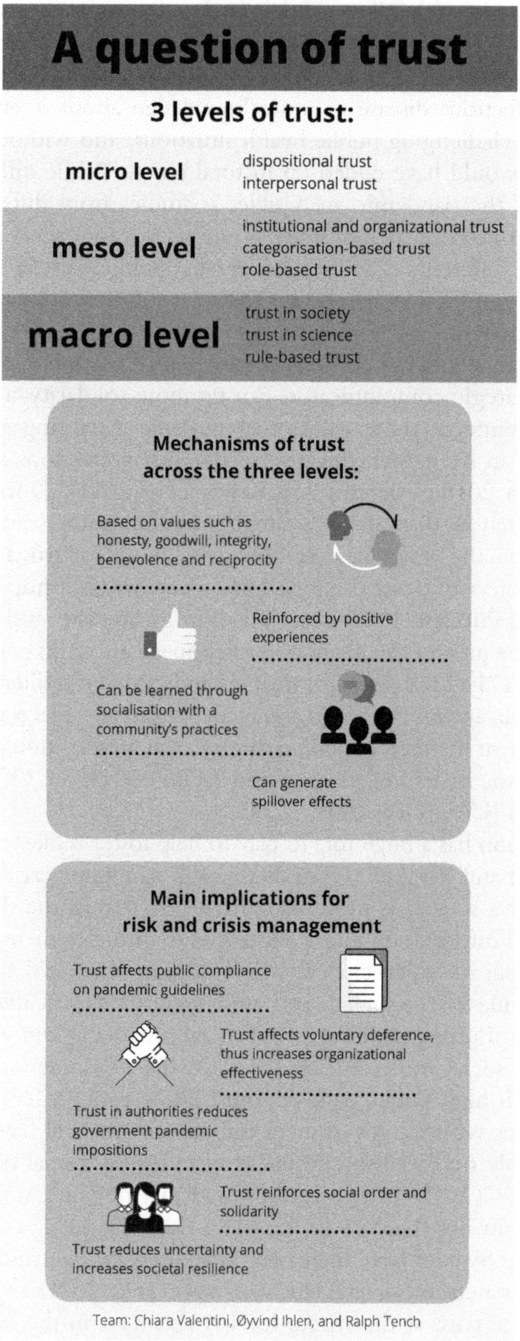

Infographic 2.1 A question of trust

pointing to how politicisation of issues reframes scientific utterings as opinions or politicised narratives. Right-wing attitudes in particular have been associated with lower trust in science, medical expertise and institutions (Baumgartner *et al.* 2018; Larson 2020). Of late, this polarisation has also been noted in the COVID-19 debate, concerning measures as well as vaccination (Lin *et al.* 2021).

Conclusion

This chapter has set the scene within the book about some of the debates and concepts relating to trust and the contextualising of these discussions against the challenging backdrop of health communication during national and international pandemics, initially from European experiences but clearly with an eye to how these principles play out in all contexts. What is clear from the discussion is that trust clearly affects behaviour in times of crisis. This leads to considerations of the sources of trust which are crucial in health pandemics when citizens are instructed to and relied upon to follow public health rules and guidelines, as COVID-19 has clearly demonstrated with core messages of hygiene, social distancing and, eventually, adherence to vaccination procedures. The chapter discusses trust at three levels, the individual (micro), the organizational and institutional (meso) and the societal (macro), to understand and explore how citizens both theoretically and practically have engaged with trust and trusting during the worldwide COVID-19 pandemic. It shows how trust formation is a rather complex, multi-layered mechanism which cannot be reduced to one form or type, particularly during pandemics, when different actors are involved and communicate at the same time.

Three learnings can be deduced. First, as societal resilience has been shown to help in critical situations, building trust in and outside organizations should be a strategic communication priority for any kind of organization oriented towards a stakeholder relationship governance (Falconi 2014). It takes time to build a trusting relationship, and during pandemics communication professionals have limited resources and time to focus on building trust, but they can, on the other hand, leverage it through authentic and transparent communications, if they have previously developed some form of trusting relations. Communication scholarship has a plethora of insights on offer in this regard (see, e.g., Ihlen *et al.* 2021).

Second, messages from the authorities do not always reach all population groups, no matter if the messages are spread through traditional means of communications or through social media. Because of the enormous consequences produced by failing to reach to some public groups – as we have seen in respect to reaching out to some groups, like immigrants, at least at the beginning of the pandemic – authorities must reach all different publics, even those who do not want to be reached. A way to do so is to leverage trust between these publics and those they trust the most. Engaging different kinds of stakeholders in risk communications – for instance, by asking them to become the intermediaries of communications about infectious disease preventive measures – can enhance public reception and acceptance of regulations and governmental measures. As a case in point, some countries, for instance Italy and Finland, have engaged social media and celebrity influencers in their emergency communication plans so as to be able to reach out to the youth (Heikkilä 2020; Reuters 2020). More of this kind of intermediary engagement is needed during emergencies.

Third, increasing dispositional trust, which essentially leads to an increase in generalised trust in others, means increasing the likelihood that individuals will exercise self-control during an infectious disease spreading period. This can be done by working on sustaining other forms of trust, for instance role- and rule-based trust. Stronger role- and rule-based trust support the development of societal norms around values such as transparency, equality, confidence, respect, cooperation and so forth. Such values can eventually institutionalise into communities and pay off during pandemics and other emergencies which often require collective actions to mitigate the spread of disease. Communication professionals can be central in building and weaving networks of social relations with different societal actors willing to lead by positive behaviours where the values at the core of trust are not just communicated but lived and practiced daily. This is particularly important, as actions speak louder than words.

With these theoretical and practical insights in mind, this chapter has highlighted the most important discussions – within the limits of a chapter length – on trust dynamics that can inform future research on risk and crisis communication and calls for new research avenues exploring the interplay between the three levels (micro, meso and macro). Trust is a key factor in risk and crisis management, but a full understanding of the role of strategic communication is still the missing piece of the puzzle that we hope colleagues will take on.

References

Arrow, K. (1974). *The limits of organization.* New York: Norton.

Baldvinsdottir, G., Andreas, H., Inga-Lill J., Kristina J., and Jan M. (2011). Accounting research and trust: A literature review. *Qualitative Research in Accounting and Management*, 8(4), pp. 382–424.

Barber, B. (1983). *The logic and limits of trust.* New Brunswick, NJ: Rutgers University Press.

Bargain, O., and Aminjonov, U. (2020). *Trust and compliance to public health policies in times of COVID-19.* IZA Discussion Paper No. 13205. Institute of Labor Economics [online]. Available from: https://ideas.repec.org/p/iza/izadps/dp13205.html [Accessed 26 April 2021].

Baumgartner, B., Carlisle, J.E., and Justwan, F. (2018). The influence of political ideology and trust on willingness to vaccinate. *PLoS One*, 13(1), e0191728. doi:10.1371/journal.pone.0191728

Baumlin, J.S., and Baumlin, T.F. (1994). On the psychology of the *pisteis*: Mapping the terrains of mind and rhetoric. In J.S. Baumlin and T.F. Baumlin, eds. *Ethos: New essays in rhetorical and critical theory.* Dallas, TX: Southern Methodist University Press, pp. 91–112.

Bentele, G.,1994. ÖffentlichesVertrauen – normative und soziale Grundlage fur public relations. In W. Armbrecht and U. Zabel, eds. *Normative Aspekte der Public Relations.*

Grunlegende Fragen und Perspektiven, Eine Einfuhrung. Opladen: Westdeutscher Verlag, pp. 131–158.

Bjornskov, C. (2010). How does social trust lead to better governance? An attempt to separate electoral and bureaucratic mechanisms. *Public Choice*, 144(1/2), pp. 323–346. Available from: www.jstor.org/stable/40661062

Block, D. (2018). *Post-truth and political discourse*. London: Palgrave Macmillan.

Bol, D., Giani, M., Blais, A., and Loewen, P.J. (2021). The effect of COVID-19 lockdowns on political support: Some good news for democracy? *European Journal of Political Research*, 60, pp. 497–505. doi:10.1111/1475–6765.12401

Brewer, M.B. (1996). In-group favoritism: The subtle side of intergroup discrimination. In D.M. Messick and A. Tenbrunsel, eds., *Behavioral research and business ethics*. New York: Russell Sage Foundation, pp. 160–171.

Canel, M.J., and Luoma-aho, V.L. (2019). *Public sector communication: Closing gaps between citizens and public organizations*. Hoboken, NJ: Wiley Blackwell.

Coleman, J.S. (1990). *Foundations of social theory*. Cambridge, MA: Belknap Press.

Colledge, B., Morgan, J., and Tench, R. (2014). The concept(s) of trust in late modernity, the relevance of realist social theory. *Journal for the Theory of Social Behaviour*, 44(4), pp. 481–503. doi:10.1111/jtsb.12064.

Coronavirus (COVID-19) in the UK (2021a). *Deaths in United Kingdom* [online]. Gov.uk. Available from: https://coronavirus.data.gov.uk/details/deaths [Accessed 14 July 2021].

Coronavirus (COVID-19) in the UK (2021b). *Vaccinations in United Kingdom* [online]. Gov.uk. Available from: https://coronavirus.data.gov.uk/details/vaccinations [Accessed 14 July 2021].

Devine, D., Gaskell, J., Jennings, W., and Stoker, G. (2021). Trust and the Coronavirus pandemic: What are the consequences of and for trust? An early review of the literature. *Political Studies Review*, 19(2), pp. 274–285. doi:10.1177/1478929920948684

Earle, T.C., and Cvetkovich, G. (1995). *Social trust: Toward a cosmopolitan society*. Westport, CT: Praeger.

Esaiasson, P., Sohlberg, J., Ghersetti, M., and Johansson, B. (2021). How the Coronavirus crisis affects citizen trust in institutions and in unknown others: Evidence from 'the Swedish experiment. *European Journal of Political Research*, 60(3), pp. 748–760.

Eurofound (2021). *Living, working and COVID-19: Mental health and trust decline across EU as pandemic enters another year*. Luxembourg: Publications Office of the European Union.

European Centre for Disease Prevention and Control (2021a). *COVID-19 situation update for the EU/EEA* [online]. Available from: www.ecdc.europa.eu/en/cases-2019-ncov-eueea [Accessed 14 July 2021].

European Centre for Disease Prevention and Control (2021b). *COVID-19 vaccine rollout overview* [online]. Available from: https://covid19-vaccine-report.ecdc.europa.eu/ [Accessed 14 July 2021].

European Commission, 2020, 24th June. *COVID-19 pandemic. Statement on scientific advice to European policy makers during the COVID-19 pandemic*. European Commission, European Group on Ethics in Science and New Technologies (EGE). doi:10.2777/190893

Falconi T.M. (2014). *Global stakeholder relationships governance: An infrastructure*. London: Palgrave Pivot.

Fancourt, D., Steptoe, A., and Wright, L. (2020). The Cummings effect: Politics, trust, and behaviours during the COVID-19 pandemic. *The Lancet*, 396(10249), pp. 464–465. doi:10.1016/s0140-6736(20)31690-1

Farjam, M., Bianchi, F., Squazzoni, F., and Bravo, G. (2021). Dangerous liaisons: An online experiment on the role of scientific experts and politicians in ensuring public support for anti-COVID measures. *Royal Society Open Science*, 8(3), p. 201310. doi:10.1098/rsos.201310

Field, J. (2002). *Social capital.* London: Routledge.

Fukuyama, F. (1995). *Trust: The social virtues and the creation of prosperity.* New York: Free Press.

Goldstein, D.A.N., and Wiedemann, J. (2021). Who do you trust? The consequences of partisanship and trust for public responsiveness to COVID-19 orders. *Perspectives on Politics*, pp. 1–27. doi:10.1017/s1537592721000049

Han, Q., Zheng, B., Cristea, M., Agostini, M., Belanger, J., Gutzkow, B., Leander, P. (2020). Trust in government and its associations with health behaviour and prosocial behaviour during the COVID-19 pandemic. *PsyArXiv.* Epub ahead of print. doi:10.31234/osf.io/p5gns

Hardin, R. (1996). Trustworthiness. *Ethics*, 107(1), pp. 26–42. doi:10.1086/233695

Hardin, R. (2002). *Trust and trustworthiness*: New York: Russell Sage Foundation.

Heath, R.L. (2018). Fully functioning society. In R. Heath and W. Johansen, eds. *The International encyclopedia of strategic communication.* New York: Wiley Blackwell. doi:10.1002/9781119010722.iesc0078

Heikkilä, M. (2020, March 31). Finland taps social media influencers during Coronavirus crisis. *Politico* [online]. Available from: www.politico.eu/article/finland-taps-influencers-as-critical-actors-amid-coronavirus-pandemic/ [Accessed 10 July 2021].

Ihlen, Ø., Toledano, M., and Just, S.N. (2021). Using rhetorical situations to examine and improve vaccination. *Communication Frontiers in Communication*, 6(130). doi:10.3389/fcomm.2021.697383

Jennings, W. (2020). *Covid-19 and the 'rally-round-the flag' effect, UK in a changing Europe* [online]. Available from: https://ukandeu.ac.uk/covid-19-and-the-rally-round-the-flag-effect/ [Accessed 23 June 2021].

Kelman, H.C. (2005). Building trust among enemies: The central challenge for international conflict resolution. *International Journal of Operational Research*, 29(6), pp. 639–650. doi:10.1016/j.ijintrel.2005.07.011

Kjeldsen, J., Ihlen, Ø., Just, S.N., and Larsson, A.O., (in press). Trust and ethos of public health promotion: Twitter debates and rhetoric on COVID-19 measures. *Health Promotion International.* doi:10.1093/heapro/daab095

Knack, S., and St Keefer, P. (1997). Does social capital have an economic payoff? A cross-country investigation. *The Quarterly Journal of Economics*, 112(4), pp. 125–1288. Available from: www.jstor.org/stable/2951271

Kramer, R.M. (1999). Trust and distrust in organizations: Emerging perspectives, enduring questions. *Annual Review of Psychology*, 50(1), pp. 569–598. doi:10.1146/annurev.psych.50.1.569

Kramer, R.M., and Tyler, T.R., eds., 1995. *Trust in organizations: Frontiers of theory and research.* Thousand Oaks, CA: Sage Publications.

Kramer, R.M., and Tyler, T.R., eds. (1996). *Trust in organizations: Frontiers of theory and research,* Thousand Oaks, CA: Sage.

Lalot, F., Heering, M.S., Rullo M.,Travaglino, G.A., and Abrams D. (2020, October). The dangers of distrustful complacency: Low concern and low political trust combine to undermine compliance with governmental restrictions in the emerging Covid-19 pandemic. *Group Processes and Intergroup Relations*, 25(1), pp. 106–121. doi:10.1177/1368430220967986

Lane, C. (1998). Introduction: Theories and issues in the study of trust. In C. Lan and R. Bachman, eds. *Trust within and between organizations, conceptual and empirical applications.* Oxford: Oxford University Press, pp. 1–30.

Larson, H.J. (2020). *Stuck: How vaccine rumors start – and why they don't go away*. Oxford: Oxford University Press.

Levi, M., and Stoker, L. (2000). Political trust and trustworthiness. *Annual Review of Political Science*, 3(1), pp. 475–507. doi:10.1146/annurev.polisci.3.1.475

Li, P. (2011). Editorial essay: The rigour, relevance balance for engaged scholarship: New frame and new agenda for trust research and beyond. *Journal of Trust Research*, 1(1), pp. 1–21. doi:10.1080/21515581.2011.550718

Lin, C., Tu, P., and Beitsch, L.M. (2021). Confidence and receptivity for COVID-19 vaccines: A rapid systematic review. *Vaccines*, 9(1), pp. 1–16. doi:10.3390/vaccines9010016

Longstaff, P.H., and Yang, S. (2008). *Communication management and trust: Their role in building resilience to 'surprises' such as natural disasters, pandemic flu, and terrorism* [online]. Available from: www.ecologyandsociety.org/vol13/iss1/art3/ [Accessed 23 June 2021].

Lorenz, E.H. (1988). Neither friends nor strangers: Informal networks of subcontracting in French industry. In D. Gambetta, ed. *Trust: Making and breaking cooperative relations*. New York: Wiley Blackwell, pp. 194–210.

Lucassen, T., and Schraagen, J.M. (2011). Factual accuracy and trust in information: The role of expertise. *Journal of American Society for Information Science and Technology*, 62(7), pp. 1232–1242. doi:10.1002/asi.21545

Lucassen, T., and Schraagen, J.M. (2012). Propensity to trust and the influence of source and medium cues in credibility evaluation. *Journal of Information Science, 38*(6), pp. 566–577. doi:10.1177/0165551512459921

Luhmann, N. (1979). *Trust and power*. Malden, MA: John Willey and Sons.

Luhmann, N. (1993). *Risk: A sociological theory*. Brunswick, NJ: Transaction Publishers.

Luhmann, N. (2000). Familiarity, confidence, trust: Problems and alternatives. In D. Gambetta, ed. *Trust: Making and breaking cooperative relations*. New York: Wiley Blackwell, pp. 94–107.

Luoma-aho, V., and Canel, M.J. eds. (2020). *The handbook of public sector communication*. New York: Wiley Blackwell.

March J.G., and Olsen J.P. (1989). *Rediscovering institutions: The organizational basis of politics*. New York: Free Press.

Mayer, R.C., Davis, J.H., and Schoorman, F.D. (1995). An integrative model of organizational trust. *Academy of Management Review* [online], 20(3), pp. 709–734. Available from: www.jstor.org/stable/258792 [Accessed 23 June 2021].

McAllister, D.J. (1995). Affect-and cognition-based trust as foundations for interpersonal cooperation in organizations. *Academy of Management Journal*, 38(1), pp. 24–59. doi:10.2307/256727

McCroskey, J.C., and Teven, J.J. (1999). Goodwill: A reexamination of the construct and its measurement. *Communication Monographs* [online], 66(1), pp. 90–103. Available from: www.informaworld.com/10.1080/03637759909376464 [Accessed 23 June 2021].

Mcintyre, L. (2018). *Post-truth*. Cambridge, MA: MIT Press.

Misztal, B. (1996). *Trust in modern societies: The search for the basis of social order*. Cambridge, MA: Polity Press.

Muethel, M., and Bond, M. (2013). National context and individual employees' trust of the out-group: The role of societal trust. *Journal of International Business Studies*, 44, pp. 312–333. doi:10.1057/jibs.2013.9

Norris, F.H., Stevens, S.P., Pfefferbaum, B., Wyche, K.F., and Pfefferbaum, R.L. (2008). Community resilience as a metaphor, theory, set of capacities, and strategy for disaster readiness. *American Journal of Community Psychology, 41*(1–2), pp. 127–150. doi:10.1007/s10464-007-9156-6

Nuremberg Institute for Market Decisions. Annual report, 2019 [online]. Available from: www.nim.org/en/publications/annual-reports [Accessed 2 June 2021].

Offerdal, T.S., Just, S.N., and Ihlen, Ø. (2021). Public ethos in the pandemic rhetorical situation: Strategies for building trust in authorities' risk communication. *Journal of International Crisis and Risk Communication Research*, 4(2), pp. 247–270. doi:10.30658/jicrcr.4.2.3

Oksanen, A., Kaakinen, M., Latikka, R., Savolanen, L., and Savela, N. (2020). Regulation and trust: 3-month follow-up study on COVID-19 mortality in 25 European countries. *JMIR Public Health and Surveillance*, 6(2), e19218. doi:10.2196/19218

Olsen, A.L., and Hjorth, F. (2020). *Willingness to distance in the COVID-19. OSF preprints* [online]. Available from: https://osf.io/xpwg2/ [Accessed 23 June 2021].

Pagliaro, S., Sacchi, S., Pacilli, MG., Brambilla, M., Lionetti, F., and Bettache, K. (2021). Trust predicts COVID-19 prescribed and discretionary behavioral intentions in 23 countries. *PLoS ONE*, 16(3), e0248334. doi:10.1371/journal.pone.0248334

Paliszkiewicz, J.O. (2011). Trust management: A literature review. *Management*, 6(4), pp. 315–331.

Prati, G., Pietrantoni, L., and Zani, B. (2011). Compliance with recommendations for pandemic influenza H1N1 2009: The role of trust and personal beliefs. *Health Education Research*, 26(5), pp. 761–769. doi:10.1093/her/cyr035

Putnam, R. (2001). *Bowling alone: The collapse and revival of American community*. New York: Simon and Schuster.

Putnam, R.D. (1993). *Making democracy work: Civic traditions in modern Italy*. Princeton, NJ: Princeton University Press.

Renn, O. (1998). Three decades of risk research: Accomplishments and new challenges. *Journal of Risk Research*, 1(1), pp. 49–71. doi:10.1080/136698798377321

Renn, O. (2008). *Risk governance: Coping with uncertainty in a complex world*. London: Earthscan.

Reuters (2020, October 20). Italian government enlists top influencers to promote COVID masks. *Reuters World News* [online]. Available from: www.reuters.com/article/uk-health-coronavirus-italy-influencers-idUKKBN27525X [Accessed 10 July 2021].

Robinson, R.V., and Jackson, E.F. (2001). Is trust in others declining in America? An age – period – cohort analysis. *Social Science Research*, 30(1), pp. 117–145. doi:10.1006/ssre.2000.0692

Rothstein, B. (2000). Trust, social dilemmas and collective memories. *Journal of Theoretical Politics*, 12(4), pp. 477–501. doi:10.1177/0951692800012004007

Rothstein, B., and Holmberg, S. (2020). *Social trust: The Nordic Gold?* (1653–8919) [online]. Available from: www.socialeurope.eu/book/re-no-11-social-trust-the-nordic-gold [Accessed 23 June 2021].

Roumeliotou, M., and Rontos, K. (2009). Social trust in local communities and its demographic, socio-economic predictors: The case of Kalloni, Lesvos, Greece. *International Journal of Criminology and Sociological Theory*, 2, pp. 230–250.

Rousseau, D.M., Sitkin, S.B., Burt, R.S., and Camerer, C. (1998). Not so different after all: A cross discipline view of trust. *Academic Management Review*, *23*(3), pp. 405–421. doi:10.5465/amr.1998.926617

Siegrist, M., and Cvetkovich, G.T. (2000). Perception of hazards: The role of social trust and knowledge. *Risk Analysis*, 20(5), pp. 713–719. doi:10.1111/0272-4332.205064

Siegrist, M., and Zingg, A. (2014). The role of public trust during pandemics. *European Psychologist*, 19(1), pp. 23–32. doi:10.1027/1016-9040/a000169

Spadaro, G., Gangl, K., Van Prooijen J-W, Van L.P., Mosso CO. (2020). Enhancing feelings of security: How institutional trust promotes interpersonal trust. *PLoS One*, 15(9), e0237934. doi:10.1371/journal.pone.0237934

Sztompka, P. (1999). *Trust: A sociological theory*. Cambridge, UK: Cambridge University Press.

Tyler, T.R. (1994). Psychological models of the justice motive: Antecedents of distributive and procedural justice. *Journal of Personal Sociology and Psychology*, 67(5), pp. 850–863. doi:10.1037/0022-3514.67.5.850

United Nations Office of Disaster Risk Reduction [UNISDR] (2009). *UNISDR terminology on disaster risk reduction*. Geneva, Switzerland: United Nations Office for Disaster Risk Reduction.

Uslaner, E.M. (2002). *The moral foundation of trust*. Cambridge, UK: Cambridge University Press.

Valentini, C. (2021). Trust research in public relations: An assessment of its conceptual, theoretical and methodological foundations. *Corporate Communications: An International Journal*, 26(1), pp. 84–106. doi:10.1108/CCIJ-01-2020-0030

Valentini, C., and Kruckeberg, D. (2011). Public relations and trust in contemporary global society: A Luhmannian perspective of the role of public relations in enhancing trust among social systems. *Central European Journal of Communication* [online], 4, 1(6), pp. 91–107. http://cejsh.icm.edu.pl/cejsh/element/bwmeta1.element.desklight-dd7146cd-6a11-46a7-9826-3570aa147f71 [Accessed 23 June 2021].

van der Bles, A.M., van der Linden, Alexandra L.J. Freeman, David J. Spiegelhalter (2020). The effects of communicating uncertainty on public trust in facts and numbers. *Proceedings of the National Academy of Sciences of the United States of America*, 117(14), pp. 7672–7683. doi:10.1073/pnas.1913678117

Waisbord, S. (2018). The elective affinity between post-truth communication and populist politics. *Communication Research and Practice*, *4*(1), pp. 17–34. doi:10.1080/22041451.2018.1428928

Warren, G.W., and Lofstedt, R. (2021). COVID-19 vaccine rollout risk communication strategies in Europe: A rapid response. *Journal of Risk Research*, 24(3–4), pp. 369–379. doi: 10.1080/13669877.2020.1870533

Williams, M. (2001). In whom we trust: Group membership as an affective context for trust development. *The Academy of Management Review*, *26*(3), pp. 377–396. doi:10.2307/259183

Wollebæk, D., Kristin Roll, Jesse Dylan Williams and Michael Carlsson (2020). *Tillit og bekymring: Hva avgjør om folk følger koronarådene? [Trust and worry: What decides if people are following the corona advice]* [online]. Oslo, Norway: Institute for Social Research.

Wong, C.M.L., and Jensen, O. (2020). The paradox of trust: Perceived risk and public compliance during the COVID-19 pandemic in Singapore. *Journal of Risk Research*, 23(7–8), pp. 1021–1030. doi:10.1080/13669877.2020.1756386

Zaheer, S., and Zaheer, A. (2006). Trust across borders. *Journal of International Business Studies* [online], 37(1), pp. 21–29. Available from: www.jstor.org/stable/3875212 [Accessed 23 June 2021].

3 Communication professionals' adaptation to COVID-19 impacts in North America

Juan Meng, Bryan H. Reber and Tong Xie

Introduction

There is no doubt that the COVID-19 pandemic has generated an ongoing and possibly long-lasting impact to many aspects of communication, the work environment and multiple business sectors worldwide. Due to the prevalence of disinformation as related to the understanding, prevention and safety guidelines to the overall problem associated with the COVID-19 pandemic (Nguyen and Catalan 2020), communication professionals are facing a particular challenge in leading effective and timely communications in this rapidly changing situation. Therefore, it is critical to explore how communication professionals adapt to COVID-19 impacts and lead to successful communication and transitions in a changing work environment.

In this chapter, we report findings based on an international survey of 1,046 full-time communication professionals in Canada and the United States (Meng *et al.* 2021). Several key topics were investigated in our survey, including the perceived impact of the pandemic to communication professionals' daily work and working environment, trusted sources they use in keeping up with the pandemic and using COVID-related information in planning, preparing and responding to the pandemic. Overall, clear evidence is found that communication professionals have paid much attention to the news about the global pandemic and they all agreed that the COVID-19 pandemic is a heavily discussed topic. In general, surveyed professionals acknowledged the pandemic is relevant to the daily work of their communication department or agency and directly affects the daily work of their communication department or agency. Communication professionals use various sources for COVID-19 information. They actively adapt their communication strategies when responding to the pandemic. Implications on how communication professionals could adapt their role as facilitators of effective communication on issues related to the COVID-19 pandemic are discussed.

Experiencing COVID-19: an overview of the COVID-19 pandemic in the region

On 20 January 2020, the United States Centers for Disease Control and Prevention (CDC) confirmed the first COVID-19 case in Snohomish County,

DOI: 10.4324/9781003184669-5

Washington (Holshue *et al.* 2020). On 29 February, the first COVID-19-related death was confirmed in the U.S. (Anderson 2020). When the World Health Organization (WHO) announced the COVID-19 outbreak as a global pandemic, President Donald Trump declared a national emergency on 13 March 2020 to allocate federal funding to fight the coronavirus outbreak in the U.S. and issued a COVID-19-related non-essential travel ban and/or travel restrictions to many countries (AJMC 2021). The coronavirus outbreak developed quickly. Consequently, the dire situation led to the cancellation of large gatherings, the shutdown of businesses and the closure of schools beginning in April 2020 (Katella 2021).

According to the trends in number of COVID-19 cases and deaths in the U.S. reported to CDC, the cumulative confirmed COVID-19 cases in the U.S. reached 43,289,203 with a cumulative death toll of 694,701 by 30 September 2021 (COVID Data Tracker 2021). As the COVID-19 pandemic generated a huge impact on almost all sectors of the country as a whole, it is critical to investigate how individuals cope with the great uncertainty and pressure caused by the pandemic. It is also important to evaluate how individuals retrieve, retain and communicate information about COVID-19, deal with the misinformation related to the disease and preventive procedures, and carry out personal hygiene and preventive health behaviours. Therefore, in this section, we reviewed some recent research and reports that have highlighted COVID-19 communication, misinformation and preventive behaviours in the U.S.

Media channels and sources for COVID-19 communication

The initial global media coverage of the COVID-19 pandemic was experienced in three stages in early 2020, namely the first rise after 20 January, a slight decline until late February and a surge starting in early March. After the Chinese government took assertive prevention measures to launch a full lockdown to the city of Wuhan on 23 January 2020, the WHO provided related information and warned international communities about the potential damage the virus may cause (WHO 2020a). When Chinese government officials confirmed the human-to-human transmission of COVID-19 (China National Health Commission 2020), there was a rise of global media coverage after 20 January (Fu and Zhu 2020; Taylor 2020). However, the media coverage experienced a slight decline until late February, before the report of confirmed COVID-19 cases in other countries, including Italy, Spain, Iran and South Korea, in March 2020 (Fu and Zhu 2020; Taylor 2020). Subsequently, the international communities witnessed a significant increase of media coverage and social media discussion on COVID-19 on a global scale (Fu and Zhu 2020; Li *et al.* 2020; Sousa-Pinto *et al.* 2020).

Although the WHO declared a public health emergency of international concern as early as 30 January 2020, international communities seemed to ignore the warning and some recommended preventive actions such as rapid testing, case tracing and social distancing (Fu and Zhu 2020, Independent Panel for Pandemic Preparedness and Response 2021, Maxmen 2021). The delayed reaction and unpreparedness reflected across international communities may have influenced how individuals perceived and responded to the pandemic.

Research and reports indicate that individuals relied on information from public health authorities and officials, governmental officials and diverse media channels to be updated on the development of the pandemic and the prevention of the infectious disease (*The Economist* 2020; Riehm *et al.* 2020). Individuals in the U.S. reported they used traditional media including different national news sources (e.g., Fox News, CNN, MSNBC, NBC, CBS and ABC) and local news sources to receive updates on the pandemic (Riehm *et al.* 2020). Social media, such as Facebook, Instagram, Twitter and TikTok, were also a main venue where communication, information dissemination and public health education occurred (Ostrovsky and Chen 2020; Riehm *et al.* 2020).

In terms of the diversity of information channels, the U.S. public were able to consult different options. When considering trusted information sources about COVID-19, the majority of U.S. residents reported they perceived the CDC as a reliable source, followed by Dr. Anthony Fauci, state government officials, WHO, President Trump, and some mainstream news media (Kirzinger *et al.* 2020). However, the perceived trustworthiness of different information sources exhibited a relatively clear bipartisan pattern, which made the response task a complex one in the U.S.

Bipartisanship and COVID-19 communication

Research indicated that many in the U.S. processed COVID-19-related information and responded in a bipartisan way during the pandemic. Although there were no significant differences between Democrats and Democratic leaners, Independents, Republicans and those who lean Republican when comparing the CDC, Dr. Anthony Fauci and state government officials as trusted information sources, Kirzinger and associates (2020) identified interesting bipartisan patterns. Their research indicates that Republicans trusted the WHO and news media less if compared to Democrats. Meanwhile, Republicans trusted President Trump more than Democrats did (Kirzinger *et al.* 2020). Overall, Democrats reported being very or somewhat concerned about the pandemic development while Republicans reported being less or not concerned at all. Republicans reported a higher confidence in the U.S. healthcare system and federal government to handle the pandemic while Democrats reported an opposite perception (Quinnipiac University Poll 2020).

Similar bipartisan trust patterns were also identified in another national poll (Kirzinger *et al.* 2020). Findings reveal that Democrats (70%) trust information from the WHO more, if compared to Republicans (57%). Trust in news media is much higher among Democrats (63%) than among Republicans (33%). Trust in President Trump also revealed a clear bipartisan pattern: 89% Republicans vs. 12% Democrats. Some other research found that Republicans were less knowledgeable about COVID-19 (Clements 2020). These bipartisan patterns exaggerated the damage of an 'infodemic', defined by the WHO as 'an overabundance of information – some accurate and some not – that makes it hard for people to find trustworthy sources and reliable guidance when they need it' (Motta *et al.* 2020; WHO 2020b).

The whole society faced not only the threats and damage brought by the pandemic but also the challenge of distinguishing and confronting COVID-19-related misinformation and disinformation. For example, a report from *The Economist* and YouGov (2020) showed 80% of surveyed U.S. adults (based on a sample of 1,500 U.S. adults) followed the COVID-19 news closely. Nearly half of surveyed U.S. adults (49%) believed or somewhat believed that the coronavirus disease was human-made. The survey also found 44% of participants believed or somewhat believed the threat of COVID-19 was exaggerated for political reasons and 13% of participants believed or somewhat believed COVID-19 was a hoax. Results of an American Trends Panel conducted by the Pew Research Center 10–16 March 2020 revealed similar trends: 22% of surveyed U.S. adults believed the lab origin conspiracy with regard to COVID-19 and 7% of participants believed that the new coronavirus was made accidentally in a lab. In addition, 24% of participants believed that a COVID-19 vaccine would be available within a few months (Motta *et al.* 2020).

COVID-19: misinformation and disinformation

Misinformation and conspiracy theories related to COVID-19 had a stronger presence through some right-leaning media, including Fox News, Fox Business, Fox Nation, Breitbart, Rush Limbaugh, and other conservative media outlets (Motta *et al.* 2020). The primary use of right-leaning media to receive COVID-19 information was correlated to at least two pieces of common misinformation: 1) COVID-19 was made in a lab intentionally or accidentally, and 2) a COVID-19 vaccine will be available soon. Particularly, the belief in a lab origin conspiracy theory was correlated with distrust in scientists and media. What's more, participants who held lab origin conspiracy beliefs were significantly more likely to believe the CDC was overplaying the risk of COVID-19 (Motta *et al.* 2020).

Research confirmed that President Trump was at the epicenter of the COVID-19 infodemic. A content analysis of more than one million pieces of news related to the topic of COVID-19 from different sources between 1 January and 26 May 2020 found that 46.6% of the media content discussed misinformation or the act of conspiracy (Evanega *et al.* 2020). Misinformation identified in the coded news spanned 11 sub-topics, including miracle cures (26.4% of total sample), new world order/deep state (4.4%), Democratic Party hoax (3.6%), Wuhan lab/bioweapon (2.6%), Bill Gates (2.5%), 5G (2.1%), antisemitic conspiracies (1.6%), population control (1.3%), Dr. Anthony Fauci (1.0%), Plandemic (0.7%), and bat soup (0.6%). Among the overall COVID-19-related misinformation and discussion, 37.9% mentioned President Trump and 26.4% related to so-called miracle cures, most notably, the use of hydroxychloroquine and chloroquine. Although the content analysis found a substantial amount of misinformation about COVID-19, only 16.4% of the conversations and discussion were subjected to fact checking. The majority of misinformation was delivered through media outlets without verification or later correction (Evanega *et al.* 2020).

COVID-19-related misinformation does not only influence individuals' perceptions of the infectious disease but also directly affects their preventive behaviours when coping with the pandemic. An *Economist*/YouGov poll (2020) collected U.S. adults' perceptions on COVID-19 preventive measures. The report found that 70% of surveyed U.S. adults did not believe medical face masks should be required. Half of participants were against closing schools, while 51% of participants thought people should not be stopped or restricted from attending in person any sporting events organized by the National Collegiate Athletic Association. In addition, 41% of participants thought most Americans were overreacting to COVID-19 and 51% of participants were not too worried or not worried at all.

The lack of science-based knowledge on COVID-19 was associated with the adoption of poor preventive measures, such as attending crowded mass events and hoarding groceries, personal hygiene products and cleaning supplies (Clements 2020). Research found that the amount and the frequency of exposure to disinformation that intentionally and deceptively misleads audiences to discredit authoritative sources were positively correlated with news avoidance (Hameleers *et al.* 2020).

Information consumption and individuals' life during the pandemic

In addition to misinformation and disinformation, research confirms that media usage and information consumption in general caused wide-ranging impacts on individuals' lives during the pandemic, especially during the lockdown period. The U.S. public reported a medium level of stress in personal life, insecurity in employment, anxiety in financial status and disruption in daily routines as consequences of the pandemic (Li *et al.* 2020; Kirzinger *et al.* 2020; Pahayahay and Khalili-Mahani 2020; Riehm *et al.* 2020; Rosen *et al.* 2020). To cope with self-isolation and quarantine, young adults were more likely to use Netflix or similar streaming services and spend more time on computer games, while older adults chose print media and network television. Video chat, telephone and streaming services were the top three media vehicles to experience a significant increase in usage and subscriptions.

It is important to note that a higher level of stress was found to be correlated with heavier usage of passive viewing behaviours such as via streaming services and YouTube (Pahayahay and Khalili-Mahani 2020). Similarly, the time individuals spent on social media and the amount of traditional media they used to learn about COVID-19 were positively associated with increased mental distress. This association was independent of participants' prior psychological stress, demographics and perceived COVID-19 impact and risk to personal life

(Riehm *et al.* 2020). It is a challenging task for individuals to balance this potential negativity and the need to stay informed about the COVID-19 preventive measures and etiology, while maintaining appropriate social interactions.

The state of play: COVID-19 communication experience and insights

Due to the prevalence of disinformation as related to the understanding, prevention and safety guides to the overall problem associated with the COVID-19 pandemic (Nguyen and Catalan-Matamoros 2020), communication professionals faced a particular challenge in leading effective and timely communications while coping with the ongoing uncertainty and complexity caused by the COVID-19 global pandemic. Particularly, we are interested in exploring how communication professionals adapted their role as facilitators of effective communication on issues related to the COVID-19 pandemic. Findings reported in this chapter are largely derived from the North American Communication Monitor (NACM) 2020–2021 (Meng *et al.* 2021).

In the 2020–2021 NACM, we designed a section focussing on the COVID-19 pandemic and its impact on several key issues related to communication professionals' responses and challenges. In this chapter, we share communication professionals' COVID-19 communication experiences and insights. Particularly, we focus on the following four sub-topics: 1) the perceived impact of the COVID-19 pandemic; 2) sources and the most trusted source for COVID-19 information; 3) using COVID-19 information to adapt communication strategies; and 4) leadership support in COVID-19 communication. The following paragraphs present the key findings addressing these four sub-topics.

An overview of the research sample

An online survey of public relations and communication professionals in Canada and the United States was employed in this study to reflect the international scope of this research, as well as to achieve a representative international sample to support the purpose of our research. We used the audience database of Qualtrics and its online platform to recruit qualified respondents. By the time the survey was closed, we were able to retain a final sample of 1,046 full-time public relations and communication professionals in Canada and the United States. All reported findings are based on the 1,046 valid responses.

The average age of our respondents is 41.2 (SD = 11.33) with a range from 19 to 86. The final sample included 545 women (52.1%) and 499 men (47.7%). We had 268 professionals from Canada (25.6%) and the rest of the respondents were in the U.S. (n = 778, 74.4%). The top areas of their job responsibilities include: communication, marketing, brand and consumer communication (n = 346, 33.1%), online communication and social media (n = 225, 21.5%), overall communication (n = 188, 18.0%), strategy and coordination of the communication function (n = 148, 14.1%), community relations (n = 134,

12.8%), internal communication and change management (n = 121, 11.6%), and monitoring, measurement and evaluation (n = 108, 10.3%). As for ethnicity, 753 respondents were white/Caucasian professionals (72.0%), 95 Black/African Americans (9.1%), 93 Asian/Asian Americans (8.9%), 57 Hispanics (5.4%), and other minorities (n = 48, 4.6%).

The impact of the COVID-19 pandemic

Our first sub-topic aimed at finding out the degree of impact the COVID-19 pandemic had on communication professionals' daily work. Results indicated that surveyed communication professionals have paid much attention to the news about the global pandemic ($M = 4.08$, $SD = 1.06$) on a scale ranging from 1 (not at all) to 5 (to a great extent) and they agreed that the COVID-19 pandemic is a heavily discussed topic in their country ($M = 4.25$, $SD = .91$). Therefore, the results confirmed the wide influence of the pandemic in the social landscape and debate. When we asked communication professionals to evaluate the direct impact of the COVID-19 pandemic on their daily communication practice, we found the impact level was not as high as it was in the social landscape and debate. In general, surveyed professionals acknowledged the pandemic is relevant to the daily work of their communication department or agency ($M = 3.86$, $SD = 1.12$) and directly affects the daily work of their communication department or agency ($M = 3.82$, $SD = 1.13$).

When we examined the gender differences, we found that male professionals rated the impact of the COVID-19 pandemic on their daily work significantly higher than female professionals ($Mean_{diff} = .16$, t-value = 2.33, $d.f.$ = 1,042, $p < .05$). They also think the pandemic is more relevant to the daily work of their communication department or agency ($Mean_{diff} = .14$, t-value = 2.07, $d.f.$ = 1,042, $p < .05$). When comparing professionals' responses by geographic location, it is surprising to find that professionals in Canada rated the impact of the global pandemic higher than their peers in the U.S. across all four questions we asked, with a significantly higher score on the relevance of the pandemic to their daily work ($Mean_{diff} = .18$, t-value = 2.38, $d.f.$ = 1,044, $p < .05$).

Another critical demographic variable we investigated is years of experience and how it related to the impact of the global pandemic. Findings revealed the general trend that as the years of experience increase, the perceived impact of the COVID-19 pandemic also increased. The group of senior professionals with more than 15 years of experience reported the highest scores in: paying attention to the news about the pandemic ($F = 9.05$, $d.f.$ = [3, 1,042], $p < .01$), considering the pandemic is a heavily discussed topic in the country ($F = 3.35$, $d.f.$ = [3, 1,042], $p < .05$), the pandemic is relevant to the daily work of the communication department or agency ($F = 6.37$, $d.f.$ = [3, 1,042], $p < .01$), and the pandemic significantly affects the daily work of the communication department or agency ($F = 4.58$, $d.f.$ = [3, 1,042], $p < .01$).

Such a pattern is also confirmed along the leadership line as we compared responses from leaders and non-leaders. Communication leaders at the levels

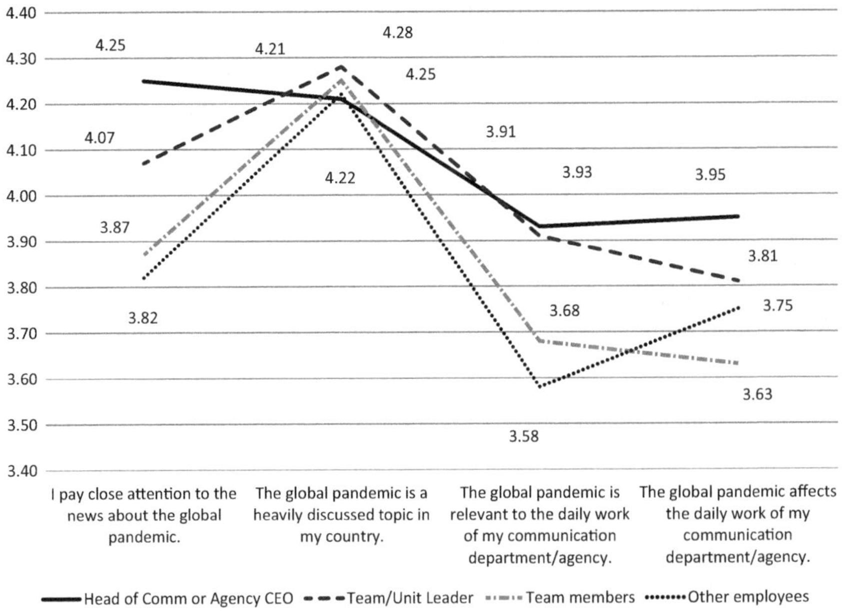

Figure 3.1 The impact of the COVID-19 pandemic as perceived by communication leaders and non-leaders

Source: Authors

of team, unit or organization expressed significantly higher concerns about the impact associated with the global pandemic, if compared with team members and other general employees in communication. Figure 3.1 displays the trend lines as reflected by the ratings from communication leaders and non-leaders.

Sources for COVID-19 information

The COVID-19 pandemic created an urgent need to digest and communicate health information to enable workplace pivot, but how can communication professionals best deliver the information, given the unique role of being a communicator on behalf of their own organization? To investigate the various sources that communication professionals used for COVID-19, we summarised and generated a list of sources for COVID-19 information based on a Pew Research Center report on COVID-19 news habits (Mitchell and Oliphant 2020). Based on the ratings on a scale ranging from 1 (not at all) to 5 (to a great extent), the top five sources communication professionals used for COVID-19 information are: 1) public health organizations and officials (M = 4.01, SD = 1.06); 2) national news outlets (M = 3.88, SD = 1.06); 3) local news outlets (M = 3.72, SD = 1.10); 4) state and local elected officials (M = 3.67, SD = 1.09); and 5) international news outlets (M = 3.58, SD = 1.22).

Gender differences were significant when it is about sources for COVID-19 information. Men rated their frequency of using most sources higher than women, with significantly higher scores on the following sources: international news outlets (t = 2.73, $p < .01$), the president or prime minister and their respective COVID-19 task force (t = 3.09, $p < .01$), social media (such as Facebook, Twitter or Instagram) (t = 3.40, $p < .01$), friends, family and neighbours (t = 2.77, $p < .01$), church or religious leaders (t = 4.14, $p < .01$), community or neighbourhood newsletter or listserv (t = 5.14, $p < .01$), social influencers and bloggers (t = 4.74, p < .01) and internet/mobile apps (t = 2.64, p < .01).

When examining the topic by country, the use of information sources did not differ significantly. Professionals in Canada are leading in getting COVID-19 information from the prime minister and their respective coronavirus task force (t = 4.67, $p < .01$) and international news outlets (t = 1.93, $p < .05$), while professionals in the U.S. showed significantly higher scores in two other sources: church or religious leaders (t = 4.36, $p < .01$) and social influencers and bloggers (t = 2.14, $p < .05$).

While communication professionals get COVID-19 information from a variety of sources, our analysis confirmed that using more information sources was associated with higher ranks along the leadership line. Top communication leaders such as head of corporate communication or agency CEO reported significantly higher scores on all listed information sources if compared to communication leaders at the team or unit level and other team members or general employees. This could be further explained by the trend-setting priorities and the strategic planning tasks associated with top communication leaders as they respond to strategic change and redirect the understanding of lower-level organizational employees toward a changing and challenging reality.

Most trusted source for COVID-19 information

To dive deep into communication professionals' information-seeking behaviour, we further asked them to select their most trusted source for COVID-19 information. Respondents reported trusting public health organizations and officials the most (n = 362, 34.6%), followed by national news outlets (n = 156, 14.9%). Trust in government (i.e., the president or prime minister and their respective COVID-19 task force) was ranked as third (n = 103, 9.8%).

A similar trust pattern was identified when comparing the answers by country, gender and leadership position. The only difference was in the category of social media: we found more professionals in the U.S. (n = 70, 9.0%) selected social media as their most trusted information source than did those in Canada (n = 15, 5.6%) (X^2 = 20.98, *d.f.* = 12, $p < .05$).

Using COVID-19 information to adapt and develop communication strategies

Communicators are constantly using information to build knowledge, enhance trust, develop strategies and guide action. Therefore, we were particularly interested in investigating how communication professionals in both countries used COVID-19 information in guiding their communication practice. We asked surveyed professionals to share how they used COVID-19 information to plan, prepare and respond to the changes and challenges caused by the global pandemic. The results revealed that the most common usage of COVID-19 information was to develop and implement formal safety guidelines, infrastructure and routines for their organization or client ($M = 3.81$, $SD = 1.13$), with 87.3% of respondents indicating their usage ranging from 'moderate' to 'a great deal'. Less than 5% of respondents expressed that they did not use COVID-19 information at all to develop safety guidelines.

Other adapting strategies included distributing COVID-19 information to employees in the organization or to the client (84.5%), using COVID-19 information to develop top-level strategies for the organization or the client (84.4%) and using COVID-19 information to develop functional strategies to support HR, IT, brands or service for the organization or the client (83.8%). The least used action was to propose a political stance for the leadership team in the organization or the client (69.9%). Two out of 10 professionals indicated that they did not use COVID-19 information at all to propose a political stance for the leadership team.

When comparing the responses between women and men, we found similar usage of COVID-19 information to develop related communication strategies. However, men rated two actions significantly higher than their female counterparts: to propose a political stance for the leadership team ($t = 4.81$, $p < .01$) and to distribute COVID-19 information to employees ($t = 2.96$, $p < .01$). No significant difference was found when comparing by country.

Consistently, we found that the higher the leadership rank, the more they would use COVID-19 information to adapt and develop communication strategies. Top communication leaders (i.e., head of corporate communication or agency CEO) reported significantly higher scores on all five communication actions, as depicted in Figure 3.2.

Leadership support in COVID-19 communication

In the NACM 2020–2021, we asked our surveyed communication professionals to evaluate the wider performance of their organization's top leadership when leading the organization to navigate through the strategic change during the global pandemic. Communication professionals confirmed several leadership initiatives were demonstrated appropriately as part of the wider organizational change effort. The top-rated one is that top leadership has stressed the importance of employee safety and health measures during the pandemic ($M = 4.18$, $SD = .99$) on a scale ranging from 1 (strongly disagree) to 5 (strongly agree), with 77.9% of respondents confirming their organization's top leadership emphasised the safety initiative.

Professionals in both countries agreed that their organization's top leadership team emphasised their commitment to effective crisis management ($M = 4.06$, $SD = .99$). The top leadership team was transparent and forthright in

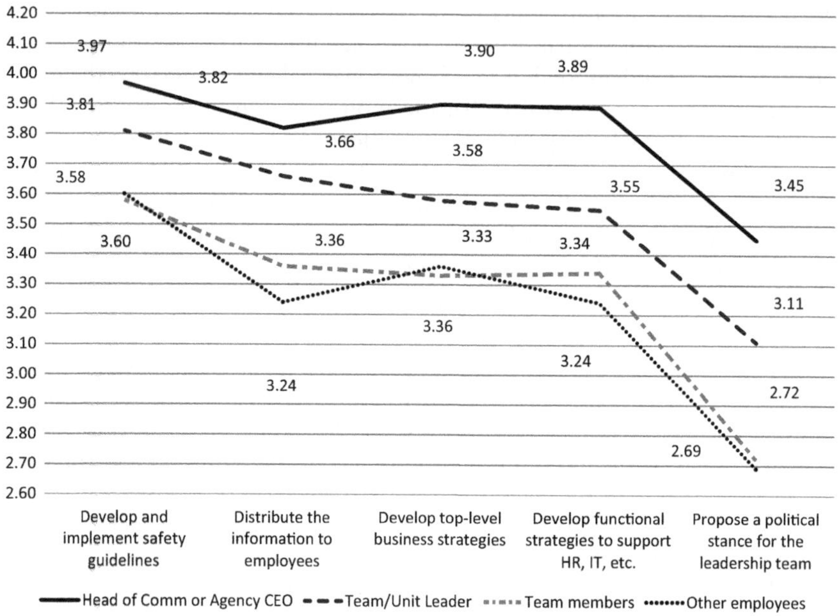

Figure 3.2 Using COVID-19 information to adapt and develop communication strategies: Differences between communication leaders and non-leaders

Source: Authors

communicating with employees about its plans in responding to the pandemic (M = 4.04, SD = .98). The top leadership team provided resources and technology to help employees maintain productivity and performance while working remotely (M = 4.04, SD = 1.01). Overall, surveyed professionals in both countries agreed that the top leadership in their organization has done sufficient work in leading organizational members to cope with the global pandemic (M = 4.03, SD = 1.00).

However, surveyed communication professionals said the top leadership can do a better job in sharing a clear vision of its post-pandemic workplace structure and culture (M = 3.88, SD = 1.04). Related to the evaluation on organizational vision, respondents also addressed more efforts are needed to develop a sense of solidarity to strengthen employees' confidence in the future (M = 3.93, SD = 1.00). They also expressed the need to have more support in maintaining a good balance between work and their living situations during the pandemic (M = 3.97, SD = 1.02). This was particularly emphasised by female professionals as the pandemic has brought a disproportionately negative impact to women in the workplace ($Mean_{diff}$ = -.13, t-value = -2.04, $d.f.$ = 1,042, $p < .05$).

The disparities in organizations' leadership support were also confirmed along the leadership line. Communication leaders rated top leadership support and performance significantly higher than non-leaders along the hierarchical line. This further indicates the importance of transparency in communication when leading organizational members to cope with a dramatically changing work environment as caused by the pandemic.

Observations and interrogation

As revealed by our research findings, it is not surprising that the COVID-19 pandemic significantly affected the daily work of communication departments and agencies. Communication professionals feel the pressure to deal with accelerated needs to provide COVID-related information to organizational leaders, co-workers and various groups of stakeholders. In general, we can confirm that the COVID-19 pandemic has significantly changed the communication environment by driving communication professionals' attention to consume more news related to it and becoming a heavily discussed social topic in the countries we investigated. By its very nature, years of experience in the profession of communication have led to higher levels of concerns on the presence of the global pandemic. Similarly, when organizations face disruptive change as caused by environmental fluctuations, it requires the leadership team to be more responsive to lead successful change.

While acting as a major source of information distribution, communication professionals also use multiple sources to collect COVID-related information, among which public health organizations and officials are rated as the most trusted source, followed by national news outlets, and the president or prime minister and their respective COVID task force. Communication professionals agree that they have gathered COVID-related information to develop and implement formal safety guidelines, distributed safety information to employees in the organization and developed top-level strategies to support organizational and business strategies in leading transitions during the pandemic.

However, when evaluating the organization's top leadership support in change management, communication professionals are unsatisfied. Some major criticism includes lacking a clear vision of the post-pandemic workplace structure and culture, not expending sufficient efforts in developing a sense of solidarity to strengthen employees' confidence in the future and not helping employees maintain a good balance between work and living situations during the pandemic. Such disparities are particularly deep between female communication professionals and their male counterparts, as well as along the leadership hierarchical line. Findings like these suggested that the implementation of transparency in communication is much needed to facilitate actions at different levels that can contribute to trust building.

Implications and conclusions

The global pandemic that is spreading COVID-19 and leaving death in its wake presents a communication problem like no other. Communication leaders are

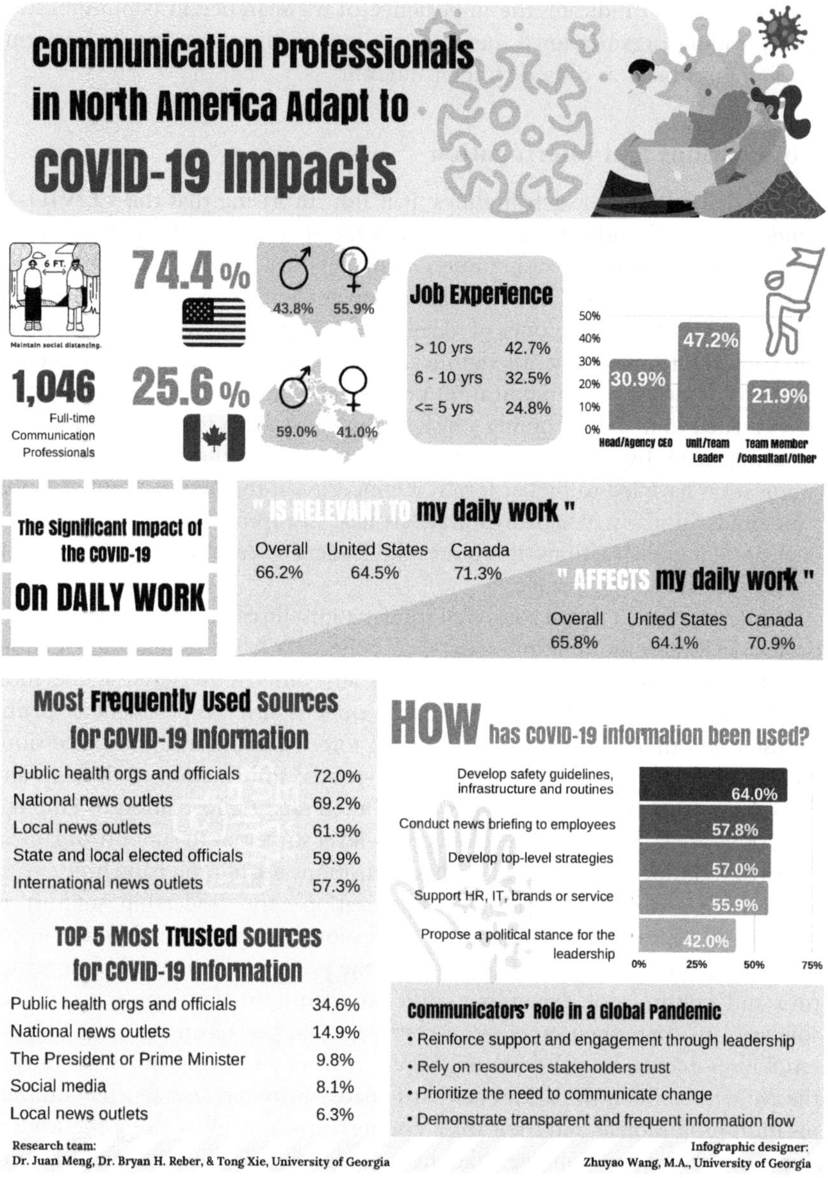

Infographic 3.1 Communication professionals in North America adapt to COVID-19 impacts

faced with a long-term and variable challenge. Not only is communication with stakeholders largely limited to virtual environments, but the information environment itself is highly unstable. What is believed to be true today may be debunked tomorrow, requiring recrafted messages with assurances of transparency and admission of uncertainty. This study reveals several implications for communication leaders, especially when facing a fast-moving, volatile and long-lasting global crisis.

1 Demographics matter. Gender, longevity in their careers and place on the hierarchy all affected responses and attitudes. This finding reinforces what good leaders already know: diversity on a team, diversity of all kinds, will improve communication response and leadership.
2 Some things cannot be delegated. Our research affirms that hierarchy matters. Respondents who identified as head of corporate communication/agency CEO were those most engaged in gathering reliable information and solving the communication problem. When a major problem arises, it is clear that the top communicator has to be completely invested and take the lead in developing and communicating solutions.
3 Rely on resources stakeholders trust. Expertise matters perhaps more than is typical during a health communication crisis. Respondents told us that their most trusted information source was public health and medical experts. Whether the problem is a global pandemic or corporate malfeasance, communication leaders face the issue of identifying and cultivating information sources that varied stakeholders trust.
4 Communicating organizational change is challenging. In the inevitable circumstances that leading business communicators find themselves in, employee communication and engagement is a special problem. Respondents reinforce the need for communicators to both manage and communicate expectations. When an employee's work rituals, and in many cases her or his environment, are so disrupted, then clear, frequent and redundant communication may be necessary.

In conclusion, results presented in this chapter share insights on communication professionals' responses as adapting their communication strategies in the face of the COVID-19 global pandemic. Our results reveal the central role of communication in a global pandemic. Nearly 9 in 10 respondents acknowledged communications' role in developing and communicating safety standards. Such findings further echo the importance of effective communication strategies during an unexpected emergency such as the COVID-19 pandemic (Mazzei 2021). It is crucial to create a sense of security by providing information on the protective measures and behaviours to be adopted by employees. It is communicators' leading responsibility to reinforce the transparency and clarification of information flow.

There will be ongoing lessons learned from communication problems and solutions encountered and generated in the face of this pandemic. Our research suggests the basic, classic and time-tested strategies and tactics still rule the day. In the topsy-turvy work environment many find themselves in, maybe there is some comfort in knowing that – though they are ratcheted up to meet the higher stakes – standard communication tactics that rely on solid information, frequent and transparent communication, trustworthy sources and lots of hard work will keep communication leaders in good stead.

Bibliography

AJMC (2021). A timeline of COVID-19 developments in 2020 [online]. *AJMC*. Available from: www.ajmc.com/view/a-timeline-of-covid19-developments-in-2020 [Accessed 29 April 2021].

Anderson, M. (2020). President Trump confirms 1st U.S. Coronavirus death; U.S. heightens travel warnings [online]. *NPR*. Available from: www.npr.org/2020/02/29/810722517/seattle-area-patient-with-coronavirus-dies, [Accessed 30 April 2021].

CDC (2021). Daily trends in number of COVID-19 cases in the United States reported to CDC [online]. *CDC*. Available from: https://covid.cdc.gov/covid-data-tracker/#trends_dailytrendscases [Accessed 30 September 2021].

China National Health Commission (2020). *Inclusion of 2019 novel Coronavirus diseases (COVID-19) into statutory infectious disease management* [online]. China National Health Commission. Available from: www.nhc.gov.cn/jkj/s7916/202001/44a3b8245e8049d2837a4f27529cd386.shtml [Accessed 30 April 2021].

Clements, J.M. (2020). Knowledge and behaviors toward COVID-19 among US residents during the early days of the pandemic: Cross-sectional online questionnaire. *JMIR Public Health and Surveillance*, 6(2), e19161.

The Economist (2020). *Toplines for March 8–10 economist/yougov poll* [online]. YouGov. Available from: https://docs.cdn.yougov.com/1ghnpqhhpu/econToplines.pdf [Accessed 29 April 2021].

Evanega, S., Lynas, M., Adams, J., Smolenyak, K., and Insights, C.G. (2020). Coronavirus misinformation: Quantifying sources and themes in the COVID-19 'infodemic'. *JMIR Preprints* [online], 19(10), p. 2020. Available from: https://allianceforscience.cornell.edu/wp-content/uploads/2020/10/Evanega-et-al-Coronavirus-misinformation-submitted_07_23_20.pdf [Accessed 29 April 2021].

Fu, K.W., and Zhu, Y. (2020). Did the world overlook the media's early warning of COVID-19? *Journal of Risk Research*, 23(7–8), pp. 1047–1051.

Hameleers, M., van der Meer, T.G., and Brosius, A. (2020). Feeling 'disinformed' lowers compliance with COVID-19 guidelines: Evidence from the US, UK, Netherlands, and Germany. *Harvard Kennedy School Misinformation Review* [online], 1(3). Available from: https://misinforeview.hks.harvard.edu/article/feeling-disinformed-lowers-compliance-with-covid-19-guidelines-evidence-from-the-us-uk-netherlands-and-germany/ [Accessed 29 April 2021].

Holshue, M.L., DeBolt, C., Lindquist, S., Lofy, K.H., Wiesman, J., Bruce, H., Spitters, C., Ericson, K., Wilkerson, S., Tural, A., and Diaz, G. (2020). First case of 2019 novel Coronavirus in the United States. *New England Journal of Medicine* [online], 382, pp. 929–936. Available from: www.nejm.org/doi/full/10.1056/NEJMoa2001191

Independent Panel for Pandemic Preparedness and Response for the WHO Executive Board (2021). *The second report prepared by the independent panel for pandemic preparedness and response for the WHO executive board* [online]. Available from: https://theindependentpanel.org/documents/ [Accessed 29 April 2021].

Katella, K. (2021). *Our pandemic year-a COVID-19 timeline* [online]. Yale Medicine. Available from: www.yalemedicine.org/news/covid-timeline [Accessed 28 April 2021].

Kirzinger, A., Kearney, A., Hamel, L., and Brodie, M. (2020). KFF health tracking poll: Early April 2020: The impact of Coronavirus on life in America [online]. *KFF*. Available from: www.kff.org/coronavirus-covid-19/report/kff-health-tracking-poll-early-april-2020/ [Accessed 29 April 2021].

Li, X., Zhou, M., Wu, J., Yuan, A., Wu, F., and Li, J. (2020). Analyzing COVID-19 on online social media: Trends, sentiments and emotions. *arXiv preprint arXiv*, 2005,14464. Available from: https://arxiv.org/pdf/2005.14464.pdf

Maxmen, A. (2021). Why did the world's pandemic warning system fail when COVID hit? [online]. *Nature*. Available from: www.nature.com/articles/d41586-021-00162-4 [Accessed 28 April 2021].

Mazzei, A. (2021). How COVID-19 taught corporations the value of internal communication [online]. *Blog Post*, The Institute for Public Relations. Available from: https://instituteforpr.org/how-covid-19-strengthened-the-value-and-importance-of-internal-communicationli/ [Accessed 29 April 2021].

Meng, J., Reber, B.H., Berger, B.K., Gower, K.K., and Zerfass, A. (2021). *North American communication monitor 2020–2021: The impact of COVID-19 pandemic, ethical challenges, gender issues, cyber security, and competence gaps in strategic communication*. Tuscaloosa, AL: The Plank Center for Leadership in Public Relations.

Mitchell, A., and Oliphant, J.B. (2020). Americans immersed in COVID-18 news; Most think media are doing fairly well covering it [online]. *Pew Research Center*. Available from: www.journalism.org/2020/03/18/americans-immersed-in-covid-19-news-most-think-media-are-doing-fairly-well-covering-it/ [Accessed 29 April 2021].

Motta, M., Stecula, D., and Farhart, C. (2020). How right-leaning media coverage of COVID-19 facilitated the spread of misinformation in the early stages of the pandemic in the US. *Canadian Journal of Political Science*, 53(2), pp. 335–342.

Nguyen, A., and Catalan, D. (2020). Digital mis/disinformation and public engagment with health and science controversies: Fresh perspectives from Covid-19. *Media and Communication*, 8(2), pp. 323–328.

Ostrovsky, A.M., and Chen, J.R. (2020). TikTok and its role in COVID-19 information propagation. *Journal of Adolescent Health*, 67(5), p. 730.

Pahayahay, A., and Khalili-Mahani, N. (2020). What media helps, what media hurts: A mixed methods survey study of coping with COVID-19 using the media repertoire framework and the appraisal theory of stress. *Journal of medical Internet research*, 22(8), e20186.

Quinnipiac University Poll (2020). *Biden crushes Sanders in Democratic race, Quinnipiac University national poll finds; More disapprove of Trump's response to Coronavirus* [online]. Quinnipiac University. Available from: https://poll.qu.edu/Poll-Release?releaseid=3771 [Accessed 29 April 2021].

Riehm, K.E., Holingue, C., Kalb, L.G., Bennett, D., Kapteyn, A., Jiang, Q., Veldhuis, C.B., Johnson, R.M., Fallin, M.D., Kreuter, F., and Stuart, E.A. (2020). Associations between media exposure and mental distress among US adults at the beginning of the COVID-19 pandemic. *American Journal of Preventive Medicine*, 59(5), pp. 630–638.

Rosen, Z., Weinberger-Litman, S.L., Rosenzweig, C., Rosmarin, D.H., Muennig, P., Carmody, E.R., Rao, S.T., and Litman, L. (2020). Anxiety and distress among the first community quarantined in the U.S due to COVID-19: Psychological implications for the unfolding crisis. *PsyArXiv Preprints*. doi:10.31234/osf.io/7eq8c

Sousa-Pinto, B., Anto, A., Czarlewski, W., Anto, J.M., Fonseca, J.A., and Bousquet, J. (2020). Assessment of the impact of media coverage on COVID-19 – related google trends data: Infodemiology Study. *Journal of Medical Internet Research*, 22(8), e19611.

Taylor, D. (2020). A timeline of the Coronavirus pandemic [online]. *The New York Times*. Available from: www.nytimes.com/article/coronavirus-timeline.html [Accessed 28 April 2021].

World Health Organization (2020a). *Timeline: WHO's COVID-19 response* [online]. World Health Organization. Available from: www.who.int/emergencies/diseases/novel-coronavirus-2019/interactive-timeline#event-3 [Accessed 29 April 2021].

World Health Organization (2020b). *Understand the infodemic and misinformation in the fight against COVID-19* [online]. World Health Organization. Available from: https://iris.paho.org/bitstream/handle/10665.2/52052/Factsheet-infodemic_eng.pdf?sequence=14 [Accessed 28 April 2021].

4 Latin America and the strategic communication dilemma in times of COVID-19

Alejandro Álvarez-Nobell, Juan-Carlos Molleda, Ángeles Moreno and Ana María Suárez-Monsalve

Introduction

Strategic communication in Latin America and the COVID-19 dilemma

March 2020 was a month on the calendar that will undoubtedly remain in memory. In a press conference on 16 March 2020, when there were barely 6,500 COVID-19 fatalities in the world, Tedros Adhanom, General Director of the World Health Organization, uttered the famous words: 'We have a simple message for all countries: Test, test, test'. This appeal has had multiple implications. Testing the population was not easy and the tensions between the need, the speculation and the real possibilities have been steady throughout these months. However, a comparable but very transcendental statement can be made. First, for the vindication of the role and value of science in everyday life, which overcame a distance that grew deeper over time (Harari 2018). Second and above all, for the importance of counting on decision-making information on the design of public policies, particularly during crisis management.

This framework should also be applicable to the scientific field of strategic communication and public relations and its resulting professional practice. It is undeniable that the COVID-19 pandemic has been a turning point for humankind, affecting different fields, practices and professions. But the current crisis may also be an opportunity to reduce inequalities and strengthen political momentum, mostly in regions as disadvantaged and kaleidoscopic as Latin America itself (CEPAL 2020a, 2020b): a region that is always in an apparent loop of unfinished progress before the eyes of the world. In the emerging world order, before the crisis, the efforts to satisfy global demands like open markets, technological development, climate change and the acknowledgement of cultural diversity were at the centre of the agenda, but they coexisted with issues like inequality, the slow growth of the middle class, the lack of social guarantees and the unequal distribution of wealth. This social, political and economic complexity in Latin America means the COVID-19 dilemma has become substantially different in its form there than in the rest of the world (CEPAL 2020, 2020b; Uzcátegui *et al.* 2021).

DOI: 10.4324/9781003184669-6

In this context, strategic communication is no exception. From a holistic viewpoint, with an interdisciplinary theoretical base and anchored in business practice (Köhler 2019), we consider this one, as all the forms of communication which contribute to the survival and success of different organization types (Zerfass *et al.* 2018), due to its intentional, planned, contextualised, monitored and evaluated nature. Many of these challenges, dilemmas and transformations had already been anticipated, for example, in the different reports of the *Global Communication Monitors* of EUPRERA, and they have accelerated during the last year. However, studies and references about the impact of the strategic management of crisis communication in Latin America, in general or in individual countries, are very scarce.

The Institute for Public Relations was one of the first to publish evidence about it: from the very beginning and on a sustained basis, it has established an online resource centre which systematises the latest research on COVID-19 in communication.

On the other hand, EUPRERA first promoted the academic research project COM-COVID in Europe in early 2020 and then extended it to other countries, as a network established to monitor the communication management of the COVID-19 crisis in various countries from various perspectives and using different methodologies, in order to understand how the information about the emergency flows through different social groups and helps to improve communication in future crisis scenarios. The countries taking part in this project are Spain, Italy, the United Kingdom, Finland, Portugal, Turkey, Croatia, the United States, Nigeria and the Latin American representatives: Brazil and Argentina (Moreno *et al.* 2020).

Regarding the background of the scientific research, we can point to the work of López-Pujalte and Nuño-Moral (2020), who analysed the phenomenon of disinformation during the coronavirus crisis comparatively in Spain and Latin America. Colombia, Argentina and Mexico (the three Latin American countries with the highest level of disinformation) participated in the sample. Data were also obtained from Uruguay, the Dominican Republic, Brazil and Ecuador, among 15 other countries.

Igartua *et al.* (2020) also included cases in Latin America (in particular Brazil, Ecuador and Mexico) in their study 'Communication use in times of the coronavirus' from the theoretical model of uses and rewards. This background provided a first snapshot of the behaviour of the users of communication in the month immediately following the declaration of the COVID-19 pandemic around the world.

Dryhurst *et al.* (2020) were the first to publish a global study about 'Risk perceptions of COVID-19' with their evaluation of the public perceptions of risk from COVID-19 all over the world, using national samples from 10 European countries, America and Asia. This evidences how risk perception was correlated significantly with the informed adoption of preventive health behaviour. Including descriptive studies and cases from specific countries, the contributions from Cabás (2020), the Social Sciences Committee of the Coronavirus COVID-19 Unit (2020) and Riorda (2020) are also relevant. Moreover, the reflections from Canel (2020), Casero-Ripollés (2020), Castillo-Esparcia *et al.* (2020), Crespo and Garrido (2020), González-Harbour (2020), Moreno *et al.* (2020), Riorda and Bentolila (2020), Xifra (2020) and Fernández-Torres *et al.* (2021) have also contributed to the debate from Spain. These collaborations are meaningful given the influence of this country in Latin America.

At the professional level or promoted by non-scientific institutions, we can refer to the contributions from Edelman's (2020) *Special Report: Trust and the Coronavirus* and from the Thomson Reuters Foundation (2021), whose report is titled 'The Impact of COVID-19 on Journalism in Emerging Economies and the Global South'. This study defines the impact of the crisis on those responsible for providing critical, balanced and precise information, hence establishing and strengthening themselves as independent and prosperous media. From Latin America, however, the evidence comes only from Brazil and Mexico (Radcliffe 2021). On the other hand, the multinational consulting firm PwC used data from the region to analyse the reconfiguration of leadership, on this occasion with the help of 'A Leadership Agenda to Take on Tomorrow: 24th Annual Global CEO Survey', which interviewed 5,050 executive directors worldwide about their plans to respond to new threats, transform their operating model and create a more sustainable future.

Clearly, the previous evidence of the crisis's impact on the communication in the region is still scant or under development. Presenting data produced practically 'hot off the press' could also be a limitation, as these may have a very basic and a descriptive quality and would clearly require deeper analysis and further discussion. The bottom line is that, although in regions such as Europe, Asia and Oceania the crisis began to moderate during 2021, in Latin America cases continued to grow.

In this regard, this chapter yields significant and necessary evidence for the discussions at hand. The chapter does so by means of a rigorous, systemised and broadly unprecedented scan of the different practices carried out by strategic communication professionals in 20 Latin American countries from May to July 2020, in the midst of the COVID-19 pandemic. The research is part of the *Latin American Communication Monitor 2020–2021* (Álvarez-Nobell *et al.* 2021), the most representative study of the perceptions from communication professionals in the region (Thelen 2021) in collaboration with the Institute for Public Relations (IPR). Specifically, 1,683 valid cases were collected, representing the viewpoint of strategic communication professionals during 2020. Two research questions were proposed to guide this chapter: 1) Does the Latin American context require a special strategic communication plan during the COVID-19 pandemic? and 2) What contributions arise from the practice in Latin America for the future management of post-pandemic strategic communication?

Research design and case study

The *Latin American Communication Monitor (LCM) 2020–2021* has been the framework for the exploration and the results presented herein. At the same time, we have taken as a reference for designing the instrument the antecedent produced by the Institute for Public Relations (IPR) with the communications company Peppercomm at the beginning of the crisis in March 2020. They analysed a sample of 300 communication executives and senior leaders to obtain an initial insight into how prepared companies were for COVID-19 and how they were handling the impacts. From the beginning of the study, a second stage was carried out, applying a group of similar variables in the *LCM* questionnaire to explore how communication professionals in the companies, non-profit and public sector organizations, including communication agencies from across Latin America, adjusted to the impacts of COVID-19.

The research has followed the highest quality standards in social sciences, and it was designed and executed by a team of 26 recognised university lecturers and national research collaborators who represent different country contexts. Dichotomous, nominal and ordinal scales were used. The research questions derive from the investigation and bibliography previously mentioned. The survey was in Spanish and Portuguese and was previously tested by 18 communication professionals in five Latin American countries. Minor changes were made and the final questionnaire was distributed during the months of May, June and July 2020. More than 20,000 professionals across Latin America were invited, with personal email accounts based on a complete database built by the research team. In addition, other invitations were sent through professional associations and national research collaborators. In total, 1,850 respondents completed the survey; 1,683 resulted in valid cases, as the answers from the participants who could not be clearly identified as being part of the population were eliminated from the data group. This strict selection of respondents sets this survey apart from many others, as it is not based on snowball sampling and does not include students, scholars and people outside the profession or region at stake.

The Statistical Package for the Social Sciences (SPSS) was used to analyse the data. The results have been tested to determine their statistical significance, depending on the variable, Chi^2, ANOVA/Scheffé Post-hoc-Test, T-Test of independent samples, Pearson correlation, Kendall rank correlation or Mann-Whitney U test. The methods applied are described in the notes of each graph. The significant results are marked with * ($p \leq 0.05$, significant) or ** ($p \leq 0.01$, highly significant) on the graphs or tables and are also mentioned in the notes.

The research was structured based on the following questions:

RQ1: To what extent has the COVID-19 pandemic had an impact on the activity of companies or organizations?

RQ2: How important was the function of communication in the crisis management of the COVID-19 pandemic?

RQ3: How prepared were companies or organizations to handle the crisis caused by the COVID-19 pandemic?
RQ4: How prepared were professionals and their communication departments to handle the crisis caused by the COVID-19 pandemic?
RQ5: When the pandemic was declared: What was the state of the crisis communication plan in companies or organizations?
RQ6: In the COVID-19 context: Did the professionals of the communication department participate in the crisis committee?
RQ7: In the COVID-19 context: How necessary was communication management in handling of the relationship between organizations and their different publics?

Most significant results

As mentioned, despite the delay of the data, the present study yields significant and necessary evidence for the discussions at hand; and it does so by means of a rigorous, systemised and broadly unprecedented scan of the different practices carried out by strategic communication professionals in 20 Latin American countries, from May to July 2020, in the midst of COVID-19 pandemic.

In this regard, an important quality of the sample is revealed by the demography, which is dominated by highly qualified professionals with a long history in the field. The majority of the survey respondents (68.5%) are from South America (Argentina, Bolivia, Brazil, Chile, Colombia, Ecuador, Paraguay, Peru, Uruguay and Venezuela), followed by Central America (22.6%: Costa Rica, Cuba, Dominican Republic, El Salvador, Guatemala, Honduras, Nicaragua and Panama), and North America (22.6%: Mexico and Puerto Rico). These roles are not exlusive i.e. can be female head and unit leader hence not 100% response women communication directors or agency CEOs, 67.8% are women team or unit leaders and 68.8% are women team members or consultants. The average age of the professionals in the region is 38.7 years. Furthermore, 4.4% have doctoral training, 43.1% have master's studies and 50% are graduates (bachelor or technical college graduate, etc.). In turn, 16.5% participate in international professional associations. When enquiries are made about the position they occupy, results show that 26.7% are directors or agency CEOs, 34.1% are team or unit leaders and 39.2% are team members or consultants. In addition, 54.9% have more than 10 years' working experience, while 21.1% have 6–10 years.

Impact on the activity of the companies and organizations and the importance of the function of communication on crisis management

Looking at what had changed or implications of the crisis, 80% of the professionals answered as expected, that COVID-19 had a great impact on the activity of their company or organization. Nevertheless, towards the end of

July 2020, 7.7% claimed they had not felt the impact, and 12.1% barely felt an impact.

The analysis by country suggests that Colombia (64.8%), Peru (63%), El Salvador and Puerto Rico (60.3%) suffered the greatest impact. Except for Uruguay, with 44.2%, all stand above 50% of the "Total Impact" assessment. Argentina and Brazil, two of the countries in the region most deeply affected by the pandemic, argued at that time, that the impact was almost zero or very low, at more than 20% (see Figure 4.1).

According to the type of organization, the communicators of the state sector, with 67.9% of the total impact, argue that they are being hit by the crisis, together with the listed companies (57.9%) and social organizations (57.6%) that moderate the assessment.

The areas with the greatest perception of the total or almost total impact of the crisis in the companies or organizations are "Strategies and Coordination" (84.4%) and those linked to "Marketing, Brand and Consumers" (79.4%). At the opposite end, with highly significant differences, is the assessment carried out by the "Online Communication" sector.

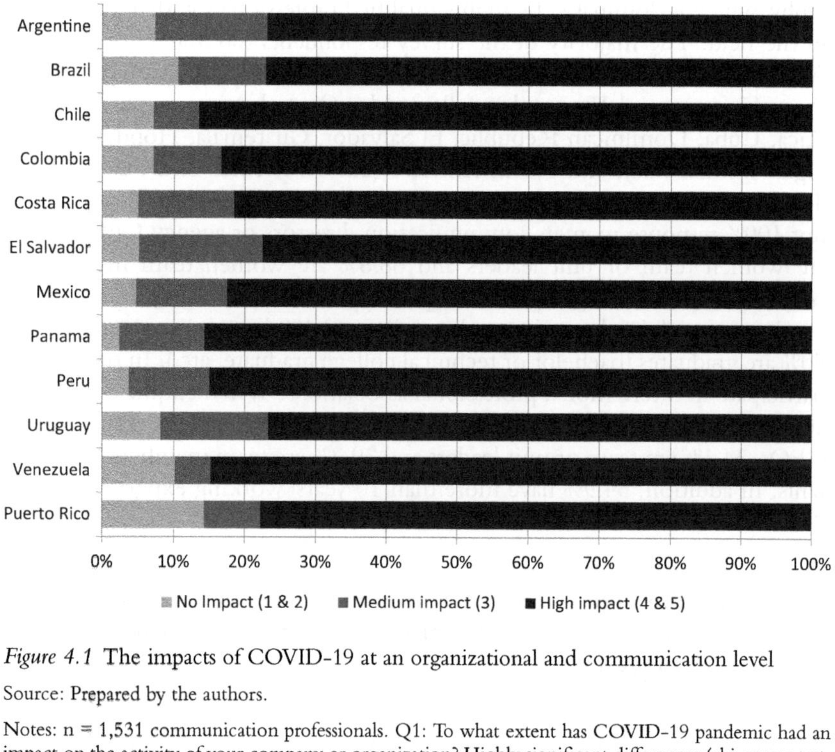

Figure 4.1 The impacts of COVID-19 at an organizational and communication level

Source: Prepared by the authors.

Notes: n = 1,531 communication professionals. Q1: To what extent has COVID-19 pandemic had an impact on the activity of your company or organization? Highly significant differences (chi-square test, $p \leq 0.01$)

Table 4.1 Importance of the communicative function

Discipline/work areas	*General communication*	*Strategy and coordination*	*Relation to the media*	*Consulting, advice, coaching, account management*	*Marketing, brand, communication with consumers*	*Online communication*
Not so important (1)	1.78%	0.29%	0.26%	1.59%	1.45%	0.54%
(2)	1.11%	1.45%	3.40%	1.90%	1.16%	1.07%
(3)	5.12%	4.35%	4.71%	4.44%	6.69%	4.29%
(4)	10.91%	9.86%	9.69%	12.70%	13.08%	12.60%
Very important (5)	81.07%	84.06%	81.94%	79.37%	77.62%	81.50%

Source: Prepared by the authors.

Notes: n = 1,531 communication professionals.

Q2: How important has the function of communication been on the crisis management of COVID-19 pandemic?

Highly significant differences (chi-square test, $p \leq 0.01$)

When the impact of the crisis on the proper function of communication is analysed, with 92% positive answers, professionals argue that their function during the crisis has been very important. In this case, the distinction by type of organization is very slight, although private companies and the public sector are those that least value their work comparatively.

Regarding the function of communication (Table 4.1), analysed through the lens of the different areas of performance, this has been very important (values 4 and 5) in the areas related to "Online Communication" (94.10%) and "Strategy and Coordination" (93.91%) and, to a lesser extent, to "Consulting, Advice, Coaching, Account Management".

Levels of prior preparation of companies or organizations and of professionals and their communication departments for crisis management

The perception of the impact of the crisis on stakeholders is usually conditioned by their level of trust in the organization in relation to an assessment of the skills and competencies necessary for crisis management. Starting from this premise, it has been interesting to analyse this aspect in organizations, their professionals and their communication teams.

Listed companies and non-profit organizations are better prepared to handle the pandemic crisis. The same is true about communication managers, 25% of whom value themselves as very prepared, against 19.1% of those team members, but over 16.1% of head profiles. There are 21.3% area heads who claim they are not prepared or very little prepared (see Figure 4.2).

When a comparative analysis between countries is made of the perception regarding how prepared the professionals and their communication departments

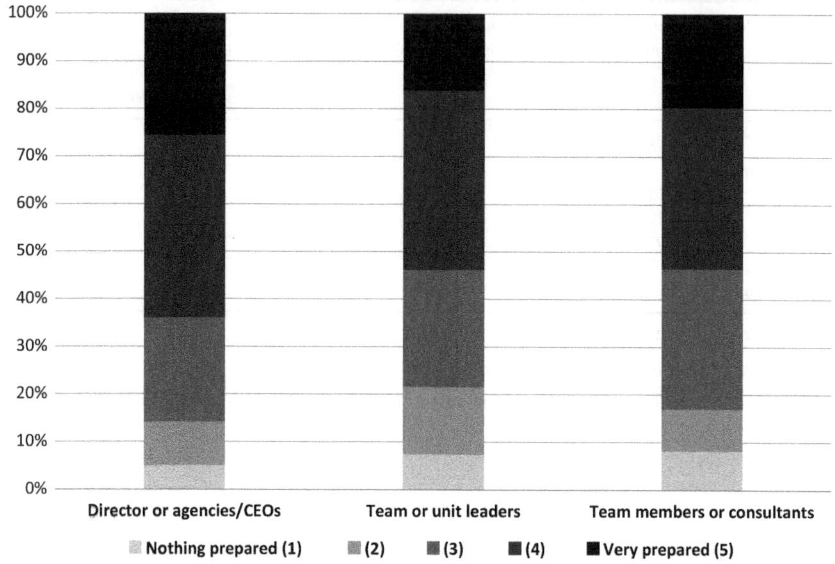

Figure 4.2 Levels of preparation to assume crisis management

Source: Prepared by the authors.

Notes: n = 839 communication professionals. Q3: How prepared is your organization to handle the crisis caused by the COVID-19 pandemic? Highly significant differences (chi-square test, $p \leq 0.01$)

were for the crisis management of the COVID-19 pandemic, the data show very significant differences. Thus, Puerto Rico reveals a high level of preparedness with 44.4%, followed by Panama (30.2%) and Argentina (24.2%). The most significant case is Brazil, 14.4% of whose professionals were very prepared. Those who state "not prepared at all" or very little (values 1 and 2) are the participants from Venezuela, totalling 24%.

Plans and crisis committees in the context of COVID-19

Questions about the status of crisis plans did not generally show highly significant differences according to the type of organization (see Table 4.2).

On the whole, 15.7% of the plans required a complete update and 22.4% required considerable updates. Only 20.5% required few updates. In short, 58.6% had to update their plans. The rest, 5%, did not update them but think they should have; 7.6% were not sure, and 25% did not have a crisis plan. Only 1.5% claimed they did not or would not update it. The most significant data are that 37.5% of the professionals who work in the public sector said that they did not have a crisis plan.

On the other hand, communication professionals from listed companies claim that they participate mostly in crisis committees (61%) and with decision-making

Table 4.2 Crisis plans in the context of COVID-19

	Listed company (multiple owners, listed on the stock exchange)	*Private company (reduced number of owners, not listed on the stock exchange)*	*State company, public sector or political organization*	*Non-profit organization or association*	*Agency, advisory or communication or public relations consultancy*	*Freelance or independent consultant*	*Total*
Required many updates	23.3%	22%	18.4%	24.3%	26.4%	19.3%	**22.4%**
Required full upgrade	16.4%	18.9%	12.3%	14.6%	12.8%	19.6%	**15.7%**
It was not updated, but required it	5.7%	4.5%	6.5%	2.8%	4.7%	5.1%	**5%**
We do not have a crisis communication plan	13.8%	26.5%	37.5%	27.1%	20.8%	22.2%	**25%**
We do not update it nor do we plan to do so	1.3%	0.8%	1.4%	3.5%	1.6%	1.3%	**1.5%**
Required few updates	27%	17.5%	15.7%	22.2%	24.4%	18.6%	**20.5%**
I do not know	11.3%	9.0%	5.8%	4.2%	6.9%	8.4%	**7.6%**
Others	1.3%	0.8%	2.4%	1.4%	2.5%	5.5%	**2.5%**

Source: Prepared by the authors.

Notes: n = 1,531 communication professionals. Q5: When the pandemic was declared, what was the status of the crisis communication plan of your organization? Highly significant differences (chi-square test, $p \leq 0.01$)

power in the organization. Consultants and the public sector are those with the least participation in these spaces. It is important to note that gender has not been a determining factor for participation or not in the crisis committee.

Importance of communication management in the handling of audiences and levels of excellence

Finally, we analysed communication management in relation to the needs and interests of the different target publics. The results exhibit significant variations according to the type of organizations, as shown in Figure 4.3. At over 86%, the management has been very necessary for consumers/clients and employees of organizations.

By analysing the alignment of communication departments in terms of excellence (Tench *et al.* 2017), the results are 19.2% strongly aligned, 64.6% aligned and 16.2% weakly aligned. Meanwhile, no existing significant differences can be found versus the preparation of the organization to handle the crises caused by the pandemic. Of respondents from excellent communication departments, 63.3% participate permanently and decisively, against 29.6% of respondents from other departments. Publics have been more essential to them.

Questions and remarks

One year after the World Health Organization declared COVID-19 a global pandemic, marking the official beginning of a period of profound disruption and suffering, Latin America does not seem to be recovering from it. The inequalities of vaccine supply plans, or even the inconvenience of having opted for vaccines which are still in the process of being recognised and authorised by the European Union (such as the Chinese and Russian vaccines), paint a bleak picture, as well as few alternatives to imagine a recovery. However, the interrogation to find solutions and regain confidence is unavoidable in every sense. For this reason, adding studies and evidence such as that provided by the *Latin American Communication Monitor*, in this case in the professional sector of strategic communication and public relations, and in particular on the impact, performance and importance of this as a key dimension of organizations, is highly significant. The data show that countries like Argentina and Brazil, even with opposing ideological profiles and governments (both populist, one left-wing and the other from the extreme right) have 'underestimated' the crisis impact even months after it took place. And today, these are the ones that mark the greatest impacts by the number of deaths, infections and social and economic consequences. Moreover, the public sector has been the first to acknowledge the impact, as well as those communication management areas linked to strategy and the relation to customers. Online communications have shown a more resilient attitude towards the situation, taking into account that, in many cases, in addition to a substantial increase in their activities, operations and range have also been reinforced with respect to budget and resources.

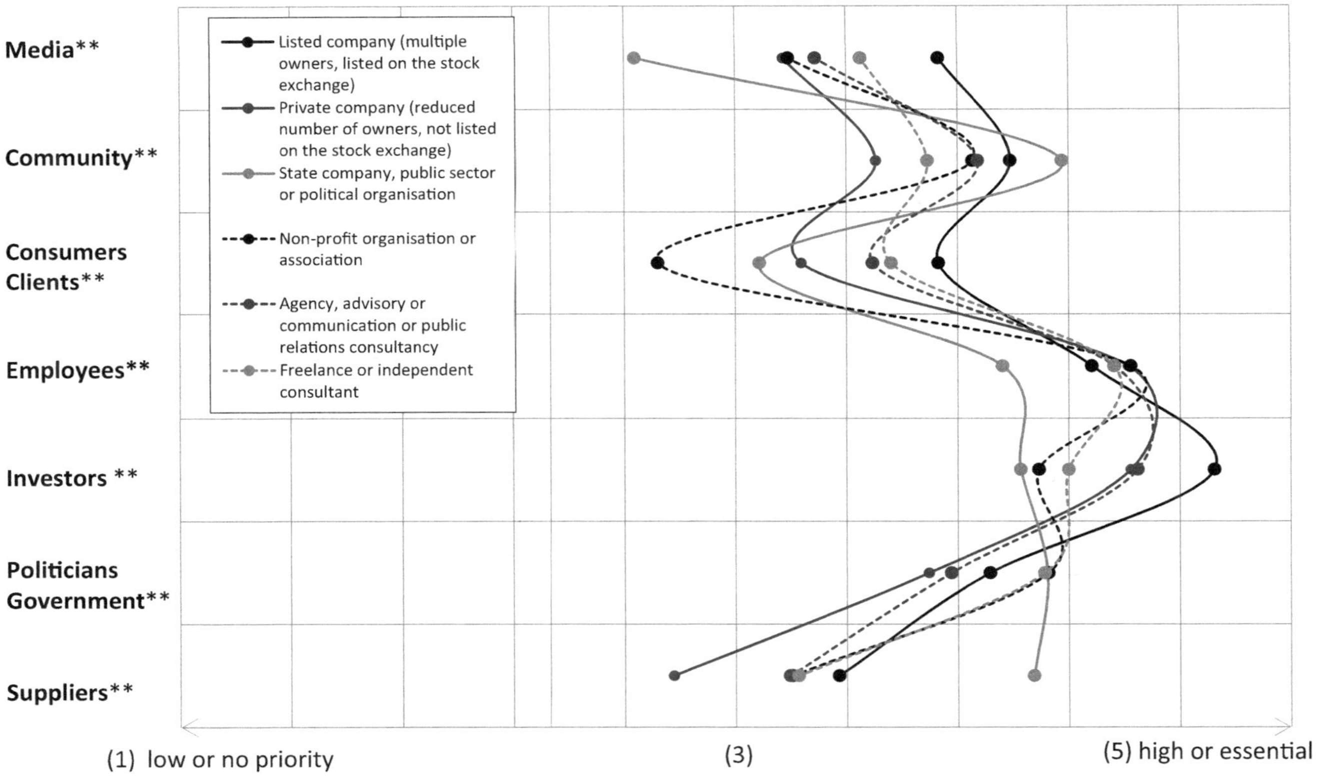

Figure 4.3 Significant differences between the different publics compared to the types of organizations

Source: Authors

Notes: n = 1,262 communication professionals. Q7: In the context of COVID-19, How necessarily has communication management been to manage the relationship of your organization with different audiences? Highly significant differences (Independent samples T-Test, $p \leq 0.01$)

Once we have analysed the impact that the crisis has had on the importance of the communication function, the levels are widely satisfactory. Relevance is almost total. Comparatively, however, private companies and the public sector are the ones that least value their importance. Public sector data are appealing because this is the sector which has claimed to have suffered the greatest impact.

Equally significant is the high valuation of the task of 'Consulting, Advice, Coaching, Account Management' in managing the crisis, a dimension that is gaining strength in the profession and becomes consolidated in extraordinary contexts such as the one experienced.

Perception of the impact of the crisis is often conditioned by trust and the assessment of the development of the skills and abilities required to cope with it. Listed companies and the third sector organizations are the ones who claim to be more prepared. Along the same line, the positive assessments made by the communication leaders are very interesting, although they barely surpass the average. Thus, the perception of having very low levels of preparation is evident – and alarming.

The pandemic has increased the focus on the communication planning process, rendering most of the existing regulatory plans obsolete. The public sector, following the sequence, shows the hardest evidence in this regard: Almost half of the professionals faced the crisis without preventive plans. At any rate, the fact that almost all professionals have felt the need to update or modify their plans constitutes a turning point in rigid communication management models and proves the value of a situational strategic perspective, especially in current contexts.

Conclusions

These findings confirm that, during processes of economic, health, political and trust crises, strategic communication, as a profession, has become a key transversal link for organizations. It influences the construction of authentic, coherent and sustainable alliances with the organizations' key publics, as well as the configuration of democracy and the adoption of coherent policies between discourse and action. Besides, its contribution is inclusively, diversely and equitably valued in the recognition of those who make up the organizations.

During the pandemic, strategic communication based on digital content and tools has posed an ethical challenge in terms of the proper use of the data provided by users and audiences in general, and also a dilemma regarding cyber security. This is no minor issue for communication professionals in Latin America, who express their ethical concerns, particularly in relation to the political instability of their countries.

Neither the details of the recovery nor the emerging profile that communications will have are clear yet, but the discussions are indeed present on a common agenda regarding topics such as the already unavoidable adoption of strategic and even prospective perspectives, a higher level of professionalisation, protagonism, and the development of resources and skills, greater involvement

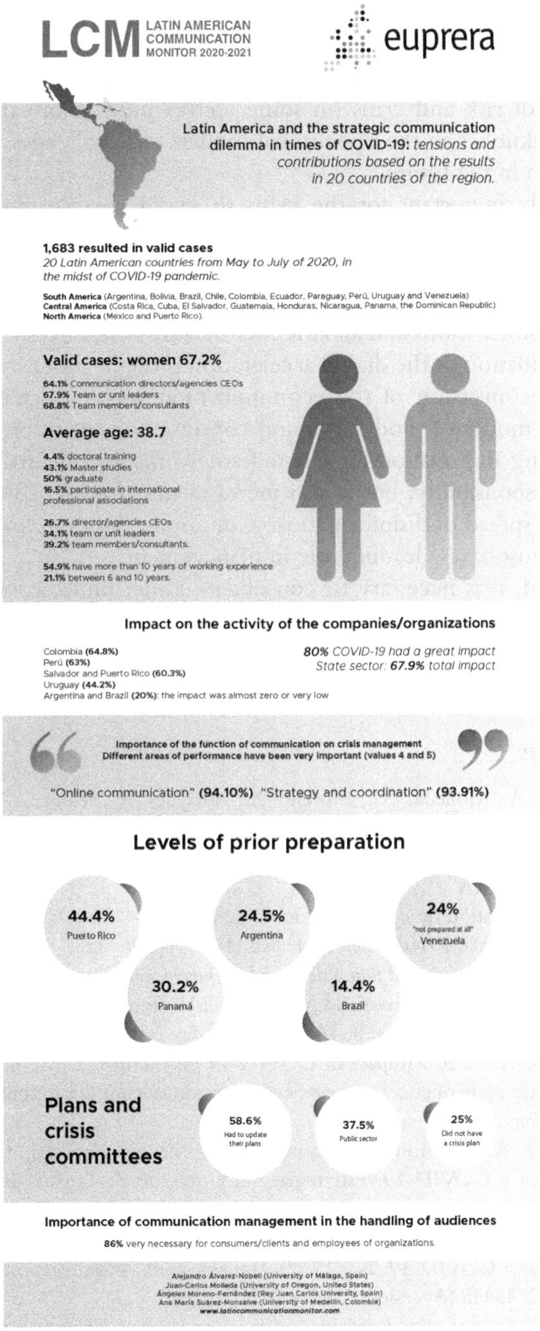

Infographic 4.1 Latin America and the strategic communication dilemma in times of COVID-19: Tensions and contributions based on the results in 20 countries of the region.

in decision-making and a reconfiguration of areas such as digital communication beyond its operational and technical role.

One thing is certain: We cannot simply return to the way things were in the past. The pandemic has exposed fundamental deficiencies of our performance in situations of risk and crisis (in some sectors much more than in others), revealing weaknesses in the operational models and challenges that will shape our profession in the future.

It is equally important for the crisis to reveal the capacity for empathy, adaptation, flexibility and creativity in the search for lasting solutions to these problems. For communication, 2022 and the years to come, will be years of powered reinvention, if we understand the lesson of the pandemic as an accelerator of transformations and an amplifier of disruptive forces.

The continuation of the digital acceleration brought about by the pandemic promises a reconversion of the economic models towards triple impact, of matrices and modes of production and consumption, new forms of distribution, marketing and relationships, new frameworks for sustainable governance and shared responsibility; but it also increases mistrust, the threat of cyberattacks and the spread of disinformation. Communication is relevant in all these aspects and must have a leading role in management.

To that end, it is necessary to consolidate leaderships capable of assuming these challenges, to broaden the critical view of the agendas and to overcome the biases of algorithmic information diets. Information in real time for the design of scenarios in ubiquitous contexts is becoming a substantial asset.

Bibliography

Álvarez-Nobell, A., Molleda, J.C., Moreno, A., Athaydes, A., Suárez, A.M., and Herrera, M. (2021). *Comunicación estratégica en América Latina: ciberseguridad, situación de las mujeres, retos éticos, nuevas competencias y crisis del COVID-19. Resultados de una encuesta en 20 países.* Bruselas, EUPRERA.

Cabás, P. (2020). Gestión de la Comunicación de crisis del COVID-19 en la isla de Tierra del Fuego, Argentina. *Revista ComHumanitas*, 11(3), pp. 96–125.

Canel, M.J. (2020). *Webinar: El futuro del branding gubernamental post COVID-19. Escuela de Posgrados en Comunicación.* Universidad Austral. Available from: www.youtube.com/watch?v=dVkqOtX15v8&feature=youtu.be [Accessed 15 May 2021].

Casero-Ripollés, A. (2020). Impact of COVID-19 on the media system. Communicative and democratic consequences of news consumption during the outbreak. *El Profesional de la información*, 29(2).

Castillo-Esparcia, A., Fernández-Souto, A.B., and Puentes-Rivera, I. (2020). Comunicación política y COVID-19. Estrategias del Gobierno de España. *El Profesional de la información*, 29(4).

CEPAL (2020a). Los efectos del COVID-19: *Dimensionar para pensar en la reactivación.* Informe especial COVID-19. *No*, 19, 2. Available from: https://repositorio.cepal.org//handle/11362/45445 [Accessed 18 May 2021].

CEPAL (2020b). *Informe sobre el impacto económico en América Latina y el Caribe de la enfermedad por Coronavirus (COVID-19).* Available from: https://repositorio.cepal.org/handle/11362/45602 [Accessed 18 May 2021].

Comisión de Ciencias Sociales de la Unidad Coronavirus COVID-19 (2020). *Comunicación y medios en COVID-19. Grupo de trabajo de Comunicación*. Septiembre – diciembre 2020, pp. 96–125. Available from: www.sociales.uba.ar/wpcontent/blogs.dir/219/files/2020/04/Informe_Final_Covid-Cs.Sociales.pdf [Accessed 25 May 2021].

Crespo, I., and Garrido, A. (2020). La pandemia del coronavirus: Estrategias de comunicación de crisis. *Más poder local*, 41, 12–19. https://dialnet.unirioja.es/descarga/articulo/7407214.pdf

Dryhurst, S., Schneider, C.R., Kerr, J., Freeman, A.L., Recchia, G., Van Der Bles, A.M., . . . and Van Der Linden, S. (2020). Risk perceptions of COVID-19 around the world. *Journal of Risk Research*, 23(7–8), pp. 994–1006.

Edelman (2020). *Special report: Trust and the Coronavirus*. Available from: https://bit.ly/2TERtFx [Accessed 10 May 2021].

Fernández-Torres, M.J., Almansa-Martínez, A., and Chamizo-Sánchez, R. (2021). Infodemic and fake news in spain during the COVID-19 pandemic. *International Journal of Environmental Research and Public Health*, 18(4), p. 1781.

González-Harbour, B. (2020). *Cinco fallos y cuatro aciertos del Gobierno en la comunicación de esta crisis*. El País. Available from: https://elpais.com/sociedad/2020-04-30/cinco-fallos-y-cuatro-aciertos-del-gobierno-en-la-comunicacion-de-esta-crisis.html [Accessed 1 May 2021].

Harari, Y.N. (2018). *21 Lessons for the 21st century*. New York: Random House.

Igartua, J.-J., Ortega-Mohedano, F., and Arcila-Calderón, C. (2020). Communication use in the times of the Coronavirus: A cross-cultural study. *Profesional de la Información*, 29(3). doi:10.3145/epi.2020.may.18

Köhler, K., and Zerfass, A. (2019). Communicating the corporate strategy: An international benchmark study in the UK, the USA, and Germany. *Journal of Communication Management*, 23(4) 348–374. doi:10.1108/JCOM-10-2018-0106

López-Pujalte, C., and Nuño-Moral, M.V. (2020). La 'infodemia' en la crisis del coronavirus: Análisis de desinformaciones en España y Latinoamérica. *Revista Española De Documentación Científica*, 43(3), e274. doi:10.3989/redc.2020.3.1807

Moreno, Á., Fuentes-Lara, C., and Navarro, C. (2020). COVID-19 communication management in Spain: Exploring the effect of information-seeking behavior and message reception in public's evaluation. *El profesional de la información*, 29(4). doi:10.3145/epi.2020.jul.02

PwC (2021). *A leadership agenda to take on tomorrow: 24th annual global CEO survey*. Available from: www.pwc.com/gx/en/ceo-agenda/ceosurvey/2021/report.html [Accessed 10 May 2021].

Radcliffe, D. (2021). *The impact of COVID-19 on journalism in Emerging Economies and the Global South*. Available from SSRN: https://ssrn.com/abstract=3796666 or http://dx.doi.org/10.2139/ssrn.3796666 [Accessed 14 January 2021].

Riorda, M. (2020). Antes de comunicar el riesgo o la crisis: hay que diferenciarlos. *Más poder local*, 41, pp. 20–23. Available from: http://maspoderlocal.es/ediciones/comunicacion-politica-COVID-19-no41

Riorda, M., and Bentolila, S. (2020). *Cualquiera tiene un plan hasta que te pegan en la cara. Aprender de las crisis*. Buenos Aires: Paidos.

Tench, R., Verčič, D., Zerfass, A., Moreno, A., and Verhoeven, P. (2017). *Communication excellence: How to develop, manage and lead exceptional communications*. London: Springer.

Thelen, P.D. (2021). The status of public relations research addressing Latin America: A content analysis of published articles from 1980 to 2020. *Public Relations Review*, 47(4), p. 102079.

Uzcátegui, J.L., Tetelboin Henrion, C., Iturrieta Henríquez, D., and Schor-Landman, C. (2021). *América Latina. Sociedad, política y salud en tiempos de pandemia.* Ciudad Autónoma de Buenos Aires: CLACSO; Xochimilco: Universidad Autónoma Metropolitana; Xalapa: Universidad Veracruzana; Cochabamba: Universidad Mayor de San Simón; Valparaíso: Universidad de Valparaíso.

WHO (2020). *Discurso de apertura del director general de la OMS en la rueda de prensa sobre Covid-19 celebrada el 16 de marzo de 2020.* Available from: www.who.int/director-general/speeches/detail/who-director-general-s-opening-remarks-at-the-media-briefing-on-covid-19---16-march-2020 [Accessed 29 May 2021].

Xifra, J. (2020). Comunicación corporativa, relaciones públicas y gestión del riesgo reputacional en tiempos del COVID-19. *El profesional de la información*, 29(2), 1–18. http://eprints.rclis.org/39942/1/xifra.pdf

Zerfass, A., Verčič, D., Nothhaft, H., and Werder, K.P. (2018). Strategic Communication: Defining the Field and its Contribution to Research and Practice. *International Journal of Strategic Communication*, 12(4), pp. 487–505. doi:10.1080/1553118X.2018.1493485

Part III

Global perspectives on COVID-19 communication

Asia

5 Assessing COVID-19 communication in China

Communication channels, sources for information and information retention

Juan Meng, Ruoyu Sun, Tong Xie and Zhao Wang

Introduction

China was the first country that reported a cluster of cases of pneumonia in Wuhan, Hubei Province, on 31 December 2019. A novel coronavirus was eventually identified and is now referred to as COVID-19. COVID-19's high transmissibility quickly turned the situation in China into a global outbreak. On 11 March 2020, the World Health Organization (WHO) declared COVID-19 a pandemic. Since then, there have been more than 233 million accumulative confirmed cases of COVID-19, including 4,771,408 deaths, globally, according to the monitoring data released by WHO as of 30 September 2021 (WHO Coronavirus Disease Dashboard 2021). The Chinese government took early responses and measures such as city lockdown, situation monitoring, large-scale surveillance at the national level and a national reporting system to reduce the COVID-19 spread with top-down collective action (AlTakarli 2020). Therefore, it is important to study key features in COVID-19 communication in China to identify communication channels the government has used, individuals' trusted sources for COVID-19 information and governmental communication and key message retention.

In this chapter, we present the findings from a national online survey of Chinese citizens (N = 1,749) about the key communication channels that they used for COVID-19 information in the times of lockdown and post-pandemic. Results showed that public health organizations and officials are the most trusted source for individuals in China to receive COVID-19 information, followed by the central government officials and government officials at the state and local level. The Chinese public also turned to friends and family to get quick updates on COVID-19. Although the level of social media consumption is high, individuals' trust in social influencers, bloggers or key opinion leaders (KOLs) is the lowest. Similarly, the public's trust in user-generated content on social media is low, if compared to the COVID-19-related content delivered via traditional media and digital media.

The chapter also presents findings on perceived impact of COVID-19, personal safety concern and information retention during the times of lockdown and post-pandemic over the four quarters of 2020. Results showed a clear

DOI: 10.4324/9781003184669-9

pattern that individuals' attention to COVID-19 news decreased significantly over the four quarters of 2020. Consequently, the perceived negative impact of COVID-19 on daily life and safety concern significantly dropped as the Chinese government has demonstrated its efficacy in controlling and reducing the disease transmission. The COVID-19 communication led by the Chinese government helped individuals retain several key messages of COVID-19 disease during the economic and city lockdown. Key message retention during the post-pandemic time was also investigated and is reported in this chapter. The chapter concludes with implications on government communication strategies addressing preventive and control measures during an ongoing global pandemic.

Experiencing COVID-19: an overview of the pandemic in China

Political structure and context

China is the second-largest economy in the world (Haini 2020), with a gross domestic product (GDP) of around US$14.72 trillion in 2020 (Statista 2021). The country has a population of 1.4 billion people, accounting for almost 20% of the world's population (Bouey 2020). The political structure in China is a one-party system, emphasising centralised and unified leadership (Xing and Zhang 2021). Over recent decades, the trend of strengthening the Chinese Communist Party's (CPC) leadership over government agencies and the civil service has continued to deepen (Ang 2020). As a result, strong central political control empowers the central government to steer local governments' actions in a top-down manner during emergency situations (He *et al.* 2020). To effectively and successfully manage major public governance issues, the regime has established a set of procedures to prioritise issues on the agenda and focus attention and resources on top priorities (Jing 2021). Such a strategy has long been proclaimed as the main institutional advantage of the Chinese regime (Jing 2021).

COVID-19 protocol introduced and implemented

According to the Johns Hopkins Coronavirus Resource Center, the accumulative number of confirmed cases of COVID-19 in China has reached 108,413, with a cumulative death toll of 4,849 as of 14 September 2021 (COVID-19 Dashboard by the Center for Systems Science and Engineering 2021). The measures to cope with the COVID-19 outbreak have been undertaken in three main stages in China (Li *et al.* 2020; World Health Organization 2020a) as explained in the following paragraphs.

The first stage (27 December 2019 – 21 January 2020)

The first phase of pandemic control focused on medical diagnosing of the virus, controlling the source of infection, and preventing infectious cases from being exported from Wuhan and other high-risk areas in Hubei Province (Jing 2021). The Wuhan city government received early warnings of four cases of unspecified pneumonia on 27 December2019 (The State Council Information Office of the People's Republic of China 2020). On 1 January 2020, the Hua-nan seafood market at Wuhan, which was closely related to most of the earliest confirmed cases, was shut down (Li *et al.* 2020). China reported the infectious cases to the World Health Organization (WHO) on 31 December 2019 and started to share information about the coronavirus outbreak with WHO on 3 January 2020 (World Health Organization 2020a). On 20 January 2020, China's National Health Commission (NHC) confirmed that the virus could be transmitted person to person. On the same day, NHC released the second edition of the Protocol on Prevention and Control of Novel Coronavirus Pneumonia (The State Council Information Office of the People's Republic of China 2020). At this stage, China launched a series of intense public health campaigns to advocate hand washing, masking when going out, and staying at home (Xu *et al.* 2020). However, all control and prevention measures at this phase were suggested only and were not enforced.

The second stage (22 January 2020 – mid-March 2020)

More stringent prevention and control measures were implemented by the Chinese central government to combat with COVID-19 (Mei 2020). On 22 January 2020, President Xi Jinping ordered strict controls over the movement of people by closing all exit channels in Hubei and Wuhan, the epicenter of China's COVID-19 outbreak. On 23 January 2020, Wuhan City Novel Coronavirus Prevention and Control Center declared an unprecedented temporary lockdown of the whole city. All public transportation within the city was suspended. Outbound routes from Wuhan's airports and railway stations were shut down, and inbound routes by road or waterway from other parts of the country were also barred (The State Council Information Office of the People's Republic of China 2020). During the strictest weeks of lockdown, only one person per household was permitted to go out to purchase necessities every three days. Some free foods were also provided by the government to Wuhan citizens (Li *et al.* 2020). In addition, similar lockdown measures were also undertaken in other high-risk regions and cities in China.

In order to relieve the overloaded medical system in Wuhan and Hubei, the central government sent medical personnel from other provinces in China and the military to Wuhan and other pandemic-hit cities in Hubei Province (Mei 2020). In Wuhan, two new temporary hospitals were built within days, and 16 convention centers or sports arenas were converted into *Fangcang* shelter hospitals (i.e., temporary treatment centers) to isolate patients with mild to moderate symptoms (Chen *et al.* 2020). Various tight measures were also implemented during this stage. These measures included the closure of schools and non-essential businesses, mandatory quarantine and mask-wearing, immediate contact tracing and large-scale free nucleic acid testing, among others

(Mei 2020). In sum, the second phase of pandemic control was characterised by mass mobilisation of healthcare and other needed resources across the country to contain the spread of the virus within the country and to treat all COVID-19 patients by any means necessary (Jing 2021; World Health Organization 2020b).

The third stage (late March 2020 – August 2020)

The stringent control measures implemented in in the second phase quickly reduced the infection rates in China. The inflection point occurred in the second half of March, with no new reported domestic cases on 19 March 2020 (Jing 2021). The Wuhan lockdown order was lifted on 8 April 2020 (He *et al.* 2020). In the third stage, the focus of pandemic control shifted to contain the importation of infectious cases from overseas and an orderly return to normal social operations (Jing 2021; Xu *et al.* 2020). For example, work was resumed, and schools were reopened in phases and batches. New technologies such as a "health code" were applied to improve contact tracing efficiency and strengthen the management of high-risk COVID-19 transmission populations (Xu *et al.* 2020). The health code system includes using QR codes for entering shops, offices and are kept on smartphone.

Economic and media responses

According to China's National Bureau of Statistics (NBS), the GDP in the first quarter of 2020 was US$2951.9 billion, a decrease of 6.8% from the same period in 2019. However, China's economy rebounded after the first quarter, with a GDP growth of 2.3% in 2020 (National Bureau of Statistics of China 2021). Although the pandemic has had a strong impact on traditional industries, such as tourism, manufacturing, wholesale/retail and transportation/storage, new and emerging industries such as digital technology–based business, online shopping and delivery services actually experienced a further boost during the pandemic (Xu *et al.* 2020).

The mainstream media in China framed the anti-pandemic campaign as a battle between human beings and the virus (He *et al.* 2020). Key terms frequently used by the media included 'Wuhan defence war', 'battle of annihilation', and 'total war' (He *et al.* 2020; Jing 2021). Such a narrative transmitted a strong sense of urgency and functioned as emotional mobilisation, propelling the Chinese public to comply with the extra strict prevention and control measures (He *et al.* 2020).

The state of play: COVID-19 communication experience and insights

The Chinese central government set several priorities when responding to the ongoing pandemic at the macro level, including public health education, risk communication and intensive media coverage (Kim *et al.* 2019; Wang *et al.* 2020). Such actions significantly helped raise the awareness of the risk associated with COVID-19 among the Chinese public (Tam *et al.* 2018), satisfied the public's need for updated COVID-19 information (Tang and Zou 2021) and increased the public's compliance with the preventive behaviours (Lin *et al.* 2014). The great uncertainty caused by the pandemic led individuals to seek information to understand the situational risk, helping to increase the knowledge of the infectious disease. It also decreased some potential mental stress associated with the uncertainty (Brashers *et al.* 2002). To examine how risk communication and education about preventive measures were introduced and implemented by the Chinese government during the pandemic, we reviewed some recent research on COVID-19 communication in China by focussing on communication channels or platforms used to disseminate the epidemic response information, sources for COVID-19 information and key preventive measures retained.

Sources for information and tools for communication: the most trusted and the most used

The sudden disruption of public services and individual routines imposed huge pressure on communications and coordination across different social entities in China. Wuhan was the first city to experience a strictly enforced lockdown, followed by another 27 cities in Hubei Province since 27 January 2020 (Xu *et al.* 2020). Although other cities in China were not required to follow the same procedure, the public were repeatedly reminded by state-run media, digital media, social media and local community services to wear masks, takesteps toward quarantine and isolation at home and avoid non-essential gatherings (Xu *et al.* 2020; Xu and Renken 2020). From the initial outbreak to later lifting of the lockdown, the public in China have actively used various media platforms to seek COVID-19 information, to satisfy their need for updates and sustain daily life (Ma *et al.* 2020).

When facing the great uncertainty during the early stage of the pandemic, the public in China largely relied on official sources, such as government officials and authorities, state-run media, and public health officials and experts as the most trusted sources for COVID-19 communication, while seeking and consuming information from diverse unofficial sources (CSM 2020; Wu and Shen 2021). The Chinese government took the first step in providing prompt epidemic information disclosure and communication (Hu *et al.* 2020). Officials from the central government reported confirmed COVID-19 cases to the WHO on 3 January 2020 and issued a warning to international communities (WHO 2020b). The China National Health Commission classified COVID-19 as a new notifiable contagious disease under the National Infectious Disease Law and took strict measures to disclose the information about the developing epidemic in two weeks (China National Health Commission 2020).

Domestically, official information about COVID-19 confirmed cases, preventive measures and important scientific findings about the coronavirus was mainly communicated through traditional Chinese media outlets, such as television, newspapers, magazines, news agencies and other government-owned media platforms (CSM 2020; Liu *et al.* 2020; Hu *et al.* 2020). Many state-owned media outlets also feature web platforms in order to compete for the attention of Chinese web users (Zhao *et al.* 2020). As the internet became one of the country's main information sources, digesting information via mobile devices has largely reshaped China's information consumption culture (China's Media Landscape 2021).

Among diverse media channels and platforms, TV viewership and the usage of WeChat, the most popular and dominant mobile messaging app developed by Tencent, experienced a significant surge since the epidemic outbreak (CSM 2020). For example, an interview with 17 participants from Hubei Province during the pandemic found individuals actively used WeChat to mobilise resources and share sensitive information and third-party critiques through one-on-one chat or audio input (Tang and Zou 2021). Although individuals in China trusted governmental official sources more than WeChat for COVID-19 information, they expressed the need to read and follow diverse information sources (Ma *et al.* 2020). Similarly, microblog sites like Weibo are also very popular among the younger generations for information consumption. Weibo was found to be one of the critical tools used by the Chinese government, KOLs and NGOs to facilitate the process of emergent response and relief (Huang *et al.* 2020; Li *et al.* 2020). At the same time, research identified that traditional print media such as newspapers and magazines were the least used media vehicles for COVID-19 information; face-to-face communication was found to rank similarly (Pan *et al.* 2020; Liu *et al.* 2020).

Information overload, mental health and compliance with preventive measures

The amount of COVID-19-related information and its accessibility changed throughout different stages of the pandemic in China (Tang and Zou 2021). According to Tang and Zou (2021), the Chinese public expressed a higher level of need for information due to uncertainty in the initial lockdown period. As the central government and state-run media delivered more information about the pandemic and etiology, the public's urgent need for more information significantly decreased, and so did the feeling of uncertainty. Interestingly, research also found that as more COVID-19 information was shared, individuals reported a negative experience of information overload and emotional burnout (Tang and Zou 2021).

These intensive media exposures also generated different effects on individuals' mental wellbeing and compliance behaviours. Research confirmed that media exposure and information sharing did raise individuals' awareness and willingness to comply with COVID-19 prevention behaviours (Pan *et al.* 2020). In addition, the amount of information received from traditional Chinese media outlets, such as television, newspapers and magazines, was associated with a better mental health condition and compliance behaviours based on self-reported data (Pan *et al.* 2020). The Chinese public believed that COVID-19 information delivered by traditional and state-owned media is more reliable, with verified sources and authorities (Pan *et al.* 2020).

Meanwhile, COVID-19 information received from unofficial web platforms and media sources was associated with a negative impact on mental health. Individuals who were inclined to think less about the veracity of the information suffered more from the negative influence of intensive media exposure, which generated a negative impact on their mental health (Pan *et al.* 2020). Another survey, with a sample of 3,063 Chinese adults, also found prevalent depression and anxiety among the Chinese public during the COVID-19 lockdown period. The consumption of COVID-19 information from social media caused some severe symptoms of anxiety based on self-reported data (Volz *et al.* 2021). In general, the Chinese public's knowledge level about the disease transmission and clinical symptoms remained low at the initial stage (Lin *et al.* 2020; Yue *et al.* 2021). Since individuals have different levels of risk tolerance, many individuals may fall prey to misinformation and disinformation, which could cause a misled or unnecessary panic (Zhang *et al.* 2020).

Overall, state-run public health campaigns on COVID-19-related knowledge and prevention further increased the public's compliance with preventive behaviours, which helped with the control of the pandemic (Sørensen *et al.* 2012). Since the initial lockdown period, the Chinese traditional media and other platforms (e.g., digital media and social media) has repeatedly emphasised pandemic prevention measures (Hu *et al.* 2020; Zhao *et al.* 2020). The higher level of trust towards the communication messages from the central government amplified the public's tendency to comply with the preventive measures (Niu *et al.* 2021; Wu and Shen 2021).

Research on COVID-19 communication in China: Findings

Based on the overall situational review of the COVID-19 pandemic in China and some recent research on the Chinese public's COVID-19 communication experience, we are inspired to continue investigating the COVID-19 pandemic's ongoing impact on government communication in China in the times of lockdown and post-pandemic. Particularly, we explored the perceived impact of COVID-19 over the span of four quarters in 2020 and the information channels individuals used to receive COVID-19 communication. In addition, we focused on examining the perceived quality of communication in three categories, namely traditional media (e.g., TV, radios, newspapers and magazines), digital media (e.g., online news websites and the web platforms of traditional media) and social media with user-generated content (e.g., Weibo, WeChat, Douyin and Zhihu). By assessing the perceived quality of communication, we further investigated the Chinese public's COVID-19 information retention, both in the times of lockdown and post-pandemic. Findings reported in this chapter are largely derived from a national online survey of COVID-19 communication among the Chinese public designed and conducted during the fourth quarter of 2020. In this chapter, we presented findings of the following four sub-topics:

1 The perceived impact of the COVID-19 pandemic during 2020;
2 The most used and trusted information channels for COVID-19 communication;
3 The perceived quality of communication through various communication channels; and
4 COVID-19 information retention in the times of lockdown and post-pandemic.

An overview of our research design

An online survey of the Chinese public using a convenient sampling strategy was employed in this study in order to increase the response rate and completion rate of the survey. The questionnaire design was largely based on the COM-COVID project initiated by the European Public Relations Education and Research Association (EUPRERA) for the purpose of consistency in international collaborative research. However, the research team has made some essential revisions to the questionnaire to ensure it fits and reflects the media landscape of today's China, as well as the developing timeline of the COVID-19 outbreak in China. The revised survey questionnaire was in English originally. Since all researchers are bilingual in English and Mandarin Chinese, it is a natural transition to have the questionnaire translated into Mandarin Chinese. The translated survey questionnaire was tested among a small group of Chinese. We used the feedback collected from the pre-test to further revise and refine the questionnaire design. The finalised survey was activated at the beginning of the fourth quarter in 2020 and remained active for six weeks.

All four researchers in the research team have reached out to multiple networks in various regions in China to recruit survey participants. The survey was distributed via personal emails and personal social media accounts, as well as professional networks. By the time the survey was closed, we were able to retain a final sample of 1,749 Chinese citizens. All findings reported in this chapter are based on the 1,749 valid responses.

Sample profiles

The final sample includes 938 women (53.6%) and 811 men (46.4%). The majority of the respondents in our survey maintained a full-time employment status (75.5%). The sample also includes some college students who are older than 18 (7.9%), self-employed individuals (5.8%) and retirees (4.1%). The average age of our respondents is 36.1 years old, with a range from 18 to 78. We had 36.2% reporting having a master's degree, followed by 33.8% having a bachelor's degree, 11.8% with an associate's degree, 11.3% with a high school diploma, 3.8% with a middle school diploma or below and 2.9% with a doctoral degree.

In terms of the geographic locations of the respondents, we were able to identify a diverse range of regions. Respondents in our study are from 22 provinces, five autonomous regions and four direct-administered municipalities, as well as Hong Kong, the special administrative region (Country Guide: China 2021). The frequency analysis indicates the top five provinces and/or municipalities from where the respondents were recruited, including Guangxi Province (21.9%), Henan Province (20.8%), Shanghai (18.7%), Yunan Province (6.2%), and Guangdong Province (4.7%). The diversity of the geographic locations further ensures the quality of the sample and the reliability of the responses.

The perceived impact of the COVID-19 pandemic during 2020

To investigate the perceived impact of the COVID-19 pandemic on the Chinese public, we asked surveyed respondents to report their assessment of the overall attention to COVID-19 communication and their overall concern. On a scale ranging from 1 (not at all) to 7 (to a great extent), our sample reported the COVID-19 outbreak is a heavily discussed topic in China (M = 6.00, SD = 1.26), the outbreak is relevant to their daily work and life (M = 5.98, SD = 1.22) and the outbreak affects their daily work and life (M = 5.66, SD = 1.38).

The consumption of COVID-19-related news is generally high. Our results indicate that 84.2% respondents followed the news on COVID-19 at the state and local levels. Similarly, the majority of them (80.4%) followed the COVID-19 news at the national level. Half of respondents (54.4%) also followed the news at the international level. In order to track the news consumption pattern as the pandemic developed, we asked the respondents to recall their information consumption by quarter (first quarter of 2020, second quarter of 2020, etc.). Our trend analysis indicated a clear pattern of decreased attention from the time of initial outbreak (i.e., first quarter of 2020) to the controlled phase (i.e., fourth quarter of 2020). To validate the pattern of decreased information consumption, we also tracked their perceived concern as the pandemic developed by using the same approach. Similarly, our trend analysis indicated another clear pattern of decreased concern of the pandemic over time. More importantly, our correlation analyses confirmed a significantly positive correlation between the COVID-19-news consumption and the perceived impact of the pandemic. Figure 5.1 displays the trend lines of the COVID-19-news consumption and the perceived impact of the pandemic by the Chinese public.

The most used and trusted information channels for COVID-19 information

To investigate the various communication channels the Chinese public used for COVID-19 information, we asked respondents to share their personal experience. We generated a list of the most popular information channels in today's

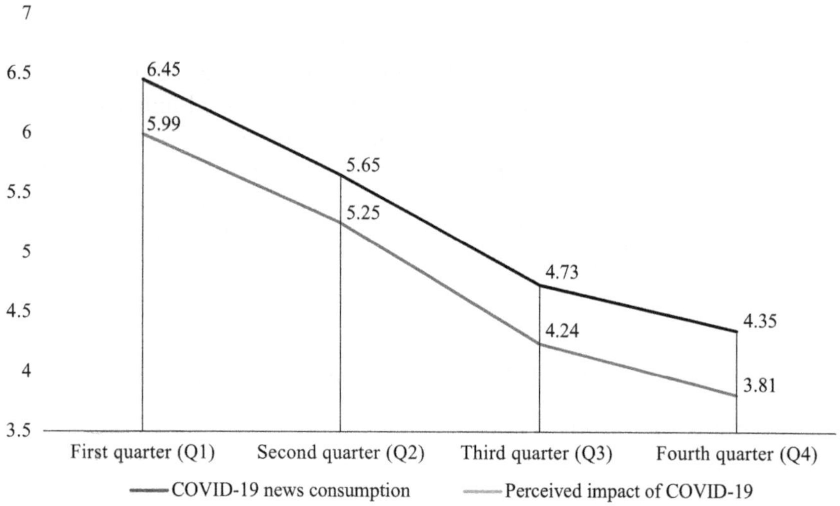

Figure 5.1 The changing patterns of COVID-19 news consumption and perceived impact of the pandemic during 2020

Source: Authors

China based on some recent trade reports of China's media landscape (China's media landscape 2021). The list includes the following major categories: 1) traditional media such as television, radio and newspapers/magazines; 2) digital media such as news websites (e.g., Sina.com.cn); 3) social media/networks for user-generated content (e.g., Weibo and Douban); 4) mobile messaging apps (e.g., WeChat and QQ); and 5) short-form mobile video platforms (e.g., Douyin).

Our data analysis identified that, during the COVID-19 pandemic, the top three most used information channels by the Chinese public are: 1) mobile messaging apps (e.g., WeChat and QQ) (76.3%); 2) news websites (e.g., Sina.com.cn) (54.2%); and 3) social media/networks for user-generated content (e.g., Weibo and Douban) (49.0%). The Chinese public also used television (42.0%) and short-from mobile video platforms (35.0%) to receive COVID-19-related information. The least used information channels are traditional media such as radio (17.8%) and newspapers/magazines (17.2%).

Are the most used information channels the most trusted ones? Results in our study reveal some opposite patterns. Traditional media such as television and newspapers/magazines led the way in building information trust among the Chinese public. Based on the findings, the top three most trusted information channels by the Chinese public are: 1) news websites (e.g., Sina.com.cn) (84.3%); 2) television (84.2%); and 3) newspapers and/or magazines (71.5%). The trust level for information from radio is also high (66.9%). Although mobile messaging apps such as WeChat and QQ are the dominant information

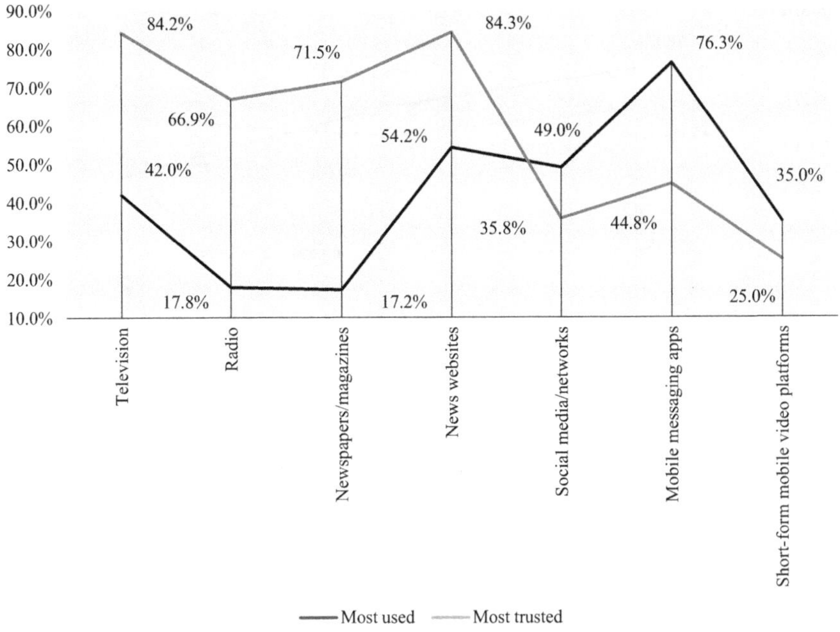

Figure 5.2 The changing patterns of the most used and most trusted information channels for COVID-19 information as rated by the Chinese public

Source: Authors

channels, less than half of respondents (44.8%) trusted them for COVID-19 information. Similarly, a low trust level was also identified for the information channel of social media and networks such as Weibo and Douban (35.8%). The short-form mobile video platform received the lowest trust score among respondents (25.0%). Figure 5.2 summarises the changing patterns of the most used and trusted information channels for COVID-19 information.

Confirming the most used and trusted information channels also helped us investigate the most trusted source for COVID-19 information. Based on our data analysis, respondents in our study indicated the highest level of trust in public health organizations and officials (M = 6.04, SD = 1.08). They also trusted the central government officials for COVID-19 information (M = 5.53, SD = 1.16) and the governmental officials at the state and local levels (M = 5.23, SD = 1.18). Respondents also trusted their friends and family when they need a quick update of the COVID-19 pandemic (M = 4.79, SD = 1.07). In general, respondents trusted sources such as social influencers, bloggers and KOLs the lowest (M = 3.80, SD = 1.30), which revealed consistent patterns when we discussed the most and least trusted information channels for COVID-19 information.

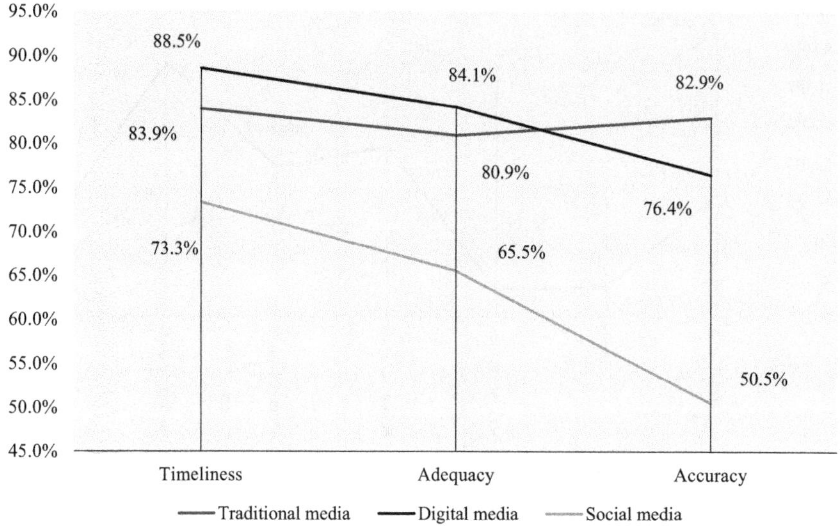

Figure 5.3 Information channels and their perceived quality of communication

Source: Authors

The perceived quality of communication on various communication channels

Research confirmed that the quality of communication affects the effectiveness of communication, which further influences trust building (Cacciatore *et al.* 2018). Therefore, we investigated the perceived quality of communication on three common groups of information channels, namely traditional media (e.g., television, radio and newspapers/magazines), digital media (e.g., news websites such as sina.com.cn) and social media with user-generated content (Weibo, WeChat, Douyin, Zhihu, etc.) on three aspects of communication quality: i.e., timeliness, adequacy and accuracy (Cacciatore *et al.* 2018, China's media landscape 2021). Results showed the group of digital media such as news websites earned the highest score on two aspects of communication quality: timeliness (M = 5.67, SD = 1.00) and adequacy (M = 5.48, SD = 1.09), while the group of traditional media took a lead on the accuracy of information (M = 5.51, SD = 1.14). It is interesting to find that social media with user-generated content received the lowest quality assessment in communication, especially in information accuracy (M = 4.51, SD = 1.39). Figure 5.3 displays the assessment of the perceived quality of communication on three common groups of information channels.

Information retention in the times of lockdown and post-pandemic

As reviewed earlier, the Chinese government set several top priorities in leading COVID-19 communication through government official and authorities, public health officials and experts, and state-run media (CSM 2020; Wu and Shen 2021). The government also took assertive steps in implementing preventive measures nationwide when responding to the ongoing pandemic (Kim *et al.* 2019; Wang *et al.* 2020). Research found that intensive media coverage on the pandemic has helped in raising awareness, communicating preventive measures and reinforcing preventive behaviours among the Chinese public (Hu *et al.* 2020). Therefore, we further investigated information retention in both the times of lockdown (e.g., Q1 and Q2 in 2020) and post-pandemic (e.g., Q4 in 2020). The top three key messages retained by the Chinese public during the times of lockdown included:

1 COVID-19 spreads easily and you must stay home so that the economy does not suffer a longer interruption (70.4%).
2 COVID-19 is dangerous and borders should be closed to persons from countries with a high level of contagion (62.7%).
3 COVID-19 will cause a state of emergency and the most important thing is to have food at home (59.9%).

The analysis of the message retention during the phase of post-pandemic revealed a different information retention pattern. The top three key messages retained by the Chinese public included:

1 Keep good hygiene habits, including taking personal protection, wearing masks, physical distancing, covering mouth and nose when coughing or sneezing, and washing hands frequently (63.1%).
2 Implement strict prevention and control measures to prevent a resurgence of the outbreak (54.0%).
3 Avoid traveling to areas experiencing ongoing transmission of COVID-19 (47.7%).

With WHO's declaration of a public health emergency of international concern in relation to COVID-19 in February 2020, the Chinese government implemented strict travel measures and activated travel bans to affected areas or denial of entry to passengers coming from affected areas (China National Health Commission 2020). Therefore, the policy reinforcement was successfully reflected in information retention among the public in China. We also found that almost half of our respondents (47.1%) agreed that economic and social activities should be carried out in a stable and orderly manner after the pandemic prevention and control measures were effectively regulated.

Implications and conclusions

As the first country to report confirmed COVID-19 cases and experience the earliest coronavirus outbreak, lessons learned from China on COVID-19 prevention and control protocol could provide practical implications to international communities. Just as revealed in our research, the repeated and intensive media

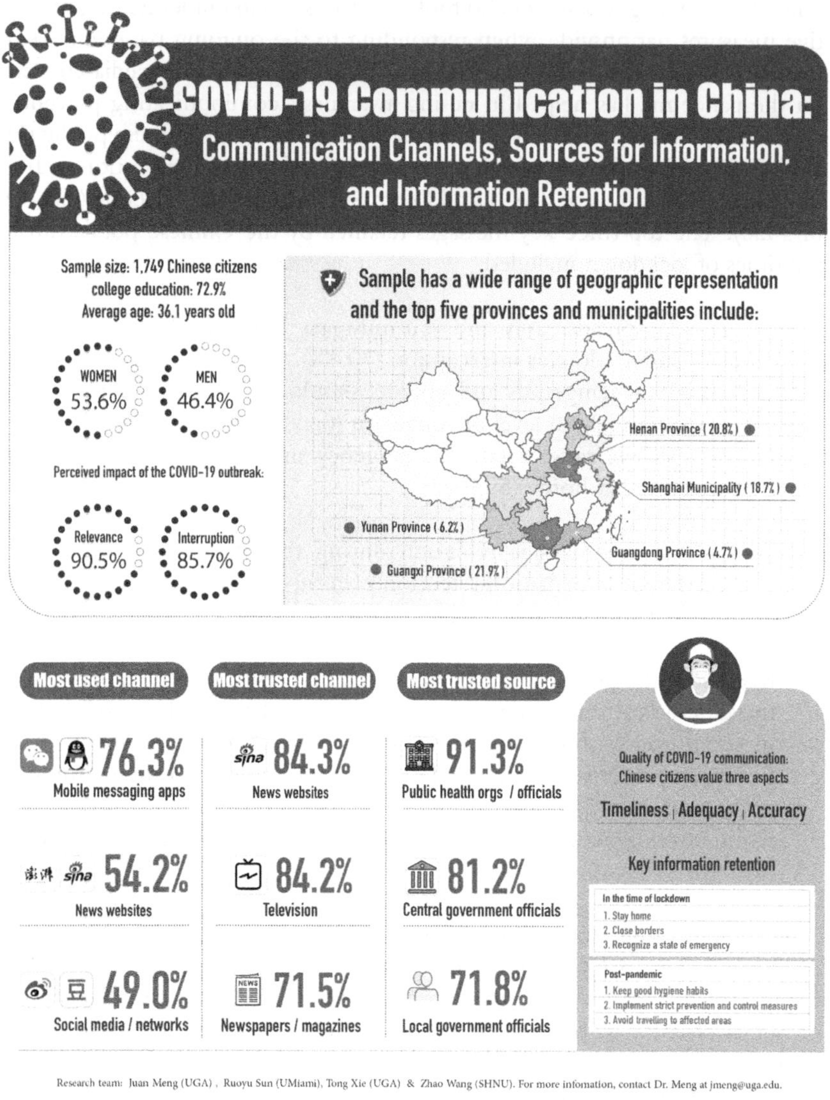

Infographic 5.1 COVID-19 communication in China: Communications channels, sources for information and information retention

coverage on public health education and risk communication during the early stage of the outbreak significantly raised the awareness of the potential risk associated with COVID-19. It also helped the Chinese public retain several key public health messages such as travel restriction, mask use and physical distancing at the preventive level.

It is important to recognise the shifting media landscape in today's China when communicating public health information to the public via diverse information channels. When the levels of anxiety and uncertainty are high, it is natural for individuals to demonstrate a significantly high level of information consumption as confirmed in our correlation analysis. When the penetration rate of mobile internet users in China achieved 99.7%, by the end of 2020 (Statista 2021), it is not surprising to confirm the majority of Chinese citizens rely heavily on mobile messaging apps such as WeChat for COVID-19 information, followed by news websites and social media with user-generated content.

However, our research also confirmed the disparity between the most used and trusted information channels. Although the Chinese public do not rely very much on traditional media for fast news consumption, their trust in those traditional media (such as television, newspapers and magazines) remains very high. Social media and popular short-form video platforms are the least trusted channels, even though individuals spend more time on those information channels. Such a disparity between usage and trust reveals important practical implications for government communication in China, especially when responding to an ongoing pandemic.

To prevent and control the spread of COVID-19, the Chinese government took assertive control actions to avoid mass gathering activities and limit transportation capacity to reduce the movement of large populations. Timely actions shall be accompanied by adequate communication. Such efforts shall not only be demonstrated in traditional media channels via state-run media; essentially, more tailored messages shall be dedicated to the most used information channels in order to reach a wide audience and build consistency and trust in communication. Timely communication matters, but so do the adequacy and the accuracy of the information being communicated. The three aspects associated with the quality of communication – timeliness, adequacy and accuracy – shall be the key measures when developing COVID-19-related preventive and control measures. In addition, the quality of communication shall demonstrate consistency across various communication channels.

In conclusion, results presented in this chapter share insights on how to build consistent communication in a country in which government communication plays a defining role when responding to an ongoing public health crisis. Such findings further echo some of the previous research on the Chinese public's attention and responses to the COVID-19 pandemic. Knowledge accumulation, information retention and the practice of preventive behaviours shall be the priorities in government communication to reinforce trust in public health.

Bibliography

AlTakarli, N.S. (2020). China's response to the COVID-19 outbreak: A model for epidemic preparedness and Management. *Dubai Medical Journal*, 3(2), pp. 44–49.

Ang, Y.Y. (2020). When COVID-19 meets centralized, personalized power. *Nature Human Behaviour*, 4(5), pp. 445–447.

Bouey, J. (2020). Strengthening China's public health response system: From SARS to COVID-19. *American Journal of Public Health*, (7), pp. 939–940.

Brashers, D.E., Goldsmith, D.J., and Hsieh, E. (2002). Information seeking and avoiding in health contexts. *Human Communication Research*, 28(2), pp. 258–271.

Buckley, C. (2020). Chinese doctor, silenced after warning of outbreak, dies form Coronavirus [online]. *The New York Times*. Available from: www.nytimes.com/2020/02/06/world/asia/chinese-doctor-Li-Wenliang-coronavirus.html?searchResultPosition=1 [Accessed 3 May 2021].

Cacciatore, M.A., Browning, N., Scheufele, D.A., Brossard, D., Xenos, M.A., and Corley, E.A. (2018). Opposing ends of the spectrum: Exploring trust in scientific and religious authorities. *Public Understanding of Science*, 27(1), pp. 11–28.

Chen, Q., Min, C., Zhang, W., Wang, G., Ma, X., and Evans, R. (2020). Unpacking the black box: How to promote citizen engagement through government social media during the COVID-19 crisis. *Computers in Human Behavior*, 110, 106380.

Chen, S., Zhang, Z., Yang, J., Wang, J., Zhai, X., Bärnighausen, T., and Wang, C. (2020). Fangcang shelter hospitals: A novel concept for responding to public health emergencies. *The Lancet*, 395(10232), pp. 1305–1314.

China National Health Commission (2020). Inclusion of 2019 novel Coronavirus diseases (COVID-19) into statutory infectious disease management [online]. *China National Health Commission*. Available from: www.nhc.gov.cn/jkj/s7916/202001/44a3b8245e8049d2837a4f27529cd386.shtml [Accessed 3 May 2021].

China's Media Landscape (2021). *AHK greater china* [online]. Available from: https://china.ahk.de/market-info/chinas-media-landscape [Accessed 3 May 2021].

Country Guide: China (2021). *The Washington Post* [online]. Available from: www.washingtonpost.com/wp-srv/world/countries/china.html [Accessed 3 May 2021].

COVID-19 Dashboard by the Center for Systems Science and Engineering (2021). *The Coronavirus resource center* [online]. Johns Hopkins University & Medicine. Available from: https://coronavirus.jhu.edu/map.html [Accessed 30 September 2021].

CSM (2020). *Expectation survey report on users' media consumption and use during the epidemic* [online]. CSM Media Research. Available from: www.csm.com.cn/Content/2020/02-25/1015314370.html [Accessed 3 May 2021].

Global Times (2020). We must avoid losses caused by fear, overreaction: Top epidemiologist [online]. *Global Times*. Available from: www.globaltimes.cn/content/1178031.shtml [Accessed 3 May 2021].

Haini, H. (2020). The evolution of China's modern economy and its implications on future growth. *Post-Communist Economies*, pp. 1–25.

He, A.J., Shi, Y., and Liu, H. (2020). Crisis governance, Chinese style: Distinctive features of china's response to the Covid-19 pandemic. *Policy Design and Practice*, 3(3), pp. 242–258.

Huang, C., Xu, X., Cai, Y., Ge, Q., Zeng, G., Li, X., . . . and Yang, L. (2020). Mining the characteristics of COVID-19 patients in China: Analysis of social media posts. *Journal of Medical Internet Research*, 22(5), e19087.

Hu, G., Li, P., Yuan, C., Tao, C., Wen, H., Liu, Q., and Qiu, W. (2020). Information disclosure during the COVID-19 epidemic in China: City-level observational study. *Journal of Medical Internet Research*, 22(8), e19572.

Jing, Y. (2021). Seeking opportunities from crisis? China's governance responses to the COVID-19 pandemic. *International Review of Administrative Sciences*, 87(3), pp. 631–650.

Kim, L., Fast, S.M., and Markuzon, N. (2019). Incorporating media data into a model of infectious disease transmission. *PloS One*, 14(2), e0197646.

Leng, Y., Zhai, Y., Sun, S., Wu, Y., Selzer, J., Strover, S., Zhang, H., Chen, A., and Ding, Y. (2021). Misinformation during the COVID-19 outbreak in China: Cultural, social and political entanglements. *IEEE Transactions on Big Data*, 7, pp. 69–80.

Lin, L., Jung, M., McCloud, R.F., and Viswanath, K. (2014). Media use and communication inequalities in a public health emergency: A case study of 2009–2010 pandemic influenza A virus subtype H1N1. *Public Health Reports*, 129(6_suppl4), pp. 49–60.

Lin, Y., Hu, Z., Alias, H., and Wong, L.P. (2020). Knowledge, attitudes, impact, and anxiety regarding COVID-19 infection among the public in China. *Frontiers in Public Health*, 8, 236.

Li, R.Y.M., Yue, X.G., and Crabbe, M.J.C. (2020). Covid-19 in Wuhan: Pressing realities and city management. *Frontiers in Public Health*, 8, 1079.

Liu, M., Zhang, H., and Huang, H. (2020). Media exposure to COVID-19 information, risk perception, social and geographical proximity, and self-rated anxiety in China. *BMC Public Health*, 20(1), pp. 1–8.

Liu, Q., Zheng, Z., Zheng, J., Chen, Q., Liu, G., Chen, S., . . . and Ming, W.K. (2020). Health communication through news media during the early stage of the COVID-19 outbreak in China: Digital topic modeling approach. *Journal of Medical Internet Research*, 22(4), e19118.

Li, Y., Chandra, Y., and Kapucu, N. (2020). Crisis coordination and the role of social media in response to COVID-19 in Wuhan, China. *The American Review of Public Administration*, 50(6–7), pp. 698–705.

Ma, R., Deng, Z., and Wu, M. (2020). Effects of health information dissemination on user follows and likes during COVID-19 outbreak in China: Data and content analysis. *International Journal of Environmental Research and Public Health*, 17(14), p. 5081.

Mei, C. (2020). Policy style, consistency and the effectiveness of the policy mix in China's fight against COVID-19. *Policy and Society*, 39(3), pp. 309–325.

National Bureau of Statistics of China (2021). *Stable recovery of the national economy in 2020, the primary objective was achieved than expectation* [online]. Available from: www.stats.gov.cn/tjsj/zxfb/202101/t20210118_1812423.html [Accessed 2 May 2021].

Niu, Z., Qin, Z., Hu, P., and Wang, T. (2021). Health beliefs, trust in media sources, health literacy, and preventive behaviors among high-risk Chinese for COVID-19. *Health Communication*, pp. 1–9.

Pan, Y., Xin, M., Zhang, C., Dong, W., Fang, Y., Wu, W., . . . and He, Y. (2020). Associations of mental health and personal preventive measure compliance with exposure to COVID-19 information during work resumption following the COVID-19 outbreak in China: Cross-sectional survey study. *Journal of Medical Internet Research*, 22(10).

Penetration rate of mobile internet users in China from 2008 to 2020 (2021). *Statista*, 2021 [online]. Available from: www.statista.com/statistics/255552/penetration-rate-of-mobile-internet-users-in-china/#:~:text=In%20December%202020%2C%20around%2099.7,going%20online%20via%20cell%20phone [Accessed 5 May 2021].

Sørensen, K., Van den Broucke, S., Fullam, J., Doyle, G., Pelikan, J., Slonska, Z., and Brand, H. (2012). Health literacy and public health: A systematic review and integration of definitions and models. *BMC Public Health*, 12(1), pp. 1–13.

The State Council Information Office of the People's Republic of China (2020). *Fighting Covid-19 China in action* [online]. Available from: http://language.chinadaily.com.cn/a/202006/08/WS5edde063a310834817251871_1.html [Accessed 5 May 2021].

Statista (2021). *Gross domestic product (GDP) at current prices in China from 1985 to 2020 with forecasts until 2026* [online]. Available from: www.statista.com/statistics/263770/gross-domestic-product-gdp-of-china/ [Accessed 5 May 2021].

Tam, G., Huang, Z., and Chan, E.Y.Y. (2018). Household preparedness and preferred communication channels in public health emergencies: A cross-sectional survey of residents in an Asian developed urban city. *International Journal of Environmental Research and Public Health*, 15(8), p. 1598.

Tang, L., and Zou, W. (2021). Health information consumption under COVID-19 lockdown: An interview study of residents of Hubei Province, China. *Health Communication*, 36(1), pp. 74–80.

Volz, M., Ladwig, S., and Werheid, K. (2021). Gender differences in post-stroke depression: A longitudinal analysis of prevalence, persistence and predictive value of known risk factors. *Neuropsychological Rehabilitation*, 31(1), pp. 1–17.

Wang, C., Horby, P.W., Hayden, F.G., and Gao, G.F. (2020). A novel Coronavirus outbreak of global health concern. *The Lancet*, 395(10223), pp. 470–473.

WHO Coronavirus Disease (COVID-19) Dashboard (2021). *Global situation* [online]. Available from: https://covid19.who.int/ [Accessed 30 September 2021].

World Health Organization (2020a). *Report of the WHO-China joint mission on Coronavirus disease 2019 (COVID-19)* [online]. Available from: www.who.int/docs/defaultsource/coronaviruse/who-china-joint-mission-on-covid-19-final-report.pdf [Accessed 2 May 2021].

World Health Organization (2020b). *Timeline: WHO's COVID-19 response* [online]. Available from: www.who.int/emergencies/diseases/novel-coronavirus-2019/interactive-timeline#event-3 [Accessed 2 May 2021].

Wu, Y., and Shen, F. (2021). Exploring the impacts of media use and media trust on health behaviors during the COVID-19 pandemic in China. *Journal of Health Psychology*, 1359105321995964.

Xing, C., and Zhang, R. (2021). COVID-19 in China: Responses, challenges and implications for the health system. *Healthcare*, 9(1), pp. 82–93.

Xu, T.L., Ao, M.Y., Zhou, X., Zhu, W.F., Nie, H.Y., Fang, J.H., . . . and Chen, X.F. (2020). China's practice to prevent and control COVID-19 in the context of large population movement. *Infectious Diseases of Poverty*, 9(1), pp. 1–14.

Xu, W., Wu, J., and Cao, L. (2020). COVID-19 pandemic in China: Context, experience and lessons. *Health Policy and Technology*, 9(4), pp. 639–648.

Xu, Y., and Renken, E. (2020). China's red banners take on Coronavirus. Even Mahjong gets a mention [online]. *NPR*. Available from: www.npr.org/sections/goatsandsoda/2020/03/01/805760905/chinas-red-banners-take-on-coronavirus-even-mahjong-gets-a-mention [Accessed 2 May 2021].

Yue, S., Zhang, J., Cao, M., and Chen, B. (2021). Knowledge, attitudes and practices of COVID-19 among urban and rural residents in China: A cross-sectional study. *Journal of Community Health*, 46(2), pp. 286–291.

Zhang, L., Li, H., and Chen, K. (2020). Effective risk communication for public health emergency: Reflection on the COVID-19 (2019-nCoV) outbreak in Wuhan, China. *Healthcare*, 8(1), p. 64.

Zhang, X., Wen, D., Liang, J., and Lei, J. (2017). How the public uses social media WeChat to obtain health information in china: A survey study. *BMC Medical Informatics and Decision Making*, 17(Suppl 2), p. 66.

Zhao, X., Fan, J., Basnyat, I., and Hu, B. (2020). Online health information seeking using '# COVID-19 patient seeking help' on Weibo in Wuhan, China: Descriptive study. *Journal of Medical Internet Research*, 22(10), e22910.

Zhao, Y., Cheng, S., Yu, X., and Xu, H. (2020). Chinese public's attention to the COVID-19 epidemic on social media: Observational descriptive study. *Journal of Medical Internet Research*, 22(5), e18825.

Europe – South

6 "I am impressed by how quickly they changed"

The impact of CSR communication initiatives during COVID-19 among millennials in Italy

Elanor Colleoni, Mirko Olivieri, Stefania Romenti and Grazia Murtarelli

Introduction

In the first wave of the COVID-19 pandemic in 2020, Italy suffered through one of the worst epidemics in the world, with more than 30,000 casualties, most of them concentrated in the north regions, and in Lombardy in particular, the most industrialised area of the country. Quickly spreading across the globe, the virus generated a world pandemic with repercussions still difficult to estimate. The severity of the pandemic has forced former Italian prime minister Giuseppe Conte – and soon after, the leaders of many other countries – to introduce several restrictive measures to limit the spread of the virus, such as social distancing and closure of non-essential shops, and in March 2020, the first national lockdown (Della Rossa *et al.* 2020). The COVID-19 pandemic has had enormous direct consequences on the economy, but also indirect effects on financial security, housing, unemployment and social isolation, which has led to an increase in emotional and psychological challenges worldwide (Statista 2021). Given this unprecedented condition, institutional communication played a critical role in reducing uncertainty, instilling trust and encouraging citizens to remain calm and stay safe (Camilleri 2021).

It is in this uncertain context that companies have decided to engage with stakeholders, including employees and customers, to restore their faith and trust, thereby providing a sense of stability to them (Camilleri 2021). Indeed, during the first wave of COVID-19 pandemic, we have witnessed business responses evolve into a variety of responsible initiatives (Gutierrez *et al.* 2020) that have been intensively communicated. Businesses such as Giorgio Armani, Louis Vuitton and Ferrari, among others, have adapted their production lines to produce medical and sanitary products and have promoted their initiatives. Gutierrez *et al.* (2020) have shown how Spanish companies' responses took the form of 'rapid responsible innovation, innovation developed in a short period of time in a state of emergency with the hope of protecting people and saving lives' (Gutierrez *et al.* 2020, p. 1) – new or significantly improved products, services, processes, organizational practices or business models whose implementation

DOI: 10.4324/9781003184669-11

in the market solves or alleviates an environmental or social problem. In Italy as well, we witnessed companies leading a responsible movement with the goal of helping to alleviate the negative impact of the outbreak. These responsible innovations were promptly communicated to the consumers and the general public through strategic responsible communication initiatives. These responsible communication initiatives in response to the health crisis derived from the COVID-19 pandemic have presented us with something unexpected that challenges numerous assumptions about corporate social responsibility (Crane and Matten 2020). Firstly, these types of business COVID-19 initiatives can be considered new forms of corporate social responsibility (CSR) as they show that companies are taking on a political and socially responsible role in supporting societies and stakeholders during a global emergency by working directly to support citizens and coordinating with governmental authorities (Crane and Matten 2020). This new role that businesses have taken on during the pandemic is radically redefining the perceptions of responsibilities of business in society. Secondly, the extensive communication of these initiatives has led to what seems to be a disruption compared to traditional models of responsible communication that interpret companies as reluctant in sharing their social commitments in fear of scepticism from stakeholders (Skarmeas and Leonidou 2013). Despite the uncertainty, companies have supported citizens, government and institutional authorities and have responsibly communicated these initiatives extensively. The results of their responsible communication are astonishing: as shown by our research, 51% of the millennials recall one or more responsible communications and 98% of them perceived these responsible communications as authentic. These results show that when a company takes action voluntarily as a social and political actor and communicates with the public's needs in mind, cynical attitudes decrease.

Hence, the aim of this book chapter is twofold: first, to investigate the main CSR communication initiatives put in place by the companies during the COVID-19 pandemic, and second, to explore Italian millennials' perceptions of these CSR communication initiatives.

This chapter provides communication scholars and practitioners with useful insights concerning millennials' perceptions of the strategic responsible communication initiatives implemented by organizations during a critical period. Additionally, it illustrates the crucial role responsible communication plays in guiding companies to develop a new social role, and in so doing, acquiring renewed legitimacy and credibility.

This chapter is organised as follows. First, we review the theories of crisis and risk management and outline the uniqueness of the companies' responses. Second, we briefly present the methodology behind the study and outline the main areas investigated, then set out the research question of the study. Third, we present the main findings of our research and try to answer our research question. Finally, in the conclusion, we summarise the results of our research, discuss implications of findings and briefly consider future avenues in strategic responsible communication.

Theoretical background

Communicating corporate social responsibility

During the past 20 years, new corporate ethical expectations have risen steadily as a response to the globalisation processes and the consequent erosion of national power. These have been accompanied by the emergence of new societal risks and citizens' perceived uncertainty – general economic, social and environmental (Beck 2000; Castells 1997). As pointed out by Colleoni (2013), corporations are increasingly treated as personified autonomous subjects, societal actors that must operate for the general wealth of society by fulfilling a set of contingent social responsibilities to various groups of stakeholders in society (Moreno and Capriotti 2009). Traditional CSR approach has emphasised the instrumental nature of corporate responsibility initiatives, inviting the examination of CSR in the context of building a competitive advantage (Porter and Kramer 2011) and increasing tangible and intangible corporate assets (Carroll 1991; Husted and Allen 2013; Lantos 2001). More recently, CSR has been conceptualised through the lenses of political-normative and ethical paradigms (Donaldson and Dunfee 1999; Scherer and Palazzo 2007), focussing on the wider societal obligations of organizations (Moreno and Capriotti 2009) and stressing the importance of building significant relationships with its stakeholders (Schultz *et al.* 2013).

This dialogical turn has been crucial in the development of the corporate social responsibility communication field, as it has put at the centre the role of communication in reaching the desired outcomes (Kim and Lee 2018).

Corporate social responsibility communication strategies

Communication is a critical part of effective CSR (Manheim and Pratt 1986), and it is mainly concerned with "how the message of CSR can be effectively conveyed from senders to recipients, how CSR activities can be understood mutually between senders and receivers and between receivers and can be perceived precisely or correctly by those receivers" (Tench *et al.* 2014).

Extant research has shown the benefits of well-communicated CSR activities, such as leading to stronger relationships with the public (Hall 2006), improving corporate legitimacy (Du and Vieira 2012) and trust (Castaldo *et al.* 2009) and building favourable stakeholders' attitudes (Du *et al.* 2010). At the same time, CSR initiatives can be perceived sceptically by the stakeholders if the engagement in CSR activities is not effectively communicated, undermining the legitimacy of the company (Illia *et al.* 2017). For instance, as shown by Du *et al.* (2010), promoting CSR initiatives aggressively results in attribution of profit-seeking motives and, in turn, in negative perception of the company. In contrast, stakeholders' trust is increased and scepticism reduced when an organization actively responds to consumers' enquiries on company blogs regarding its CSR initiatives, leading consumers to advocate for the organization (Rim and Song 2013), or when a company engages in CSR as a long-term partnership to support a certain social cause, rather than as an ad hoc promotional campaign (Lafferty and Goldsmith 1999).

In order for CSR initiatives to be effective, it is crucial to understand where, how and to whom CSR initiatives should be communicated. Accordingly, extant research in the field has been focused on three main strategic areas (Tench *et al.* 2014): communicative subjects; the communication forms and means; and the development of effective communication content. The first aspect concerns the identification of the stakeholders with whom the company wishes to communicate, as different stakeholders might have different interests in and concerns with CSR issues. The second aspect concerns the identification of appropriate channels and sources to convey the desired message to the stakeholders, such as formal CSR reports, media (including social media), advertising, direct dialogue and other methods. The third aspect concerns the development of effective content. To create effective CSR content, four aspects should be made explicit: the values of the company, and their relationship with the CSR initiatives, the concrete actions taken to implement the CSR initiatives and the stakeholders whose concern they are addressing through these CSR initiatives.

CSR communication initiatives during a societal crisis

Recently, Crane and Matten (2020) have emphasised how the COVID-19 pandemic and the business responses to it are forcing scholars to rethink CSR theory. In particular, two elements about the COVID-19 pandemic need scholars' attention.

The advent of the societal risk

To date, little attention has been paid to the notion of societal risk in the CSR literature. Traditionally, risk has been conceptualised at the company level and CSR often has been presented as a tool to manage this risk (Crane and Matten 2020). This focus on risk centred on individual company risks to the bottom line. Indeed, CSR has been conceived and managed to buffer an organization from crises (Diers-Lawson *et al.* 2020). However, the societal risks created by COVID-19 pandemic are not directly connected to corporate action, and yet companies, as citizens, are part of it. CSR research is needed to shift from an individual to a societal conception of risk and examine how companies can strategically work under this new framework.

The political role of business

The severity of the COVID-19 pandemic crisis has put governments under great pressure, and the need to successfully manage the crisis have seen traditional political actors, civil society organizations, companies and others working together in unprecedented ways. In this sense, companies have taken on a political and socially responsible role in supporting societies and stakeholders during a global emergency by working directly to support citizens and coordinating with governmental authorities (Crane and Matten 2020). In a similar context, the strategic communication of the responsible initiatives by the companies seems to play a relevant role in helping organizations successfully address societal challenges. However, to date, little is known about what forms strategic communication of responsible initiatives will take, and whether this communication needs to be accompanied by a reconceptualisation of the notion of strategic responsible communication.

Research questions

Based on the theoretical open questions we have outlined, it is crucial to investigate the main strategic responsible communication initiatives put in place by companies during the COVID-19 pandemic and to explore millennials' perception of these CSR communication initiatives. In particular, in our empirical analysis we focused on communication channels, credible sources of information, type of shared messages and effectiveness of CSR communication initiatives. More specifically, the research aims to answer the following research questions:

RQs: What are the main CSR communication initiatives put in place by the companies during the COVID-19 pandemic as perceived by millennials? How do millennials evaluate these CSR communication initiatives?

Methodology

A quantitative survey based on an online questionnaire consisting of 15 questions was carried out during the initial phase of the COVID-19 pandemic in the period between March and May 2020. The survey was conducted at an international level in collaboration with IULM University (Milan, Italy), Rey Juan Carlos University (Madrid, Spain) and Leeds Beckett University (Leeds, UK) and provides unique data about the millennials' perceptions of the CSR communication initiatives adopted by companies during the COVID-19 emergency. In particular, the results presented in the chapter refer to Italian millennials. The questionnaire was sent to undergraduate and graduate students at selected universities in Milan. A total of 468 millennials completed the survey. Nominal and ordinal response scales have been used throughout the questionnaire. Figure 6.1 summarises the research framework characterising the survey.

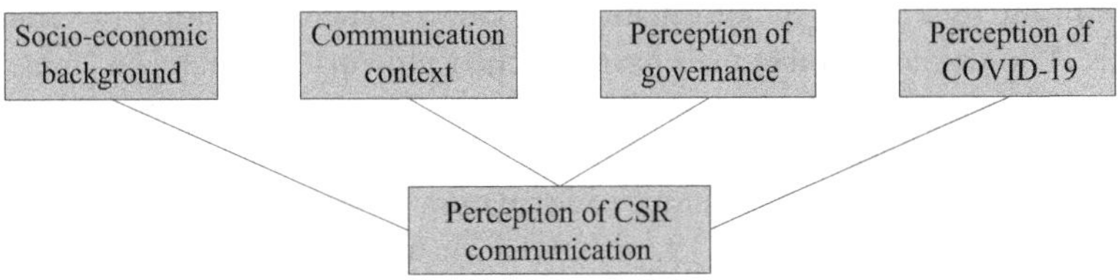

Figure 6.1 COVID-19 survey framework

Source: Authors

As illustrated in Figure 6.1, the survey has analysed five areas: the communication context in which the respondents are embedded, their social and economic background and resulting perceptions towards COVID-19, the government and effectiveness of its communication, and perception of the responsible communication initiatives carried out by the companies. In order to explore the communication context in which millennials are embedded, questions were asked about what channels have been used for information retrieval around COVID-19, the sources of information and the trust towards these sources. The perception of COVID-19 includes questions about COVID-19 knowledge, perceived uncertainty and perceived self-efficacy. Concerning the perception of businesses' responsible communication initiatives, respondents were asked to name the most effective communication initiatives implemented during the COVID-19 emergency and to explain why in their own words. In order to identify the main goals of the responsible communication initiatives, the open-ended responses were classified through content analysis. The coding was carried out independently by three researchers and the percentage of agreement reached was 90%. The open-ended responses were also analysed to extract the most recurrent words used to describe the CSR communication initiatives.

Research findings

Descriptive statistics

The survey has collected 468 answers with an average respondent age of 25. Most of the respondents are female (78.4%), still living with their parents (45.9%) and in the northern regions (75.6%).

Figure 6.2 shows the most used channels for collecting information about COVID-19 among millennials in Italy. The figure shows that traditional channels have been the most proactively used channels. Indeed, 61% of respondents declared they have used TV for collecting information; 50.4% of respondents searched and collected information by using online newspapers; 31.2% used websites and institutional blogs; while 14.3% read a printed newspaper. Radio has been used by 48.5% of respondents. Social networks have been used less than traditional channels: 54.3% of respondents used Facebook to look for information and only 5% of respondents used Twitter for reading news. Moreover, Instagram has been used for informative reasons by 63.6% of millennials.

However, when looking at age, educational level and income, we can find significant differences in information-seeking behaviours among the millennials. The youngest millennials have searched information more on Instagram (r=-.251, p<0.05) and online newspapers (r=-.119, p<0.05), while the oldest millennials have mostly used radio (r=.232, p<0.01). Millennials with a higher level of education have searched information more on Facebook (r=.176, p<0.05) and magazines (r=.119, p<0.05) than millennials with lower levels of education. Finally, millennials with higher levels of income have preferred to use websites and blogs about alternative therapies (r=.108, p<0.05) compared to millennials with lower levels of income.

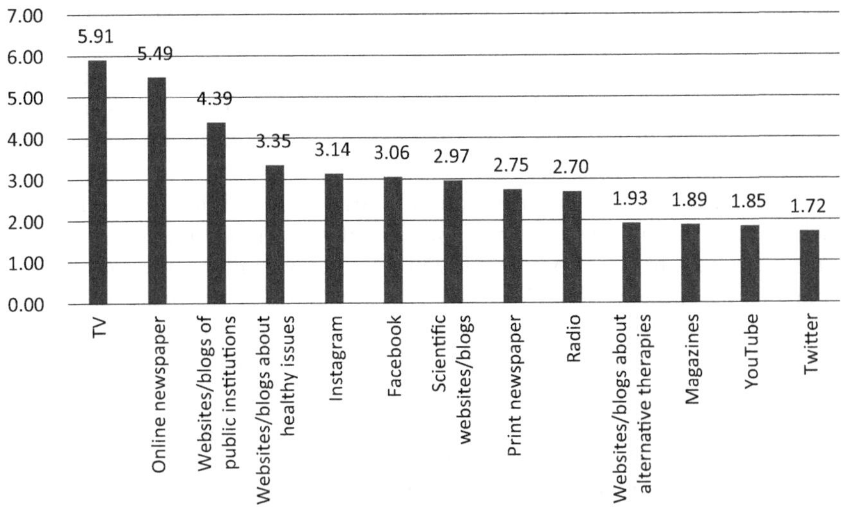

Figure 6.2 Channels used for information retrieval

Source: Authors

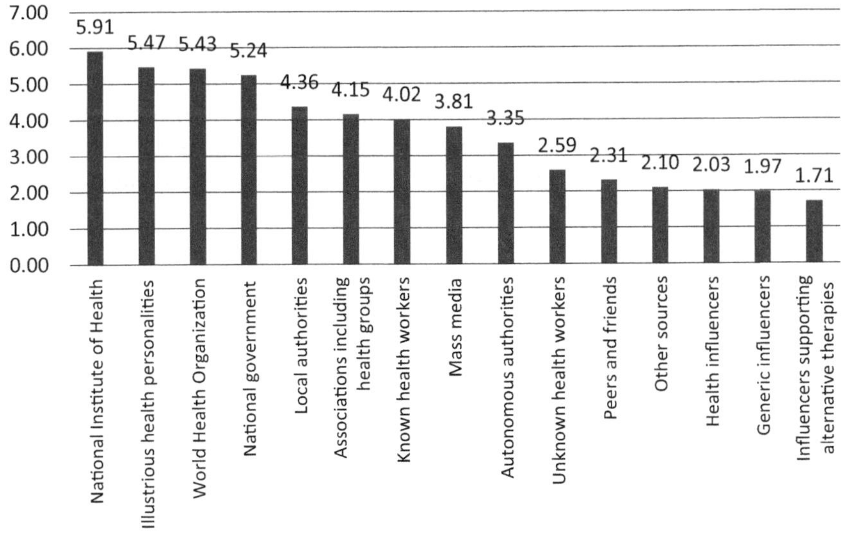

Figure 6.3 Trust in sources of information

Source: Authors

Figure 6.3 shows the most trusted sources of information about COVID-19 among the millennials in Italy. The figure shows that 51% of respondents fully trusted the National Institute of Health, 408% showed trust towards the World Health Organization and 29.3% trusted the Italian government. Peers and friends have been considered as not credible unless they work within the health context. Of the respondents, 80% have questioned what peers and friends were able to say about the health emergency. Medical and health influencers obtained the lowest score in terms of credibility: 69% of respondents have declared they do not trust influencers promoting alternative therapies and 59.4% of respondents do not believe medical or health influencers. And, as shown in the graph, 24.4% put their trust in illustrious health personalities such as epidemiologists.

Concerning trust towards sources, significant differences emerged when considering age, income and use of specific channels for searching information. The youngest millennials show higher trust towards the Italian government (r=-.157, p<0.01), the National Institute of Health (r=-.191, p<0.05), generic influencers (r=-.123, p<0.05) and the World Health Organization (r=.183, p<0.05), compared to the oldest millennials. Millennials with higher levels of income show higher levels of trust towards the Italian government (r=-.095, p<0.05), compared to millennials with lower levels of income. Finally, differences have emerged based on the channels used for collecting information. Millennials who have used Twitter as a preferred channel for seeking information regarding COVID-19 show higher levels of trust towards unknown health workers (r=.091, p<0.05), illustrious health personalities (r=.108, p<0.05) and the World Health Organization (r=.118, p<0.05). Those who have mostly used Instagram show a general confidence towards multiple sources of information, such as the National Institute of Health (r=.125, p<0.01), autonomous authorities (r=.146, p<0.01), local authorities (r=.145, p<0.01), mass media (r=.091, p<0.05), peers and friends (r=.091, p<0.05), unknown health workers (r=.091, p<0.05), health influencers (r=.091, p<0.05), generic influencers (r=.091, p<0.05) and influencers supporting alternative therapies (r=.091, p<0.05).

RQ: Millennials' perceptions of CSR communication initiatives

When asked about CSR communication initiatives, 51% of the millennials recalled one or more responsible communication initiatives. Among those who identified at least one CSR communication initiative, 97% evaluated it positively, while only 3% perceived it as not authentic or instrumental. This means that these communication initiatives were not only extremely effective, with a recall rate more than double standard recall rate for advertising (Angell *et al.* 2016), but also that when taking on a political role supporting citizens and institutions during the crisis, companies are perceived as authentic, overcoming traditional problems of scepticism (Illia *et al.* 2013).

Figure 6.4 shows the most recurring terms used by the respondents for describing perceptions of the responsible communication initiatives implemented by the companies. Most of these words have a positive connotation, such as donating/collecting, solidarity/supportive, clear, informative, effective and impactful.

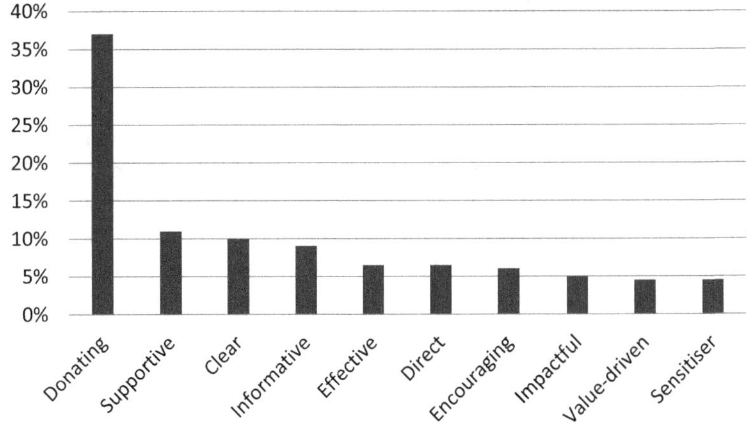

Figure 6.4 Most recurring words describing respondents' perception of responsible communication initiatives

Source: Authors.

From the content analysis on the CSR communication initiatives mentioned by the respondents, is possible to identify four different communication strategies: 1) social and economic support, 2) promoting appropriate social behaviour, 3) promoting community values and 4) informing.

Next we review these four strategies and in the final part of the paragraph we summarise differences and similarities.

Social and economic support

In 33% of cases, the CSR communication initiatives were perceived as a sincere attempt to alleviate economic and/or social problems (Halme and Korpela 2014). Reducing the onerous work done by health facilities and ensuring that resources are used to increase assistance and care is, for example, the message spread by Armani Group when it announced that it would be one of the first Italian companies to join the anti-COVID-19 vaccination campaign. The Armani Group, in fact, has made available its own theatre for the vaccination campaign, which traditionally hosts the brand's fashion shows and which in February 2020 was the setting for the first high-fashion show closed to the public. As a matter of fact, respondents affirmed:

> *I am impressed by how quickly they changed their production to support citizens.*
> *(21-year-old female)*

> *I love the world of fashion and I was very impressed with how Giorgio Armani concerned himself with the health situation by closing the doors of the show to the public during fashion week and how he cared about his employees.*
> *(22-year-old male)*

The initiative to support health facilities in vaccination activities was strongly supported by Giorgio Armani, with a view to service and proximity to his employees at a time that is still critical for everyone's health. Already during the first lockdown, the humanity of the Armani brand and its economic and social support had been widely recognised. For example, on social media a photo of Giorgio Armani had gone viral, showing him intent on arranging his shop window in Milan, after having converted his haute couture production to produce protective gowns and masks to be donated to healthcare personnel. The evocative power of that photograph circulated on social media highlighted the company as a living body of society which must participate in the events of humanity and become the instrument of a message of value. In fact, the values of solidarity, closeness and the common good have been enhanced by the COVID emergency, especially in the most dramatic moments of the lockdown. With these values in mind, Armani promoted a reflection of the entire fashion world on the sustainability of business models, which were already beginning to spread in the pre-COVID era. Today, a solid value proposition reflected both in business and marketing and communication strategies that goes beyond emergencies has been demonstrated by Armani.

At the same time, there has been a strengthening of omni-channel CSR communication. On the one hand, the use of social media and general channels has grown exponentially because of social distancing; on the other hand, companies like Armani have felt the need to be present on several fronts, focussing not only on digital communication but taking advantage of all possible touchpoints. For example, as shown in Figure 6.5, a message signed by Giorgio Armani appeared on a mural in the centre of Milan: 'I am there for Milan, with the Milan citizens, with feeling'.

COVID-19, therefore, represents a push towards an even more integrated communication which mixes traditional channels with the growing role of digital: hence, the need for many companies such as Armani Group to spread their messages on several outlets.

Promoting appropriate social behaviour

Reiterating the importance of the rules fundamental to countering the spread of COVID-19 is another CSR communication strategy that emerged from our study. In particular, 28% of respondents stressed that companies have used their communication to reinforce the importance of these rules, such as social distancing and wearing masks. Among the CSR communication initiatives related to the promotion of appropriate social behaviour, Coca-Cola was remembered by the respondents involved in this research:

> *The Coca-Cola ad in Times Square, because they changed the logo to convey the idea of being separated.*
>
> *(25-year-old male)*

Figure 6.5 Message from Giorgio Armani to Milan citizens
Source: Ansa (2020)

As shown in Figure 6.6, Coca-Cola, with the aim of reiterating the importance of social distancing, changed its logo by spacing the elements that compose it.

With the claim 'Staying apart is the best way to stay united', Coca-Cola sent an essential message to combat the spread of the COVID-19 by targeting consumers around the world through an outdoor campaign aimed, above all, at those who were still away from home for various reasons. In this way, Coca-Cola developed an educational branding strategy aimed at encouraging careful behaviour, simultaneously announcing on its social media the absolute suspension of advertising activities as a sign of solidarity. The company was in fact engaging in emergency management and support for facilities and health personnel with cash donations, supplies of protective equipment, food and drinks. Consequently, corporate communication has undergone changes dictated by a historical event and has not turned to a chosen target, as traditionally happened. In other words, the Coca-Cola communication strategy aims to educate and contribute to overcoming a shared difficulty, no longer only to sell products. Communication campaigns to promote appropriate social behaviour have been implemented by many companies. Among these, the respondents of our research also remember McDonald's which, like Coca-Cola, separated the elements of its logo (see Figure 6.7). As a matter of fact, the respondents stated:

Figure 6.6 Coca-Cola logo

Source: Media4Growth (2020)

Figure 6.7 McDonald's logo

Source: Corriere.it (2020)

> *McDonald's logo change, because I didn't think a company belonging to such a distant sector would take the field to encourage compliance with the rules. Diligently, the company has implemented strategic marketing measures to also show itself socially close to consumers and increase its reputation.*
>
> *(20-year-old female)*
>
> *McDonald's – I was struck by the two 'humps' of the M that show how important it is to respect the safety distance.*
>
> *(21-year-old female)*

Hence, the graphic rendition of social distancing that has resulted in the redesign of the logo of many brands has had a strong communicative power, highlighting the importance of the evocative aspect of a brand and the effectiveness of adapting it in temporary rebranding initiatives. Among the other CSR communication initiatives functioning to promote appropriate social behaviour, our results also allow us to focus on initiatives launched by institutions and taken up by several companies. This is the case of the hashtag #Istayathome, launched by the Italian government in the first weeks of the pandemic to sensitise citizens to leave their homes only for proven needs and then echoed by many companies. According to one respondent, 'The #Istayathome campaign was intended to raise awareness among the population and enclose us all in a hug and a sense of solidarity'. For example, Eni SpA, a multinational company operating in the gas and electricity supply sector, has dedicated a section of its website to the #Istayathome campaign, in which it reiterates, "in addition to compliance with all the requirements of the Ministry, the importance to stay at home during this period and – in the case of respiratory symptoms, cough or cold – to call your family doctor before going to the office or to a unit of the national health system' (Eni.com 2020). In practice, this company, by relaunching a communication campaign disseminated by institutional sources, has tried to promote correct behaviour in the population by explaining how to behave and providing useful information on who to contact in case of COVID-19 symptoms.

Promoting community values

From this research, it emerged that 20% of the respondents reported CSR communication initiatives whose goal was to build or bolster a sense of community by delivering a message of true hope. Indeed, many brands have decided to adapt their communications to the historical moment we are experiencing due to the spread of COVID-19 by promoting community values. Nike, for example, has devised an effective communication strategy which is consistent with the situation we are seeing. In the first weeks of the coronavirus emergency, the brand tweeted a new motto adopted for this particular moment: 'Play inside, play for the world' (see Figure 6.8).

In this way, Nike, while keeping its identity and tone of voice intact, has shown its community that it is aware of the emergency and reiterated the importance of staying at home to benefit the whole world. The promotion of community values which emerged from Nike's communication campaign was highly appreciated by millennials:

> *I was struck by the fact that Nike's message is direct and always refers to the values of the brand. A fitting message with a few words that makes us understand the importance of team play necessary in this situation.*
>
> *(23-year-old female)*

> *Nike is one of the companies that I follow the most and has made an engaging campaign.*
>
> *(21-year-old male)*

Figure 6.8 Nike motto

Source: Nike Twitter page (2020)

> *Nike with the latest Instagram post exploits a common dream for a common good, very interesting in my opinion!*
>
> *(22-year-old female)*

Even at national level, many companies have opted for CSR communication initiatives with the aim of promoting community values. For example, Barilla in Italy quickly rethought its communication strategies, bearing in mind the spread of COVID-19. Barilla's communication in the first weeks of the lockdown was addressed to the company's employees. With two pages in *Corriere della Sera*, the largest Italian newspaper by circulation, Barilla thanked its employees for the sacrifices they were making and for continuing to work uninterrupted even during a health emergency. Furthermore, Barilla, addressing consumers, launched a TV spot that was broadcast during the first Italian lockdown, designed specifically for this particular period. The Barilla TV spot recounted the experiences of the many Italians who continued to sacrifice themselves for the community, such as medical doctors, nurses and other health personnel, and thanking the Italians for the closeness and affection shown when they sang from the balconies, spreading positive messages and hope. The aim of Barilla's communication was therefore to promote a sense of belonging to the Italian community, also expressed by the national identity symbol of the flag. For example, on Barilla social media pages, the Italian flag, next to the mask and two hands (with a visual reference to Michelangelo's "Creation of Adam") which come close without being able to touch each other, communicates a strong closeness to the workers in the health sector in times of social distancing (see Figure 6.9).

Also, on the occasion of Father's Day in Italy, 19 March 2020, the brand, on its social media platforms, addressed good wishes to all the fathers of Italy with

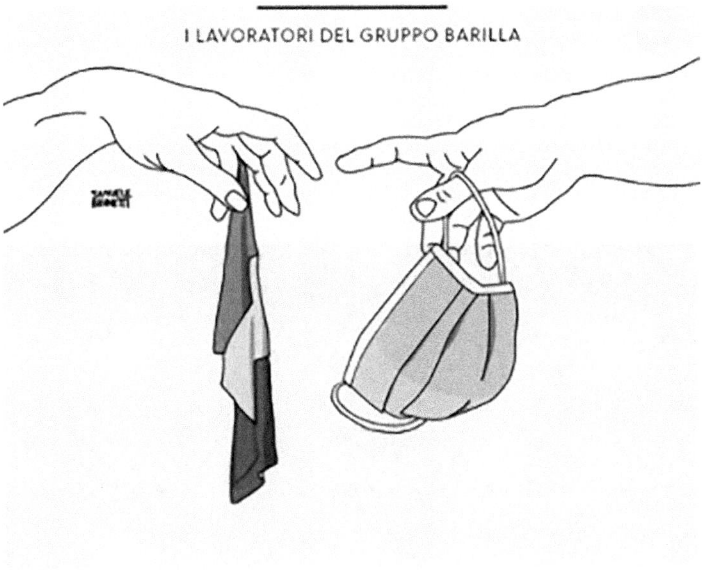

Figure 6.9 Barilla Facebook post (translation: Barilla Group Employees).
Source: Barilla Facebook page (2020)

the image of the Barilla plant illuminated with the colours of the Italian flag (see Figure 6.10).

Barilla's initiative to illuminate its factories with the colours of Italy did not stop at Father's Day but continued in the following weeks, involving various company facilities. With a Tweet on 10 April, Barilla shared images of its factories scattered throughout the peninsula, writing that the aim of the initiative is 'to express pride and encouragement to the Italy that resists and to the communities we belong to' (see Figure 6.11).

Hence, the CSR communication initiative of Barilla, which aimed to strengthen Italians' sense of community, was appreciated by the millennials who described it as 'a reminder of Italian values'.

Informing

Of the respondents involved in this study, 17% mentioned CSR communication initiatives with the goal of providing correct information related to COVID-19. Companies identified in this area operate mainly in the infomedia industry and public sector. For example, our respondents recalled the communication campaign for information purposes promoted by Rai Radiotelevisione Italiana S.p.A., which is the exclusive concessionaire of the public radio and television service in Italy and the second largest Italian television group, after Mediaset.

Figure 6.10 Barilla Facebook post (translation: This is dedicated to all our Dads. Those who are working in the hospitals; those who are working in our factories. Note the original post was in colour and reflected the factories being illuminated in the Itaian flag's colours).

Source: Barilla Facebook page (2020)

> *The campaign promoted by Rai in which images related to doctors working in contact with serious patients are shown and in which the importance of various things (solidarity, empathy) is reiterated, as well as the importance of funds to purchase tools to operate, such as masks and gloves.*
>
> *(23-year-old male)*

Rai, in fact, has often produced television commercials in collaboration with the Presidency of the Council of Ministers and with the Ministry of Health. As stated on the Rai website, among the objectives of its communication initiatives, we find recommendations for compliance with the rules aimed at preventing the spread of the virus (for example, frequent and careful washing of hands, not touching eyes, nose and mouth with hands, cover your mouth and nose if you sneeze or cough); the importance of using the ministry website and other institutional sources as a source of information; the invitation to all citizens to be responsible and supportive in dealing with this emergency, as

Figure 6.11 Barilla Twitter post

Source: Barilla Twitter page (2020)

evidenced by the final message of the spot, 'Let's help each other. Together we can do it'. Mediaset also made its contribution to convey information messages during the health emergency. With the institutional campaign 'Mediaset cares about the future', for which Mediaset created an ad hoc logo (see Figure 6.12), the company spread a message focussed on the fight against fake news on various traditional and digital channels.

Our research reveals that Mediaset's informative message has been fully grasped by millennials. A respondent stated:

> *Mediaset. Its schedule is communicating in every way how to behave in the face of the virus and recently it is debunking fake news by inviting all users to ascertain the source. Today, in addition to the emergency, many people tend to let themselves be overwhelmed by a vortex of negative emotions . . . . Having truthful news helps everyone to have a concrete and real overview of what is happening and how we must behave in order not to harm others and ourselves.*
>
> *(21-year-old female)*

In addition, many private companies operating in different sectors have supported the dissemination of correct information during the pandemic. Pampers,

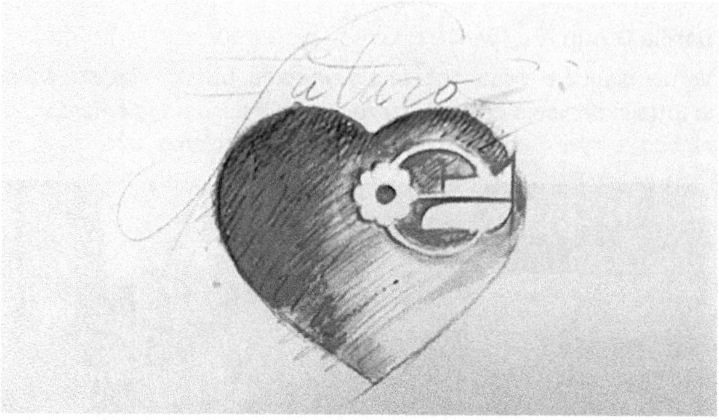

Figure 6.12 Mediaset logo for Covid-19 (translation: Future).
Source: Mediasetplay.mediaset.it (2021)

for example, was remembered by our respondents because with its communications 'it convinced the little ones to wash their hands frequently'. Finally, the results of our research show that millennials positively remember the responsible messages conveyed by influencers. For example, our respondents recalled communications from Chiara Ferragni and Fedez, who were committed to disseminating correct information during the health emergency by addressing social media users around the world. They conveyed information from institutional sources, as well as promoting fund-raising campaigns to help healthcare structures cope with the emergency:

> *Awareness and fundraising campaign by Chiara Ferragni and Fedez. The use of their personal social channels has helped to disseminate updated news and the behaviours to be adopted, to raise funds [of] 4 million euros and have sensitised the foreign public.*
>
> *(23-year-old female)*

In conclusion, the millennials involved in this research have perceived the importance of CSR communication initiatives which aim to inform correctly, calmly and reassuringly through various channels, focussing on the difficulty of containing the spread of COVID- 19 and on the hygiene rules that must be followed. Hence, strategic and transparent communication by private, public and influencers has been appreciated by the millennials.

Discussion

Following the classification (2004) of CSR communication activities by Tench *et al.*, in Table 6.1 we summarise the key elements of the different CSR initiatives identified.

Table 6.1 CSR communication activities during COVID-19

CSR communication content	*CSR communication means*	*CSR subjects*
Social and economic support	Public billboards Corporate website	Local community (local level)
Promote appropriate behaviour	Corporate Digital channels	Consumers (global level)
Community building	National newspapers TV Physical buildings	Employees (national level)
Informing	TV Social media Digital channels	Citizens (global level)

Source: Authors

The first aspect concerns the identification of the stakeholders with whom the company wishes to communicate, as different people might have different interests in and concerns with CSR issues. The second aspect is related to the identification of appropriate channels and sources to convey the desired message to the stakeholders, such as formal CSR reports, media (including social media), advertising, direct dialogue and other methods. The third and last aspect is about the development of effective content. To create effective CSR content, four aspects should be made explicit: the values of the company, their relationship with the CSR initiatives, the concrete actions taken to implement the CSR initiatives, and the stakeholders whose concerns they are addressing through these CSR initiatives.

Communication campaigns aimed at promoting social and economic support to a local community need to strengthen omni-channel responsible communication by mixing *murales* (public billboards) and social media. These campaigns often make visible concrete corporate actions, such as donations of goods and services to the community. When companies make an effort to promote appropriate behaviours among the public, educational branding strategies should be deployed, with particular attention to creativity in order to capture the attention of and engage younger generations, who remain largely neglected. Community-building might be a further goal of communication campaigns. In this chapter, we have seen examples of initiatives done to promote a sense of belonging to the Italian national community, to express pride in being Italian and to encourage people to react and fight against adversity. By recalling the importance of social relationships and reciprocal support, campaigns focused on community values are also effective for involving employees. Finally, companies could defend the quality of information released about delicate and sensitive health issues. A communication campaign could play an important role even when it merely informs, in this way taking away space for disinformation and fake news.

Conclusions

This chapter investigates the emergence of CSR communication initiatives during COVID-19 among millennials in Italy. We present evidence that these

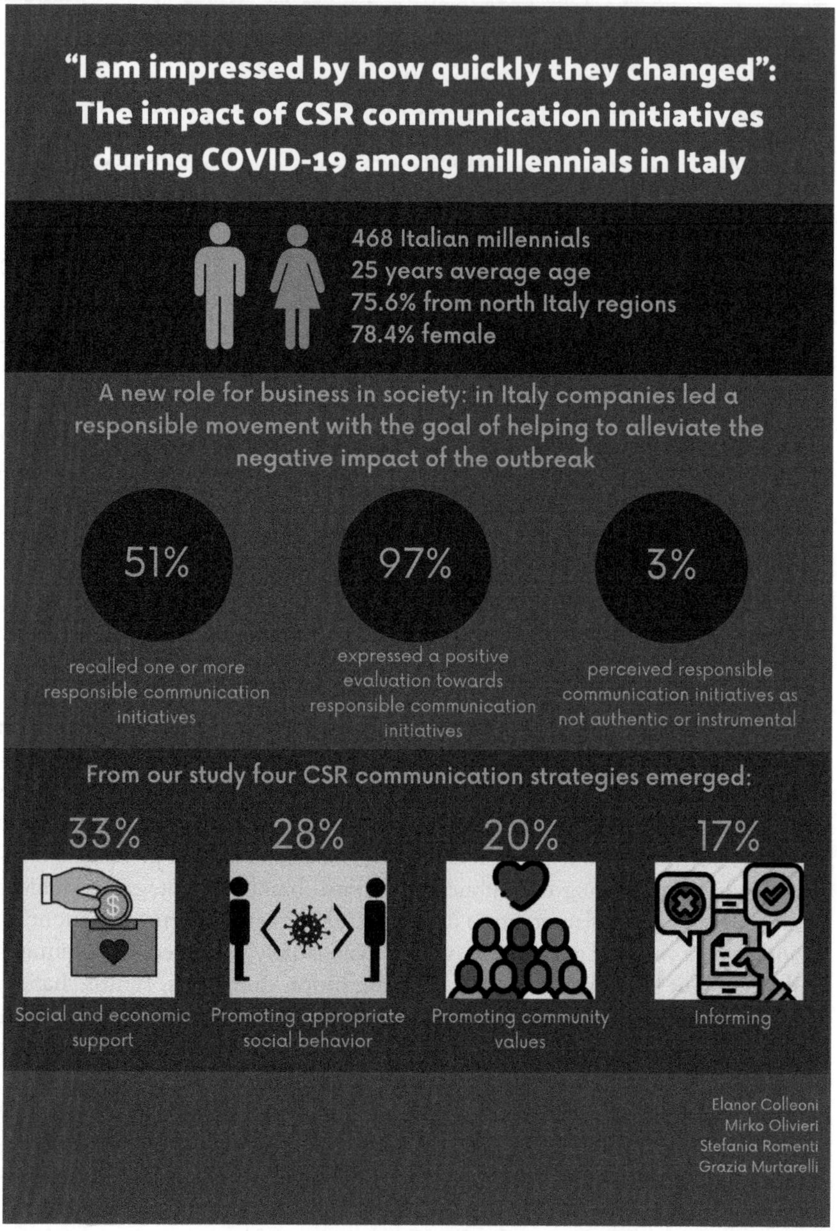

Infographic 6.1 "I am impressed by how quickly they changed": The impact of CSR communication initiatives during Covid-19 among millennials in Italy

initiatives were positively perceived by millennials who recognised the authenticity of the goals of this communication. We identify four different goals of these CSR communication initiatives, which are not only related to responsible innovations but also to the creation and dissemination of information and values for the social good.

Our in-depth analysis of the strategic CSR communication initiatives enacted by companies in Italy suggest worthwhile reflections about both managerial implications and future fruitful research avenues.

Concerning managerial implications, this research shows how during a pervasive and global crisis that deeply affects a society, being sustainable means putting aside the goal of companies to massively communicate how good and green they are. Being sustainable during a global pandemic crisis has meant demonstrating businesses' relationship to citizens, families, local and national communities. Those Italian companies perceived as the most authentic by younger generations effectively communicated empathy and focused their narratives on the concept of support, both emotional and concrete. From a communication management point of view, that means developing communication initiatives targeted to society in general, instead of narrower, segmented publics. Another implication concerns the fact that brand personality and values are indirectly expressed, since consumers will be more inclined to perceive as the most sustainable those companies which are able to manifest concerns for the community rather than for their customers and the market. In other words, the more sustainable a company is perceived, the more 'how green are its products and services' claims remain in the background.

From a conceptual point of view, this study opens the route for new reflections about the role of strategic communication within the *societalisation* process of hot issues (Alexander 2018), like promoting good behaviour to contain the spread of diseases or social malaise caused by COVID-19 (Brammer *et al.* 2020). *Societalisation* entails 'a significant social upheaval in which a problem or issue that may have been endemic for some time transcends its traditional institutional boundaries, leading to widespread anguish and a fundamental crisis within society' (Alexander 2018, p. 1050). Among conditions that foster *societalisation* of hot issues, there is the need for communication that supports activism and promotes information disclosure on key topics and public awareness. The Italian experience depicted in this chapter also envisages significant opportunities for further scholarship to theorise how corporate agencies could affect the process of *societalisation* through communication practices in relation to specific contexts and issues. Finally, as the data discussed in this chapter refer to younger generations, our results might stimulate further considerations when expecting millennials to perceive a brand as authentic during a global and pervasive crisis.

References

Alexander, J.C. (2018). The societalization of social problems: Church pedophilia, phone hacking, and the financial crisis. *American Sociological Review*, 83, pp. 1049–1078.

Angell, R., Gorton, M., Sauer, J., Bottomley, P., and White, J. (2016). Don't distract me when i'm media multitasking: Towards a theory for raising advertising recall and recognition. *Journal of Advertising*, 45(2), pp. 198–210.

Beck, U. (2000). *Risk society. Towards a new modernity*. Thousand Oaks, CA: Sage.

Brammer, S., Branicki, L., and Linnenluecke, M. (2020). COVID-19, societalization and the future of business in society. *Academy of Management Perspective*, 34(4). In press.

Camilleri, M.A. (2021). Evaluating service quality and performance of higher education institutions: A systematic review and a post-COVID-19 outlook. *International Journal of Quality and Service Sciences*, 13(2), pp. 268–281.

Strategic corporate communication in the digital age. Bingley, UK: Emerald.

Carroll, A.B. (1991). The pyramid of corporate social responsibility. *Business Horizons*, 7, pp. 39–48.

Castaldo, S., Perrini, F., Misani, N., and Tencati, A. (2009). The missing link between corporate social responsibility and consumer trust: The case of fair trade products. *Journal of Business Ethics*, 84(1), pp. 1–15.

Castells, M. (1997). *The power of identity, the information age: Economy, society and culture vol. II*. Cambridge, MA: Blackwell.

Colleoni, E. (2013). CSR communication for organizational legitimacy in social media. *Corporate Communications: An International Journal*, 18(2), pp. 228–248.

Crane, A., and Matten, D. (2020). COVID-19 and the future of CSR research. *Journal of Management Studies*, 58(1), pp. 278–282.

Della Rossa, F., Salzano, D., Di Meglio, A., De Lellis, F., Coraggio, M., Calabrese, C., Guarino, A., Cardona-Rivera, R., De Lellis, P., Liuzza, D., Lo Iudice, F., Russo, G., and Di Bernardo, M. (2020). A network model of Italy shows that intermittent regional strategies can alleviate the COVID-19 epidemic. *Nature Communications*, 11, pp. 1–10.

Diers-Lawson, A., Coope, K., and Tench, R. (2020). Why can CSR seem like putting lipstick on a pig? Evaluating CSR authenticity by comparing practitioner and consumer perspectives. *Journal of Global Responsibility*, 11(4), pp. 329–246.

Donaldson, T., and Dunfee, T.W. (1999). When ethics travel: The promise and peril of global business ethics. *California Management Review*, 41(4), pp. 45–63.

Du, S., Bhattacharya, C.B., and Sen, S. (2010). Maximizing business returns to corporate social responsibility (CSR): The role of CSR communication. *International Journal of Management Reviews*, 12(1), pp. 8–19.

Du, S., and Vieira, E., Jr. (2012). Striving for legitimacy through corporate social responsibility: Insights from oil companies. *Journal of Business Ethics*, 110(4), pp. 413–427.

Eni.com 2020 (2020). Available from https://www.eni.com/assets/documents/eng/reports/2020/Annual-Report-2020.pdf [Accessed 22 June 2022].

Gutierrez, L., Castillo, A., and Montiel, I. (2020). Companies vs Coronavirus: A call for rapid responsible innovation. Covid-19 Insights from business sustainability scholars. *Organizations & Natural Environment, Academy of Management*. Available from: https://one.aom.org/covid-19-insights-from-business-sustainability-scholars

Hall, M.R. (2006). Corporate philanthropy and corporate community relations: Measuring relationship-building results. *Journal of Public Relations Research*, 18, 1–21. doi:10.1207/s1532754xjprr1801_1

Halme, M., and Korpela, M. (2014). Responsible Innovation toward sustainable development in small and medium-sized enterprises: A resource perspective. *Business Strategy and the Environment*, 23(8), pp. 547–566.

Illia, L., Romenti, S., Rodríguez-Cánovas, B., Murtarelli , G., and Carroll, C.E. (2017). Exploring corporations' dialogue about CSR in the digital era. *Journal of Business Ethics*, 146(1), pp. 39–58.

Illia, L., Zyglidopoulos, S.C., Romenti, S., Rodríguez-Cánovas, B., and del Valle Brena, A.G. (2013). Communicating corporate social responsibility to a cynical public. *MIT Sloan Management Review*, 54(3), p. 2.

Lafferty, B.A., and Goldsmith, R.E. (1999). Corporate credibility's role in consumers' attitudes and purchase intentions when a high versus a low credibility endorser is used in the ad. *Journal of Business Research*, 44(2), pp. 109–116.

Lantos, G.P. (2001). The boundaries of strategic corporate social responsibility. *Journal of Consumer Marketing*, 18(7), pp. 595–632.

Husted, B.W., and Allen, D.B. (2013). Responsibility multinational enterprise: Strategic. *Journal of International Business Studies*, 37(6), pp. 838–849.

Kim, H., and Lee, T.H. (2018). Strategic CSR communication: A moderating role of transparency in trust building. *International Journal of Strategic Communication*, 12(2), pp. 107–124.

Manheim, J.B., and Pratt, C.B. (1986). Communicating corporate social responsibility. *Public Relations Review*, 12(2), pp. 9–18.

Moreno, A., and Capriotti, P. (2009). Communicating CST: Citizenship and sustainability on the Web. *Journal of Communication Management*, 13(2), pp. 157–175.

Porter, M.E., and Kramer, M.R. (2011). Creating shared value. *Harvard Business Review*, 89(1/2), pp. 62–77.

Rim, H., and Song, D. (2013). The ability of corporate blog communication to enhance CSR effectiveness: The role of prior company reputation and blog responsiveness. *International Journal of Strategic Communication*, 7(3), pp. 165–185.

Scherer, A., and Palazzo, G. (2007). Toward a political conception of corporate responsibility: Business and society seen from a Habermasian perspective. *Academy of Management Review*, 32(4), pp. 1096–120.

Schultz, F., Castello, I., and Morsing, M. (2013). The construction of corporate social responsibility in network societies: A communication view. *Journal of Business Ethics*, 115, pp. 681–92.

Skarmeas, D., and Leonidou, C.N. (2013). When consumers doubt, watch out! The role of CSR skepticism. *Journal of Business Research*, 66(10), pp. 1831–1838.

Statista (2021). *COVID-19 and mental health* [online]. Available from: www.statista.com/topics/7106/covid-19-and-mental-health/

Tench, R., Sun, W., and Jones, B. (2014). *Communicating corporate social responsibility: Perspectives and practice*. Bingley, UK: Emerald.

7 Risk communication and disinformation in Portugal

How media consumption affects the understanding of COVID-19 health-protective messages

Gisela Gonçalves, Valeriano Piñeiro-Naval and Sónia de Sá

Introduction

The World Health Organization (WHO) has characterised the COVID-19 information landscape as a massive 'infodemic': an overabundance of information – some accurate and some not – that makes it hard for people to find trustworthy sources and reliable guidance when they need it. Likewise, the proliferation of disinformation, misinformation and medical mistrust, including conspiracy beliefs, undermines health authorities' and governmental risk communication efforts (Baines and Elliott 2020; Mubarak *et al.* 2021).

The audience choices regarding sources of information and their perception of the reliability of the information are relevant predictors for the degree of adherence towards recommended preventive behaviours (Park *et al.* 2019). Thus, several studies have focused on the role of information and social mediated channels regarding health-related crisis (Parmer *et al.* 2016; Jin *et al.* 2019; Zhang and Zhou 2019). COVID-19-related research applied in the first wave of the pandemic has shown an increase in health information seeking, both online and in mainstream media (Edelman 2020), as well as widespread concern about the phenomenon of fake news and disinformation (Ceron *et al.* 2021; Falcone and Sapienza 2020; Mubarak 2021; Skarpa *et al.* 2021).

In the context of uncertainty characteristic of a pandemic, there are several motivations that encourages people to seek informational content (Austin *et al.* 2012; Lu and Jin 2020). Some authors claim that traditional media are primarily used for information needs because citizens perceive them to be more credible than social media (Austin *et al.* 2012; Moreno *et al.* 2020). Others claim that social media are increasingly important in crisis contexts because they provide access to unfiltered information (Tai and Sun 2007; Lu and Jin 2012) and emotional support (Fraustino *et al.* 2017). In fact, the reach of the so-called *legacy media* was fostered in the digital media and much news content is today read online and shared by many followers. Consequently, studies show that online news consumption did not replace but instead complemented the consumption of traditional news (Dutta-Bergman 2004).

DOI: 10.4324/9781003184669-12

Based on the assumption that access to (in)accurate information and (un)trustworthy sources is directly linked to the perception of risk (Devine *et al.* 2020), and that the propagation of misinformation on social media undermines the COVID-19 individual responses (Barua *et al.* 2020), we discuss in this chapter the specific case of Portugal during the second wave of the disease. The main aim is to assess how media consumption by the Portuguese influences their perception of (mis)information, including the awareness of self-protective messages. Starting with an overview of the COVID-19 pandemic in Portugal, we then reflect upon the theoretical-practical implications of the data obtained in this country, which are also highlighted in the infographic at the end of the chapter.

Overview of the COVID-19 pandemic in Portugal

Communication policies

Since the beginning of the pandemic, governments and health authorities around the world have sought to contain the contagion figures through the imposition of preventive measures and awareness communication strategies oriented towards individual and collective risk. The public response to lockdown measures and other policies varies greatly depending on the country, the pandemic development and the age groups (Hale *et al.* 2020).

In the Portuguese case, as highlighted by the *Financial Times* (2020), although the country received the international praise for its fast response to the pandemic's first wave, it was also, in January 2021, one of the most affected countries by the second wave in Europe and one of the slowest to mitigate the growth rate of new infections. In the peak of the pandemic, Portugal, a country with a population just over 10 million, reported daily figures around 15,000 new cases and 180 deaths.

As far as communication policies of the government and the Portuguese Directorate General of Health (Direção-Geral da Saúde, or DGS) are concerned, it is important to highlight, from the very first moment, the dissemination of daily briefings to society through press conferences, the creation of a website (covid19.min-saude.pt) dedicated to the pandemic and the definition of guiding standards for risk communication (Arriaga *et al.* 2020).

The regular meetings between DGS and government officers with the press began on 9 March 2020, right at the beginning of the pandemic, when the country had only 39 people infected with COVID-19. From that day on, there would be two daily moments where information was made available: in the morning, through the bulletin of the epidemiological situation in the country, and in the late afternoon, through a press conference in DGS's headquarters or in the Ministry of Health's central office. On 15 June 2020, and after more than 100 daily press conferences usually led by the Minister of Health, Director-General of Health and the State Secretary, these started taking place just three times per week. These highly politicised and tally-focused press conferences were criticised by experts (Barata 2020). In the beginning of January 2021, a period in which contagion figures were showing an exponential growth, DGS chose to cancel press conferences – without any justification – keeping only the daily publication of the epidemiological bulletin on their website and social media accounts.

One of the core problems of misinformation and post-trust societies is trust in communications (Moreno *et al.* 2021). DGS also joined WHO in the fight against fake news and misinformation. DGS published a 'Recommendation for the press', advising on the importance of seeking official institutions as sources of information, 'with facts that fight biased or contradictory information' (DGS 2020). Creating campaigns with celebrities, DGS alerted the population to the significance of referring to reliable institutions for information. It should also be noted that DGS partnered with Polígrafo SIC (2020), an online Portuguese fact-checking platform. This project had considerable visibility in SIC's TV show, broadcast in prime time right after the news on Mondays.

The importance of partnerships between health authorities and fact-checking platforms is emphasised by the case of Italy, one of the most affected countries in the first wave of the pandemic, and it is considered a positive example in the fight against misinformation (Lovari 2020). In April 2020, the Italian government created a task force to promote cooperation with fact-checkers, encouraging citizen activism to flag misinformation. This was an teaching moment for the media that served as an example to 'increase the skills and competences necessary to interact effectively while negotiating the pitfalls of misinformation' (Lovari 2020, p. 460). In Portugal, the creation of a task force to manage communication efforts with the population was announced only on 11 March 2021. This task force is made up of behavioural scientists, not including strategic communication experts, and its results are yet to be proven.

Experts believe that this and many other government initiatives were more a response to critics – regarding low-performance communication, confusing messages coming from spokespersons and lack of transparency – and less well-founded and planned strategies to face the pandemic crisis (Araújo 2020; Oliveira 2021). In fact, during the initial phase, public risk communication in Portugal was characterised by an informational superabundance by DGS and the government, which even resulted in conflicting statements. The lack of clarity on the recommendations regarding the use of masks and face shields is one example. While the Director-General of Health stated that the use of masks by the population was not recommended, the press, experts and doctors defended its use as the best way of protecting oneself (Pina 2020).

Both source credibility and communicational transparency affect the perception of risk messages, as highlighted by the risk communication literature (Renn and Levine 1991; Llewellyn 2020; Lundgren and McMakin 2013; Seeger *et al.* 2018). While credibility depends on the degree of technical expertise attributed to the source of information – its credentials and experience – transparency can stem from its history itself, that is, the source's previous behaviour in analogous situations (Earle and Siegrist 2008). If there are reports of data omission or manipulation, for example, subsequent messages are less likely to be trusted. In the aforementioned case of masks, the DGS would later clarify that it advised against their use, not because of their lack of effectiveness, but because there was a lack of material on the market for everyone (Antunes 2020).

The discussion on the transparency of public policies in the face of a pandemic is visible in two public policies which have been strongly criticised in the public space. In September 2020, STAYAWAY COVID was launched, a smartphone application that sends notifications when the user is near someone who is infected with COVID-19. While the government defended that installing the application was a 'civic duty', public opinion stood against the requirement, perceiving it as aconsequential privacy violation of citizens (Carvalho 2020). The initiative was a failure. Six months after the launch, just over 3,000 people were notified. On March 2021, the government decided to broadcast live the meeting of experts that took place at the headquarters of Infarmed, the Portuguese agency for medicines and medical devices. The absence of the press, significant to help contextualising, prioritising and interpreting information conveyed by experts, was seen as the proof of 'the demagogy of transparency' (Oliveira 2021). It should be noted that in Portugal, the burden of limited health literacy is higher than in other European countries. Studies estimate than 3 in 4 Portuguese between 16 and 79 years old (about 73% of the population) struggle to understand and make use of information concerning healthcare (Paiva *et al.* 2017).

Media consumption in Portugal in pandemic times

Risk communication experts have long emphasised the significance of monitoring the needs and expectations of population groups, providing timely, accurate, specific, sufficient, consistent and intelligible information (Anderson and Spitzberg 2009). This guideline is also underscored by WHO: 'The capacity to relay information quickly and clearly on different media platforms (television, radio, print, web), [. . .] is essential to the effective management of a public-health emergency' (2011, p. 116). As such, having awareness of communication preferences (i.e., how and where information is consumed by the audiences), is essential for any effective risk communication plan.

According to the pre-pandemic study Reuters Digital News Report Portugal (RDNR 2020), in a set of 40 markets analysed, Portugal is the country where news is most trusted, along with Finland, with 56% of the Portuguese saying they trust news in general. Facebook, YouTube and WhatsApp are the most widely used social media platforms by the Portuguese to get news or for any other purpose, but television is still the main source of news for 55.8% of the Portuguese population. The Portuguese reveal themselves as one of the people most concerned about the legitimacy of online content, with 75% of the national sample saying they are worried about what is real and what is fake on the internet. Social networks in general, and the Facebook network in particular, reveal themselves as the sources that generate the most concern for Portuguese respondents.

The Edelman research (2020), which took place in 12 countries – not including Portugal – in the beginning of the pandemic, showed that the consumption of information immensely increased, particularly news related to the evolution of the outbreak. Focussing on information seeking related to the pandemic, 64% of the respondents stated they seek information from the main news organizations; 70% of the population followed COVID-19 news at least once a day or several times a day, while 45% claimed to struggle to find trustworthy sources and reliable guidance when they needed it (Edelman 2020). Data from Marktest, collected through the Coronavirus Trends Report from Dentsue Aegis (2021) support a peak of online news consumption that also took place in Portugal.

The study 'Pandemic and media consumption' (*Pandemia e consumos mediáticos*) from Obercom and Intercampus (Cardoso *et al.* 2020) shows the Portuguese case. This report, featuring data collected in June 2020, shows changes in media consumption patterns throughout the pandemic. The most used sources for COVID-19 information were search engines (used by 31% of the respondents) and Facebook (used by 20%); Instagram was more used than Twitter during the lockdown, when Portuguese frequently shared with their groups of friends (through WhatsApp, for example) news, newspapers in digital format or podcasts. Activities on social media networks, through posts or comments, were more frequent during the lockdown period than in the post-lockdown period. The reading of opinion articles saw an increase, with preference being given to opinion articles shared by news brands on Facebook, based on information provided by experts, such as researchers or epidemiologists. Regarding misinformation, 43.6% of respondents said they had difficulty distinguishing truths from false information, and more than a third of the Portuguese said they avoid news about the pandemic. This last data point is a clear indicator of 'information avoidance' (Soroya *et al.* 2021), a symptom of 'pandemic fatigue' phenomenon, forewarned by WHO (2020).

Although existing research on health-related crisis has addressed the role of information channels and media consumption patterns, few studies have evaluated how information channels and sources influence the retention of information during health crisis events and the public's perceived risks. Given the significance that news media have in health emergency contexts – spreading reliable, up-to-date and accurate messages in a high-misinformation context – our research was guided by two main research questions:

RQ1: Which communication/information channels were the most used by the Portuguese to obtain information regarding COVID-19?

RQ2: How much accurate information has been available to the Portuguese regarding COVID-19?

The first research question aims at understanding the behaviour of the Portuguese while searching for information on COVID-19, and the frequency with which they used different information media and channels compared, in particular, with traditional or legacy media (e.g., TV, radio, press), but also social media and scientific and institutional sources.

The second research question aims at understanding the main knowledge points retained by the Portuguese about COVID-19, and whether they are true or false. As a way to introduce the variable on misinformation, we intended to measure the Portuguese acceptance of propositions widely disseminated through the media, including the origin of the virus and the treatment of the disease. From the list of 'false news about the coronavirus' listed by Fuchs (2020, p. 392), we selected the one addressed the origin of the virus: 'Coronavirus is a Chinese biological weapon developed by the Wuhan Institute of Technology'. From the list of news regarding cure or treatment, we selected the following pieces: 'Taking medicinal herbs kills coronavirus' and 'COVID-19 can be treated with chloroquine'. The misstatement in both news pieces was also reported by the fact-checking platform Polígrafo SIC (2020). We sought to assess the acceptance of these statements. Therefore, we proposed the following main hypothesis to guide our study:

H1: The greater the consumption of traditional media is, the lower the belief in misinformation will be.

Methodology: sample and questionnaire

In the context of the EUPRERA COM-COVID project, a survey was applied to Portuguese citizens (*n* = 460) between 7 October and 11 November 2020. This period corresponds to a non-lockdown period, at the beginning of the school year, when in-person teaching returned. Portugal was in a state of contingency due to the increase in new cases and was now entering the second wave of the pandemic.

The sample has a confidence level of 95% and a margin of error of 4.6% over the population of the country (*N* = 10,295,909 inhabitants). It is composed of 65.7% women and 34.3% men, with a mean age of 41.01 years (*SD* = 12.09). This sample was recruited by using the snowball sampling technique. Invitations with a link to the online survey were sent out via email and social media, in particular WhatsApp and Facebook. The invitation encouraged people to complete and disseminate the questionnaire to their contacts, and there was no compensation for participating in the research.

The online questionnaire included questions regarding information-seeking behaviour, trust in different sources and channels, perception of government communication management, message retention, and demographic questions. The overall results of this study can be seen in the infographic at the end of this chapter. For this particular chapter, we examine the sections of the survey relating to the frequency of use of different media and information channels, and the key pieces of information about COVID-19 that respondents recall.

To answer RQ1, participants were asked to indicate which channel they used to obtain COVID-19 information (e.g., 'How often do you read or listen to information about COVID-19 in the following media?' There were 14 channels listed: WhatsApp, Facebook, Twitter, Instagram, YouTube, television, radio news, print newspapers, online newspapers, syndicated magazines, public institutions websites and other. To answer RQ2, participants had to select among 27 statements related to COVID-19 risks, treatments or preventive measures those that were correct (12 items). The listed true statements were selected from the analysis of DGS press conferences and government briefings in September 2020. In the group of false statements, 3 of them correspond to false information, identified by fact-checking platforms, and the other 12 are incorrect statements.

In regard to RQ1, the response options for each of the 14 items were operationalised by 7-point Likert-type scales, with 1 being the lowest point (frequency = never) and 7 the highest (frequency = always). To reduce the scale dimensions, the items were included in an exploratory factor analysis (EFA) to detect associations among them and create *a posteriori* aggregate variables or factors.

As shown in Table 7.1, each of the 14 items regarding the frequency of use of different media and information channels has a significant bearing on some of the three factors, suggesting that the EFA is a latent structure (explained variance = 58.96%, KMO = .84, Bartlett's test: $p < .001$). The internal consistency of each factor, assessed with the Cronbach's alpha statistical parameter (α_c), displayed an adequate reliability in all cases (Hair *et al.* 2010; Robinson *et al.* 1991).

Results

All surveys were conducted using Google Forms, and then coded and entered into the statistical software SPSS (Statistical Package for Social Sciences, version 24). For each factor, an indicator was calculated based on the average of the items that compose it, detected in the EFA (Table 7.1). These new indices were used, in turn, to carry out different descriptive and inferential tests.

After the statistical treatment was carried out with extracted data from the 460 questionnaires, it is possible to establish three types of main media or information channels, presented in Table 7.2 next to the specific items that compose them, ordered according to the average of the frequency of use by the respondents:

After performing a repeated measures analysis of variance, we observe that the differences between media and channels are statistically significant [λ_w = .294, F (2, 458) = 549.39, $p < .001$, η^2 = . 706], with 'media' being the most used by the Portuguese population (PI_1) above 'scientific and institutional sources' [t (459) = 29.053, $p < .001$, d = 1.456] and 'social media' [t (459) = 31.057, $p < .001$, d = 1.721]. If we compare 'scientific and institutional sources' with 'social media', there are also significant differences between them [t (459) = 2.73, $p < .01$, d = 0.127], but of smaller effect sizes (Cohen 1988; Johnson *et al.* 2008). In isolation, television (M = 5.83, SD = 1.74) is the medium most used by citizens, followed by online press (M = 5.36, SD = 2.01) and radio (M = 4.70, SD = 2.11).

Table 7.1 Media channels used to obtain COVID-19 information

Media and channels	*Scientific and institutional sources (factor 1)*	*Media (factor 2)*	*Social media (factor 3)*
Scientific websites	.842		
Scientific magazines	.789		
Healthcare websites	.724		
Institutional websites	.658		
Alternative treatments websites	.645		
Television		.860	
Radio		.760	
Online press		.670	
Print press		.596	
Instagram			.835
YouTube			.764
Twitter			.661
WhatsApp			.543
Facebook			.436
Eigenvalue	4.924	1.983	1.348
Explained variance	35.17%	14.16%	9.63%
Cronbach's alpha	.85	.75	.71

Source: Authors

Note: Dimensions of the use of different media and information channels through EFA (varimax rotation and reliability test).

Table 7.2 Frequency of use of media and information channels

Frequency of use of media and channels	*n*	*M*	*SD*	*% high frequency**
Scientific and institutional sources (factor 1)	*460*	*2.73*	*1.54*	
Public institutions websites	460	3.46	2.16	35.2
Healthcare-specialised websites/blogs	460	3.07	2.11	27.0
Scientific publications	460	2.92	2.07	26.5
Science websites/blogs	460	2.29	1.77	14.7
Alternative therapies websites/blogs	460	1.90	1.58	10.3
Media (factor 2)	*460*	*4.98*	*1.55*	
Television	460	5.83	1.74	80.5
Online press	460	5.36	2.01	73.3
Radio	460	4.70	2.11	59.4
Print press	460	4.03	2.31	46.0
Social media (factor 3)	*460*	*2.55*	*1.26*	
Facebook	460	4.26	2.25	49.9
WhatsApp	460	2.23	1.80	14.6
Instagram	460	2.20	1.79	13.6
YouTube	460	2.08	1.67	12.2
Twitter	460	1.96	1.75	12.6

Source: Authors

Note: Descriptive statistical data on the frequency of use of media and information channels, as well as of the items that compose them.

* Combined percentage of respondents who expressed quite (5), a lot (6) or total (7) frequency in using information media or channels.

With regard to age, the initial quantitative variable was recoded into an ordinal variable so that the frequency of use of the different media and channels could be compared according to the three age groups:

As we can see in Table 7.3, there are no differences in the frequency of use of traditional media. However, there are differences regarding institutional sources (more commonly used by older persons) and social networks (preferred by young people). In terms of academic background, the initial variable (nominal polytomous) was recoded into another dichotomous (0 = academic degree, 1 = no academic degree). In Table 7.4 we can observe the values of the two groups regarding their use of media and channels:

We observe statistically significant differences in the use of media and channels. Respondents with an academic background use media more intensively. However, these differences are smaller regarding social media. With regard to gender, there are only significant differences in access to media, used more by men than women.

As for the Portuguese population's general knowledge about COVID-19, they are gathered in Table 7.5 in relation to the percentage of respondents who were aware of this information or, put in other words, who found these messages to be true:

As can be seen in Table 7.5, the most widespread information among respondents relates to washing hands and keeping distance as effective ways of protection (95.4%), as well as COVID-19 being transmitted by touching infected surfaces (90%). Tests were also carried out with demographic variables, but they did not return significative results. On the other hand, it is relevant to observe possible correlations between the consumption of different media and information channels and all this knowledge, as displayed in Table 7.6.

Table 7.3 Frequency of use of media and channels during COVID-19 crisis by age

Media and Channels	*Young*	*Adults*	*Mature*	*Total*	*ANOVA*
Scientific and institutional sources	2.29 (1.54)	2.58 (1.53)	2.61 (1.52)	2.72 (1.54)	F (2, 457) = 8.13, p = .032, η^2 = .015
Media	4.98 (1.67)	4.82 (1.51)	5.15 (1.45)	4.97 (1.55)	F (2, 457) = 1.68, p = .188, η^2 = .007
Social media	3.05 (1.35)	2.34 (1.16)	2.26 (1.12)	2.55 (1.26)	F (2, 457) = 28.37, $p < .001$, η^2 = .077
n	149	168	143	460	

Source: Authors

Note: Comparisons of age groups according to the frequency of use of media and channels (ANOVA). The recoding of the initial quantitative variable 'age' into another ordinal qualitative one based on three age groups of homogeneous sizes was possible thanks to the calculation of the P33 and P66 percentiles. 1 = young (n = 149), 18–36 years; 2 = adults (n = 168), 37–47; and 3 = mature (n = 143), 48–79 years (age of the oldest respondent in the sample).

Table 7.4 Frequency of use of media and channels during COVID-19 crisis by academic level

Media and channels	*No academic degree*	*Academic degree*	*Total*	*Student's t*
Scientific and institutional sources	2.15 (1.59)	2.89 (1.49)	2.72 (1.54)	t (458) = -4.35, $p < .001$, d = -0.48
Media	4.38 (1.71)	5.14 (1.46)	4.97 (1.55)	t (458) = -4.46, $p < .001$, d = -0.48
Social media	2.29 (1.23)	2.62 (1.27)	2.55 (1.26)	t (458) = -2.28, p = .023, d = -0.26
n	102	358	460	
	Men	*Women*	*Total*	*Student's t*
Scientific and institutional sources	2.76 (1.52)	2.71 (1.55)	2.72 (1.54)	t (458) = .369, p = .712, d = .032
Media	5.17 (1.41)	4.87 (1.61)	4.97 (1.55)	t (458) = 1.99, p = .047, d = .198
Social media	2.57 (1.36)	2.53 (1.21)	2.55 (1.26)	t (458) = .286, p = .775, d = .03
n	158	302	460	

Source: Authors

Note: Comparisons of the academic level according to use frequency of the media and channels (Student's t).

Table 7.5 General knowledge of the Portuguese population on COVID-19 (%)

General knowledge of the Portuguese population on COVID-19	*%*
Washing hands and keeping distance are effective ways of protection	95.4
COVID-19 can be transmitted by touching infected surfaces	90
Studies predict that the second wave will be more severe	82.2
In order to be tested, I must call SNS24*	77.6
3 in 4 Portuguese wish to be vaccinated	67.2
The vaccine is the only way to end the pandemic	65.9
A vaccine will be commercialised in less than a year	54.3
It spreads much faster when schools and universities are open	52.4
For most of the population, it's like a flu	47.8
I should stay home if I have severe symptoms	44.1
The use of the STAYAWAY app decreases contagion figures	40
It's more contagious than any other disease	35.7
Only those who are positive should be in isolation	32.2

(*Continued*)

Table 7.5 (Continued)

General knowledge of the Portuguese population on COVID-19	%
Portugal has a low level of testing, when compared with other countries	27.2
The coronavirus was created in a laboratory	23.3
I should only go to the hospital with a COVID-19-related condition	14.1
It kills more than any other disease	12
It can be treated with chloroquine	10
The isolation of the elderly in nursing homes is unnecessary	9.8
I should go to the hospital if I have mild symptoms	9.6
Staying at home does not help decreasing contagion figures	8
Masks provide 100% protection from infection	5.9
There are home and homeopathic remedies for it	5.4
It only affects older and sick people	4.6
If you're not old and you're not sick, you can lead a normal life	4.3
If you do not have symptoms, you're not contagious	3.7
It's only lethal in the elderly	3.7

Source: Authors

Note: Grey shading indicates false statements; no shading indicates true statements.

* SNS24 is the Portuguese toll-free emergency helpline (808242424).

Table 7.6 Correlation between general knowledge of the Portuguese population on COVID-19 and frequency of use of media and channels (r_{pb})

General knowledge of the Portuguese population on COVID-19	*Scientific and institutional sources*	*Media*	*Social media*
Washing hands and keeping distance are effective ways of protection	.032	.031	.042
COVID-19 can be transmitted by touching infected surfaces	-.01	.066	.012
Studies predict that the second wave will be more severe	.019	.035	.053
In order to be tested, I must call SNS24	.007	-.012	.025
3 in 4 Portuguese wish to be vaccinated	.075	.04	.088
The vaccine is the only way to end the pandemic	-.063	.018	-.062
A vaccine will be commercialised in less than a year	.048	.028	.01
It spreads much faster when schools and universities are open	-.031	-.036	.071
For most of the population, it's like a flu	.017	-.051	.056
I should stay home if I have severe symptoms	-.061	-.02	-.069

The use of the STAYAWAY app decreases contagion figures	.039	.017	.026
It's more contagious than any other disease	-.035	-.023	-.054
Only those who are positive should be in isolation	-.075	-.033	-.07
Portugal has low level of testing, when compared with other countries	.076	-.018	.148***
The coronavirus was created in a laboratory	.02	-.056	.081
I should only go to the hospital with a COVID-19 related condition	-.012	-.06	-.008
It kills more than any other disease	-.041	-.071	-.045
It can be treated with chloroquine	.10*	.06	.098*
The isolation of the elderly in nursing homes is unnecessary	-.087	-.148***	-.078
I should go to the hospital if I have mild symptoms	.044	-.084	.035
Staying at home does not help decreasing contagion figures	-.045	-.085	.007
Masks provide 100% protection from infection	-.104*	-.062	-.054
There are home and homeopathic remedies for it	-.123**	-.117*	-.031
It only affects older and sick people	.072	-.135**	.048
If you're not old and you're not sick, you can lead a normal life	.028	-.049	.029
If you do not have symptoms, you're not contagious	-.031	-.022	-.034
It's only lethal in the elderly	.012	.051	.051

Source: Authors.

Note: * $p < .05$, ** $p < .01$, *** $p < .001$.

The highest and most statistically significant correlations have to do with the following elements:

- The higher the use of social media, the higher the knowledge that Portugal has tested little compared to other countries [r_{pb} (458) = .148, $p < .001$], and the higher the belief that COVID-19 can be treated with chloroquine [r_{pb} (458) = .98, $p < .05$].
- The higher the media use, the lower the belief that confinement of the elderly in nursing homes is an unnecessary measure [r_{pb} (458) = -.148, $p < .001$] and that the virus affects only elderly and sick people [r_{pb} (458) = -.135, $p < .01$].
- Lastly, the greater the use of scientific and institutional sources, the lower the belief that there are home and homeopathic remedies [r_{pb} (458) = -.123, $p < .01$], and the lower the perception that masks provide 100% protection from infection [r_{pb} (458) = -.104, $p < .05$].

Therefore, we note that a greater employment of media and scientific sources usually decreases certain false knowledge or beliefs. In fact, if we establish an aggregate indicator from the sum of all items relating to false knowledge,[1] this indicator will correlate negatively with media consumption [r (458) = -.13, p = .005], which means that media consumption decreases misinformation (H1).

Discussion

The findings allow us to discuss the medium and the message, and the relation therein. The analysis related to the most used media by the Portuguese was split across three main groups: media, scientific and institutional sources and social media. The main and first evidence is that three in four of the most used channels to seek information on the pandemic are among the so-called mainstream media: television (80.5%) is the medium most used by citizens, followed by online press (73.3%) and radio (59.4%). This is in line with previous studies that stress that traditional media are primarily used for information needs, as people perceive them – especially broadcast news and newspapers – to be more credible than social media (Austin *et al.* 2012). The importance of radio should also be emphasised, given that it was not stressed in other recent studies regarding the Portuguese (RDNR 2020) and international (Edelman 2020) media contexts.

The second highlight pertains to seeking information in scientific and institutional sources (e.g., public institutions or healthcare institution websites, scientific journals). Despite this kind of sources being less frequently sought than media, they were more accessed than social media. More concretely, the preference of respondents falls on public and healthcare institutions' websites, well above websites on alternative therapies, which are the less visited channels. The relevance attributed to public and healthcare institutions' websites (35.2%) is also emphasised if we focus the analysis on the most sought online media, although it is still clearly below access to online press (73.3%) and Facebook (49.9%). Facebook, in the overall compilation of information sources, was the fourth most used channel (after TV, online press and radio) and the most accessed social media (above WhatsApp and others). This is also highlighted by the Obercom study (Cardoso *et al.* 2020).

From the point of view of crisis communication management in times of pandemic, these data underline the importance, for public authorities, of optimising the institutional website on the pandemic. Findings show that official websites are preferred by the oldest people but accessed by all respondents. It is not the object of this chapter to analyse the opinion of the Portuguese about the contents of the DGS website, but this is a possible future line of research, for example, in the light of Kent and Taylor's (2002) theory of dialogic communication.

Regarding the discussion about the message, the main knowledge points of the Portuguese population regarding COVID-19 relate to prevention measures, of which 'washing hands and keeping social distance' stands out. This conclusion is corroborated by the fact that only 5.9% of the respondents considered that masks provide 100% protection from infection, a false statement. Given that the survey was conducted six months after the beginning of the pandemic in Portugal, these data are not surprising. The general protective measures – hand hygiene, social distancing and masks – were and still are the main message of prevention and the most widespread across all channels. Furthermore, the statement that the STAYAWAY app decreases contagion, despite the controversy associated to its use, was considered true by 40% of the respondents.

The third evidence to be drawn from this study is therefore that the Portuguese have mainly internalised messages concerning protective measures. The false statements regarding possible ways of treatment were indicated as true by a small number of respondents: only 5.4% believe that there are home and homeopathic remedies that prevent and cure COVID-19; and 10% believe that it can be treated with chloroquine. In the same vein, it is interesting to note that 23.3% believe that 'the new coronavirus was created in a laboratory to sink Western economies'. These data corroborate a recent study on information consumption applied in Portugal during the first lockdown, where 27% of respondents agreed with the same thesis (Gonçalves *et al.* 2021, p. 44). One of the most disseminated conspiracy theories since the beginning of the pandemic (Fuchs 2020) seems to have survived over time.

Finally, arising from the analysis of the correlations between media consumption and the messages recalled, we can stress that, overall, people who claim to use mainly traditional media and institutional or scientific sources are the ones who retain less misinformation about the pandemic. In the specific case of the claim 'The coronavirus was created in a laboratory', there was no significant correlation with the type of media most used. However, some misinformation about the treatment and prevention of COVID-19 stood out, defended by those who access the information mainly on social media. This is the case of those who believe that COVID-19 can be treated with chloroquine. Conversely, it can be highlighted that those who seek information mainly on media consider it important to isolate to protect the elderly and believe that the virus does not only attack people in this age group. In the case of those who access mainly scientific and institutional sources, the perception that the mask does not provide 100% protection against infection stands out.

Conclusion and implications

This chapter introduces new empirical knowledge on the relation between media consumption and health-related messages in a pandemic context. Evidence shows that a greater employment of media informative sources usually decreases certain false knowledge or beliefs. We can see implications for risk communication management but also for journalism itself. In fact, the pandemic has posed an unprecedented challenge to journalism, to the extent that it has been pointed out as an antidote to the pandemic of misinformation (Brennen *et al.* 2020). However, previous studies have shown that during public health crises, many of the messages disseminated by the media did not follow journalistic 'good practice' or contained misinformation (Parmer *et al.* 2016), whether in mainstream or digital media (Malecki *et al.* 2021).

A final reflection is therefore needed on audiences' media dependency during a public health crisis (Tai and Sun 2007). One the one hand, if citizens seek COVID-19 information from the media, it is up to journalism brands, in

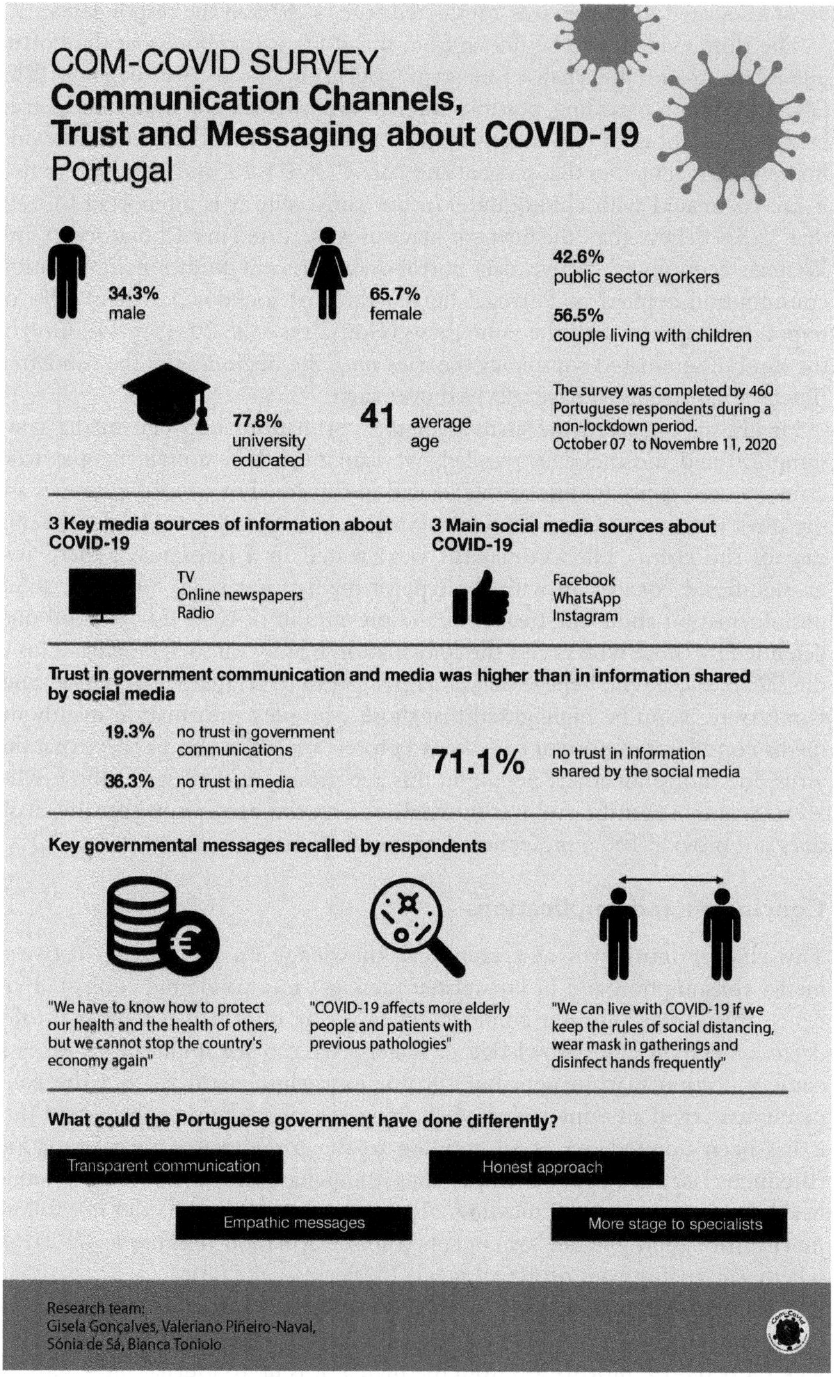

Infographic 7.1 Communication channels, trust and messaging about COVID-19 in Portugal

line with the authorities, to do everything possible to fulfil these expectations by offering credible, impartial and timely content. The media and journalists are not obviously alone in this endeavour. The fight against misinformation requires a 'crowdsourcing call-to-arms' (Alam *et al.* 2020), a holistic approach to the detection and correction of false information, combining the perspectives of journalists, fact-checkers, policy makers, government entities, social media platforms and all society.

On the other hand, scientists and public health experts, in particular, can be given greater prominence in media coverage in order to avoid inadvertent dissemination of misinformation (Jaiswal *et al.* 2020). Based on the EUPRERA COM-COVID survey, Gonçalves *et al.* (2021) conclude that there is a somehow positive perception of government communication in Portugal, but that people trust more in healthcare personnel to be reliable sources of information, particularly doctors and epidemiologists. Findings also show that mainstream media are the most trusted, more than social media, and, that government information is less trusted than media. This is in line with the information-seeking behaviour discussed in this chapter, once the respondents stress searching COVID-19-related information on multiple channels, but mainly on the informative media. Hence, the Portuguese government could have had more transparent and honest communication, as well as giving more stage to the experts in media and other channels. Moreover, the government and authorities could have benefited from public relations specialists' advice. As stated by the EUPRERA Declaration (2021), simply informing audiences is not enough. The capacity to relay the right information quickly and clearly across different media platforms is essential to manage a public health emergency in an unbounded media landscape.

Note

1 The 'Aggregate Indicator of False Knowledge' (AIFK) would be composed of the 15 dichotomous (or dummy) items of the questionnaire that assume false knowledge about the pandemic (shaded in Table 7.5 and Table 7.6). The alphanumeric expression that represents its creation is: AIFK = Σ 15 items/15; therefore, its ratio is '0–1'. From the point of view of internal consistency, Cronbach's alpha was relatively low: $\alpha_c = .50$.

Bibliography

Alam, F., Dalvi, F., Shaar, S., Durrani, N., Mubarak, H., Nikolov, A., Da San Martino, G., Abdelali, A., Sajjad, H., Darwish, K., and Nakov, P. (2020). Fighting the COVID- 19 infodemic in social media: A holistic perspective and a call to arms. *ArXiv* preprint available in arXiv:2007.07996

Anderson, P., and Spitzberg, B. (2009). Myths and maxims of risks and crisis communication. In Robert L. Heath and H. Dan O'Hair, eds. *Handbook of risks and crisis communication*. New York: Routledge, pp. 205–226.

Antunes, R. (2020, March 20). DGS não ensina a usar máscaras porque não há para todos. *Jornal Observador*. Available from: (in Portuguese): https://observador.pt/2020/03/20/dgs-nao-ensina-a-usar-mascaras-porque-nao-ha-para-todos-nao-vale-a-pena-dizer-que-ha-nao-ha/ [Accessed 17 June 2021].

Araújo, R. (2020, November 12). Continuamos à espera de um 'milagre' na comunicação da Covid-19. *Jornal Público*. Available from: (in Portuguese) www.publico.pt/2020/11/12/sociedade/opiniao/continuamos-espera-milagre-comunicacao-covid19-1938975 [Accessed 17 June 2021].

Arriaga, M.T., Ângelo, R., Gaspar, R., Espassandim, T., and Leiras, G. (2020). *Princípios orientadores para comunicação de riscos e crise, baseados na perceção de riscos*. Lisboa: Direção Geral da Saúde. Available from: (in Portuguese) https://covid19.min-saude.pt/wp-content/uploads/2020/03/Principios-Orientadores-Comunicac%CC%A7a%CC%83o-Crise-2020-.pdf [Accessed 17 June 2021].

Austin, L., Liu, B., and Jin, Y. (2012). How audiences seek out crisis information: Exploring the social-mediated crisis communication model. *Journal of Applied Communication Research*, 40(2), pp. 188–207. doi:10.1080/00909882.2012.654498

Baines, D., and Elliott, R. (2020). Defining misinformation, disinformation and malinformation: An urgent need for clarity during the COVID-19 infodemic. *Discussion Papers*, 20(06), RePEc:bir:birmec:20–06.

Barata, C. (2020, November 9). Precisa-se de quem saiba falar de Covid-19. Entrada imediata. *Jornal Público*. Available from: (in Portuguese) www.publico.pt/2020/11/09/sociedade/noticia/precisase-saiba-falar-covid19-entrada-imediata-1938321 [Accessed 17 June 2021].

Barua, Z., Barua, S., Aktar, S., Kabir, N., and Li, M. (2020). Effects of misinformation on COVID-19 individual responses and recommendations for resilience of disastrous consequences of misinformation. *Progress in Disaster Science*, Elsevier, 8. doi:10.1016/j.pdisas.2020.100119

Brennen, J., Simon, F., Howard, P., and Nielsen, R. (2020). Types, sources, and claims of COVID-19 misinformation. *Reuters Institute for the Study of Journalism*. Available from: https://reutersinstitute.politics.ox.ac.uk/types-sources-and-claims-covid-19-misinformation#references [Accessed 17 June 2021].

Cardoso, G., Baldi, V., Paisana, M., and Quintanilha (2020). *Pandemia e consumos mediáticos, Ober-Com – Observatório de Comunicação*. Available from: (in Portuguese) https://obercom.pt/wp-content/uploads/2020/10/Final_Pandemia_media_Geral.pdf [Accessed 17 June 2021].

Cardoso, G., Paisana, M., and Pinto-Marinho, A. (2020). *Reuters news report 2020 – Portugal, OberCom – Observatório de Comunicação*. Available from: (in Portuguese) https://obercom.pt/wp-content/uploads/2020/06/DNR_PT_2020_19Jun.pdf [Accessed 17 June 2021] (in Portuguese).

Carvalho, M. (2020, October 16). Enterre-se já a proposta absurda da Stayaway Covid. *Jornal Público*. Available from: www.publico.pt/2020/10/16/sociedade/noticia/enterrese-ja-proposta-absurda-stayaway-covid-1935594

Ceron, W., Lima-Santos, M.F., and Quiles, M. (2021). Fake news agenda in the era of COVID-19: Identifying trends through fact-checking content. *Online Social Networks and Media*, 21, pp. 1–14. doi:10.1016/j.osnem.2020.100116

Ceron, W., de-Lima-Santos, M.F., and Quiles, M.G. (2021). Fake news agenda in the era of COVID-19: Identifying trends through fact-checking content. *Online Social Networks and Media*, 21, 100116.

Cohen, J. (1988). *Statistical power analysis for the behavioral sciences*, 2nd ed. Hillsdale, NJ: Lawrence Earlbaum.

Dentsue Aegis (2021). *Coronavírus trends report*. Available from: https://www.dentsu.com/covid-19-hub#top [Accessed 23 June 2022].

Devine, D., Gaskell, J., Jennings, W., and Stoker, G. (2020 August). Trust and the Coronavirus pandemic: What are the consequences of and for trust? An early review of the literature. *Political Studies Review*. doi:10.1177/1478929920948684

DGS (2020). *Recomendações para os media*. Available from: https://covid19.min-saude.pt/wp-content/uploads/2020/03/Folheto-MEDIA-PDF.pdf (in Portuguese).

Dutta-Bergman, Mohan, J. (2004). Complementarity in consumption of news types across traditional and new media. *Journal of Broadcasting & Electronic Media*, 48(1), pp. 41–60. doi:10.1207/s15506878jobem4801_3

Earle, T., and Siegrist, M. (2008). Trust, confidence and cooperation model: A framework for understanding the relation between trust and risk perception. *International Journal of Global Environmental Issues*, 8(1–2), pp. 17–29.

Edelman (2020). *Special report: Trust and the Coronavirus*. Available from: www.edelman.com/sites/g/files/aatuss191/files/2020-03/2020%20Edelman%20Trust%20Barometer%20Coronavirus%20Special%20Report_0.pdf

Euprera (2021). *Communication save lives. Statement on Communication of Covid-19 Pandemic*. Available from: https://euprera.org/covid-comm-statement/

Falcone, R., and Sapienza, A. (2020). How COVID-19 Changed the information needs of Italian Citizens. *International Journal of Environmental Research and Public Health*, 17(6988), 6988. doi:10.3390/ijerph17196988.

Financial Times (2020, January 20). *Portugal suffers surging Covid-19 deaths after mastering first wave*. Available from: www.ft.com/content/fbeb622e-0a69-4f5c-a6fe-6653a72d2377

Fraustino, J., Liu, B-F., and Jin, Y. (2017). Social media during disasters: A research synthesis and road map. In Lucinda L. Austin and Y. Jin, eds. *Social media and crisis communication*. New York, NY: Routledge, pp. 283–295.

Fuchs, C. (2020). Everyday life and everyday communication in coronavirus capitalism. *TripleC: Communication, Capitalism & Critique. Open Access Journal for a Global Sustainable Information Society*, 18(1), pp. 375–399. doi:10.31269/triplec.v18i1.1167

Gonçalves, G., Piñeiro-Naval, V., and Toniolo, B. (2021) (forthcoming). Who do the Portuguese trust? Government communication management in the Covid-19 pandemic. *Comunicação e Sociedade*, 40.

Hair, J.F., Black, W.C., Babin, B.J., and Anderson, R.E. (2010). *Multivariate data analysis*, 7th ed. Upper Saddle River, NJ: Pearson Prentice Hall.

Hale, T., Angrist, N., Kira, B., Petherick, A., Phillips, T., and Webster, S. (2020). *Variation in government responses to COVID-19* [Internet]. Available from: www.bsg.ox.ac.uk/covidtracker

Jaiswal, J., LoSchiavo, C., and Perlman, D.C. (2020). Disinformation, misinformation and inequality-driven mistrust in the time of COVID-19: Lessons unlearned from AIDS Denialism. *AIDS and Behavior*, 24, pp. 2776–2780. doi:10.1007/s10461-020-02925-y

Jin, Y., Austin, L., Vijaykumar, S., Jun, H., and Nowak, G. (2019). Communicating about infectious disease threats: Insights from public health information officers. *Public Relations Review*, 45(1), pp. 167–177.

Johnson, B.T., Scott-Sheldon, L.A.J., Snyder, L.B., Noar, S.M., and Huedo-Medina, T.B. (2008). Contemporary approaches to meta-analysis in communication research. In A.F. Hayes, M.D. Slater, and L.B. Snyder, eds. *The SAGE sourcebook of advanced data analysis methods for communication research*. Thousand Oaks, California: Sage, pp. 311–347.

Kent, M.L., and Taylor, M. (2002). Toward a dialogic theory of public relations. *Public Relations Review*, 28(1), pp. 21–37.

Llewellyn, S. (2020). Covid-19: How to be careful with trust and expertise on social media. *BMJ*, 368, m1160. doi:10.1136/bmj.m1160

Lovari, A. (2020). Spreading (dis)trust: Covid-19 misinformation and government intervention in Italy. *Media and Communication*, 8(2), pp. 458–461 doi:10.17645/mac.v8i2.3219

Lundgren, R.E., and McMakin, A.H. (2013). *Risk communication: A handbook for communicating environmental, safety and health risks*. Hoboken, NJ: Wiley.

Lu, X., and Jin, Y. (2020). Information vetting as a key component in social-mediated crisis communication: An exploratory study to examine the initial conceptualization. *Public Relations Review*, 46(2), p. 101891. doi:10.1016/j.pubrev.2020.101891

Malecki, K.M., Keating, J.A., and Safdar, N. (2021). Crisis communication and public perception of COVID-19 risk in the era of social media. *Clinical Infectious Diseases*, 72(4), pp. 697–702.

Moreno, Á., Fuentes-Lara, C., and Navarro, C. (2020). Covid-19 communication management in Spain: Exploring the effect of information-seeking behavior and message reception in public's evaluation. *El profesional de la información*, 29(4), e290402. doi:10.3145/epi.2020.jul.02

Moreno, Á., Tench, R., and Verhoeven, P. (2021). Trust in public relations in the age of mistrusted media: A European perspective. *Publications*, 9(7). doi:10.3390/publications9010007

Mubarak, H., Nikolov, A., Shaar, S., Alam, F., Dalvi, F., Durrani, N., Da San Martino, G., Abdelali, A., Sajjad, H., Darwish, K., and Nakov, P. (2021). *Fighting the COVID-19 infodemic in social media: A holistic perspective and a call to arms*. Association for the Advancement of Artificial Intelligence, arXiv:2007.07996.

Oliveira, D. (2021, March 3). O nosso ruído. *Expresso*. https://expresso.pt/opiniao/2021-03-03-O-nosso-ruido (in Portuguese).

Paiva, D., Silva, S., Severo, M., Moura-Ferreira, Lunet, N., and Azevedo, A. (2017). Limited health literacy in portugal assessed with the newest vital sign. *Acta Medica Portuguesa*, 30(12), pp. 861–869. doi:10.20344/amp.9135

Park, S., Boatwright, B., and Johnson-Avery, E. (2019). Information channel preference in health crisis: Exploring the roles of perceived risk, preparedness, knowledge, and intent to follow directives. *Public Relations Review*, 45(5), p. 101794. doi:10.1016/j.pubrev.2019.05.015

Parmer, J., Baur, C., Eroglu, D., Lubell, K., Prue, C., B Reynolds, B., and Weaver, J. (2016). Crisis and emergency risk messaging in mass media news stories: Is the public getting the information they need to protect their health? *Health Commun*, 31, pp. 1215–1222.

Pina, J. (2020, November 4). Covid-19, como chegámos aqui: da iliteracia em saúde à má estratégia comunicacional. *Jornal Público*. Available from: www.publico.pt/2020/11/04/opiniao/opiniao/covid19-chegamos-aqui-iliteracia-saude-ma-estrategia-comunicacional-1937808 (in Portuguese).

Polígrafo SIC (2020). Coronavírus: Polígrafo e Direção-Geral da Saúde estabelecem parceria contra as fake news. *Jornal Polígrafo SIC*. Available from: www.dgs.pt/em-destaque/coronavirus-poligrafo-e-direcao-geral-da-saude-estabelecem-parceria-contra-as-fake-news.aspx (in Portuguese).

RDNR (2020). https://reutersinstitute.politics.ox.ac.uk/sites/default/files/2020-06/DNR_2020_FINAL.pdf [Accessed 23 June 2022].

Renn, O., and Levine, D. (1991). Credibility and trust in risk communication. *Communicating Risks to the Public: International perspectives*, 4, pp. 175–218.

Robinson, J.P., Shaver, P.R., and Wrightsman, L.S. (1991). Criteria for scale selection and Evaluation. In J.P. Robinson, P.R. Shaver, and L.S. Wrightsman, eds. *Measures of personality and social psychological attitudes*. San Diego: Academic Press, pp. 1–16.

Seeger, M.W., Pechta, L., Price, S., Lubell, K.M., Rose, D.A., Sapru, S., Chansky, M.C., and Smith, B.J. (2018). A conceptual model for evaluating emergency risk communication in public health. *Health Security*, 16(3), pp. 193–203.

Skarpa, P.E., and Garoufallou, E. (2021 Apr 15). Information seeking behavior and COVID-19 pandemic: A snapshot of young, middle aged and senior individuals in Greece. *International Journal of Medical Informatics*, 150, 104465. doi:10.1016/j.ijmedinf.2021.104465

Soroya, S.H., Farooq, A., Mahmood, K., Isoaho, J., and Zara, S. (2021, March). From information seeking to information avoidance: Understanding the health information behavior during a global health crisis. *Information Processing and Management*, 58(2) doi:10.1016/j.ipm.2020.102440

Tai, Z., and Sun, T. (2007). Media dependencies in a changing media environment: The case of the 2003 SARS epidemic in China. *New Media & Society*, 9(6), pp. 987–1009. doi:10.1177/1461444807082691

WHO (2011). *Report of the review committee on the functioning of the international health regulations (2005) in relation to pandemic (H1N1) 2009*. Geneva, Switzerland: World Health Organization. Available from: https://apps.who.int/gb/ebwha/pdf_files/WHA64/A64_10-en.pdf [Accessed 17 June 2021].

WHO (2020). *Pandemic fatigue: Reinvigorating the public to prevent COVID-19. Policy framework for supporting pandemic prevention and management*. Copenhagen: WHO Regional Office for Europe. Available from: https://apps.who.int/iris/bitstream/handle/10665/335820/WHO-EURO-2020-1160-40906-55390-eng.pdf [Accessed 17 June 2021].

Zhang, X., and Zhou, S. (2019). Clicking health risk messages on social media: Moderated mediation paths through perceived threat, perceived efficacy, and fear arousal. *Health Communication*, 34(11), pp. 1359–1368. doi:10.1080/10410236.2018.1489202

8 COVID-19 information seeking in Spain

How media use affects trust in the government

Cristina Navarro, Ángeles Moreno and Cristina Fuentes-Lara

Introduction

In March 2020, the fast-rising infections and death toll from COVID-19 led the Spanish government to declare a State of Alarm, implementing a series of extraordinary and unprecedented measures to contain the spread of the virus. The political response was a strict national lockdown of more than three months that greatly restricted social activities and freedom of movement. In July 2021, one and a half years since the first case of COVID-19 was detected in the Canary Islands, the country faces a fifth wave, less lethal than the previous ones thanks to the vaccination campaign, but with an increase of cases among the younger population and hospitals still under severe pressure. With this scenario on the table, the country's regions – which are in charge of coronavirus measures – are opting to reintroduce the toughest restrictions seen so far during the health crisis (Mouzo 2021). Spain now ranks 11th worldwide in terms of absolute number of cases, and 31st if measurement of the frequency of officially acknowledged cases is calculated relative to the population (Worldometers 2021).

Immediately after the citizens learnt of a public health–related outbreak, they started seeking and processing information from all kinds of sources of information and media channels. The government responded to the increasing demand for information, offering updated information through the websites of the ministries, but also holding press conferences, granting interviews to officials in national and international media or making statements daily (Castillo-Esparcia *et al.* 2020). However, the confidence of Spanish citizens in the government's management of the pandemic has remained at low levels since the beginning of 2020. According to a survey conducted in September 2020, 56.8% of the population had little or no confidence in the government's ability to handle the outbreak of the novel coronavirus (CIS 2020). Reuters Institute (2020) also pointed out that the national authorities did not play a positive role in helping citizens understand the pandemic.

Previous research found that trust in government has a big impact on how citizens follow public health authorities' recommendations. Trust consists of

DOI: 10.4324/9781003184669-13

judgments about the competence, fairness, honesty, caring, accountability, and transparency of leaders or risk managers. It can be influenced by the characteristics and performance of official spokespersons and by message content during the outbreak (Vaughan and Tinker 2009). Existing research on health-related crises have partially addressed the role of information channels (e.g., Reifegerste *et al.* 2017; Wang and Ahern 2015; Wedderhoff *et al.* 2018; Zhang and Zhou 2019), but few studies have adopted a comprehensive approach to evaluate how information channels and sources influence the public's perceived risks and their evaluation of the government's response. While crisis communication is a burgeoning field, several questions remain to be answered about how people consume, process, retain and evaluate information during health crisis events (Austin and Jin 2016).

Experiencing COVID-19 in Spain

COVID-19 first made its appearance in Spain on 31 January when a German tourist tested positive in La Gomera (Canary Islands). The day before, the World Health Organization (WHO) had declared the 2019-nCoV outbreak a public health emergency of international concern under the International Health Regulations (IHR). In March 2020, the Prime Minister of Spain, Pedro Sánchez, announced a nationwide State of Alarm, banning all trips that were not force majeure, cancelling every on-site educational activity from kindergartens to the universities and confining the population to their homes to contain the epidemic. Spain managed to stop having the worst coronavirus incidence in Europe only between the last weeks of spring and the first of summer (Linde 2020). The virus drastically changed the work situation and the public's daily lives in a matter of days. Many people temporarily or permanently lost their jobs, many have been working from home, sometimes with insufficient preparation for doing so, and those who work in sectors considered essential have experienced heavy workloads, increased levels of stress and a greater exposure to the virus.

The Spanish health system was overwhelmed at the beginning of the pandemic and there were shortages of space in the hospitals (mostly in the emergency rooms and in the intensive care units), of health equipment (mostly ventilators) and of personal protective equipment (Rodríguez-Rey *et al.* 2020). With the end of the State of Alarm on 9 May 2021, experts increasingly worried about what impact this might have on efforts to curb the spread of the coronavirus. Epidemiologists also expressed fears that the disparities between Spain's 17 regions, when it comes to introducing restrictions, will be exacerbated without emergency measures such as night-time curfews. There is also concern that delays due to legal or administrative processes will hurt the effort to control the pandemic (Rincón 2021).

The COVID-19 crisis led the country into an unprecedented downturn in economic activities, with GDP falling by 10.8% in 2020 (BBVA Research 2021), the deepest recession in 80 years and the harshest in Europe. The number of international tourists plummeted from 83.7 million in 2019 to less than 20 million in 2020, the lowest figure since the late 1960s and generating just 4% of GDP, compared with the usual 12%. Small to Medium-sized Enterprises (SMEs), which contribute to over 70% of employment, have been struggling to stay afloat (Santander Trade 2021). The pandemic also widened inequalities in the labour market, with disruptions among young, low-skilled and temporary workers being particularly harsh. The overall unemployment rate, which stood at 14% when the pandemic started, close to double the EU average, rose to 16.2% at the end of 2020.

In terms of governance, a widespread problem in Spain was a lack of coordination, whether among experts and decision makers or among the various agencies and levels of administration, hampered by the decentralised nature of the Spanish political system. For example, as explained by Royo (2020), the autonomous regions had the responsibility for collecting statistics, which left the country without a central data source, making accurate performance comparisons between regions essentially impossible to undertake (Elcano Royal Institute 2020). Moreover, the health services in each region were quickly overwhelmed in the realms of monitoring and control tasks. The National Center for Epidemiology's computer platform was seen to be far from adequate and there was a lack of personnel, especially in contact tracing.

Despite the creation in 2004 of a Centre for Coordination of Health Alerts and Emergency, a Health Ministry department with fewer than a dozen workers, the pandemic laid bare the country's weak surveillance systems, low capacity for PCR tests and scarcity of personal protective equipment and critical care equipment. Moreover, a group of 20 Spanish public health leaders also criticised the delayed reaction by central and regional authorities, the slow decision-making processes, the poor coordination among central and regional authorities, the low reliance on scientific advice and the lack of preparedness in nursing homes (García-Basteiro *et al.* 2020). Another factor that intensified the challenges of fighting the pandemic was the politicisation of the crisis, and the missing solidarity as regions largely acted independently to protect their own citizens. The decentralisation also led to a mosaic of different rules (for instance, some authorities closed nightclubs again within weeks of reopening, imposed earlier closing times for bars and banned smoking in public spaces, while others did not go that far), and wide disparities in the levels of testing and tracing.

The unexpected emergence and rapid spread of the virus triggered government officials' efforts to provide information about the rate of transmission, the best means of containment, treatment, the de-escalation process and so on. However, despite the task force's daily briefings, numerous press conferences and speeches by members of the government, the management of communication has been widely questioned by professional organizations (FAPE 2020; RSF 2020) and experts in political communication (González-Harbour 2020). The main criticisms had to do with the delay in offering information, the lack of consistent and sufficient data, as well as the lack of clarity and empathy on the part of the Prime Minister. The presentation of a negative reality through positive metaphors was a questionable communication strategy. The lockdown was called the 'hibernation' of the economy; the facilities to host thousands of asymptomatic patients were called 'Noah's arks', and the number of deceased and infected became the 'curve' (Elías and Catalán-Matamoros 2020). These communication mistakes negatively affected the government's approval ratings (Costa-Sánchez and López-García 2020; Crespo and Garrido 2020).

The Spanish prime minister also failed to develop and maintain good relations with the media. In March 2020, more than 400 journalists published an open letter entitled 'The Freedom to Ask', proposing a new system based on videoconferences granting a more transparent flow of information (RSF 2020). The daily appearances of government representatives and the technical committee in charge of managing the health emergency received harsh criticism due to the filtering of questions by the Secretary of State for Communication. Unlike authorities of other European countries, such as Italy, Germany, the United Kingdom and France, neither the president nor any other member of the government agreed during the first three weeks of the State of Alarm to answer questions asked directly by journalists electronically. The government argued, instead, that the formula followed was 'simple and efficient', and guaranteed the right of participation and information (González-Harbour 2020). Finally, under pressure from the media and public opinion, the Secretary of State for Communication agreed to hold press conferences with journalists by videoconference and allowed them to reformulate questions.

Media consumption increased considerably during the first lockdown, particularly news related to the evolution of the outbreak. Online newspapers and television were the main sources of information, far ahead of social media, messaging services and radio (Blasco *et al.* 2020). Citizens of all ages preferred obtaining information via traditional media, confirming the trend for taking shelter in recognised media, mainly news programs on public television networks and the digital versions of traditional newspapers (Masip *et al.* 2020). Daily records were set for television consumption, at four viewing hours a day, along with an increase in audience figures for news services, especially among the younger population (Barlovento 2020). According to Gevers (2020), during the last week of March 2020, the consumption of information from social networks grew in Spain by 55%. In comparison to this data, the growth was 30% in Italy, 11% in Germany, 18% in the United Kingdom, and 14% in France. Regarding the role played by the media during the first weeks of the pandemic, Spanish citizens have a negative opinion. The main complaints are related to the overabundance of information, the ideological biases and the tendency toward sensationalism (Masip *et al.* 2020). Members of the scientific community consider that – in general terms – rigor and realism have been lacking in the media and that there has been an excess of sensationalism (Sola 2021).

Even if there were genuine uncertainties, Spanish authorities misjudged the gravity of the threat (Crespo and Garrido 2020). Costa-Sánchez and López-García (2020) point out that the government and the COVID-19 task force did not prepare the citizens for the most negative scenario, overprotecting them with a message of calm in the initial stages. Royo (2020) also explains that the public statements of government officials who sought to downplay the risk of the pandemic until mid-March were a blunt testament of how woefully unprepared and unwilling the authorities were to deal with the crisis. These mistakes negatively influenced the citizens' assessments of the government (Elcano Royal Institute 2021), which highlights the importance of effectively managing any crisis. Perceptions of credibility and trust in public authorities also influences risk perception. Building trust requires not just expertise in implementing rescue activities and mitigating harmful consequences but also openness and empathy when explaining decisions and alternatives (Palttala *et al.* 2012).

Media consumption and trust

The main goal of this research is to assess how information forms and sources influenced the perception of government's crisis response strategies during the pandemic. There is extensive literature on crisis management in Spain, especially reputational crisis management. However, because the COVID-19 health crisis is something unprecedented in the recent history of the country, this research provides valuable information on the ability of Spanish public authorities to communicate effectively. An online survey was conducted between 14 March and 14 April 2020, the first four weeks after the declaration of the State of Alarm in Spain. The online questionnaire included questions regarding information-seeking behaviour, trust in different sources and channels, perception of government communication management, message retention and demographic questions. In total, 1,216 respondents began the survey. The data for this study were cleaned by following Morrow and Skolits' (2014) process to bolster data quality. For example, participants with incomplete answers or those who took less than two minutes to complete the survey were excluded from the analysis. The final sample for analysis was based on 546 completed questionnaires by the target population. In the sample, 71.1% are women, 28% men, and 0.9% nonbinary-gender. All age groups were in the sample, with 36.6% under 30 years old. Regarding their education, 43.7% are undergraduates and 28.3% graduates.

Television (86.2%), WhatsApp (77.6%) and online newspapers (75%) were the most frequent information channels, while magazines (7.4%), Telegram (5.7%), and websites/blogs specialised in alternative therapies (4.6%) were the least used ones. The low consumption of traditional media such as printed newspapers (17.8%) and magazines (7.4%) could be linked to the strict confinement decreed by the government and the closure of non-essential businesses.

These information-seeking trends do not reveal important differences regarding gender and education level of the respondents. Women had a higher use of media in general, especially Instagram and health websites and blogs, while men received more information from radio stations. Young people under the age of 29 got more information than the rest of the age groups from Twitter

Table 8.1 Information sources during the COVID-19 health crisis

Information source	*Percentage*
Television	86.2%
WhatsApp	77.6%
Online newspapers	75.0%
Radio	42.6%
Websites/blogs of public institutions	41.9%
Twitter	40.2%
Facebook	36.6%
Instagram	34.9%
Health websites/blogs	26.1%
Scientific websites/blogs	20.2%
Print newspapers	17.8%
YouTube	16.8%
Magazines	7.4%
Telegram	5.7%
Alternative therapies websites/blogs	4.6%

Source: Authors.

Note: Q1: Which of the following information channels do you rely on to get COVID-19 information? Scale 1 (Never) – 7 (A great deal). Percentages: Frequency based on scale points 5–7.

Table 8.2 Information sources during the COVID-19 health crisis by age

	Age				
	29 or younger	*30–39 years*	*40–49 years*	*50–59 years*	*60 or older*
Television**	87.5%	84.6%	81.9%	89.2%	90%
WhatsApp**	77.0%	78.1%	77.1%	81.1%	65%
Online newspapers**	76.5%	79.5%	73.3%	70.3%	55%
Websites/blogs from public institutions**	48.0%	44.5%	37.2%	37.9%	10%
Twitter**	63.0%	38.7%	20.1%	17.6%	15%

Source: Authors.

Notes: **Highly significant difference (chi-squared $p \leq 0.01$). Scale 1 (Never) – 7 (A great deal). Percentages: Frequency based on scale points 5–7.

(63%, $p \leq 0.01$) and websites/blogs from public institutions (48%, $p \leq 0.01$). Older participants reported a highly significant use of television (90%, $p \leq 0.01$) and a very limited consumption of information from social media and online media channels. People with higher levels of education read the print press more frequently.

In the first month of confinement, the government was a highly trusted source for half of the Spanish citizens. Seen as even more credible was the government's COVID-19 Committee (58.3%), led by Fernando Simon, one of the most popular figures during the pandemic in Spain but who widely criticised for his vacillation during certain phases of the crisis.

Both the government and the COVID-19 task force enjoyed greater trust from women than from men. Conversely, regional (37%) and local authorities (33.6%) do not pass the exam of public trust. WHO (79.3%) and health staff were the most trusted sources of information. They stand out in comparison to prestigious health staff figures (75.1%), personally known health staff (73.5%), and health bodies and associations (61.4%). Other health personnel not personally known who disseminated messages via social media were credible for only half of the population, while influencers on health topics were irrelevant. Notwithstanding the high consumption of information, trust in the media's coverage of COVID-19 was relatively low. Only four out of 10 respondents considered news media a trusted source, with people aged 29 and under showing the least confidence in the media (9%).

A detailed comparison between the first and the second fortnights of confinement indicate a general descent of trust in sources as time went by (see Table 8.3). Only local authorities gained trust from citizens (from 33.2% to 40.1%, $p \leq 0.01$). Media experienced a smaller increase in trust, from 42.5% to 42.9% ($p \leq 0.01$). Personal information from health personnel retained the highest credibility, while the government and the COVID-19 committee lost 20 points in the second fortnight. It is worth highlighting that the largest drop in trust was in the WHO, which declined from 80.9% to 54.3% ($p \leq 0.01$).

During the 30 days of the State of Alarm, 38% of the citizens claimed that the government was the most reliable source of information. More than one-third

Table 8.3 Trust in information sources by fortnight

	First fortnight	*Second fortnight*
Government	51.9%	31.4%
COVID-19 committee	59.6%	39.9%
Regional authorities	37.6%	31.4%
Local authorities	33.2%	40.1%
Media	42.5%	42.9%
Friends on social networks	18.0%	14.7%
Unknown health personnel who have spread on social networks	50.4%	45.7%
Personal information from the health sector	73.8%	70.6%
Health influencers	15.5%	11.5%
Influencers on alternative therapies	2.6%	0.0%
Influencers of other topics (not health) on social networks	3.8%	2.9%
World Health Organization	80.9%	53.4%
Associations of health groups (professional medical associations, etc.)	61.8%	53.4%
Prestigious healthcare personalities (e.g., epidemiologists)	75.2%	74.3%

Source: Authors.

Notes: Scale 1 (Strongly disagree) – 7 (Strongly agree). Percentages: Frequency based on scale points 5–7.

** Highly significant difference (independent simple T-test $p \leq 0.01$).

of the respondents (33.8%, $p \leq 0.01$) evaluated this information as clear and sufficient at all times, and 22.8% ($p \leq 0.01$) thought that it was timely. Nevertheless, 52.8% of the citizens believed that the whole truth was not revealed, 45.9% that the information confused the population, and 48.4% that it had caused social alarm.

Half of the Spanish citizens stated that the government had not revealed the whole truth (52.8%), followed by those who thought that had caused social alarm (48.4%) and had confused the population (45.9%). Nevertheless, four out of 10 citizens strongly believed that the government was 'the most reliable information source' (38.4%), and every one out of three thought it was clear and sufficient (33.8%). The timing of communication was the most critical aspect: Only 22.8% thought the information was timely. Moreover, the statement regarding appropriate timing of communication was the one that showed a bigger variation between the first and the second fortnights of the State of Alarm. Even through only 21.4% ($p \leq 0.01$) of the people thought that the government had correctly timed communication, the percentage doubles in the second fortnight (42.9%, $p \leq 0.01$).

Furthermore, increasing criticism of government communication management took place in the second fortnight. There was a three-percentage-point decrease in people who believed 'the information was clear and enough' and a smaller decrease in people who believed 'the information was the most reliable' (from 38.6% to 37.1%, $p \leq 0.01$). Altogether, more people believed the whole truth was not revealed (from 52.7% to 54.2%, $p \leq 0.01$). There were no significant differences by gender or age between the two fortnights of the State of Alarm.

The more favourable assessments of government crisis communication management and its specialised committee were mainly made by people who use the traditional media extensively. Indeed, print newspaper consumption shows the highest values for these three favourable statements about government communication. By contrast, most people who had a stronger use of social media believed that government communication caused social alarm and confused the population. People who were mainly informed through Twitter (53.4%,

Table 8.4 Perception of the government's communication strategy by fortnight

	First fortnight	*Second fortnight*
Has always been clear and sufficient**	34.1%	31.4%
Has not revealed the whole truth**	52.7%	54.2%
Has been scheduled at the appropriate times**	21.4%	42.9%
Has confused the population**	46.4%	40.0%
Has been the most reliable information**	38.6%	37.1%
Has generated social alarm**	48.3%	48.6%

Source: Authors.

Notes: Scale 1 (Strongly disagree) – 7 (Strongly agree). Percentages: Frequency based on scale points 5–7.
**Highly significant difference (independent simple T test $p \leq 0.01$).

$p \leq 0.01$) and Facebook (52.5%, $p \leq 0.01$) strongly believed that the government's communication caused social alarm and confused the population (50.7% and 49.5%, respectively). However, most audiences for all media agree with the statement 'The government has not revealed the whole truth', especially Twitter users (57.1%, $p \leq 0.01$) and print press readers (56.7%, $p \leq 0.01$).

Finally, most citizens had a correct retention of governmental messages. Nevertheless, despite moderate criticism, it does not appear that all citizens correctly attributed some of the messages disseminated by the government before the declaration of the State of Alarm. Citizens more critical of the government were less able to correctly identify messages displayed by leaders of the government or the task force before the State of Alarm declaration. Most people who believed the government did not reveal the whole truth also thought that the most important thing was to have food at home (54.1%, $p \leq 0.01$) and that borders should have been closed to people from countries with a high level of contagiousness (59.7%, $p \leq 0.01$). However, neither message was displayed by the government before the State of Alarm. On the contrary, those who had a more positive assessment of government communication, such as those who thought the information was clear and enough or was the most reliable information, made fewer mistakes in attributing statements.

Observations and interrogation

In risk and crisis communication, channel selection and trustworthiness are important predictors of information processing and adherence to recommended preventative behaviours (Park *et al.* 2019). Although this topic has been extensively studied over the past decades, the emergence of social media channels, with their ability to amplify rumors and questionable information, makes it more necessary than ever to explore the relationship between media consumption and trust in the authorities.

As COVID-19 swept Spain, the population were forced to dramatically change their purchasing and media behaviours, looking for information about the magnitude of a crisis, checking on family and friends and fostering emotional support. However, despite the growth of social media platforms, legacy media played an important role during the first months of the outbreak. Traditional media are still primarily used for information needs because citizens perceive them – especially broadcast news and newspapers – to be more credible than social media. These findings are also consistent with the Edelman COVID-19 survey (2020). This research showed that although the media had scored poorly in recent years, trust in traditional media rose 7 percentage points, to 69%, as people sought reliable information about the pandemic. The inclusive reach and capacity for information dissemination makes mainstream media, particularly television, an ideal resource for sharing instructional messages during crises (Frisby *et al.* 2014).

Understanding media use is especially important during crisis times because of the potentially dramatic consequences that may arise as a result of how the public understands and frames the crisis (Van der Meer 2018). This research

Table 8.5 Perception of the government's communication strategy by media consumption

	WhatsApp	*Facebook*	*Twitter*	*Websites/blogs from public institutions*	*Print press*	*Online newspapers*	*Television*	*Radio*
Has always been clear and sufficient**	32.4%	31.5%	33.3%	35.4%	40.2%	34.5%	35.7%	36.5%
Has not revealed the whole truth**	54.6%	53.5%	57.1%	53.3%	56.7%	54.5%	54.1%	49.8%
Has been scheduled at the appropriate times**	22.9%	23.5%	23.7%	24.9%	29.3%	24.0%	23.8%	27.5%
Has confused the population**	47.8%	49.5%	50.7%	44.1%	45.4%	46.7%	45.9%	43.8%
Has been the most reliable information**	39.0%	37.5%	43.3%	43.2%	43.3%	39.4%	39.9%	42.5%
Has generated social alarm**	50.8%	52.0%	53.4%	47.2%	51.5%	47.9%	48.8%	44.6%

Source: Authors.

Notes: Q1: Which of the following information channels do you rely on to get COVID-19 information? Q2. To what extent do you agree with the following statements regarding the government's communication on COVID-19? Scale 1 (Strongly disagree) – 7 (Strongly agree). Percentages: Frequency based on scale points 5–7.

**Highly significant difference (independent simple T test $p \leq 0.01$).

confirms the high use of mainstream mass media channels during the pandemic, such as television, newspapers and radio, and corroborates that the choice of medium influences the government's credibility in the fight against COVID-19. In general, people who got news from mainstream news media expressed more positive opinions of the government's crisis response. However, findings suggest that classical crisis theories based on type of crisis and responses are not enough for understanding citizens' responses today, and more factors related to media choice need to be operationalised for risk and crisis communication research.

When public health depends on people understanding the actions they need to take, the possibility of lessening harm highly depends on trust in the sources of information, and particularly trust in public authorities. However, trust cannot be suddenly built just when a crisis arises. Professional public relations and strategic communication specialists are mandatory for a successful crisis committee, but an instrumental use of communication is not enough (Moreno *et al.* 2020). Building trust requires deep understanding, two-way communication and transparency. Our research confirmed low rates of confidence in most information sources, except for doctors and healthcare experts. One of the most interesting findings is that print newspaper consumption is related to more favourable assessments of the government crisis communication strategy.

Results also proved the expected decline in trust in public authorities as the weeks went by. There was a higher decline in trust regarding the WHO, the Spanish government and the COVID-19 committee. This indicates a highly deceived public and raises a new question: how inter-agenda of public authorities could also have an inter-effect on trust assessment. Further research is needed to explore this issue, which may be very important in a global context. Moreover, cross-cultural research will allow us to corroborate whether the same problems arise in other countries and what consequences would follow.

On the other hand, the high simultaneous and multiplatform consumption of information can explain why many people were unable to attribute correctly the information provided by public authorities. Incorrect retention and false attribution contribute to the biggest problems that authorities face in the multiplatform scenario: how to deal with rumours and fake news, especially on certain social media platforms. Findings prove that people less able to make correct attributions of governmental information were the most critical of the government's crisis response. Even if the information of the authorities were correctly constructed, over-information and contra-information make some citizens unable to discern wayward messages. Thus, additional factors regarding message retention and source identification also need to be operationalised for a multivariable analysis of risk and crisis communication.

Conclusions

Mistrust in government authorities is affecting countries' responses to the global pandemic by undermining trust, amplifying fears and sometimes leading to

Infographic 8.1 COVID-19 in Spain: Information seeking and trust in the government

harmful behaviours. During public-health emergencies, such as the COVID-19 pandemic, a well-coordinated and efficient communications strategy helps stakeholders to define risks, identify hazards, assess weaknesses and promote community resilience, thereby increasing the capacity to cope with the difficulties. In an uncertain world, where crises will be part of the new normal and pandemics will emerge again, preparedness is vital to administrations and goes beyond unique efficient responses. People are more likely to follow advice if they understand the rationale behind it. Experts in risk and crisis communication stress the importance of monitoring the needs and expectations of citizen groups, offering timely, accurate, specific, sufficient, consistent, and understandable information.

Although television, radio and online newspapers played a key role in the dissemination of information about the pandemic during the national lockdown, it should not be forgotten that the younger population, especially those under 40 years old, used social media intensively. Undoubtedly, the fact that social media is the source of 88% of the misinformation (Reuters Institute 2020) should serve as a call to rethink future communication strategies. Thus, the government and public authorities must educate the population to find reliable sources of information. A strategic approach entails matching the content, form and style of communication with the media, timing and frequency so that information will reach the intended audience and serve the intended purpose.

In Spain, an initial hesitancy to communicate decisively, even about the uncertainty and unknowns surrounding the pandemic, left space for misinformation to proliferate as people searched for answers. While changes in communications are inevitable, it is crucial to act fast and to adopt a bidirectional communications approach to deliver clear messages tailored to different social groups via multiple media so that everyone in the country receives the correct information, and to ensure community input on the messages to ensure their effectiveness. Mechanisms also need to be developed to ensure honest, transparent, compassionate, and scientificially reliable information sources. When communicating, leaders should listen to the community's needs and concerns and express genuine empathy and concern (Hyland-Wood *et al.* 2021). But above all, communication should be issued through trusted sources, mainly scientists and healthcare workers, and adapted to the social context.

Bibliography

Austin, L., and Jin, Y. (2016). Social media and crisis communication: Explicating the social-mediated crisis communication model. In A. Dudo, and L. Kahlor, eds., *Strategic communication: New agendas in communication*. New York: Routledge, pp. 175–198.

Barlovento Comunicación (2020). *Cambio de hábitos y preferencias de la ciudadanía española frente al televisor por la crisis del coronavirus* [online]. Available from: www.barloventocomunicacion.es [Accessed 12 January 2021].

BBVA Research (2021). *Spain economic outlook. Second quarter 2021* [online]. Available from: www.bbvaresearch.com/en/publicaciones/spain-economic-outlook-second-quarter-2021/ [Accessed 12 April 2021].

Blasco, M.M., Castella, C.O., and Raso, M.L. (2020). Impact of the covid-19 pandemic on media consumption in Spain. *Revista Latina de Comunicacion Social*, 78, 155–167. doi:10.4185/RLCS-2020-1472

Brennen, S., Simon, F., Howard, P.N., and Nielsen, R.K. (2020). Types, sources, and claims of COVID-19 misinformation. *Reuter Institute* [online]. Available from: https://reutersinstitute.politics.ox.ac.uk/types-sources-and-claims-covid-19-misinformation [Accessed 1 March 2021].

Castillo-Esparcia, A., Fernández-Souto, A.B., and Puentes-Rivera, I. (2020). Comunicación política y Covid-19. Estrategias del Gobierno de España//Political communication and Covid-19: Strategies of the Government of Spain. *Profesional de la información (EPI)*, 29(4).

CIS (2020). *Barómetro Especial de Abril 2020. Estudio 3279* [online]. Available from: http://datos.cis.es/pdf/Es3279mar_A.pdf [Accessed 12 January 2021].

Costa-Sánchez, C., and López-García, X. (2020). Comunicación y crisis del coronavirus en España. Primeras lecciones. *El profesional de la información (EPI)*, 29(3). doi:10.3145/epi.2020.may.04

Crespo, I., and Garrido, A. (2020). La pandemia del coronavirus: estrategias de comunicación de crisis. *Más poder local*, 41, 12–19.

Edelman (2020). *Special report: Trust and the Coronavirus* [online]. Available from: www.edelman.com/sites/g/files/aatuss191/files/2020- 03/2020%20Edelman%20Trust%20Barometer%20Coronavirus%20Special%20Report_0.pdf [Accessed 3 April 2021].

Elcano Royal Institute (2020). *Has Spain's management of COVID-19 been a failure? Errors, lessons and recommendations* [online]. Available from: www.realinstitutoelcano.org/wps/wcm/connect/a632f4bb-00aa-480a-82fd-d2aee4b44cca/WP-16-2020-Otero-Molina-Martinez-Has-Spains-management-of-COVID-19-been-a-failure.pdf?MOD=AJPERES&CACHEID=a632f4bb-00aa-480a-82fd-d2aee4b44cca [Accessed 12 April 2021].

Elcano Royal Institute (2021). *Barómetro de la imagen de España (BIE). 9a oleada* [online]. Available from: www.realinstitutoelcano.org/wps/wcm/connect/4bb6daf2-8a0f-4d8e-b1e2-94ef157d6403/9BIE_Informe_abril2021.pdf?MOD=AJPERES&CACHEID=4bb6daf2-8a0f-4d8e-b1e2-94ef157d6403 [Accessed 17 May 2021; 12 April 2021].

Elías, C., and Catalan-Matamoros, D. (2020). Coronavirus in Spain: Fear of 'official'fake news boosts WhatsApp and alternative sources. *Media and Communication*, 8(2), 462–466.

FAPE (2020). *La APM y la FAPE proponen al Gobierno ruedas de prensa con periodistas por videoconferencia* [online]. Available from: http://fape.es/la-apm-y-la-fape-proponen-al-gobierno-ruedas-de-prensa-con-periodistas-por-videoconferencia/ [Accessed 17 January 2021].

Frisby, B., Veil, S., and Sellnow, T. (2014). Instructional messages during health-related crises: Essential con- tent for self-protection. *Health Communication*, 29(4), pp. 347–354. https://doi.org/10.1080/10410236.2012.755604

García-Basteiro, A., Alvarez-Dardet, C., Arenas, A., Bengoa, R., Borrell, C., Del Val, M., Franco, M., Gea-Sánchez, M., Otero, J.J.G., Valcárcel, B.G.L., and Hernández, I. (2020). The need for an independent evaluation of the COVID-19 response in Spain. *The Lancet*, 396(10250), 529–530.

Gevers, A. (2020). What consumers in Europe do online during the lockdown [online]. *ComScore*. Available from: www.comscore.com/esl/Prensa-y-Eventos/Blog/What-consumers-in-Europe-do-online-during-the-lockdown [Accessed 11 April 2021].

González-Harbour, B. (2020, May 1). Cinco fallos y cuatro aciertos del Gobierno en la comunicación de esta crisis [online]. *El País*. Available from: https://elpais.com/sociedad/2020-04-30/cinco-fallos-y-cuatro-aciertos-del-gobierno-en-la-comunicacion-de-esta-crisis.html [Accessed 12 January 2021].

Hughes, E., Kitzinger, J., and Murdock, G. (2006). The media and risk. In P. Taylor-Gooby and J. Zinn, eds., *Risk in social science*. Oxford: Oxford University Press, pp. 250–270.

Hyland-Wood, B., Gardner, J., Leask, J., and Ecker, U.K. (2021). Toward effective government communication strategies in the era of COVID-19. *Humanities and Social Sciences Communications*, 8(1), 1–11.

Jurkowitz, M., and Mitchell, A. (2020). Older Americans continue to follow COVID-19 news more closely than younger adults [online]. *Pew Research Center*. Available from: www.journalism.org/2020/04/22/older-americans-continue-to-follow-Covid-19-news-more-closely-than-younger-adults/ [Accessed 6 April 2021].

Krimsky, S. (2007). Risk communication in the internet age: The rise of disorganized skepticism. *Environmental Hazards*, 7(2), 157–164.

Linde, P. (2020, September 28). Why has Spain failed to contain the Coronavirus pandemic? [online]. *El País*. Available from: https://english.elpais.com/society/2020-09-28/why-has-spain-failed-to-contain-the-coronavirus-pandemic.html [Accessed 6 May 2021].

Masip, P., Aran-Ramspott, S., Ruiz-Caballero, C., Suau, J., Almenar, E., and Puertas-Graell, D. (2020). Consumo informativo y cobertura mediática durante el confinamiento por el Covid-19: sobreinformación, sesgo ideológico y sensacionalismo. *El profesional de la información (EPI)*, 29(3). doi:10.3145/epi.2020.may.12

Moreno, Á., Fuentes Lara, C.M., and Navarro, C. (2020). Covid-19 communication management in Spain: Exploring the effect of information-seeking behavior and message reception in public's evaluation. *El profesional de la información (EPI)*, 9(4), e290402. doi:10.3145/epi.2020.jul.02

Morrow, J.-A., and Skolits, G.-J. (2014). The twelve steps of data cleaning: Strategies for dealing with dirty data. In Workshop conducted at the *28*th *Annual conference of the American Evaluation Association*, Denver, CO. https://www.eval.org/evaluation2014.

Mouzo, J. (2021, July 13). Spain's regions reintroduce Coronavirus restrictions as fifth wave gains pace [online]. *El País*. https://english.elpais.com/society/2021-07-13/spains-regions-reintroduce-coronavirus-restrictions-as-fifth-wave-gains-pace.html [Accessed 15 July 2021].

Nerlich, B., and Koteyko, N. (2012). Crying wolf? Biosecurity and metacommunication in the context of the 2009 swine flu pandemic. *Health & Place*, 18(4), 710–717.

Palttala, P., Boano, C., Lund, R., and Vos, M. (2012). Communication gaps in disaster management: Perceptions by experts from governmental and non-governmental organizations. *Journal of contingencies and crisis management*, 20(1), pp. 2–12.

Park, S., Boatwright, B., and Avery, E.J. (2019). Information channel preference in health crisis: Exploring the roles of perceived risk, preparedness, knowledge, and intent to follow directives. *Public Relations Review*, 45(5), 101794.

Reifegerste, D., Bachl, M., and Baumann, E. (2017). Surrogate health information seeking in Europe: Influence of source type and social network variables. *International Journal of Medical Informatics*, 103, 7–14.

Reuters Institute (2020). Reuters Digitial News Report, Spain. https://www.digitalnews-report.org/survey/2020/spain-2020/ [Accessed 23 June 2022].

Rincón, R. (2021, May 6). What will happen when Spain's state of alarm expires? Supreme Court set to take key role with express rulings [online]. *El País*. Available from: https://english.elpais.com/society/2021-05-06/what-will-happen-when-spains-state-of-alarm-expires-supreme-court-set-to-take-key-role-with-express-rulings.html [Accessed 17 May 2021].

Rodríguez-Rey, R., Garrido-Hernansaiz, H., and Collado, S. (2020). Psychological impact and associated factors during the initial stage of the Coronavirus (COVID-19) pandemic among the general population in Spain. *Frontiers in Psychology*, 11, 15–40.

Royo, S (2020). Responding to COVID-19: The case of Spain. *European Policy Analysis*, 6(2), 180–190.

RSF (2020). Coronavirus: *Spanish government yields to the pressure of journalists and agrees to live press conferences* [online]. Available from: https://rsf.org/en/news/coronavirus-spanish-government-yields-pressure-journalists-and-agrees-live-press-conferences-0 [Accessed 1 April 2021].

Santander Trade (2021). *Spain: Economic and political outline* [online]. Available from: https://santandertrade.com/en/portal/analyse-markets/spain/economic-political-outline [Accessed 20 Febuary 2021].

Sola, J. (2021). Science in the media: The scientific community's perception of the COVID-19 media coverage in Spain. *Journal of Science Communication*, 20(2), A08.

Van der Meer, T.G. (2018). Public frame building: The role of source usage in times of crisis. *Communication Research*, 45(6), 956–981.

Vaughan, E., and Tinker, T. (2009). Effective health risk communication about pandemic influenza for vulnerable populations. *American Journal of Public Health*, 99(S2), 324–332.

Wang, W., and Ahern, L. (2015). Acting on surprise: Emotional response, multiple-channel information seeking and vaccination in the H1N1 flu epidemic. *Social Influence*, 10(3), 137–148.

Wedderhoff, O., Chasiotis, A., Rosman, T., and Mayer, A.K. (2018). Unveiling the subjective perception of health information sources: A three-dimensional source taxonomy based on similarity judgements. *Frontiers in Communication*, 3, 57. doi:10.3389/fcomm.2018.00057

WHO (2011). *Report of the review committee on the functioning of the international health regulations (2005) in relation to Pandemic (H1N1) 2009*. Geneva, Switzerland: World Health Organization [online]. Available from: https://apps.who.int/gb/ebwha/pdf_files/WHA64/A64_10-en.pdf [Accessed 16 December 2020].

WHO (2020). *2019 novel Coronavirus (2019-nCoV): Strategic preparedness and response plan* [online]. Available from: www.who.int/docs/default-source/coronaviruse/srp-04022020.pdf [Accessed 16 March 2021].

Worldometers (2021). *Spain* [online]. Available from: www.worldometers.info/coronavirus/country/spain/ [Accessed 16 May 2021].

Xifra, J. (2020). Comunicación corporativa, relaciones públicas y gestión del riesgo reputacional en tiempos del Covid-19. *El Profesional de la Información*, 29(2), e290220. doi:10.3145/epi.2020.mar.20

Zhang, X., and Zhou, S. (2019). Clicking health risk messages on social media: Moderated Mediation paths through perceived threat, perceived efficacy, and fear arousal. *Health communication*, 34(11), pp. 1359–1368.

Europe – North

9 The good, the bad and the ugly

Learning lessons from the UK's COVID-19 communication

Ralph Tench and Gemma Bridge

Introduction: COVID-19 in the UK

The COVID-19 pandemic has had an enormous impact globally, affecting economies and societies as a result of the health impacts of the virus itself and also the policy decisions made amidst uncertainty (Smith *et al.* 2020). Attempts to control the spread of the virus have had to be carefully managed by national governments against negative impacts on economies and public freedoms (Wright *et al.* 2021). However, the effectiveness of such actions, assessed in terms of infection rates and public opinion, has varied. For instance, consider the variation in disease burden between New Zealand, where disease burden was low and the country was able to achieve COVID-19 elimination (Jefferies *et al.* 2020), against that of the United Kingdom, which has been one of the countries hardest hit by COVID-19, as measured by infection rates, deaths and lost economic production (Worldometer 2021).

Effective and timely communication and leadership are central to the successful management of the COVID-19 pandemic, playing an important role in the complex relationship between scientific knowledge and individuals' beliefs and behaviours. In this vein, it could be argued that messaging about the COVID-19 outbreak by national governments could have played, and will continue to play, a critical role in limiting the spread of disease. However, attempts to inform and educate the public about COVID-19, and the effective prevention measures that should be followed, can be impacted by the volume of information available and the prevalence of misinformation, especially online. This is because we live in a world of information overload, whereby information is shared across multiple platforms, by numerous people and organizations, and there are multiple interpretations of the same information (Bettis-Outland 2012). Therefore, ensuring the information that the public receives is true, complete and accurate is a challenge (Wiesenberg and Tench 2020). It is also relevant to consider other factors that can affect compliance with information, such as trust and confidence in the communicator (Spiegelhalter 2017; Turcotte *et al.* 2015).

To assess the UK government's communication management of the COVID-19 crisis, and the public's perceptions of this communication and the

DOI: 10.4324/9781003184669-15

communications from other platforms and sources, two online surveys were developed. In this chapter, we discuss the results of both surveys. We also discuss implications of the research and highlight how communication professionals could adapt to become more effective communicators when sharing information related to the COVID-19 pandemic, and future health crises.

Experiencing COVID-19 in the UK

On 23 January 2020, the Foreign and Commonwealth Office in the UK advised against all but essential travel to the city of Wuhan, in China, the original epicentre of the COVID-19 outbreak. This was extended to the rest of mainland China by 29 January (Gov.UK 2020). On 31 January the first two cases of COVID-19 were confirmed in the UK (BBC News 2020a), and on 28 February the first British death from COVID-19 was confirmed (Weaver 2020). By 2 March, the number of cases had jumped to 36, so the government held meetings to discuss preparations and responses to the virus (BBC News 2020c). On 16 March Prime Minister Boris Johnson advised everyone in the UK against non-essential travel and contact with others. He also advised people with certain health conditions to self-isolate (BBC News 2020b). To curb the number of cases and deaths from COVID-19, on 23 March Boris Johnson announced a national lockdown with new, strict 'stay at home' rules in the UK (Legislation.gov.uk 2020). The lockdown was accompanied by the closure of all non-essential shops and services. Restrictions were eased in May 2020, and a tiered system was put in place. However, later waves of COVID-19 infection meant that a further two national lockdowns were enforced, first in November 2020 and then in January 2021. Despite the range of restrictions in the UK, trend data indicates that by 9 May 2021, there had been 4.43 million cases of COVID-19 and 128,000 deaths (Our World in Data 2021). In addition, the COVID-19 pandemic resulted in wide-ranging impacts on the country as a whole, affecting the economy, education and physical and mental health care. As a result of these wide-ranging effects, their long-lasting impact and the likelihood of other similar crises in the future, it is essential to explore how the public respond to and perceive communication during the pandemic.

COVID-19 communication experience and insights from the UK

As the COVID-19 pandemic spread in early 2020, media coverage and social media discussion increased significantly. Communications professionals faced a challenge in terms of communicating important information effectively, whilst also dealing with the rapidly changing nature of the crisis. There were also challenges for communicators in terms of navigating the volume of misinformation, and ensuring public behavioural responses were in line with scientific advice. To explore communications about the COVID-19 pandemic in the UK and how they were perceived by the UK public, two surveys were conducted. These surveys, which were carried out at two time points, focussed on the most used channels for information receipt and searching, the most credible sources of information, the types of messages received and remembered and the effectiveness of the messages.

The first survey was delivered during the first UK national lockdown in March and April 2020. Recruitment was via convenience and snowball sampling using the researchers' personal and work networks and social media (Twitter and Facebook). The survey included 20 questions and was shared during the first three weeks of lockdown. To increase response rates, a post on Facebook, with a link to the survey, was promoted for five days using £100 credit. The survey was completed by 609 adults, 16 years or over, living in the UK. Most of the participants (n= 290, 48.1%) were 40–60 years old, female (n= 373, 62.27%) and educated to bachelor's degree or equivalent and above (n= 308, 51%), not currently employed (e.g., unemployed/ retired) (n= 253, 41.89%), white (n= 576, 95.36%) and living in England (n= 581, 96.18%).

The second survey was run in February 2021, as the country was in the depths of the third national lockdown. Due to the availability of additional funding and the intention to explore perspectives from a more diverse population, recruitment for the second survey was carried out via Prolific, an online participant pool. The survey was completed by a demographically varied population of 422 adults across England. Most respondents were female (n=200, 63%) and white (n=346, 82%). Of those respondents who provided their age, 23% (n=97) were aged 16–24, 40% (n=171) were aged 25–39, 33% (n=138) were aged 40–60 and 3% (n=14) were over 61 years. Most respondents work full time (n=187, 44%). Of the remaining respondents, many were students (n=63, 15%) or worked part time (n=58, 14%); 7% (n=30) were unemployed, 7% (n=31) were furloughed and 2% (n=10) were retired. In terms of academic qualifications, 7 (1.5%) respondents reported that they had no academic qualifications, 3% (n=14) stated that they had less than five General Certificates of Secondary Education (GCSEs) or equivalent, with a similar proportion of respondents holding a doctorate degree or equivalent (n=13, 3%). Five GCSEs or equivalent were held by 8% (n=35), but most respondents held two or more General Certificate of Education Advanced Level (A Levels) or equivalent level 3 certifications (n=126, 30%), or had gained a bachelor's degree or equivalent (n=168, 40%). Most respondents reported that they were living in a household as a couple with children (n=149, 35%), with a substantial proportion of the remaining respondents living in a household as part of a couple without children (n=96, 28%).

Use of multiple media and platforms

Previous research indicates that audiences have drifted away from traditional media platforms for information retrieval, especially related to health (Anderson 2017; Stroud 2011), instead retrieving information from online news sources (Cuan-Baltazar *et al.* 2020). This pattern was evident during previous national and global health crises, such as Ebola or Zika infections. Findings from both surveys discussed here reveal a synchronous use of multiple media and platforms throughout the COVID-19 pandemic. These channels included social media, television, radio and printed newspapers. In the first survey, TV was most frequently used as a platform to receive information about COVID-19 (n= 386, 66%), but Facebook and radio were also frequently or very frequently used (n=364, 62.9% and n=237, 43.6% respectively). In the second survey, TV and radio were again an important source of information, but Twitter was mentioned more frequently than Facebook as a source of information.

The use of multiple sources of information supports recent research that identified an increase in media consumption during the COVID-19 pandemic (Hernández-García and Giménez-Júlvez 2020). The data from the two surveys also indicated that online sources of information, such as websites, blogs and social media, were particularly important platforms for the public, reflecting a growing reliance on the internet. In support, Nielsen *et al.* (2020b) found that news use increased throughout the pandemic across a range of countries, and that online platforms such as social media and messaging applications were particularly important sources of information. However, this trend towards preferring online news sites was also noted prior to the pandemic, when research indicated that they were the main source of news for over 40% of people in the UK (Statista 2021).

Paying attention to the news

In survey 2, respondents were asked about the extent to which they paid attention to the news throughout the COVID-19 pandemic. Most respondents (n=257/422, 60.9%) paid attention to local news to a great extent, with many also stating that they had paid attention to the regional news to a great extent (n=148/422, 35%). Most also paid attention to the national news to a great extent (n=257/422, 60.9%), whilst over half of respondents (n=224/422, 53%) also reported that they 'somewhat paid attention' to international news on the COVID-19 pandemic, but fewer paid attention to a great extent (n=99/422, 23%). Also in survey 2, respondents were asked about the extent to which they watched the news. Results indicated that this changed throughout the pandemic. During the first quarter of 2020 (January to March), most respondents (n=183/422, 43%) followed the news to 'a great extent', with only 3% (n=15) not following the news at all. This trend continued into the second quarter of 2020 (April to June), with over half of respondents (n=213/422, 50.5%) following the news to a great extent. In the fourth quarter of 2020 and the first quarter of 2021, most respondents were again following the news to a good or great extent (n=236/422, 55.6% and n=243/422, 57.6% respectively).

The pattern of news seeking identified in the second survey may relate to the extent to which respondents were concerned about the pandemic at different time points. Findings suggest that in the first quarter of 2020, just over a third of respondents (n=152, 36%) were 'concerned to a great extent' about the COVID-19 pandemic. This proportion increased to 54% (n=229/422) by the second quarter of 2020. By the third quarter of 2020, concern appeared to have decreased, with 41.4% (n=175/422) somewhat concerned, compared to 30% who were concerned to a great extent. Concern peaked in the first quarter of 2021, when 54% (n=226/422) of respondents stated that they were concerned to a great extent.

Infodemic: perceived accuracy and timeliness of information

Within weeks of the disease outbreak, COVID-19 became a trending topic worldwide, creating an 'infodemic' (Cuan-Baltazar *et al.* 2020; Rothkopf 2003; World Health Organization 2020). Due to the volume of information online, not all information shared is accurate, true (Oyeyemi *et al.* 2014; Venkatraman *et al.* 2016) or trusted (European Commission 2018), and much does not adhere to official guidance, such as that by the World Health Organization (WHO) (Hernández-García and Giménez-Júlvez 2020). People tend not to critically assess information but still use that information to make important decisions regarding their lives and health (Cuan-Baltazar *et al.* 2020). In relation to the COVID-19 outbreak, misinformation has been associated with stockpiling, buying unnecessary medical supplies and not adhering to official guidance (Cuan-Baltazar *et al.* 2020; Oxford Internet Institute 2018). Whilst misinformation can be shared offline too, traditionally healthcare professionals were the primary source of health information, serving as gatekeepers of information that their publics receive, helping to reduce the sharing of inaccurate data (Hesse *et al.* 2005).

When levels of perceived accuracy of information were explored in survey 2, it was revealed that perceived accuracy was significantly different between media outlets. Figure 9.1 summarises these differences and shows that differences were found between broadcast news outlets, websites and social media ($p = <0.0001$), with broadcast being perceived as more accurate than websites, and both broadcast media and websites being more accurate than social media. Perceived timeliness of information was also significantly different across these three media outlets with broadcast media being perceived as the timeliest source of information, followed by social media and then websites ($p = <0.0001$).

Lack of trust in information

Trust is a key motivator for individuals preferring one source of information over the other (Glik 2007; Rains 2007; Zerfass *et al.* 2019a). Despite the high consumption of information from online sources, respondents reported low trust in this form of information from online platforms. In survey 1, most respondents reported no trust in information shared by the media (n=404, 69.3%). Findings from survey 2 show that there was a significant difference in perceived trustworthiness in the information shared by broadcast media,

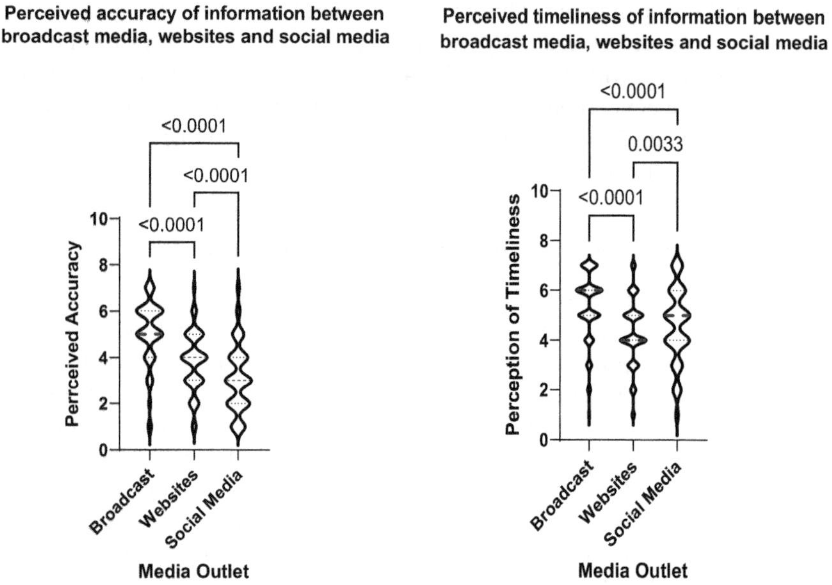

Figure 9.1 Perceived accuracy and timeliness of information shared across media outlets

Source: Authors

websites and social media (p=<0.0001), with broadcast media trusted more than both websites and social media. The lack of trust in online sources of information supports previous research (Glik 2007; Rains 2007; Zerfass *et al.* 2019b). It also reflects the downward trend in trust in traditional mass media (European Commission 2020; Turcotte *et al.* 2015), which, it has been suggested, has led to the public becoming less attentive to mainstream news (Gilens *et al.* 2007; Ladd 2011). Findings from survey 2 also indicate that trust in information shared by both politicians and social influencers was low, but politicians were better trusted than social influencers (p=<0.0001). A similar lack of trust in influencers was seen in survey 1, as respondents reported to have had the lowest trust in information shared by non-health influencers (n=545, 95.3% (no trust)). The respondents in both surveys also had low levels of trust in the information shared by government civil servants, and this trust was significantly lower than that in public health organizations.

In terms of government communication, trust in the messages shared has been deteriorating across the world (OECD 2015; Stokes 2020). Trust in the UK government during the COVID-19 pandemic has declined further still, with polls suggesting that over 30% of the population do not trust the government's management of the crisis (Patel 2020). In a similar vein, in both surveys, many respondents reported that government communication was untrustworthy, unreliable, confusing and a cause of social alarm. In survey 1, most respondents reported no trust (n=288, 48.9%) in government communications. When explored by education level, a significant difference was found between those with no education and those with a bachelor's degree (p= 0.03), as well as between those with five GCSEs or a bachelor's degree (p= .001), and those with a master's degree or doctorate (p= 0.006), with those with fewer qualifications reporting greater trust.

When explored by age groups in survey 2, all age groups were just as likely to state that government messages had been unclear and insufficient, but there was a significant difference in the perceived clarity between 16–24-year-olds and those aged 40–60, with the older age group being more likely to perceive the information as being insufficient and unclear (see Figure 9.2). Similarly, in survey 1 a significant difference was found in terms of perceived clarity between age groups, with those aged 40–60 more likely to consider government communication to be clear than those over age 61 (p = <0.01). Such findings concerning government communication of key information should be central to how people anticipate, understand, prepare for and respond to an emergency such as the COVID-19 pandemic (Enright 2020; Wang *et al.* 2020).

Despite the lack of trust and perceived reliability of government messages, key messages about effective behavioural responses to COVID-19, such as hand washing frequently, were retained by most respondents in both surveys. Moreover, despite the lack of trust in the communication and the volume of information received from social media, most of the false messages appear to have been recognised and disregarded. For instance, in survey 2, when respondents were asked if it is true that COVID-19 affects only the elderly and those with pre-existing health conditions, most (n=395/449, 88%) correctly disagreed. Similarly, when asked if they had to call 999 (the number for the emergency

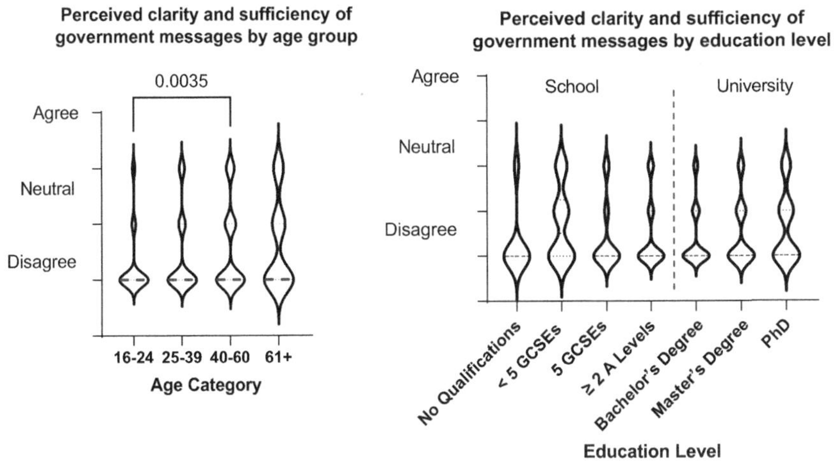

Figure 9.2 Perceived clarity of information shared during the COVID-19 pandemic

Source: Authors

services in the UK) to receive a test for COVID-19, most (n=410/434, 94.5%) also correctly disagreed.

Survey observations and findings from the UK

During a public health crisis, such as the global COVID-19 pandemic, effectively sharing evidence-informed, accurate communication is important in ensuring that the public are equipped with information about the virus itself and how to promote individual and societal health. Two surveys were conducted, the first at the start of the pandemic and the second in the third national lockdown. The surveys explored COVID-19 communications in the UK.

Respondents used several sources of information during the COVID-19 pandemic. This finding is in line with complementarity theory which states information seekers utilise multiple sources when acquiring information to fulfil that information need (Dutta-Bergman 2004). It also corroborates previous research that indicates that people consult multiple sources, including television, radio and social media, when searching for health information (Hjarvard 2013; McCaughan and McKenna 2007; Rains and Ruppel 2016), and used a range of sources throughout the COVID-19 pandemic (Nielsen *et al.* 2020a). Previous research suggests that different platforms are used to varying degrees by those in different demographic groups (Lorence and Park 2007). For instance, previous data suggests that older adults are more likely to receive information from TV, whilst younger people are more likely to use online platforms such as social media (Oxford University 2017). However, in our surveys, no significant differences in information source preference was found between demographic groups in the surveys. This may reflect societal changes in technology access over the course of the COVID-19 pandemic or may reflect the changes in media access that have occurred over recent years.

Trust is a key motivator for preferring one source of information over the other (Rains 2007). It is also an important factor in terms of how likely audiences are to attend to and adhere to messages that are shared. Most respondents reported no trust in information shared by the media, which reflects existing literature (Gilens *et al.* 2007). The findings of this survey suggest little difference between demographic groups, which contrasts with previous research (Stroud and Lee 2013), but may relate to the specific context of the COVID-19 pandemic and its rapidly changing nature and uncertainty.

The survey results also highlight that most respondents have little trust in government communications relating to COVID-19. This supports research which reveals declining trust in the government and reflects the polls carried out by UK national newspapers of public trust (OECD 2015; Patel 2020; Stokes 2020). The lack of trust in government communication could be in part due to the volume of misinformation that exists, with previous studies revealing that misinformation can undermine trust in institutions (Pummerer *et al.* 2021). It is also possible that the government communicators lacked credibility, due to the misdemeanours that were reported in the media, with an important example being Dominic Cummings, the Prime Minister's chief adviser during the COVID-19 pandemic, who was seen near his parents' home in the north of England despite Downing Street saying he was self-isolating at home in London (Fancourt *et al.* 2020). The perceived credibility of communicators is important to consider since credibility plays an important role in behavioural responses (Spiegelhalter 2017; Turcotte *et al.* 2015).

Moreover, trust is crucial to how people respond to guidance, such as that related to COVID-19 vaccinations – a critical next step in fighting the COVID-19 disease (Loomba *et al.* 2021). As such, it is important to identify ways to reduce the prevalence of misinformation, especially online, and find effective methods to support the public in assessing what information is true and what is not. This is particularly important since previous research indicates that some sociodemographic groups are more severely impacted by exposure to misinformation than others, and this could have ramifications to public health outcomes.

Despite the lack of trust in government communications, most respondents have a good or average working knowledge about the pandemic and how to prevent spread, with no differences by education level, income or employment status. This finding differs from previous research, which found that those with higher educational levels were better informed about the risks of a pandemic (Lin *et al.* 2014). This finding from the current survey may suggest that the communication during the COVID-19 pandemic has been delivered at appropriate health literacy levels. In support, most important messages appear to have been retained by the public, such as the importance of key concepts around COVID-19, including hand washing and physical distancing to keep people safe, which indicates that the delivery of essential and basic health messaging was successful.

Finally, survey findings indicate that the extent of the attention that has been paid to the news has ebbed and flowed over the course of the pandemic. This may reflect the changes in level of concern about the pandemic at different time points, with findings indicating that there was a relation between levels of concern and attention given to the news. This ebbing of attention may also reflect the extent to which the pandemic was discussed by government, as there were daily press briefings at the start of the pandemic, which slowed down as the urgency dissipated and were stopped when the first lockdown was lifted in the UK.

Takeaways, lessons learned and future recommendations from the UK experience

COVID-19 has impacted millions of lives across the globe. Governments have responded to the pandemic with extensive restrictions on public movement and freedoms, which have helped to reduce cases and in turn, limit deaths from the virus. In addition to restrictions imposed by governments, limiting the

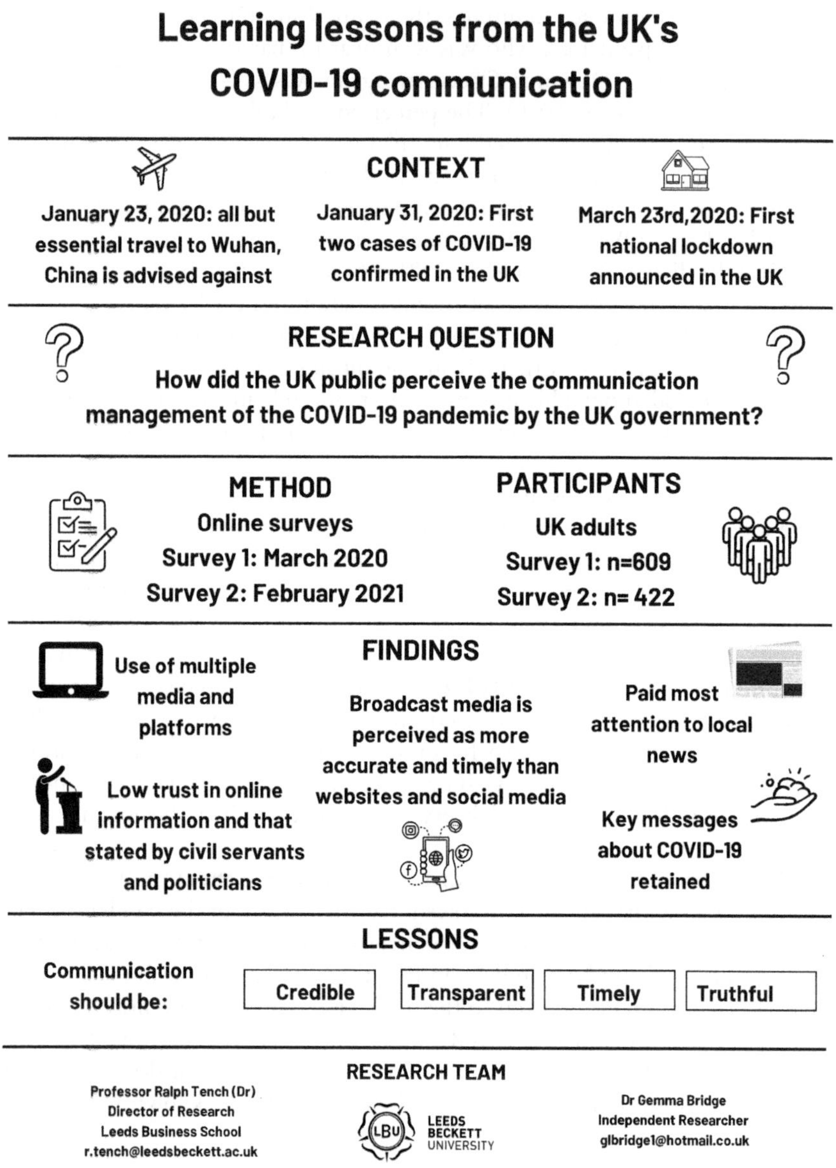

Infographic 9.1 Learning lessons from the UK's COVID-19 communication

negative impact of COVID-19 has relied on the public's awareness and acceptance of scientific knowledge, as this has impacted their beliefs and behaviours. However, communicators who have tried to inform and educate the public about COVID-19 and effective prevention measures have had to compete with huge amounts of information and large volumes of persuasive misinformation, especially online.

The research discussed in this chapter revealed that people in the UK have access to and use many different sources of information about the COVID-19 pandemic, with a focus on information from online sources and TV. Although trust was low in the media and government communications, most key messages, such as the importance of social distancing and hand washing, appear to have been retained, which signals a success of public health messaging and is a promising finding considering the importance of behavioural strategies to control the virus.

The findings presented in this chapter could be relevant to communicators seeking insights for improvement and more effective future management of communication in similar global public health crises. Importantly, practitioners should look to ensure that messages are: 1) consistent, as this improves perceived legitimacy (Massey 2001); 2) clear and transparent, as this can improve public motivation and intention to adopt or maintain recommended self-protective actions (Vaughan and Tinker 2009); and 3) honest, as the complete presentation of known and unknown factors can positively affect people's knowledge, attitudes and beliefs, including trust in the way the government is handling the emergency (Lin *et al.* 2014). By doing so, communicators would be able to better ensure that public trust in the information shared is high. This would help to ensure that the public trust the information that they are given, that their willingness to comply with guidance is high and that they are able to anticipate, understand, prepare for and respond to an emergency such as the COVID-19 pandemic, supporting public health and societal wellbeing.

Bibliography

Anderson, K. (2017). *Beyond the article: Frontiers of editorial and commercial innovation* [online]. Oxford: Reuters Institute for the Study of Journalism. Available from: https://reutersinstitute.politics.ox.ac.uk/sites/default/files/2017-10/Beyond%20the%20Article%20-%20Frontiers%20of%20Editorial%20and%20Commercial%20Innovation.pdf

BBC News (2020a, January 31). Coronavirus: Two cases confirmed in UK. *BBC News* [online]. Available from: www.bbc.com/news/health-51325192 [Accessed 8 May 2021].

Bettis-Outland, H. (2012). Decision-making's impact on organizational learning and information overload. *Journal of Business Research*, 65(6), pp. 814-820.

Coronavirus: PM says everyone should avoid office, pubs and travelling (2020b, March 16). *BBC News* [online]. Available from: www.bbc.com/news/uk-51917562 [Accessed 8 May 2021].

Coronavirus: Widespread transmission in UK 'highly likely' (2020c, March 2). *BBC News* [online]. Available from: www.bbc.com/news/uk-51700604 [Accessed 8 May 2021].

Cuan-Baltazar, J.Y., Cuan-Baltazar, J.Y., Muñoz-Perez M.J., Robledo-Vega C., Pérez-Zepeda M.F., and Soto-Vega, E. (2020). Misinformation of COVID-19 on the internet: Infodemiology study. *JMIR Public Health and Surveillance* [Online], 6(2) April. Available from: www.ncbi.nlm.nih.gov/pmc/articles/PMC7147328/ [Accessed 29 April 2020].

Dutta-Bergman, M.J. (2004). Complementarity in consumption of news types across traditional and new media. *Journal of Broadcasting & Electronic Media*, 48(1) March, pp. 41–60.

Enright, S. (2020). Emergency communications: Leading communities through an unforeseen crisis: Local government association [online]. *Local Government Association*. Available from: www.local.gov.uk/our-support/guidance-and-resources/comms-hub-communications-support/futurecomms-building-local-11 [Accessed 17 February 2021].

European Commission (2018). *Public opinion in the European Union* [online]. Brussels, Belgium: Eurobarometer. Available from: https://ec.europa.eu/commfrontoffice/publicopinion/index.cfm/Survey/index#p=1&instruments=standard&yearFrom=1974&yearTo=2006

European Commission (2020). *Coronavirus: Parliament's green light for new resources* [online]. European Commission – European Commission. Available from: https://ec.europa.eu/commission/presscorner/detail/en/IP_20_685 [Accessed 29 April 2020].

Fancourt, D., Steptoe, A., and Wright, L. (2020). The cummings effect: Politics, trust, and behaviours during the COVID-19 pandemic. *The Lancet*, 396(10249) August, pp. 464–465.

Gilens, M., Vavreck, L., and Cohen, M. (2007). The mass media and the public's assessments of presidential candidates, pp. 1952–2000. *Journal of Politics*, 69(4), 1160–1175.

Glik, D.C. (2007). Risk communication for public health emergencies. *Annual Review of Public Health*, 28, 33–54.

Gov.UK (2020). Foreign office advises against all but essential travel to Mainland China [online]. *GOV.UK*. Available from: www.gov.uk/government/news/fco-advises-against-all-but-essential-travel-to-mainland-china [Accessed 8 May 2021].

Hernández-García, I., and Giménez-Júlvez, T. (2020). Assessment of health information about COVID-19 Prevention on the internet: Infodemiological study. *JMIR Public Health and Surveillance* [Online], 6(2) April. Available from: www.ncbi.nlm.nih.gov/pmc/articles/PMC7117090/ [Accessed 29 April 2020].

Hesse, B.W., Nelson, D.E., Kreps, L.G., Croyle, T.R., Arora, N.K., Rimer, B.K., and Viswanath, K. (2005). Trust and sources of health information: The impact of the internet and its implications for health care providers: Findings from the first health information national trends survey. *Archives of Internal Medicine*, 165(22) December, pp. 2618–2624.

Hjarvard, S. (2013). *The mediatization of culture and society* [online]. Routledge. Available from: www.routledge.com/The-Mediatization-of-Culture-and-Society/Hjarvard/p/book/9780415692373 [Accessed 2 April 2021].

Jefferies, S., French, N., Gilkison, C., Graham, G., Hope, V., Marshall, J., McElnay, C., McNeill, A., Muellner, P., Paine, S., Prasad, N., Scott, J., Sherwood, J.,Yang, L., and Priest, P. (2020). COVID-19 in New Zealand and the impact of the national response: A descriptive epidemiological study. *The Lancet Public Health*, 5(11) November, e612 – e623.

Ladd, J.M. (2011). *Why Americans hate the media and how it matters* [online]. Available from: https://press.princeton.edu/books/paperback/9780691147864/why-americans-hate-the-media-and-how-it-matters [Accessed 29 April 2020].

Legislation.gov.uk (2020). *The health protection (Coronavirus, restrictions) (England) regulations 2020* [online]. Legislation.gov.uk. Available from: www.legislation.gov.uk/uksi/2020/350/contents/made/data.htm [Accessed 8 May 2021].

Lin, L., Savoia, E., Agboola, F., and Viswanath, V. (2014). What have we learned about communication inequalities during the H1N1 pandemic: A systematic review of the literature. *BMC Public Health*, 14(1) May, p. 484.

Loomba, S., Figueiredo, A.D., Piatek, S.J., Graaf, K.D., and Larson, H.J. (2021). Measuring the impact of COVID-19 vaccine misinformation on vaccination intent in the UK and USA. *Nature Human Behaviour*, 5(3) March, pp. 337–348.

Lorence, D., and Park, H. (2007). Study of education disparities and health information seeking behavior. *Cyberpsychology & Behavior: The Impact of the Internet, Multimedia and Virtual Reality on Behavior and Society*, 10(1) February, pp. 149–151.

Massey, J.E. (2001). Managing organizational legitimacy: Communication strategies for organizations in crisis. *The Journal of Business Communication (1973)*, 38(2) April, pp. 153–182.

McCaughan, E., and McKenna, H. (2007). Never-ending making sense: Towards a substantive theory of the information-seeking behaviour of newly diagnosed cancer patients. *Journal of Clinical Nursing*, 16(11) November, pp. 2096–2104.

Nielsen, Fletcher, Newman, Brennen and Howard (2020a). Navigating the 'infodemic': How people in six countries access and rate news and information about Coronavirus [online]. *Reuters Institute for the Study of Journalism*. Available from: https://reutersinstitute.politics.ox.ac.uk/infodemic-how-people-six-countries-access-and-rate-news-and-information-about-coronavirus [Accessed 29 April 2020].

Nielsen, R., Fletcher R., Newman, N., and Howard, P.N. (2020b). Navigating the 'infodemic': How people in six countries access and rate news and information about Coronavirus. *Reuters Institute for the Study of Journalism* [online]. Available from: https://reutersinstitute.politics.ox.ac.uk/infodemic-how-people-six-countries-access-and-rate-news-and-information-about-coronavirus [Accessed 29 April 2020].

OECD (2015). *Trust in government – OECD* [online]. OECD: Better policies for better lives. Available from: www.oecd.org/gov/trust-in-government.htm [Accessed 29 April 2020].

Our World in Data (2021). *Coronavirus pandemic (COVID-19) – the data – statistics and research* [online]. Our World in Data. Available from: https://ourworldindata.org/coronavirus-data [Accessed 9 May 2021].

Oxford Internet Institute (2018). *The Computational propaganda project* [online]. The Computational Propaganda Project. Available from: https://comprop.oii.ox.ac.uk/ [Accessed 29 April 2020].

Oxford University (2017). *Where do people get their news? – Oxford University – Medium* [online]. Medium. Available from: https://medium.com/oxford-university/where-do-people-get-their-news-8e850a0dea03 [Accessed 29 April 2020].

Oyeyemi, S.O., Gabarron, E., and Wynn, R. (2014, October). Ebola, twitter, and misinformation: A dangerous combination? *BMJ (Clinical Research Ed.)*, 349, 6178.

Patel, B. (2020). Trust in government's handling of covid crisis plummets. *Daily Mail Online* [online]. Available from: www.dailymail.co.uk/news/article-8258029/Trust-governments-handling-covid-crisis-plummets.html [Accessed 29 April 2020].

Pummerer, L., Böhm, R., Lilleholt, L., Winter, K., Zettler, I., and Sassenberg, K. (2021, March). Conspiracy theories and their societal effects during the COVID-19 pandemic. *Social Psychological and Personality Science*, pp. 1–11. doi:10.1177/19485506211000217

Rains, S.A. (2007). Perceptions of traditional information sources and use of the world wide web to seek health information: Findings from the health information national trends survey. *Journal of Health Communication*, 12(7) November, pp. 667–680.

Rains, S.A., and Ruppel, E.K. (2016). Channel complementarity theory and the health information-seeking process: Further investigating the implications of source characteristic complementarity. *Communication Research*, 43(2) March, pp. 232–252.

Rothkopf, D. (2003). When the buzz bites back. *Washington Post* [online]. Available from: http://www1.udel.edu/globalagenda/2004/student/readings/infodemic.html [Accessed 29 April 2020].

Smith, G.D., Blastland, M., and Munafò, M. (2020, October). Covid-19's known unknowns. *BMJ*, 371, m3979.

Spiegelhalter, D. (2017). Risk and uncertainty communication. *Annual Review of Statistics and Its Application*, 4(1), 31–60.

Statista (2021). Main sources of news in the UK [online]. *Statista.* Available from: www.statista.com/statistics/1099758/main-sources-of-news-in-the-uk/ [Accessed 2 April 2021].
Stokes, K. (2020). The 2020 Edelman trust barometer report [online], 78. Available from: www.edelman.com/trust/2020-trust-barometer [Accessed 23 July 2021].
Stroud, N.J. (2011). *Niche news: The politics of news choice* [online]. Oxford University Press. Available from: www.oxfordscholarship.com/view/10.1093/acprof:oso/9780199755509.001.0001/acprof-9780199755509 [Accessed 29 April 2020].
Stroud, N.J., and Lee, J.K. (2013). Perceptions of cable news credibility. *Mass Communication and Society* [Online], 16(1). Available from: www.tandfonline.com/doi/abs/10.1080/15205436.2011.646449 [Accessed 29 April 2020].
Turcotte, J., York, C., Irving, J., Scholl, R.M., and Pingree, R.J. (2015). News recommendations from social media opinion leaders: Effects on media trust and information seeking. *Journal of Computer-Mediated Communication*, 20(5) September, pp. 520–535.
Vaughan, E., and Tinker, T. (2009). Effective health risk communication about pandemic influenza for vulnerable populations. *American Journal of Public Health*, 99(S2) October, S324–S332.
Venkatraman, A., Mukhija, D., Kumar, N., and Nagpal, S.S. (2016). Zika virus misinformation on the internet. *Travel Medicine and Infectious Disease*, 14(4) August, pp. 421–422.
Wang, H., Cleary, P.D., Little, J., and Auffray, C. (2020). Communicating in a public health crisis. *The Lancet Digital Health*, 2(10) October, e503.
Weaver, M. (2020). First British Coronavirus death confirmed [online]. *The Guardian*. Available from: www.theguardian.com/world/2020/feb/28/first-briton-dies-from-coronavirus-japanese-media-report-diamond-princess [Accessed 8 May 2021].
WHO (2020). *Munich security conference* [online]. WHO. Available from: www.who.int/dg/speeches/detail/munich-security-conference [Accessed 29 April 2020].
Wiesenberg, M., and Tench, R. (2020, April). Deep strategic mediatization: Organizational leaders' knowledge and usage of social bots in an era of disinformation. *International Journal of Information Management*, 51, 102042.
Worldometer (2021). *UK Coronavirus cases and deaths* [online]. Worldometer. Available from: www.worldometers.info/coronavirus/country/uk/ [Accessed 8 April 2021].
Wright, L., Burton, A., McKinlay, A., Steptoe, A., and Fancourt, D. (2021, March). Public opinion about the UK government during COVID-19 and implications for public health: A topic modelling analysis of open-ended survey response data. *medRxiv*, 2021.03.24.21254094.
Zerfass, A., *Verčič, D., Verhoeven, P., Moreno, Á., and Tench, R.* (2019a). *European communication monitor 2019. Exploring trust in the profession, transparency, artificial intelligence and new content strategies. results of a survey in 46 countries*. Brussels, Belgium: EUPRERA/EACD.
Zerfass, A., *Verčič, D., Verhoeven, P., Moreno, Á., and Tench, R.* (2019b). Trust in communicators 2019 study: How the general population trusts . . . [online]. Available from: www.slideshare.net/communicationmonitor/trust-in-communicators-2019-study-how-the-general-population-trusts-journalists-public-relations-professionals-marketeers-and-other-communicators-a-comparative-study-in-germany-italy-and-the-united-kingdom [Accessed 29 April 2020].

10 Public trust in governments' communicating with intermediaries

Finnish and Swedish governments during the COVID-19 pandemic

Chiara Valentini and Mark Badham

Introduction

The Finnish and Swedish governments handled the COVID-19 pandemic very differently in 2020, with contrasting results in terms of number of deaths and infected people. Given that in the Nordic region citizens' trust in their governments generally ranks very high (Andreasson 2017), did Finns and Swedes trust their governments' COVID-19 response strategies towards the end of 2020?

Trust in national governments is especially important during infectious disease outbreaks (Balog-Way and McComas 2020). Trust can influence the public's perception of risk (Flynn *et al.* 1992; Slovic 1993; Cvetkovich 1999; Siegrist *et al.* 2000; Bronfman *et al.* 2009) and intentions to adopt government-recommended guidelines (Blair *et al.* 2017; Vinck *et al.* 2019).

In this chapter we draw on conceptualisation of intermediaries (Deephouse and Heugens 2009; Fombrun 1996; Frandsen and Johansen 2015; Rindova and Fombrun 1999) in strategic communication studies and organizational studies to shed light on the role and importance of intermediaries in building trust during risk communication processes. Strategic communicators within government may turn to intermediaries as government-endorsed sources of risk information, who hold varying levels of public trust, to help disseminate risk messages to the wide range of stakeholders affected by a health crisis. Studying the mediating role of different strategic communication intermediaries in risk management during global pandemics such as COVID-19 is thus timely and important.

In this chapter we focus on two Nordic countries, Finland and Sweden, as illustrative examples of two very different government response strategies that both include intermediaries. The Finnish and Swedish cases can offer insights into differences and similarities of how national governments in two countries with high citizen trust in authorities communicated risk messages via intermediaries and the resulting implications for citizens' trust in their governments and in their communication intermediaries.

After presenting the main theoretical premises of this comparative study, and introducing the reader to the main events in the two analysed countries, the

DOI: 10.4324/9781003184669-16

chapter presents empirical data pertaining to public trust in different sources of information, perceived quality of government communication, public risk perceptions and compliance with government recommendations. For this part, primary data collected through a web survey conducted in autumn 2020 in these respective countries is used. The chapter concludes with recommendations for strategic communication scholars and practitioners on ways to use intermediaries during health crisis situations, particularly to build and manage trust.

Literature review

Given the important mediating role of trust in public compliance with government recommendations during pandemics, in the following section we elaborate on the role of trust and of intermediaries during health crises from the most prominent literature primarily on risk, health and crisis communication and stakeholder relations.

Trust as main factor influencing risk communication success

The trust people have in their government, health authority and fellow citizens is an important variable during public health crises. Trust is a multifaceted concept often related to a state, belief or positive expectation (Valentini 2021). Trust is essentially understood as the public confidence in a government's intentions and capacity to act to limit negative health effects on the population (Esaiasson *et al.* 2020; Levi and Stoker 2000; Taylor *et al.* 2009). Particularly during health pandemics, such as COVID-19, in which individual human behaviour strongly determines the transmission of the disease, public compliance with health recommendations is an essential feature of effective risk management by governments.

Several studies show that when people trust the source of information, they most likely find the information to be credible (Bickham and Francis 2021; Lucassen and Schraagen 2012), evaluate its quality and comprehensiveness in a positive light (Cairns *et al.* 2013) and tend to follow the instructions provided by that source to prevent or limit risks (Quinn *et al.* 2013). This ultimately means that when people trust a source they are more willing to follow its rules and guidelines (Han *et al.* 2020; Olsen and Hjorth 2020). The public's trust in a government's capacity to manage a public health situation has been shown to highly correlate with the public's behaviour during situations characterised by high health crisis (Fancourt *et al.* 2020) and this therefore has impacted the effectiveness of governments' risk management plan during pandemics (Bargain and Aminjonov 2020). Studies show that greater trust in government leads to more compliance with health policies (Van Bavel *et al.* 2020), such as measures relating to quarantining, testing and restrictions on mass gatherings. Indeed, high levels of institutional trust are a necessary condition for the implementation of restrictive policies and for public compliance with them (Van Bavel *et al.* 2020). Effective risk management during a health crisis helps increase and reinforce public trust in a government managing that crisis (Siegrist and Zingg 2014), but people's perception of that government's lack of effectiveness in managing a health crisis also may hinder public trust in it (van der Weerd *et al.* 2011).

Another type of trust important to public risk management is trust in intermediaries. Research shows that trust in intermediaries such as health agencies, medical organizations and the scientific community positively influences people's willingness to adopt recommended behaviour in health crises (Battiston *et al.* 2021; Gilles *et al.* 2011; Siegrist and Zingg 2014). As a result, government use of experts as intermediary communicators during health crises could potentially amplify the reach of other risk information, particularly among those groups of individuals who hold high trust in these intermediaries (Siegrist and Zingg 2014). In the next section we elaborate on the specific role of intermediaries as strategic communicators engaged by the government in risk communications.

Intermediary communicators in health crises

Global health crises affect a very broad and diverse set of stakeholders. Therefore, governments' risk management has numerous challenges in reaching all these diversified groups of stakeholders and persuading them to embrace health recommendations. In the case of the COVID-19 pandemic, it is paramount that government communicators address and reach out to each stakeholder group via their preferred channels and sources. Since stakeholders may have different levels of trust in sources of health information, communication with them needs to reflect the sources they trust most, which may or may not be government-based. These can be disease experts and scientists (Battiston *et al.* 2021). These social actors, together with medical practitioners and experts from different health organizations, such as a national pharmaceutical agency, act as intermediaries of pandemic communications.

Organizational studies shed light on the role of intermediaries in communication contexts (Deephouse and Heugens 2009; Fombrun 1996; Rindova and Fombrun 1999). In the context of frequent information exchanges between organizations and their stakeholders, some types of organizations take on professional third-party roles to mediate these information flows between organizations and stakeholders and thus provide mediated information to audiences (Hirsch 1977; Shoemaker and Reese 1996). Examples include trade unions and news media organizations. In strategic communication literature, Frandsen and Johansen (2015) define an intermediary as:

> an individual, a group of individuals, an organization, or a meta-organization, that belongs to a specific area in society (e.g., a specific industry, a specific organizational field, and/or a specific sector), and whose primary function or mission is to mediate; that is, to represent an organization and/

> or a specific stakeholder group, and/or to intervene in the relationship between them either by furthering or by impeding the interests and activities of the organization in question and/or its stakeholders in a specific situation or over time.
>
> (Frandsen and Johansen 2015, p. 257)

Since intermediaries are so heterogenous, it is important to select the most relevant ones based on the issue at stake and some formal characteristics they show. Frandsen and Johansen (2015) propose six main elements to classify intermediaries which, we argue, can be used to select the most appropriate ones in risk communication management planning. These are: 1) the areas of society where the intermediary is active (and thus influential), 2) its organizational form, 3) status, 4) representation, 5) intervention and 6) its strategic communications.

First, intermediaries are active at both societal and organizational levels, and each of these contexts has its own structure, rules and norms of behaviours. Hence each of these contexts affects what an intermediary can do and how. Therefore, Frandsen and Johansen (2015) suggest paying attention to the industry or sector as well as the organizational field where the intermediary operates. Second, the very nature (i.e., the organizational form) of the intermediary can tell a lot about what it can do and through what means. Intermediaries can, in fact, be individuals (e.g., social media influencers), organizations (e.g., trade unions and professional associations) and meta-organizations (i.e., organizations of organizations, such as consortiums) (Ahrne and Brunsson 2008). Third, status indicates the types of roles the intermediary can play. It can act as a pure intermediary of an organization or of a stakeholder group. It can also be considered a stakeholder of an organization while acting as intermediary for another.

Fourth, the representation of the intermediary is also an important element. Frandsen and Johansen (2015) describe this as 'the relationship between the intermediary and the focal organization; that is, to act or speak on behalf of an organization or a group of stakeholders' (p. 264). In this chapter we understand representation as *alignment*. Intermediaries are situated along a spectrum between close alignment with the focal organization and close alignment with a specific stakeholder group. For example, an association of medical practitioners is established to represent medical workers and in a crisis situation they would be more aligned with this group than with a government managing a crisis impacting this group. When an intermediary is closely aligned with an organization, the organization may request that it act as a spokesperson for the organization, thus endorsing the organization.

This question of intermediary alignment is important to organizations planning which intermediaries to work with when communicating about a crisis with all stakeholders. From an organizational perspective, they can be positioned anywhere between acting as a hateholder and faithholder of the organization (Luoma-aho 2015). Accordingly their communicative intervention could be either vouching for the organization/stakeholder group and advocate for its interests (furthering intervention) or else hindering the organization/stakeholder group's interests (impending intervention) through, for example, campaigns against it. This is the fifth element of Frandsen and Johansen's classification (2015). Finally, the strategic communication of the intermediary offers insight into its reputation and is an important element to understanding how an intermediary operates, forms collaborations and alliances, and eventually represents the interests of other organizations or groups of stakeholders. All in all, literature shows that intermediaries can play an important role in the management of communications, and thus they deserve to be investigated when studying risk communication processes such as those related to COVID-19.

Method and data

This study is comparative, employing a mixed method approach; data in the two countries were collected and contrasted to identify similarities and differences in each government's risk communication strategy during the pandemic. The case was researched using news coverage from leading Finnish, Swedish and international media and official information from the Finnish and Swedish governments' websites and respective authorities' websites in charge of the management of the COVID-19 disease. To identify relevant information, we searched for a combination of the following keywords: 'COVID-19' and 'government' and 'Finland' or 'Sweden' in English, Finnish and Swedish in the LexisNexis database and the official governments' and authorities' websites during the period March–November 2020. This material was used to compile the case narrative describing the events and to gather information on these governments' communication strategies, their pandemic management actions and involved stakeholders.

We approached the analysis through a close reading of news articles and official media resources against our research purpose to generate insights and knowledge on the Finnish and Swedish governments' official strategic communication strategies and the involved stakeholders with no intention to quantify the contents but rather using them as background to understand the situation. To understand whether the governments' actions in these two countries were perceived appropriately by the general population, we employed a computer-assisted web interviewing (CAWI) methodology and collected primary data through a web-based survey during fall 2020 in these respective countries. The data comprises over 1,000 valid answers from a representative sample of adults (over 18 years old). Descriptive statistics were run to show public perceptions across key elements identified in the literature.

COVID-19 situation in Finland and Sweden

In this section we first present a comparative analysis of the different approaches that the Finnish and Swedish governments took when responding to the first wave of the COVID-19 pandemic between February and November 2020. We show how both national governments communicated during this period of the pandemic and how their main intermediary stakeholders became involved in this process.

Differing approaches to managing COVID-19

The first confirmed cases of COVID-19 in Finland were found in Lapland in late January 2020 when two Chinese tourists developed flu-like symptoms and tested positive (Yle 2021). At the same time, Sweden had its first case when a young woman returned from Wuhan, China, to Jönköping and entered hospital for treatment on 31 January 2020 (The Local 2021). Both the Swedish and Finnish governments recognised the severity of the novel disease for society, imposing a state of emergency for each of these countries. The Swedish government started taking some actions in February. The Finnish government response came only on 16 March 2020, a week after the WHO declared COVID-19 a world pandemic. However, beyond this action, each country took very different strategic approaches.

Finnish government responses

Finland is one of a few European countries with fewer COVID-19 casualties (Euractiv 2020), around 19,900 cases and 374 deaths as of 19 November 2020 (Höppner 2020). The Ministry of Social Affairs and Health has been responsible for the general planning, guidance and monitoring of the prevention of infectious diseases. It supported the efforts of multiple state agencies to prevent the spread of the coronavirus, such as the Finnish Institute for Health and Welfare (THL), the Finnish Medicines Agency (Fimea), the National Supervisory Authority for Welfare and Health (Valvira), the regional state administrative agencies and the municipalities and joint municipal authorities. In May 2020, the Finnish government announced that its response strategy would be based on a 'hybrid' approach, aiming at curbing the epidemic while minimising the adverse impact on people, businesses, society and the exercise of fundamental rights. The hybrid strategy used a 'test, trace, isolate and treat' approach to contain the pandemic's spread (Government Communications Department, Ministry of Social Affairs and Health, Finnish Government 2020). The government restricted public and private gatherings to no more than six people (THL 2020). These restrictions, however, have rarely lasted for more than three consecutive weeks.

As of 1 June, gatherings of up to 50 persons were permitted and public premises reopened. Restaurants, cafés and bars reopened, with temporary restrictions relating to requirements on hygiene and social distancing and limiting the number of customer seats and opening and licensing hours. On 15 June 2020, the Finnish government decided to lift the state of emergency, and to manage the COVID-19 epidemic using regular powers.

Swedish government responses

In Sweden, the government response was rather different. The Swedish management model is based on the division of executive power between elected politicians and state authorities. State authorities such as the Public Health Agency – known in Sweden as Folkhälsomyndigheten (FHM), which historically has plenty of freedom – are partly self-governing bodies. Politicians follow the advice of the experts working for state agencies such as FHM. This gives FHM's state epidemiologist, Anders Tegnell, a special position (Cederblad 2020) enjoying immense public and state support in Sweden.

Unlike Finland, Sweden did not implement a state of emergency to deal with the pandemic. The basic principles of Swedish democracy are manifested in the Instrument of Government (one of the fundamental laws that make up the constitution) and this makes no specific reference to a 'state of emergency'. Workplaces, primary schools, shops and restaurants have generally remained open. FHM issued strong recommendations for Swedish citizens, such as to maintain social distance and hand hygiene, work and study from home if possible, abstain from unnecessary domestic travel, avoid going to work with symptoms and avoid visiting people at risk. Shops and stores were advised to limit the number of visitors. Upper secondary schools, higher institutions of education and adult learning were recommended to carry out distance learning.

In March 2020, at the request of FHM, the government made various revised decisions to restrict public gatherings. It was not until 18 December 2020 that the Swedish government gave directives to use face masks in public transportation, starting on 7 January 2021 (Regeringskansliet 2020a). This policy came relatively late compared to Finland and other neighbouring countries (Our World in Data 2021). The Swedish approach to coronavirus risk management relied more on voluntary cooperation from citizens than on mandatory regulations imposed by the governments (Fund and Hay 2020; Pierre 2020; Strang 2020). Critics, however, believe that the weak government response was planned to embark on a de facto herd immunity approach, allowing community transmission to occur relatively unchecked (Claeson and Hanson 2020). No mandatory measures were taken to limit crowds on public transport, in shopping malls or in other crowded places, while a limit of 50 people was recommended for gatherings as of 29 March 2020 (Regeringskansliet 2020b). These measures were based on hygiene and social distancing. Most businesses, schools and restaurants remained open even during the peak of the pandemic (DW 2020). By November 2020 Sweden had recorded 196,000 infections – ten times that of Finland – and about 6,000 deaths (Höppner 2020).

Government COVID-19 communication alongside intermediaries

Like many Western democratic countries, the Finnish and Swedish governments held frequent press conferences to maintain regular communication about the government's COVID-19 messages, including updates about the spread of the virus and government strategies to contain it. These press conferences gave each country's media frequent opportunities to question the government's decisions, statistics and messages. Representatives of each government's intermediary stakeholders often took part. The most important ones were state agencies, associations of medical professionals and news media. In the following we elaborate on these key intermediaries, comparing Finnish and Swedish situations.

State agencies

Both the Finnish and Swedish governments worked closely with their respective state agencies during the pandemic. The Finnish government mainly relied on THL, an independent expert agency working under the Ministry of Social Affairs and Health. It serves the government, municipal and provincial decision makers, the research community and the public. It was heavily involved in communicating about the pandemic alongside the Finnish government. The Swedish government mainly relied on FHM and its state epidemiologist, Tegnell, to communicate COVID-19 messages. Another state agency is the Swedish National Board of Health and Welfare (Socialstyrelsen) positioned under the Ministry of Health and Social Affairs. It is an important intermediary stakeholder providing support to the health system and social services during the Swedish COVID-19 response. It supports and coordinates crisis preparedness across the 21 Swedish regions. It too played a vital COVID-19 communication role alongside the Swedish government.

Associations of medical professionals

Key intermediary stakeholders in both countries include associations of medical professionals. This intermediary holds a high reputation among the general public and is the interface between doctors, health experts and medical staff, and the government. The Finnish Medical Association (FMA) is a professional organization representing all doctors in Finland in their common professional, social and economic interests. On four occasions in April 2020 the FMA issued press releases critical of aspects of the Finnish government's handling of the pandemic. On 2 April 2020 it demanded adequate protection for healthcare personnel. It reiterated this message on 9 April, calling for a national response to the protection of healthcare workers. A similar message was conveyed in a 20 April press statement. Interestingly, no FMA public statements after April were about COVID-19 – either critical or supportive.

Similarly, the Swedish Association of Health Professionals (SAHP) is the national trade union and professional organization for nurses, midwives, biomedical scientists and radiographers, representing 80% of the workforce in Sweden. On two occasions between February and December 2020, the SAHP made public statements somewhat critical of the Swedish government's COVID-19 management. On 3 July a press statement called for the government to stop punishing healthcare workers financially for staying home when they were ill during the pandemic. A 2 November press release called for the government and its COVID-19 stakeholders to stop blaming healthcare workers caring for the elderly for the spread of the virus.

News media

While not expected to be an ally and aligned with the government response strategy, the news media have traditionally been central in informing the public and setting an agenda on matters of high importance, such as the spread of novel infectious diseases. Thus, news media have had intermediary status between focal organizations (as sources of news information) and their own constituents (consumers of their news output) while also being stakeholders of focal organizations (see Frandsen and Johansen 2015), which in this study are the Finnish and Swedish governments.

For the most part, the Swedish media did not seem to question the government's handling of the pandemic (Orange 2020). This predominantly positive coverage indicates that the news media in Sweden were communication intermediaries aligned more or less closely with the Swedish government when disseminating the government's COVID-19 messages. However, there were instances when media representatives pushed back against the government. In March 2020, Peter Wolodarski from *Dagens Nyheter* criticised the Swedish government's management of the pandemic, stating that high-risk groups received warnings far too late about avoiding large crowd gatherings and that there were no entry restrictions on people travelling from high-risk areas (Wolodarski 2020). That same month Ewa Stenberg from *Dagens Nyheter* criticised the way that Sweden's management model was different from those of many other countries. She stated that the Swedish decentralisation of responsibility could not solve the acute shortage of protective equipment, which limited the healthcare system's ability to curb the epidemic (Stenberg 2020).

Similar to the Swedish situation, in the first few months of the Finnish government's response to the pandemic, the news media in Finland tended to be very supportive and less critical of the Finnish government's COVID-19 messages (Seuri 2020). At that time one of Finland's leading newspapers, *Helsingin Sanomat* (HS), experienced some hesitation in how it should respond to government communication about the pandemic. According to Jussi Pullinen, a member of the policy editorial office at HS, the newspaper found it difficult to locate experts willing to criticise the government's decision over closing one of its internal borders to contain the spread of the virus. Experts advised the newspaper that this was not the time for criticism. However, this opinion began to change in May when HS noticed that Finns were becoming more open to public criticism of the government (Seuri 2020). Thus media coverage of the government's handling of the pandemic began to take on more of a critical perspective.

Given this situation in which two governments adopted varying COVID-19 response strategies and involved intermediaries in their communication of COVID-19 messages, how did the public respond? In the next section, we introduce some empirical findings from a survey showing how much publics in both these countries trusted their government's capacity to manage the pandemic, their evaluation of the quality of communication disseminated by the two governments and their intermediaries, their overall perception of the severity of the situation and their compliance with preventive behaviours.

Public trust in Finnish and Swedish government and intermediaries

According to our data[1] in Finland, trust in the national government and local administrations in Finland has continued to be high even during the pandemic. Our data show that 47.7% of Finns trust their government, and specifically hold confidence in the capacity of their political leaders, with Prime Minister Sanna Marin holding 42.9% of trust, followed by the regional authorities (37.2%). While local authorities, such as municipalities, are closer to people's day-to-day businesses and concerns, they are the least trusted governmental institution, with 24.5% of the population trusting them as source of COVID-19 information.

Looking at the key intermediaries of the Finnish government strategy, one of the key players of the government, THL, received the highest trust (62.5% of those strongly agree and agree). This is not surprising, as this intermediary is the leading public authority for health and welfare in the country. But what is interesting is that its spokesperson, Professor Mika Salminen, received almost the same level of trust (47.9%) as the prime minister, which means that Finns trust a politician as much as a non-political figure, that has – we would argue – higher expertise on the disease. Media trust has remained overall stable with most Finns trusting the news information they received (31.1% of those who agree and strongly agree). A high level of trust (48.6%) was also shown in those intermediaries that are considered highly reputed, such as the Finnish associations of health professionals, which includes the Finnish Medical Association (FMA) health experts that Finns personally know also received high levels of trust (47.6%).

Concerning the perceived quality of government communications during the pandemic, 26.5% considered government communication about COVID-19 to have always been clear and sufficient, 29.6% believed that it has been scheduled at appropriate times, and 33.3% that has provided the most reliable information.

Swedes also showed high trust in their government (42.8%), albeit less than the Finns' relatively high trust in their national government. Similarly, their trust in Prime Minister Stefan Löfven (33%) was significantly lower than for the Finnish Prime Minister. Regional authorities received higher levels of trust by the population (40.1%), followed by local municipalities (28.1%).

Among the key intermediaries, Socialstyrelsen attracted 42.7% trust and FHM's spokesperson, state epidemiologist Anders Tegnell, received higher trust (53.6%). While this was overall a high level of trust in a public agency, it was much less than the Finnish counterpart. Media trust in Sweden was also lower than that of the Finnish news media, but it still captured the majority of Swedes' confidence, with almost one out of three highly trusting them (28.3%). Information provided by health experts who Swedes know personally was trusted less (25.4%) than that provided by the Swedish Associations of Health Professionals (SAHP) (45.1%). As for the perceived quality of Swedish government communications, about 28.8% considered government communication on COVID-19 to have always been clear and sufficient, 25.3% believed it has been scheduled at appropriate times and 35.1% felt it had provided the most reliable information.

The strategy of using intermediaries to communicate about COVID-19 information has been successful given that a great number of respondents in both countries expressed positive intentions to follow the government recommendations regarding preventive behaviours. Our aggregated data on people's intention to perform preventive behaviours show that 63.4% of all Finns and of all Swedes intend to act or are actually acting as recommended by the authorities. Moreover, COVID-19 communications promoted by the government and its intermediaries has helped to draw attention to the seriousness of the novel disease. 35.3% of all Finns and 34.5% of all Swedes believe that COVID-19 poses a serious personal threat and 25.7% of Finns and 45.2% of Swedes are afraid to get infected. This last finding on Sweden particularly seems to indicate a greater concern of contracting COVID-19, which can be explained by the government strategy of allowing the virus to circulate to gain herd immunity.

Discussion

Taking into consideration how these two governments managed the pandemic during the first wave of 2020 and the empirical data on public perceptions, it becomes clear that public trust at the institutional level has played an important role in the way citizens have perceived their respective governments' capacity in managing the pandemic. The high confidence placed in these governments, coupled with a high level of trust in their key intermediary stakeholders in the pandemic management planning, resulted in high levels of public compliance with government guidelines and overall clear public understanding of the severity of the pandemic. Our study does not show whether public trust in the government mediated public perception of the quality of information received or the other way around. However, it does offer some important points of reflections concerning the use of intermediary stakeholders in communicating risk and health issues.

Different forms of trust enhance the effectiveness of public compliance with government guidelines

It is clear that people have put a lot of confidence in authorities, despite the fact that some government decisions have come late or have failed to control the spread of the disease and despite the results related to the number of deaths and spread of infectious diseases. Yet, in the case of Sweden, interpersonal trust has favoured a sort of self-regulating mechanism among citizens, thus filling the government's gaps in appropriately imposing restrictive preventive measures. In the case of Finland, institutional trust played a bigger role, as most Finns followed the suggested recommendations without the need for more restrictive impositions like those that occurred in other countries. Trust in sources (Lucassen and Schraagen 2012), including key government communication intermediaries, is also an indicator that different forms of trust enhance the effectiveness of public compliance with the government's recommended guidelines.

Importance of selecting the right intermediaries during a pandemic

We make two points about strategic choice over the involvement of intermediaries. First, there are differences between intermediaries as spokespersons (close alignment with focal organization) and intermediaries as channels (distant alignment with focal organization), such as news media. Thus organizations can choose intermediaries based on this alignment factor. A news media outlet may be considered an intermediary whose alignment vacillates between corporate and government interests and the interests of their own constituents. A news media outlet in a democratic society typically is considered less aligned with focal organizations (as sources of news) and more closely aligned with its own constituents (i.e., consumers of news).

Second, the choice of relying on intermediary stakeholders who have generally a strong reputation in the country and who are considered the authority in their specific industry, such as pharmaceutical and medical associations, has paid off for these two governments' strategic management. As shown in this study, public trust in both governments' prime ministers (especially in Sweden) was lower than the public trust in their health authorities and experts and this justified these governments' involvement of these agencies and experts as intermediaries. Therefore, leaning heavily on these high trust agencies and experts as communication intermediaries makes sense. Because they are set up primarily to serve the interests of their democratic governments, suggesting that they take on an 'intermediary of the organization' status (Frandsen and Johansen 2015), these governments can make use of them as spokespersons rather than as channels of communication, which in this case they did on a regular basis throughout 2020.

So, there were intermediaries who acted as spokespersons and others as channels of government communications (i.e., news media). Their involvement was genuine and authentic rather than imposed. Particularly, the Swedish case shows that the Swedish government's intermediaries also opposed some of the government decisions and suggested different courses of actions. Thus, while they were overall aligned with the pandemic management, they also offered impending interventions (Frandsen and Johansen 2015). In a certain way this helped increase their authenticity and credibility as independent institutions among the general public.

We argue that the news media can be considered a communication intermediary for governments facing a major risk situation. Despite the media in Finland and Sweden having relatively low levels of trust compared to government health agencies and experts, governments should continue to use media as intermediaries during pandemic situations for reasons other than trust-building. Indeed, treating media as a communication channel for organizational messages is an important practice even as media trust is falling. In times of national emergency, such as during a pandemic or war, media outlets sometimes adopt a collaborative role (Christians *et al.* 2009); in this role they work closely with the government as a public service to ensure news reports reflect government narratives. We argue that this is what took place among Finnish and Swedish media outlets during 2020 when covering government COVID-19 messages. Thus, discarding their institutional tendency for independence from external influences, in the name of a shared effort to restore public health they took on a supportive intermediary role, which Frandsen and Johansen (2015) refer to as a 'shared intermediary' status, recognising allegiance to both the public (news consumers) and the government (as a primary news source).

One of the most important advantages of strategically engaging different types of intermediaries to act as spokespersons of a government's risk management plan is that these intermediaries can assist governments in influencing people's attitudes and behaviours during health crises. In other words, during pandemics, intermediaries' involvement in risk communications can lead to megaphoning effects in the diffusion of persuasive information on the novel infectious disease.

Conclusions

In this chapter we examined Finnish and Swedish governments' response strategies and the role of intermediary stakeholders in the management of the COVID-19 pandemic during the period March–November 2020. We argue that the two selected cases are particularly interesting because, despite similarities in the Nordic models of welfare, the general public's trust towards authorities, and the way they used intermediaries as communication stakeholders to build public trust in these governments during the pandemic, these respective governments chose very different risk management approaches, but obtained similar public perceptions in terms of compliance with government recommendations, perceived severity of the disease and overall evaluation of

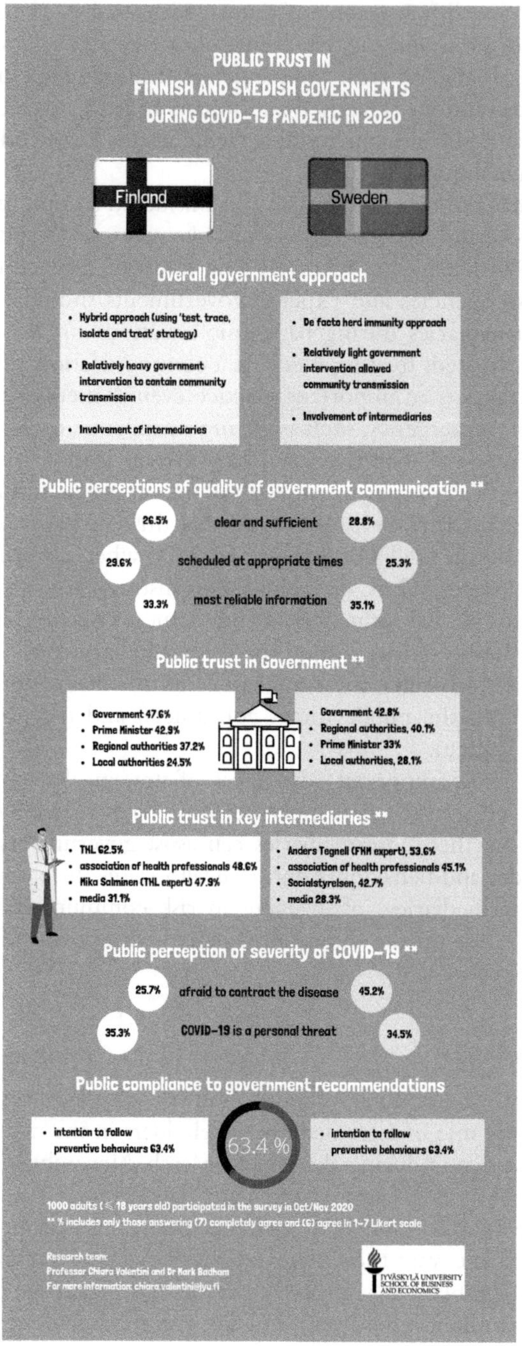

Infographic 10.1 Public trust in Finnish and Swedish governments during the COVID-19 pandemic in 2020

the pandemic's principal sources of information. Since the Swedish management response was less effective in reducing the number of deaths and diffusion of infection in the country, one would have expected lower levels of public trust in the government's capacity. However, this was not the case. In part, we argue this is due to the general high level of institutional trust that citizens in Sweden hold in their authorities. Furthermore, the strategic involvement of intermediary stakeholders as communicators during the pandemic paid off. To aid governments in communicating to build and manage public trust during a major public health crisis, strategic communicators are able to make use of a range of intermediary stakeholders, from their own government agencies and health experts, to medical associations and even news outlets. These can be used to varying degrees to communicatively mediate between the government and the public.

Strategic communicators working for governments build public trust by aligning with trusted intermediaries such as scientific experts (Balog-Way and McComas 2020). Aligning with expert intermediaries like these 'publicly signals a strategic affirmation of trust' between elected political leaders, one of the least trusted professions, and scientists, one of the most trusted professions (Balog-Way and McComas 2020, p. 840). Government communicators can involve intermediaries to generate megaphoning effects and increase the influence of communicated messages in changing people's risk behaviors. In doing so, their mediating role between the different stakeholders (subjects of trust) and the government handling a health crisis (object of trust) can be boosted (Bentele 1994). The reputation of intermediaries, tied to the public's trust in them as an important source of information, is paramount to the effect of their mediating role during a health crisis.

Limitations and future research

This study is based on the analysis of publicly available documents from the Finnish and Swedish governments, selected national and international news articles and enriched with some of the data collected through a survey in fall 2020. There are limits on what this data can show and further studies could, for instance, investigate the role of intermediaries by examining each intermediary's strategic communications, for example by analysing their framing strategies and how the crisis frames travel from one source to another or change based on what other intermediaries do and say. The role of news media as a shared intermediary could also be studied qualitatively to shed more light on the factors influencing the editorial decisions to follow different types of media roles. Another important research avenue is related to the different levels of trust: societal, interpersonal, institutional and mediated (i.e., via news media). Further investigation could look at the possible causal relationships between these different types of trust and their role in public perceptions and compliance with government recommendations.

Note

1 We employed Reichheld's (2003) approach and reported aggregated results of top favourable percentages, meaning only those who responded within the range of agree (6) to strongly agree (7) in a Likert scale ranging 1–7 points.

Bibliography

Andreasson, U. (2017). *Trust – The Nordic Gold*. Copenhagen: Nordic Council of Ministers.

Ahrne, G., and Brunsson, N. (2008). *Meta-organizations*. Cheltenham: Edward Elgar Publishing.

Balog-Way, D.H.P., and McComas, K.A. (2020). COVID-19: Reflections on trust, tradeoffs, and preparedness. *Journal of Risk Research*, 23(7/8), pp. 838–848. doi:10.1080/13669877.2020.1758192

Bargain, O., and Aminjonov, U. (2020). Trust and compliance to public health policies in times of COVID-19. *IZA Discussion Paper No. 13205, Institute of Labor Economics* (IZA). Available from: https://ideas.repec.org/p/iza/izadps/dp13205.html [Accessed 26 April 2021].

Battiston, P., Kashyap, R., and Rotondi, V. (2021). Reliance on scientists and experts during an epidemic: Evidence from the COVID-19 outbreak in Italy. *SSM – Population Health*, 13, 100721. doi:10.1016/j.ssmph.2020.100721

Bentele, G. (1994). ÖffentlichesVertrauen – normative und sozialeGrundlagefur public relations. In W. Armbrecht and U. Zabel, eds. *Normative Aspekte der Public Relations. GrunlegendeFragen und Perspektiven*. Eine Einfuhrung, Westdeutscher Verlag, Opladen, pp. 131–158.

Bickham, S.B., and Francis, D.B. (2021, April). The public's perceptions of government officials' communication in the wake of the COVID-19 pandemic. *Journal of Creative Communications*, 16(2), pp. 190–202. doi:10.1177/09732586211003856

Blair, R.A., Morse, B.S., and Tsai, L.L. (2017). Public health and public trust: Survey evidence from the ebola virus disease epidemic in Liberia. *Social Science & Medicine*, 172, pp. 89–97. doi:10.1016/j.socscimed.2016.11.016

Bronfman, N.C., Vázquez, E.L., and Dorantes, G. (2009). An empirical study for the direct and indirect links between trust in regulatory institutions and acceptability of hazards. *Safety Science*, 47(5), pp. 686–692. doi:10.1016/j.ssci.2008.09.006

Cairns, G., de Andrade, M., and MacDonald, L. (2013). Reputation, relationships, risk communication, and the role of trust in the prevention and control of communicable disease: A Review. *Journal of Health Communication*, 18(12), pp. 1550–1565. doi:10.1080/10810730.2013.840696

Cederblad, J. (2020, March 28). We epidemiologists have been given a little too much power. *Göteborgs-Posten*. Available from: www.gp.se/nyheter/sverige/vi-epidemiologer-har-f%C3%A5tt-lite-f%C3%B6r-stor-makt-1.26081990 [Accessed 26 April 2021].

Christians, C.G., Glasser, T.L., McQuail, D., Nordenstreng, K., and White, R.A. (2009). *Normative theories of the media: Journalism in democratic societies*. Champaign, IL: University of Illinois Press.

Claeson, M., and Hanson, S. (2020). COVID-10 and the Swedish enigma. *The Lancet*, 397(10271), pp. 259–261. doi:10.1016/S0140-6736(20)32750-1

Cvetkovich, G. (1999). The attribution of social trust. In G. Cvetkovich and R. Lofstedt, eds. *Social trust and the management of risk*. London: Earthscan, pp. 53–61.

Deephouse, D.L., and Heugens, P.P.M.A.R. (2009). Linking social issues to organizational impact: The role of infomediaries and the infomediary process. *Journal of Business Ethics*, 86(4), pp. 541–553. doi:10.1007/s10551-008-9864-3

DW (2020, June 1). Sweden launches probe into handling of pandemic. *DW*. Available from: www.dw.com/en/sweden-launches-probe-into-handling-of-pandemic/a-53651574 [Accessed 26 April 2021].

Esaiasson, P., Sohlberg, J., Ghersetti M., and Johansson, B. (2020). How the Coronavirus crisis affects citizen trust in institutions and in unknown others: Evidence from 'the Swedish experiment'. *European Journal of Political Research*, 60(3), pp. 748–760. doi:10.1111/1475-6765.12419

Euractiv (2020, November 4). *Finland: Europe's quiet success in COVID-19 fight*. Available from: www.euractiv.com/section/languages-culture/news/finland-europes-quiet-success-in-COVID-19-fight/ [Accessed 22 April 2021].

Fancourt, D., Steptoe, A., and Wright, L. (2020). The cummings effect: Politics, trust, and behaviours during the COVID-19 pandemic. *The Lancet*, 396(10249), pp. 464–465. doi:10.1016/s0140-6736(20)31690-1

Flynn, J., Burns, W., Mertz, C.K., and Slovic, P. (1992). Trust as a determinant of opposition to a high-level radioactive waste repository: Analysis of a structural model. *Risk Analysis*, 12(3), pp. 417–429.

Fombrun, C. (1996). *Reputation: Realizing value from the corporate image*. Boston: Harvard Business School Press.

Frandsen, F., and Johansen, W. (2015). Organizations, stakeholders, and intermediaries: Towards a general theory. *International Journal of Strategic Communication*, 9(4), pp. 253–271.

Fund, J., and Hay, J. (2020). Has Sweden found the right solution to the Coronavirus? Available from: www.nationalreview.com/2020/04/coronavirus-response-sweden-avoids-isolation-economic-ruin/amp/?__twitter_impression=true&fbclid=IwAR1yIA0sHQoJwWkF8o2TYH9JFkFdQpyKc4HgRySy0zUkfhHvngr_e0cJqVE [Accessed 22 April 2021].

Gilles, I., Bangerter, A., Clémence, A., Green, E. Krings, F., Staerklé, C., and Wagner-Egger, P. (2011). Trust in medical organizations predicts pandemic (H1N1) 2009 vaccination behavior and perceived efficacy of protection measures in the Swiss public. *European Journal of Epidemiology*, 26, pp. 203–210. doi:10.1007/s10654-011-9577-2

Government Communications Department, Ministry of Social Affairs and Health, Finnish Government (2020, May 6). *Government resolution on a plan for a hybrid strategy to manage the COVID-19 crisis* (Press release). Available from: https://stm.fi/-/10616/valtioneuvoston-periaatepaatos-suunnitelmasta-koronakriisin-hallinnan-hybridistrategiaksi?languageId=en_US [Accessed 26 April 2021].

Han, Z., Liu, J., and Wu, W.N. (2020). Trust and confidence in authorities, responsibility attribution, and natural hazards risk perception. *Risks Hazards Crisis Public Policy*, pp. 1–17.

Hirsch, P.M. (1977). Occupational, organizational and institutional models in mass communication. In P. Hirsch, P.V. Miller, and F.G. Kline, eds. *Strategies for communication research*. Beverly Hills, CA: Sage, pp. 13–42.

Höppner, S. (2020, November 19). Why is Finland coping so well with the Coronavirus crisis? *DW*. Available from: www.dw.com/en/coronavirus-finland-sweden-role-model/a-55664117 [Accessed 13 May 2021].

Levi, M., and Stoker, L. (2000). Political trust and trustworthiness. *Annual Review of Political Science*, 3(1), pp. 475–507. doi:10.1146/annurev.polisci.3.1.475

The Local (2021, February 1). How we got here: The defining events of the Coronavirus pandemic in Sweden. *The Local*. Available from: www.thelocal.se/20210201/timeline-heres-what-happened-in-the-year-since-swedens-first-coronavirus-case/ [Accessed 22 April 2021].

Lucassen, T., and Schraagen, J.M. (2012). Propensity to trust and the influence of source and medium cues in credibility evaluation. *Journal of Information Science*, 38(6), pp. 566–577. doi:10.1177/0165551512459921

Luoma-aho, V. (2015). Understanding stakeholder engagement: Faith-holders, hateholders and fakeholders. *Research Journal of the Insitute for Public Relations*, 2(1). Available from: https://instituteforpr.org/understanding-stakeholder-engagement-faith-holders-hateholders-fakeholders/ [Accessed 7 May 2021].

Ministry of Social Affairs and Health (2020, May 6). *Government resolution on a plan for a hybrid strategy to manage the COVID-19 crisis*. Available from: https://stm.fi/-/10616/valtioneuvoston-periaatepaatos-suunnitelmasta-koronakriisin-hallinnan-hybridistrategiaksi?languageId=en_US [Accessed 7 May 2021].

Ministry of Social Affairs and Health (2021, March 23). *Preparedness for the COVID-19 disease*. Available from: https://stm.fi/en/coronavirus-preparedness [Accessed 7 May 2021].

Olsen, A.L., and Hjorth, F. (2020). Willingness to Distance in the COVID-19 Pandemic. Retreived from https://osf.io/xpwg2/.

Orange, R. (2020, June 5). Sweden starts to doubt its outlier Coronavirus strategy. *DW*. Available from: www.dw.com/en/sweden-starts-to-doubt-its-outlier-coronavirus-strategy/a-53696565 [Accessed 26 April 2021].

Our World in Data (2021, April 24). *Face covering policies during the COVID-19 pandemic*. Available from: https://ourworldindata.org/grapher/face-covering-policies-COVID?time=2021-04-24&region=Europe [Accessed 26 April 2021].

Pierre, J. (2020). Nudges against pandemics: Sweden's COVID-19 containment strategy in perspective. *Policy and Society*, 39(3), pp. 478–493. doi:10.1080/14494035.2020.1783787

Quinn, S.C., Parmer, J., Freimuth, V.S., Hilyard, K.M., Musa, D., and Kim K.H. (2013). Exploring communication, trust in government, and vaccination intention later in the 2009 H1N1 pandemic: Results of a national survey. *Biosecurity and Bioterrorism: Biodefense Strategy, Practice, and Science*, 11(2), pp. 96–106. doi:10.1089/bsp.2012.0048

Regeringskansliet (2020a, December 18). *Additional national restrictions to stop the spread of infection* (Press release). *Regeringskansliet*. Available from: www.regeringen.se/artiklar/2020/12/ytterligare-nationella-restriktioner-for-att-hejda-smittspridning/ [Accessed 26 April 2021].

Regeringskansliet (2020b, March 27). *Förbud mot allmänna sammankomster eller offentliga tillställningar med fler än 50 deltagare* [trans. 'Prohibition of public gatherings or public events with more than 50 participants']. *Regeringskansliet*. Available from: www.regeringen.se/artiklar/2020/03/forbud-mot-allmanna-sammankomster-eller-offentliga-tillstallningar-med-fler-an-50-deltagare/ [Accessed 22 April 2021].

Reichheld, F.F. (2003). The one number you need to grow. *Harvard Business Review*, 81(12), pp. 46–54.

Rindova, V.P., and Fombrun, C.J. (1999). Constructing competitive advantage: The role of firm-constituent interactions. *Strategic Management Journal*, 20(8), pp. 691–710. Available from: www.jstor.org/stable/3094244

Robinson, R.V., and Jackson, E.F. (2001). Is trust in others declining in America? An age – period – cohort analysis. *Social Science Research*, 30(1), pp. 117–145. doi:10.1006/ssre.2000.0692

Seuri, V. (2020, May 16). Political scientist on border mess: Government makes people believe border is closed – media even added rounds to order. *YLE*. Available from: https://yle.fi/uutiset/3-11355420 [Accessed 14 May 2021].

Shoemaker, P.J., and Reese, S.D. (1996). *Mediating the message: Theories of influences on mass media content*. New York: Longman.

Siegrist, M., and Cvetkovich, G.T. (2000). Perception of hazards: The role of social trust and knowledge. *Risk Analysis*, 20(5), pp. 713–719. doi:10.1111/0272-4332.205064

Siegrist, M., Cvetkovich, G., and Roth, C. (2000). Salient value similarity, social trust, and risk/benefit perception. *Risk Analysis*, 20(3), pp. 353–362. doi:10.1111/0272-4332.203034

Siegrist, M., and Zingg, A. (2014). The role of public trust during pandemics: Implications for crisis communication. *European Psychologist*, 19(1), pp. 23–32. doi:10.1027/1016-9040/a000169

Slovic, P. (1993). Perceived risk, trust, and democracy. *Risk Analysis*, 13(6), pp. 673–682. doi:10.1111/j.1539-6924.1993.tb01329.x

Stenberg, E. (2020, March 15). Ewa Stenberg: Den svenska krisberedskapen skakar i grunden. *Dagens Nyheter*. Available from: www.dn.se/nyheter/sverige/ewa-stenberg-pandemin-kommer-andra-krisberedskapens-grundbultar/ [Accessed 26 April 2021].

Strang, J. (2020). *Why do the Nordic countries react differently to the COVID-19 crisis?* Available from: https://nordics.info/show/artikel/the-nordic-countries-react-differently-to-the-COVID-19-crisis/?fbclid=IwAR382GJQy-3krMGyDxVLDKVxgqX5yG9d3riaw5CF2UKejJjXLchJLMbc414 [Accessed 22 April 2021].

Taylor, M., Raphael, B., Barr, M., Agho, K., Stevens, G., and Jorm, L. (2009). Public health measures during an anticipated influenza pandemic: Factors influencing willingness to comply. *Risk Management and Healthcare Policy*, 9(2), pp. 9–20. doi:10.2147/RMHP.S4810

THL (2020, August 13). *THL suosittaa kasvomaskin käyttöä toisten suojaamiseksi – käsienpesu ja turvavälit ovat tärkeimmät keinot ehkäistä koronatartuntoja*. Available from: https://thl.fi/fi/-/thl-suosittaa-kasvomaskin-kayttoa-toisten-suojaamiseksi-kasienpesu-ja-turvavalit-ovat-tarkeimmat-keinot-ehkaista-koronatartuntoja [Accessed 22 April 2021].

Valentini, C. (2021). Trust research in public relations: An assessment of its conceptual, theoretical and methodological foundations. *Corporate Communications: An International Journal*, ahead of print. doi:10.1108/CCIJ-01-2020-0030.

Van Bavel, J.J., Baicker, K., Boggio, P.S., Capraro, V., Cichocka, A., Cikara, M., Crockett, M.J., Crum, A.J., Douglas, K.M., Druckman, J.N., Drury, J., Dube, O., Ellemers, N., Finkel, E. J., Fowler, J. H., Gelfand, M., Han, S., Haslam, S.A., Jetten, J.,Kitayama, S., Mobbs, D., Napper, L.E., Packer, D.J., Pennycook, G., Peters, E., Petty, R.E., Rand, D.G., Reicher, S.D., Schnall, S., Shariff, A., Skitka, L.J., Smith, S.S., Sunstein, C.R., Tabri, N., Tucker, J.A., van der Linden, S., van Lange, P., Weeden, K.A., Wohl, M.J., Zaki, J., Zion, S.R., and Willer R. (2020). Using social and behavioural science to support COVID-19 Pandemic Response. *Nature Human Behaviour*. Advance online publication. doi:10.31234/osf.io/y38m9

van der Weerd, W., Baicker, K., Boggio, P.S., Capraro, V., Cichocka, A., Cikara, A., Crockett, M.J., Crum, A.J., Douglas, K.M., Druckman, J.N., Drury, J., Dube, O., Ellemers, N., Finkel, E.J., Fowler, J.H., Gelfand, M., Han, S., Haslam, S.A., Jetten, J., Kitayama, S., Mobbs, D., Napper, L.E., Packer, D.J., Pennycook, G., Peters, E., Petty, R.E., Rand, D.G., Reicher, S.D., Schnall, S., Shariff, A., Skitka, L.J., Smith, S.S., Sunstein, C.R.,Tabri, N., Tucker, J.A., der Linden, S.V., Lange, P.V., Weeden, K.A., Wohl, M.J., Zaki, J., Zion S.R., and Willer, R. (2011). Monitoring the level of government trust, risk perception and intention of the general public to adopt protective measures during the influenza A (H1N1) pandemic in the Netherlands. *BMC Public Health*, 11(575), pp. 1–12. doi:10.1186/1471-2458-11-575

Vinck, P., Pham, P.N., Bindu, K.K., Bedford, J., and Nilles, E.J. (2019). Institutional trust and misinformation in the response to the 2018–19 Ebola outbreak in North Kivu, DR Congo: A population-based survey. *The Lancet Infectious Diseases*, 19(5), pp. 529–536. doi:10.1016/S1473-3099(19)30063-5

Wolodarski, P. (2020, March 13). Peter Wolodarski: Shut down Sweden to protect Sweden. *Dagens Nyheter*. Available from: www.dn.se/ledare/peter-wolodarski-stang-ned-sverige-for-att-skydda-sverige/ [Accessed 26 April 2021].

Yle (2021, January 29). One year since Finland's first confirmed COVID-19 case. *YLE*. Available from: https://yle.fi/news/3-12240838 [Accessed 22 April 2021].

11 Experiencing COVID-19 in Denmark, Norway and Sweden

The role of the Nordic Model

Øyvind Ihlen, Bengt Johansson and Mark Blach-Ørsten

Introduction

Society needs trust between citizens as well as some level of trust in its authorities. Such trust is put to the test in a crisis like COVID-19. This chapter looks at three similar so-called high-trust societies – the Scandinavian countries of Denmark, Norway and Sweden – and the ways strategic communication has been used in these countries during the pandemic. What makes a comparison of these countries particularly compelling is that Sweden famously chose a different strategy than most other nations. As of 2 July 2021, the death toll related to COVID-19 was 14,630 in Sweden (population 10.2 million), compared to 2,535 in Denmark (population of 5.8 million) and 794 in Norway (population of 5.5 million) (European Centre for Disease Prevention and Control 2021).

Despite these differences, surveys of trust in the authorities have shown remarkably high figures in all three countries, particularly during the early phases. During the later phases, trust had declined somewhat, particularly in Sweden. The "rally around the flag" effect has been mentioned as one explanation for the public reaction during the initial phase (Johansson and Vigsø 2021; Esaiasson *et al.* 2020). This chapter focusses on how Scandinavian public health authorities have communicated during COVID-19, particularly exploring the role of what has been called *the Nordic model*. The Nordic model is a particular brand of economic and social policies, as well as cultural practices, often linked to high level performance on economic and social indicators (e.g., Hilson 2008; Ervasti *et al.* 2008). The relationship with societal trust has been pinpointed by several authors (e.g., Andreasson 2017). Thus, we argue that the Nordic model should be seen in relation to the high levels of trust both before and during the pandemic; something also maintained by the public Norwegian Corona Commission (NOU 2021). In general, trust serves as a reservoir for strategic crisis communication (Earle 2010; Lee 2009; Siegrist and Zingg 2014) and has increasingly been placed in focus for crisis communication research (e.g., Liu and Mehta 2020; Offerdal *et al.* in press; Johansson *et al.* in press).

We start by giving an overview of the COVID-19 experience and some survey figures from the three countries. Then we provide a short overview of the Nordic model before we pinpoint some of the crucial principles used in

DOI: 10.4324/9781003184669-17

the Nordic crisis communication during the pandemic. Finally, we see these aspects in relation to each other and spell out some implications for future pandemics.

Experiencing COVID-19

The first instances of COVID-19 in Scandinavia were reported on 31 January 2020, in Sweden, 26 February 2020, in Norway, and 27 February 2020, in Denmark. On 11 March 2020, the Danish government chose to shut down the country, with Norway following suit the next day. Strict measures were introduced, such as closing down many shops, schools and leisure activities. Sweden, on the other hand, chose a different strategy. In the following, the situation in each country is described.

Sweden: The Swedish strategy to manage the COVID-19 pandemic caught international attention (Andersson and Aylott 2020; Johansson and Vigsø 2021; Pierre 2020). The declared strategy was to meet the crisis with recommendations instead of regulations and trusting citizens' sense of responsibility. To keep primary and secondary schools, restaurants, shops and malls open and rely on citizens' sound judgement was in the beginning of the pandemic seen by some as an example to follow. Mainly, however, it was perceived as a dangerous experiment, particularly among the Nordic neighbours (Johansson and Vigsø 2021; Pierre 2020; Claeson and Hanson 2021).

To understand the Swedish choice, we need to consider both governance and path dependency (Pierre 2020; Andersson and Aylott 2020). First, the government decided to follow the same protocol as for previous crises, which meant to rely on their autonomous expert public authorities. From this perspective, it did not appear strange to give the Public Health Agency (PHA) a leading role in the effort to mitigate COVID-19. Second, the PHA also followed the protocol for how to mitigate similar infections – tracing the spread and breaking chains of infection. However, when the disease was considered to have reached community spread (11 March), the strategy changed – as planned – to containing the spread of the virus to avoid overloading hospitals with patients ('flattening the curve'). COVID-19 was at the time perceived as a mortal threat to high-risk groups (the elderly and those with underlying illnesses), and it was believed that a lockdown would cause more severe problems for the whole population. Another important prerequisite for choice of strategy was the limited legal possibilities. Until January 2021, when a new law was passed, Sweden could not legally restrict and close down society.

While some voiced criticism early on, Sweden experienced a strong rally-around-the-flag effect, with a spike in support for the ruling Social Democratic Party and public health authorities (see Figures 11.1 and 11.2) (Esaiasson *et al.* 2020). This support declined as the death toll raised and more criticism became visible, stemming from the political opposition, external audits and investigative media reporting (Johansson *et al.* in press; Ghersetti 2021). A main focus of the criticism has been the failure to protect the elderly. Of COVID-19-related

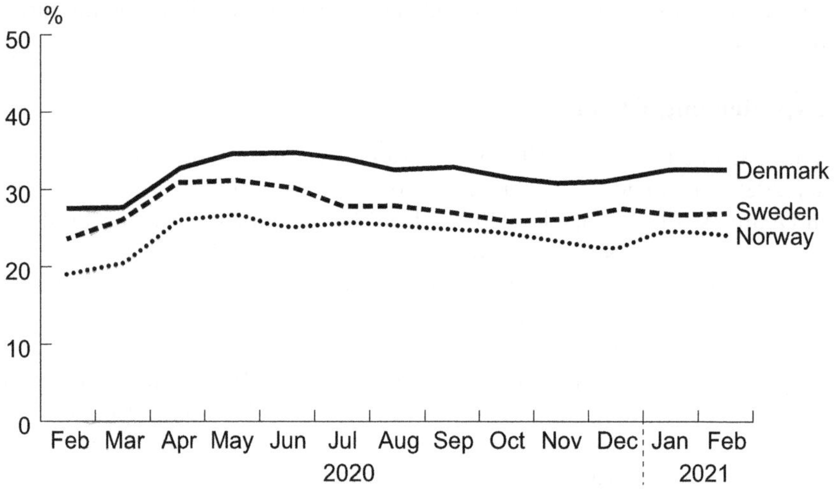

Figure 11.1 Support for leading government party

Sources: Berlingske (2021), Poll of polls (2021), Datastory (2021)

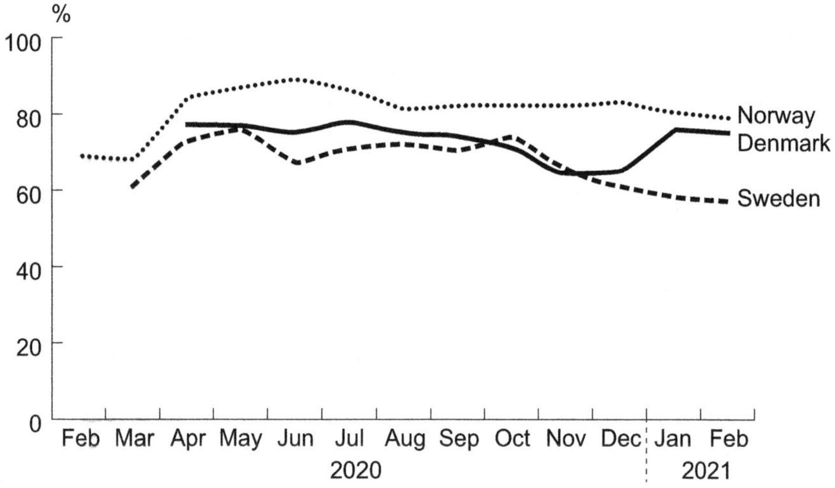

Figure 11.2 Evaluation and trust

Sources: HOPE Project (2021), The Norwegian Directorate of Health – Koronatracker (internal document), NOVUS (2021), Kantar/Sifo (2021)

deaths, 92% were in persons over 70 years of age (SOU 2020, p. 80). In June 2020, the government decided to appoint an evaluation commission looking into this (SOU 2020, p. 80). Structural shortcomings in the healthcare system, such as fragmented organization, privatisation and poor working conditions, as well as lack of sufficient competence among the staff, were pointed out. Measures were introduced too late and were somewhat insufficient. This included limited testing capacity and bans to visit care homes (SOU 2020, p. 80). Over time, the Swedish strategy changed to be more like the strategy of other countries. Face masks were now recommended in crowded public settings and on public transportation, strict limitations of public gatherings were implemented and bars and restaurants were partially closed for periods of time.

With higher death tolls compared to Denmark and Norway, one could assume a steep decline in support for those responsible for managing the crisis. This is partly true, as the support for the ruling Social Democrats has declined. Still, the polls showed higher numbers in the spring of 2021 compared with the numbers before the pandemic. The support for the PHA has also declined, but it is still high. Results indicate both a higher general trust in government authorities and interpersonal trust among citizens compared with the situation before COVID-19 (Esaiasson *et al.* 2021; Kantar/Sifo 2020/2021). In terms of economic consequences, the pandemic resulted in a GNP decline of 2.8 (Statistics Sweden 2021, February 2) and unemployment increased from 6.8% to 8.3% in 2020 (Statistics Sweden 2021, March 25).

Denmark: In Denmark, the various lockdowns have been particularly hard on children, young people and the elderly, who have been isolated or have had their access to kindergartens, schools, universities or outside visitors restricted during most of 2020 and also off and on during 2021. As mentioned, the death toll has been lower than in many other countries, with most deaths occurring in the oldest part of the population, those over 80 years of age. The economic consequences, which at the beginning of the pandemic were projected to be very severe, have turned out to be less so. Thus, the Danish GNP fell just 2.7% (Danmarks Statistik 2021, March 31), and all in all, unemployment rose just one point, to 4.6% (Ohlsson *et al.* 2021).

In the midst of the pandemic, the Danish Parliament commissioned a report from an expert group on how the Danish government and health authorities had handled the pandemic so far. The report was published on 29 January 2021, and concludes that both the government and the health authorities all in all did a good job in guiding the Danish society through an unprecedented health crisis (Folketinget 2021). Still, the report also describes a conflict between the government, especially the Office of the Prime Minister, and the health authorities. While the health authorities at the beginning of the pandemic hesitated to engage, the government and the Prime Minister wanted a stronger, proactive strategy, with more testing. The differences in strategies led to behind-the-scenes conflicts and to communication from the Prime Minister stating that different actions, such as imposing lockdowns, were taken due to advice from 'authorities', when in fact it was mostly a political decision (Folketinget 2021). Despite this critique and a continuing public debate focussing on the arguments for and against lockdowns, the public trust in government, health authorities and politicians has almost continuously been high (see Figures 11.2 and 11.3). However, as of late, the positive evaluation has dropped, indicating a shift in the population's response to the government policy (HOPE Project 2021).

Norway: As mentioned, Norway reacted to the COVID-19 pandemic by introducing lockdown periods and strict measures, closing restaurants and bars, limiting private visits, and so forth. Face masks became recommended on public transportation and in crowded places. As in many other countries, Norway has also felt the adverse effects, not least for children, young people and precarious groups. The number of unemployed has almost doubled. The immigrant population from non-Western countries experienced disproportionally high levels of hospitalisation and mortality during the COVID-19 pandemic (Indseth *et al.* 2021). Still, Norway has enjoyed relative success in the handling of COVID-19. The death toll is comparatively low, many have survived after intensive care and the economic consequences have not been as severe as in many other countries (Christensen and Laegreid 2020a; Ursin *et al.* 2020; NOU 2021). The nation has been able to mitigate some of the social concerns and some of the impact on the economy due to its Sovereign Wealth Fund (Ursin *et al.* 2020). Mainland GDP fell by 2.5% in 2020 (Norway 2021, February 12).

The mentioned Corona Commission chastised the government for its lack of preparedness but also concluded that 'the Norwegian authorities have handled the COVID-19 pandemic well' (NOU 2021). The report also highlighted how this success hinged on public cooperation and support made possible by 'distinctive features of Norwegian society that we believe make it resilient' (p. 22). The high level of trust was explicitly tied to the Nordic model, which also facilitated compliance with advice and regulations. For instance, it was pointed out that the welfare schemes provided full sick pay, allowing employees to stay home when sick. The tripartite cooperation has laid the ground for trust among the work life organizations. During the pandemic, regular meetings have provided arenas for discussions of the need for and consequences of measures (NOU 2021).

The levels of trust have been high throughout most of the pandemic (see Figures 11.1 and 11.2). Early February 2020, the Norwegian Directorate of Health started weekly national surveys asking, 'To what extent to you trust the public health authorities' handling of the corona virus'? Although the trust results took a dive that month, they climbed after the lockdown. Throughout the rest of 2020 and the first months of 2021, an average of 83% expressed high and very high trust. During the early phase of the pandemic, other surveys showed high levels of trust in the authorities' ability to manage the outbreak, as well as high levels of compliance (Zickfeld *et al.* 2020; Helsingen *et al.* 2020). One of these surveys also indicated an even stronger effect in Sweden (Helsingen *et al.* 2020).

In 2021, however, a more complicated picture emerged. In March 2021, 65%expressed trust in the information given by the government and 67% in the information given by the public health authorities (Norwegian Corona Monitor 2021). Like the Corona Commission, academic publications have also pinpointed trust as a major reason for these results. One study, for instance, highlighted factors such as 'competent politicians, a high-trust society with a reliable and professional bureaucracy, a strong state, a good economic situation, a big welfare state, and low population density' (Christensen and Laegreid 2020a). In other words, the study pointed to the importance of the Nordic model.

The Nordic model

The Nordic countries perform well on a number of economic and social indicators, which has led to debate and research seeking to identify what has been called the Nordic model (Hilson 2008; Skogerbø *et al.* 2021; Bengtsson *et al.* 2014; Ervasti *et al.* 2008). Of the Nordic countries, the trio of Denmark, Norway and Sweden have been described as social-democratic welfare regimes with long democratic traditions (Esping-Andersen 1990). Three main components have been cited (see Figure 11.3): a particular economic policy with an active state, tax revenues and open trade; organised work life coordinating wage

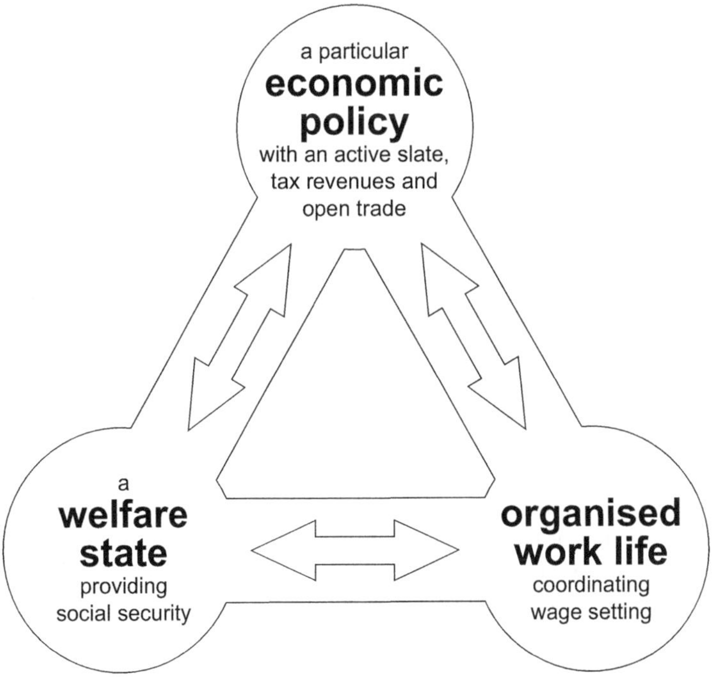

Figure 11.3 The Nordic model

Source: Adapted from Fløtten, T., and Trygstad, S. (Eds.), 2020. *Post korona – en ny fase for den nordiske modellen? [Post corona – A new phase for the Nordic model?].* Oslo, Norway: FAFO and SAMAK, (2016). *The Nordic Model for Dummies.* Oslo, Norway: The Joint Committee of the Nordic Social Democratic Labour Movement.

setting; and a welfare state providing a social security net (Fløtten and Trygstad 2020). Economically speaking, they are depicted as having 'high work effort, small wage differentials, high productivity, and a generous welfare state' (Barth *et al.* 2015). The State has a crucial role in the welfare model, which builds on principles such as universalism and equality.

In general, there has been consensus around the Nordic model (Arter 2016). Much has also been made of the corporatist tradition whereby interest groups partake in the preparation and/or implementation of public policies. This tradition has been strong in the Scandinavian countries (Christiansen *et al.* 2010). A tripartite cooperation with employers, trade unions and employer associations has been another hallmark of the Nordic model, which has been instrumental in, for instance, limiting workplace conflict (Brandal *et al.* 2013).

In Norway, for instance, the national union and the employers' federation reached an agreement in 1935 on the regulation of relations between management and employees, establishing rules for conflict resolution (Ibsen 1996). These two organizations have cooperated, attempting to strike a balance between conflicting and common interests (Kjelstadli 1998). A similar agreement was struck in Sweden in 1938 (Casparsson 1966). Comparative studies have also shown higher levels of trust between the employer and employee representatives in, for instance, Denmark and Sweden, than in the rest of Europe (Brandl 2020).

The Scandinavian countries are small, and the power distance is relatively low, with open political systems. As such, the Scandinavian countries have had relatively low levels of conflict, compared with, for instance, the UK or France, which have huge and sometimes violent strikes. The political culture has been inclusive, also described as a form of co-optation. One example is how the environmental organizations, while criticising the state, have also received public funding and membership in public committees. This has led the environmental organizations in a pragmatic and moderate direction, making the environmental movement part of the mainstream political culture (Bortne *et al.* 2002; Christensen *et al.* 2002). Historically, divergent opinions and revolutionary threats have been met with an '*open hand strategy* . . . based on democratic compromises and a policing of consent ideology' (Dahlen and Skirbekk 2021, emphasis in original). In general, there has been an emphasis on pragmatic policy making and finding consensus solutions (Lewin 1998).

Taken together, it has been argued that the way that the Scandinavian institutions work helps create social capital – a vital civil society (Rothstein 2001; Christiansen and Petersen 2001). The high levels of social capital and trust have been explained as an effect of '(a) the high degree of economic equality, (b) the low level of patronage and corruption and (c) the predominance of universal non-discriminating welfare programmes' (Rothstein and Stolle 2003).

Still, the very existence of the Nordic model has been under debate. Some argue that it is mostly a myth, driven by journalists in particular (Arter 2016), leading to an unwarranted idea of exceptionalism (Bengtsson *et al.* 2014). Some also argue that the differences between the countries have become so large over time that it is difficult to talk about a Nordic model (Calmfors 2014). Still, the levels of *trust* have been said to set the Nordic countries apart. Trust surveys, such as the ones conducted by the European Social Survey, consistently show the Nordic countries at the top (European Social Survey Round 9 Data 2018).

It is, of course, possible to discuss whether the societal traits discussed here are the sources or the consequences of societal trust. It has, however, been described as creating a positive spiral. Economic growth can lead to increased trust, which in turn promotes economic growth. Declining economic growth can have the opposite effect (Andreasson 2017). Generally, small wage differentials are thought to contribute to trust (Rothstein 2011).

Somewhat obviously, there are also other contributing factors to the high levels of trust. Homogeneity is another aspect that is frequently mentioned, which extends to ethnic and linguistic similarities (Andreasson 2017; Fukuyama 1995). Thus, the political arrangements of the Nordic model are not the sole explanation of the high levels of trust.

What is certain is that the Scandinavian countries had a good starting point in their already high levels of trust when the COVID-19 pandemic hit in 2020. For instance, a comparative study of seven European countries highlighted how the Swedish focus group informants felt 'confident that crises could be overcome if they followed the right instructions, which they expected to receive from the trustworthy authorities' (Cornia *et al.* 2016). In other words, the public authorities cannot only rely on a reservoir of established trust but have to communicate actively.

The state of play: COVID-19 communication in Scandinavia

Despite the similarities described in the section on the Nordic model, the Scandinavian countries differed in their management of the COVID-19 communication. In Sweden, during the early phases, the PHA chief epidemiologist took centre stage, with the Prime Minister taking a back seat. The situation was the opposite in Denmark, with the Prime Minister taking a leading role early on and the public health authorities following suit and being hesitant. In Norway, it was more of a mixture between the government and the public health institutions (Just *et al.* 2021, May). In the later phases, journalists revealed tensions between government bureaucrats and politicians as well as among the health bureaucrats. In the Norwegian setting, some of the disagreement was handled by explicitly pointing out that public health experts had provided a recommendation, but that the final decision was a political one, also taking into consideration other concerns. Next we provide more details about each country.

Sweden: The Swedish Prime Minister addressed the importance of solidarity in the few speeches he gave in the first year of the pandemic. However, speeches and politicians were not in the centre of crisis communication. Instead, the PHA chief epidemiologist, Anders Tegnell, personified the pandemic communication in daily press conferences at 2 p.m. (Andersson and Aylott 2020).

Tegnell predominantly used ethos-based rhetoric, emphasising the PHA's own approach to deal with the pandemic. Consequently, the communication about COVID-19 was framed more clearly by arguments based on medical – epidemiological – warrant (Bjørkdahl *et al.* 2021). Tegnell also gained status as a popular icon for his calm communication style and his steady appeal to react according to 'what we know in the scientific community'. No recommendations were issued until the PHA deemed it had solid scientific proof to back them up. This positive public image was increasingly problematised as the death tolls were rising, which resulted in less positive news media coverage and an emerging debate about the main strategy (Ghersetti 2021; Johansson and Vigsø 2021). Critics –politicians, experts and editors – have repeatedly argued for implementing more and stronger protective measures, and the recommendations have from time to time been described as contradictory and difficult to interpret (Brorström *et al.* 2021). Still, in general, citizens have been positive towards the news coverage of the pandemic and its handling by the authorities (Ghersetti and Odén 2021). The population has largely complied, by keeping social distance, washing hands and staying at home when feeling sick, even though reports have also warned about 'COVID-19 fatigue' (citizens growing tired of mask wearing and maintain social distance), especially among the young. Research has also pointed out how trust in government authorities seems to be crucial for citizens' willingness to follow recommendations (Johansson *et al.* in press).

Denmark: The commissioned expert report in Denmark described a situation where the Prime Minister was particularly engaged and kept control of the communication (Folketinget 2021). The report also stresses the differences of opinion on strategy and communication between the Office of the Prime Minister and the health authorities. In a study of the early part of the pandemic, Rubin and de Vries (2020) address this conflict through sense-making theory and argue that the root of the conflict stems from the different kinds of understanding of the pandemic that separated the lead actors. According to them, the Prime Minister relied on a sense-making frame where 'major decisions needed to be made fast to avoid an impending disaster, and where scientific evidence alone could not be trusted to reach the right policy conclusions' (p. 4). The public health authorities, however, based their judgements on a 'frame where evidence-based decision-making was still the modus operandum, and where policy recommendations were continuously updated as new scientific information became available' (Rubin and de Vries 2020).

This, they conclude, led to conflicts and unclear communication in the early parts of the pandemic. A study of the communication via press releases by the health authorities in Denmark, Norway and Sweden (Schnaider *et al.* 2021) finds several differences between the three countries. For Denmark's part, communication from the health authorities focusses on monitoring statistics, on the spread of the epidemic and on illness (p. 13). They also conclude 'that the politicians are more directly in charge of administration (of the pandemic response) in Norway and Denmark' (p. 14). They describe the Danish strategy as 'act fast and with force' (p. 15), which allows Denmark to react faster with political discission and sometimes even overrule health authorities and their expertise.

Norway: The Norwegian crisis communication during the COVID-19 pandemic has been characterised as being 'clear, timely and repeating messages and advice for actions informed by expert knowledge and delivered by credible political and administrative executives and experts' (Christensen and Laegreid 2020a). Much attention has also been directed towards the use of the meta-narrative *dugnad* – communal work that has a long cultural tradition and that 'nurtures prosocial and cooperative activities' (Simon and Mobekk 2019; Moss and Sandbakken 2021; Christensen and Laegreid 2020b). Some have also argued that the social control mechanism afforded by the *dugnad* has been successfully scaled up to the national level, contributing to high levels of trust and a well-functioning society (Wilson and Hessen 2014). It has been claimed that during the early phases of the pandemic, at least, 'the effectiveness of the government in controlling the pandemic was enhanced by successful meaning-making and communication with the public, and to the high level of citizens' trust in government' (Christensen and Laegreid 2020b). Focus group research indicates that the authorities managed to build trust by communicating uncertainty (Moss and Sandbakken 2021). The firm action of the first lockdown was favourably received, as the trust survey previously referenced also shows.

These and similar points were also repeated by the mentioned Corona Commission, which presented the overall conclusion that 'the authorities have largely succeeded in communicating to the population' (NOU 2021). In particular, the commission highlighted the positive consequence for trust of communicating uncertainties as well as being explicit about recommendations from public health experts being different from political decisions. Communication professionals in the Norwegian Institute of Public Health (NIPH) talked explicitly about the need to be transparent (Offerdal *et al.* in press). Another strategic value for the NIPH was that this also helped the institute signal its professional independence, something that was of particular importance when the government did not follow the recommendations of the institute.

Discussion and conclusion

In this chapter, we have detailed how the Scandinavian countries have fared through the COVID-19 pandemic and how the authorities have communicated. In Denmark, the narrative of 'fast and decisive action' by the government has dominated. In Norway, the government followed a similar course, but one much more in concert with the health authorities and with appeals to the people to pull together – 'join the *dugnad*' and local versions like 'Do it for [the capital] Oslo'. In Sweden, the faith in science and the autonomy of the public health authorities was striking. A narrative of 'let science prevail' characterised the first phase.

As mentioned, surveys in all three countries have shown remarkably high trust figures despite the different mitigation strategies and results, as well as the different communication strategies (see Figures 11.1 and 11.2). While the trust levels have fallen, particularly in Sweden, they still remain high. Our argument is that this must be seen in the context of how the Scandinavian countries are fundamentally high-trust societies. As mentioned, there might be several factors contributing to this, such as low levels of corruption (Rothstein and Stolle 2003) and high ethnic and linguistic similarities (Andreasson 2017; Fukuyama 1995). Here, however, we have highlighted the role of the Nordic model and how it has contributed to trust by creating equality through small wage differences, a comprehensive and universal welfare system, as well as a political culture for consensus and cooperation inside and outside work life (Fløtten and Trygstad 2020; Brandal *et al.* 2013; Barth *et al.* 2015). This has also been described as having produced high levels of social capital (Rothstein 2001). Such social capital and trust have in turn been an important factor for the ability to deal with the COVID-19 pandemic, particularly in regard to compliance. It has also fuelled the national rhetoric providing political leaders the possibility to make appeals to the tradition of solidarity (Bjørkdahl *et al.* 2021). In Denmark, references have been made to *samfunnsind* (societal spirit) – chosen 'word of the year' in 2020 (Morovati 2020, December 18) in Norway – *dugnad* (communal work), and in Sweden – '*Folkhemmet* (the people's home). Again, we argue that the success of this strategy is premised on high societal trust, which is not something that can be created in an instant or in a crisis. Rather, it is tied to larger political, economic, social and cultural traditions and structures. In short, we see the Nordic model as a contributing factor for the handling and the communication in the COVID-19 pandemic and the described outcomes.

The COVID-19 pandemic has increased existing social differences. As such, this represents a potential threat to the Nordic model and in turn to societal trust and resilience. Some researchers argue that they see cracks in the pillar of the model (Fløtten and Trygstad 2020). Increasing unemployment rates and a decline in union membership could, according to these researchers, lead to destabilisation and reduce economic growth and trust. Cooperation and coordination have been a hallmark of the Nordic model, making the Nordic countries resilient. Despite the lack of preparedness, the Nordic countries have been able to utilise societal trust to manage and communicate in the pandemic.

Bibliography

Andersson, S., and Aylott, N. (2020). Sweden and Coronavirus: Unexceptional exceptionalism. *Social Sciences*, 9(12), p. 232.

Andreasson, U. (2017). *Trust – The Nordic gold.* Copenhagen, Denmark: Nordic Council of Ministers.

Arter, D. (2016). *Scandinavian politics today*, 3 ed. Manchester: Manchester University Press.

Barth, E., Moene, K.O., and Willumsen, F. (2015). The Scandinavian model – An interpretation. *Journal of Public Economics*, 127, pp. 17–29.

Bengtsson, Å., Hansen, K.M., Harðarson, Ó.þ., Narud, H.M., and Oscarsson, H. (2014). *The Nordic voter: Myths of exceptionalism.* Colchester, UK: ECPR Press.

Berlingske (2021). *Berlingske barometer* [online]. Available from: www.berlingske.dk/barometeret2021.

Bjørkdahl, K., Kjeldsen, J.E., Villadsen, L., and Vigsø O. (2021). Argumentum ad Solidarietatem: Rhetorical Strategies of Scandinavian Political Leaders during COVID-19. In M. Lewis, E. Govender, and K. Holland, eds. *Communication Covid-19: Interdisciplinary perspectives*. London: Palgrave Macmillan.

Bortne, Ø., Selle, P., and Strømsnes, K. (2002). *Miljøvern uten grenser? [Environmental conservation without boundaries?]*. Oslo, Norway: Gyldendal.

Brandal, N., Bratberg, Ø., and Thorsen, D. (2013). *The Nordic model of social democracy*. London: Macmillan.

Brandl, B. (2020). Variations and (a) symmetries in trust between employees and employers in Europe: Some (not so) well-known stylized facts. *European Journal of Industrial Relations*, 26(3), pp. 313–329.

Brorström, B., Johansson, B., and Kastberg, G. (2021). *Godkänt, men med förbehåll: Västra Götalandsregionens hantering av coronapandemin. En utvärdering med fokus på styrning, organisation och ledning [Approved, but conditional: The handling of the Corona Pandemic in the region of Region Västra Götaland: An evaluation of handling, organisation and management]*. Gothenburg: KFI, University of Gothenburg.

Calmfors, L. (2014). How well is the Nordic model doing? Recent performance and future challenges. In T. Valkonen and V. Vihriälä, eds. *The Nordic model – Challenged but capable of reform*. Copenhagen: Nordic Council of Ministers.

Casparsson, R. (1966). *Saltsjöbadsavtalet i historisk belysning [The Saltsjöbad agreement in a historical perspective]*. Stockholm, Sweden: Tiden.

Christensen, T., *Lægreid, P., Egeberg, M., Aars, J.* (2002). *Forvaltning og politikk [Administration and politics]*. Bergen, Norway: Fagbokforlaget.

Christensen, T., and Laegreid, P. (2020a). Balancing governance capacity and legitimacy – how the Norwegian government handled the COVID-19 crisis as a high performer. *Public Administration Review*, 80(5), pp. 774–779.

Christensen, T., and Laegreid, P. (2020b). The Coronavirus crisis – crisis communication, meaning-making, and reputation management. *International Public Management Journal*, 23(5), pp. 713–729.

Christiansen, N.F., and Petersen, K. (2001). The dynamics of social solidarity: The Danish welfare state, pp. 1900–2000. *Scandinavian journal of history*, 26(3), pp. 177–196.

Christiansen, P.M., Nørgaard, A.S., Rommetvedt, H., Svensson, T., Thesen, G. and Öberg, P. (2010). Varieties of democracy: Interest groups and corporatist committees in Scandinavian policy making. *Voluntas: International Journal of Voluntary and Nonprofit Organizations*, 21(1), pp. 22–40.

Claeson, M., and Hanson, S. (2021). COVID-19 and the Swedish enigma. *The Lancet*, 397(10271), pp. 259–261.

Cornia, A., Dressel, K., and Pfeil, P. (2016). Risk cultures and dominant approaches towards disasters in seven European countries. *Journal of Risk Research*, 19(3), pp. 288–304.

Dahlen, Ø.P., and Skirbekk, H. (2021). How trust was maintained in Scandinavia through the first crisis of modernity. *Corporate Communications: An International Journal*, 26(1), pp. 23–39.

Danmarks Statistik (2021, March 31). *Stor nedgang i få erhverv bag BNP-fald i 2020 [Big decline in few professions behind GNP-fall in 2020]* [online]. Available from: www.dst.dk/da/Statistik/nyt/NytHtml?cid=35394

Datastory (2021). *Your guide to the Swedish election polls* [online]. Available from: www.datastory.org/services/poll-of-polls-sweden

Earle, T.C. (2010). Trust in risk management: A model-based review of empirical research. *Risk Analysis*, 30(4), pp. 541–574.

Ervasti, H., Fridberg, T., Hjerm, M., Ringdal, K. (2008). The Nordic model. In H. Ervasti, et al. eds. *Nordic social attitudes in a European perspective*. Cheltenham, UK: Edward Elgar Publishing, pp. 1–22.

Esaiasson, P., Sohlberg, J., Ghersetti, M., and Johansson, B. (2021). How the Coronavirus crisis affects citizen trust in institutions and in unknown others: Evidence from 'the Swedish experiment'. *European Journal of Political Research*, 60(3), pp. 748–760.

Esping-Andersen, G. (1990). *The three worlds of welfare capitalism*. London: Polity Press.

European Centre for Disease Prevention and Control (2021). *COVID-19 situation update for the EU/EEA* [online]. Available from: www.ecdc.europa.eu/en/cases-2019-ncov-eueea

European Social Survey Round 9 Data (2018). Data file edition 2.0. NSD – Norwegian for Research Data, Norway – Data Archive and distributor of ESS data for ESS.

Fløtten, T., and Trygstad, S., eds. (2020). *Post korona – en ny fase for den nordiske modellen? [Post corona – A new phase for the Nordic model?]*. Oslo, Norway: FAFO.

Folketinget (2021). *Håndteringen af covid-19 i foråret 2020 [The handling of COVID-19 in the spring of 2020]*. Copenhagen, Denmark: Folketinget.

Fukuyama, F. (1995). *Trust: The social virtues and the creation of prosperity*. New York: Free Press.

Ghersetti, M. (2021). Den största nyheten [The biggest news]. In B. Johansson and L. Truedson, eds. *Journalistik i coronas tid [Journalism in the age of Corona]*. Gothenburg, Sweden: JMG/MSB.

Ghersetti, M., and Odén, T. (2021). *Coronapandemin våren 2020: En undersökning av nyheter och opinion [The Corona Pandemic Spring 2000: An investigation of news and opinon]*. Gothenburg, Sweden: JMG/MSB.

Helsingen, L.M., Refsum, E., Gjøstein, D.K., Løberg, M., Bretthauer, M., Kalager, M., and Emilsson, L. (2020). The COVID-19 pandemic in Norway and Sweden – threats, trust, and impact on daily life: A comparative survey. *BMC Public Health*, 20(1), p. 1597.

Hilson, M. (2008). *The Nordic model: Scandinavia since 1945*. London: Reaktion Books.

HOPE Project (2021). *HOPE dashboard* [online]. Aarhus, Denmark: HOPE Project. Available from: https://hope-project.dk/dashboard/ [Accessed 20 April 2021].

Ibsen, H. (1996). *Mellom profitt og moral: Bedriftsvelferd ved A/S Freia sjokoladefabrikk, J.L. Tiedemanns Tobaksfabrik og Christiania Portland Cementfabrik A/S 1910–1970 [Between profit and moral: Worker welfare at A/S Freia sjokoladefabrikk, J.L. Tiedemanns Tobaksfabrik og Christiania Portland Cementfabrik A/S 1910–1970]*. Oslo, Norway: Tano Aschehoug.

Indseth, T., Grøsland, M., Arnesen, T., Skyrud, K., Kløvstad, H., Lamprini V., Telle, K., Kjøllesdal, A. (2021). COVID-19 among immigrants in Norway, notified infections, related hospitalizations and associated mortality: A register-based study. *Scandinavian Journal of Public Health*, 1403494820984026.

Johansson, B., Sohlberg, J., Esaiasson, P., and Ghersetti, M., in press. Why Swedes don't wear face masks. A case of blindly trusting the government. *Journal of International Crisis and Risk Communication Research*.

Johansson, B., and Vigsø, O. (2021). Sweden: Lone hero of stubborn outlier? In D. Lilleker, *et al.* eds. *Political communication and COVID-19: Governance and rhetoric in times of crisis*. London: Routledge, pp. 155–164.

Just, S.N., *Kjeldsen, J., Mølster, R., Rasmussen, J., Skogerbø, E., & Ihlen, Ø.* (2021, May). Pandemic rhetoric: COVID-19 and communication strategies in a changing media landscape in Scandinavia. *The 71st International Communication Association Conference*, Washington [online].

Kantar/Sifo, (2020/2021). *Rapporter om förtroende, oro och beteende under coronakrisen. 21 mars-15 juni: Rapport till MSB [Reports on trust, concerns and behaviour during the corona crisis. March 21-June 15: Report to MSB]*. Stockholm, Sweden: Kantar/Sifo.

Kantar/Sifo (2021). *Kantar Sifos rapport om förtroende, oro och beteende under pandemin [The report from Kantar Sifo on trust, worry and behaviour during the pandemic]* [online]. Available from: www.msb.se/sv/aktuellt/pagaende-handelser-och-insatser/msbs-arbete-med-anledning-av-coronaviruset/kantar-sifos-rapport-om-fortroende-oro-och-beteende-under-coronakrisen.

Kjelstadli, K. (1998). *Et splittet samfunn: 1905–1935*. Oslo: Aschehoug.

Lee, K. (2009). How the Hong Kong government lost the public trust in SARS: Insights for government communication in a health crisis. *Public Relations Review*, 35(1), pp. 74–76.

Lewin, L. (1998). Majoritarian and consensus democracy: The Swedish experience. *Scandinavian Political Studies*, 21(3), pp. 195–206.

Liu, B.F., and Mehta, A.M. (2020). From the periphery and toward a centralized model for trust in government risk and disaster communication. *Journal of Risk Research*, pp. 1–17.

Morovati, S. (2020, December 18). 'Samfundssind' er Årets Ord i 2020 ['Society spirit' is Word of the Year 2020]. *Journalisten*, p.

Moss, S.M., and Sandbakken, E.M. (2021). Everybody needs to do their part, so we can get this under control. Reactions to the norwegian government meta-narratives on COVID-19 Measures. *Political Psychology*, 42(5), pp. 881–898.

Norway, S. (2021, February 12). *Fastlands-BNP falt 2,5 prosent i 2020 [Mainland GNP fell by 2,5 percent in 2020]* [online]. Available from: www.ssb.no/nasjonalregnskap-og-konjunkturer/artikler-og-publikasjoner/fastlands-bnp-falt-2-5-prosent-i-2020

Norwegian Corona Monitor (2021). Tilliten til myndighetene faller [Trust in authorities in decline] [online]. *Opinion*. Available from: https://opinion.no/2021/03/tilliten-til-myndighetene-faller/

NOU (2021). *NOU 2021:6 Myndighetenes håndtering av koronapandemien [NOU 2021:6 The authorities' handling of the COVID-19 pandemic]*. Oslo, Norway.

NOVUS (2021). *Novus coronastatus* [online]. Available from: https://novus.se/novus-coronastatus/

Offerdal, T.S., Just, S.N., and Ihlen, Ø. in press. Public ethos in the pandemic rhetorical situation: Strategies for building trust in authorities' risk communication. *Journal of International Crisis and Risk Communication Research*.

Ohlsson, J., Blach-Ørsten, M., and Willig, I., eds. (2021). *Covid-19 och de nordiska nyhetsmedierna*. Gothenburg: NORDICOM.

Pierre, J. (2020). Nudges against pandemics: Sweden's COVID-19 containment strategy in perspective. *Policy and Society*, 39(3), pp. 478–493.

Poll of polls (2021). *Gjennomsnitt av nasjonale meningsmålinger om stortingsvalg [Average of national surveys of parliament elections]* [online]. Available from: www.pollofpolls.no/?cmd=Stortinget&do=visallesnitt

Rothstein, B. (2001). Social capital in the social democratic welfare state. *Politics & Society*, 29(2), pp. 207–241.

Rothstein, B. (2011). *The quality of government: Corruption, social trust, and inequality in international perspective*. Chicago, IL: University of Chicago Press.

Rothstein, B., and Stolle, D. (2003). Introduction: Social capital in scandinavia. *Scandinavian Political Studies*, 26(1), pp. 1–26.

Rubin, O., and de Vries, D.H. (2020). Diverging sensemaking frames during the initial phases of the COVID-19 outbreak in Denmark. *Policy Design and Practice*, 3(3), pp. 277–296.

Schnaider, K., Schiavetto, S., Meier, F., Wasson, B., Allsopp, B.B., and Spikol, D. (2021). Governmental response to the COVID-19 pandemic – A quantitative ethnographic comparison of public health authorities' communication in Denmark, Norway, and Sweden. ed. *Advances in Quantitative Ethnography*, 2021//2021 Cham, pp. 406–421.

Siegrist, M., and Zingg, A. (2014). The role of public trust during pandemics. *European Psychologist*, 19(1), pp. 23–32.

Simon, C., and Mobekk, H. (2019). Dugnad: A fact and a narrative of norwegian prosocial behavior. *Perspectives on Behavior Science*, 42(4), pp. 815–834.

Skogerbø, E., *Kristensen, N.N., Nord, L., and Ihlen, Ø.* (2021). Introduction: A Nordic model for political communication? In E. Skogerbø*, et al.* eds. *Power, communication, and politics in the Nordic countries.* Gothenburg: NORDICOM, pp. 13–27.

SOU, 2020:80. *The Corona commission. Elderly care during the pandemic.* Stockholm, Sweden: Ministry of Health and Social Affairs.

Statistics Sweden (2021, March 25). *Arbetslöshet i Sverige [Unemployment in Sweden]* [online]. Available from: www.scb.se/hitta-statistik/sverige-i-siffror/samhallets-ekonomi/arbetsloshet-i-sverige/

Sweden Sweden. (2021, February 2). *BNP-indikatorn: Försiktig återhämtning fjärde kvartalet* [GNP indicator: Slight recovery in fourth q]. Available from https://www.scb.se/contentassets/c63c858f7c014073bc209edda9c4daf2/the-nordics-and-covid-19.pdf

Ursin, G., Skjesol, I., and Tritter, J. (2020). The COVID-19 pandemic in Norway: The dominance of social implications in framing the policy response. *Health Policy and Technology*, 9(4), pp. 663–672.

Wilson, D.S., and Hessen, D.O. (2014). Blueprint for the global village. *Cliodynamics: The Journal of Quantitative History and Cultural Evolution*, 5(1).

Zickfeld, J.H., Schubert, T.W., Herting, A.K., Grahe, J., and Faasse, K. (2020). Correlates of health-protective behavior during the initial days of the covid-19 outbreak in Norway. *Frontiers in Psychology*, 11, 564083.

America – South

12 Strategic communication and left-wing populist governments

The paradigmatic case of crisis management due to COVID-19 in Argentina

Alejandro Álvarez-Nobell

Introduction

Do I govern well but communicate badly? COVID-19, a change of track

Edgar Morin, the outstanding complexity theoretician, defines COVID-19 as a mega-crisis, one that intertwines, feeds back on and interrelates with other political, economic, social, ecological, national and planetary crises and, although he does not explicitly mention this, communicative crises. With a touch of sarcasm about reality, he states: 'A tiny virus, which suddenly emerged in a very far away city in China, has triggered a worldwide cataclysm' (Morin 2020, p. 19). In fact, in 2020, the whole of society was at risk, perhaps never better defined than by Ulrich Beck several decades earlier: the imperceptibility of dangers, dependency with respect to knowledge, supranationalism, ecological expropriation and a step from the normal to the absurd, among other characteristics (Beck 1998, p. 13). The pandemic accelerated some processes that were foreseen by some, denied by others and bypassed or simply relativised by still others.

Riorda and Bentolila, from the viewpoint of political communication, with one foot in Latin America, but with a global perspective, have been more conclusive, with the well-known phrase and metaphor from boxing – and quoted by former world champion Mike Tyson – 'Anyone has a plan until you are punched in the face'. And they constantly revise categories, such as conflict, crisis, risk and communication, fundamentally applied to the public sector and the role of governments, where clearly the strategic management of communication during the COVID-19 pandemic has played a fundamental role in controlling the spread of the disease. Unlike conflict, which is pure strain but intrinsic to social, political and personal relationships, crises are exceptional situations. They constitute the 'end of the world', in the words of Riorda and Bentolila (2020). Crises are 'when the value system that sustains you, your power, your representation, your foresight ability, your legitimacy, ends. Technically, what sustains you, disappears' (p. 16). This is what began at the end of 2019, when a new coronavirus (SARS-CoV-2) was identified in China, called

DOI: 10.4324/9781003184669-19

COVID-19, which due to its gravity and the speed at which it spread, forced the World Health Organization (WHO) to declare a pandemic on 11 March 2020, under the International Health Regulations (IHR).

In political communication, Riorda introduced a kind of 'negative hypothesis' that the political class often uses to justify its failures: 'I govern well but communicate badly' (2008, p. 1). In fact, it has allowed him to analyse and make an issue of government communication routines, in order to distinguish, for example, crisis communication from risk communication. Accordingly, they argue, on the one hand, that risk implies alertness to a threat or potential dangers, and serves to create preventive awareness and behavioural change, in the face of anticipated damage:

> [T]here is a prior hypothetical risk, which works before a crisis takes place, to raise awareness, if it were to occur, or to try to avoid it. And another type of risk occurs once the crisis arises, which requires acting in the face of inevitable phenomena.
>
> (Riorda 2020, p. 21)

On the other hand, the crisis takes place when the risk is present and implies a recovery of at least one part of the disruptive situation, normalising that exceptionality, trying to find an order, a future forecast (Riorda and Bentolila 2020). It does not necessarily work on behaviour, but on the idea of establishing future trajectories that give certainty in an uncertain context.

Most authors of the extensive literature on crisis and communication have made their contributions from a reputation perspective (Coombs 1995; Reynolds 2002; Reynolds and Seeger 2005; Gaspar *et al.* 2014; González-Herrero and Smith 2008; Moreno-Millán 2008). Moreover, at a theoretical and conceptual level, other aspects are considered important, such as strategic communication itself (Zerfass *et al.* 2018), the management of information sources and their impact (Van-der-Meer 2018; WHO 2018), the selection of channels and media, trust building and reputation management (Xifra 2020) and the adoption of preventive recommendations attributed to behaviours (Park *et al.* 2019), among others.

In the case of COVID-19, the sudden emergence of the risk and its rapid global propagation forced governments to improvise, in the best scenarios, communication plans at all levels and to inform about the infection, preventive measures, possible treatments, the lockdown stages and de-escalation. Strict perspectives and planning regulations collapsed.

But at the same time, the exceptional situation and chaos require administrative communication or service strategies, something considered coherent in the face of citizens' increasing demand for reliable information (Castillo-Esparcia *et al.* 2020; Casero-Ripolles 2000). The dramatic progress and the severity of the impact evidenced a lack of transparency, coordination and coherence, insufficient data and a lack of clarity and empathy in many political leaders.

Generally speaking, despite the narrative and even propagandist efforts of the media, in particular, the management of the communication has been questioned by organizations (namely, Reporters Without Borders and the Inter American Press Association) and by experts in political communication (González-Harbour 2020; Moreno *et al.* 2020; Riorda 2020; Crespo and Garrido 2020, among others). In the particular case of Latin America, low levels of excellence were evidenced in the communication departments, especially at the political level, as reports on the development of the profession had already been anticipating (Álvarez Nobell *et al.* 2021; Tench *et al.* 2017). However, news consumption grew exponentially with the evolution of the outbreak (Edelman 2020; WHO 2020), which provided unprecedented empirical proof that one of the most common ways of dealing with risk, crisis and the resulting uncertainty is the active search for information (Austin *et al.* 2012; Zhao *et al.* 2018; Zhu *et al.* 2017).

In this framework, the present chapter proposes to analyse and discussthis topic in the context of empirical research carried out in Argentina during October and November 2020, in which we study the public communication strategies developed by the left-wing populist government and its impact on the population, in relation to the current health, social and economic situation. The research is part of the international project EUPRERA COM-COVID network, which aims to provide evidence from this unprecedented crisis, as well as valuable information on the ability of the authorities to communicate effectively in risk, crisis and emergency situations.

In Argentina, the first case of the disease was confirmed on 5 March 2020. One year later, there were more than 3 million confirmed cases and 70,000 deaths, according to data from the Center for Systems Science and Engineering at Johns Hopkins University. In the Bloomberg report of January 2021, Argentina was classified among the five worst countries to live in during the pandemic.

A few days after the worldwide escalation, Argentina was the first South American country to apply and maintain various measures for COVID prevention over time, aligned with the European position. 'Preventive and Mandatory Social Isolation' was the measure with the greatest social impact as of 20 March 2020. The pandemic was a disruptive event which produced high social, economic and health costs and consequently brought about even greater uncertainty. In addition, the government agreed, like Russia, to carry out vaccine trials despite a lack of clear scientific evidence.

A few months before the pandemic, a left-wing populist government regained power in Argentina after four unsuccessful years of a centre-right coalition led by Macri. With a new government headed by President Alberto Fernández and Vice President Cristina Fernández de Kirchner, some people were thrilled with the idea of Latin America being capable of regaining the 'glories' of the so-called golden decade they had led. Some of the leaders had already retired, while others faced trials for corruption: Lula and Rousseff in Brazil, Chávez and Maduro in Venezuela, Castro in Cuba, Morales in Bolivia, Mujica in Uruguay, Bachelet in Chile and Correa in Ecuador, among others.

It is therefore a question of evaluating the role communication has played from a strategic perspective, controlling the spread of the disease, taking into account the different factors at play (Zerfass *et al.* 2018), in a case which stands out in the reality of a region of the world marked by political and ideological diversity and clashes (for instance, Trump's leadership and influence on far-right governments, namely President Bolsonaro's in Brazil), which has simultaneously configured various contexts and scenarios that have conditioned this management and its main associated issues.

This empirical study has theoretical effects, since the findings will contribute to the literature in the field of risk and crisis communication. At the same time, the empirical results will shed light on how information procedures and sources influence the information-seeking processes of the public and the perception frameworks that are built therefrom.

Experiencing COVID-19: Argentina, the end of the world

Argentina represents a paradigmatic case. It is a country of contradictions, of the vast tracts of agricultural and cattle-raising land, a wide variety of ecosystems, one of the lowest levels of illiteracy in the region, a melting pot of races and cultures, with no war or civil strife and more than 40 years of uninterrupted democracy. It is the only South American country to have produced a pope, football stars like Maradona and Messi, a Dutch queen and even Nobel Prize and Oscar winners. Nevertheless insecurity, rampant corruption, political instability and cyclical economic crises tarnish its evident potential.

Argentina faced the arrival of the pandemic at a very particular time. In late 2019, poverty reached 40% of the population: 16,000,000 people. The political scene was dominated by a serious deterioration of the living conditions of broad sectors of the population. The issue of poverty was the centre of the activity of the new government, while the current opposition pointed out the dangers of falling back into 'populism'. The issue of the foreign debt – expressed in the re-negotiation with the so-called bondholders – was at the centre of the economic and political scene in the middle of a profound recession. After the first recorded case of COVID-19 was diagnosed in Argentina, in a traveller from Milan, Italy, on 8 March, the first death from coronavirus was verified in Argentina and Latin America: In this case, a person from France (Prado *et al.* 2021).

The government adopted an early quarantine, following the guidelines of the World Health Organization (WHO) by way of a 'Necessity and Urgency Decree' that established the so-called Preventive and Mandatory Social Isolation. Together with the quarantine, other territorial measures were taken, like the closure of the national and interprovincial borders, and a series of social schemes, such as food aid, complementary contributions, the Universal Allowance for Child and Pregnancy and the establishment of the Emergency

Family Income. Support schemes were also activated for small- and medium-size companies, in the forms of assistance with the payment of 50% of salaries and low-rate loans. A great effort was made to strengthen and increase public health services and state resources were articulated with powerful union social insurance plans and social security. In perspective, a clear increase in response was achieved in organizational and functional aspects, the availability of personnel and of medical supplies. Community responses were strengthened and multiplied, gaining importance among the poor.

Indeed, the Commission of Experts in Social Sciences of the Coronavirus COVID-19 Unit prepared a special report on the role of the media and communication during the first months of the pandemic for the National Ministry of Science, Technology and Innovation. As regards the press coverage, experts agree that for the first time in recent years, a topic outside politics and economy dominated the media agenda: 'COVID-19 captures 9 out of 10 news headlines published on the main digital media front pages in the country' (*Comisión de Expertos en Ciencias Sociales de la Unidad Coronavirus COVID-19* 2020, p. 138). On average, journalistic pieces have two sources, which surpasses the average citation of sources of the media agenda in Argentina. Most of these sources are institutional and governmental. Positive framing clearly dominates the media evaluation of government initiatives on COVID-19. The aforementioned aspects contrast with the coverage of other matters in the public agenda, in this case, by the media, which mostly evaluate government activity negatively.

Other relevant aspects of the report include highlighting several recommendations regarding official/government communication (Comisión de Ciencias Sociales de la Unidad Coronavirus COVID-19 2020):

- Avoiding a lack of coordination and foreseeing possible mistakes that, in the context of the pandemic, could be serious.
- Seeking balance, calm, coherence, consensus building and support by specialists; strengthening presidential authority and its image.
- Regulating the exposure of the president and planning his media appearances, bearing in mind that the health emergency will be long and economic and social aspect will follow.
- Defining strategic guidelines and measures to tackle rumours and disinformation with specific interventions.
- Guaranteeing the right to the protection of personal data and the right to privacy.

Analysing the communicational aspect of how the Argentine government began tackling the pandemic, three significant wise decisions can be highlighted: early action, multilevel political action and generalised technical consensus. Early on, all of this led to very high levels of support. However, experts on political communication (Cabás 2020; Riorda 2020) argue that during the management of the crisis, the government confused crisis communication with risk communication, something that is often the case throughout Latin America.

Leaders confused risk management with crisis management, and all the time they should have spent 'building risk' to modify habits and behaviours to prevent this vulnerability was spent building political power showcased through exacerbated decisionism, exaggerated voluntarism and overexposure of the president, which ended up eroding his image. In addition, there were 'feelings of victory or near-victory generated against COVID-19 in comparative perspective, noting that Argentina was being able to contain the pandemic better than other countries or generating optimistic scenarios that never arrived' (Riorda and Bentolila 2020, p. 155).

Research design and case study

The state of play: the paradigmatic case of the management of COVID-19 crisis in Argentina

The general goal of the research was to study public communication strategies during the COVID-19 crisis carried out by the Argentine national government to help understand how information about the emergency flows among different social groups and to help improve communication for future crisis scenarios. For this purpose, five research questions were proposed to guide this specific study:

RQ1: What are the means through which you have read or heard information about COVID-19?

RQ2: How do you rate the government's communication regarding COVID-19?

RQ3: What are the main messages that the government has given through the specialised committee and government leaders on COVID-19 before declaring preventive and mandatory social isolation?

RQ4: Which sources do you trust the most for COVID-19 information?

RQ5: What do you know about COVID-19?

The study focused on the combined notions of risk communication and crisis communication based on the contributions of different authors and conceptualisations indicated in the introduction, and also on the following study variables: credibility of the news (Yale *et al.* 2015), diversity of sources and diversity of content (Zhang and Zhou 2019), channel complementarity (Dutta-Bergman 2004, 2006), diversity of opinion (van der Wurff 2011; Newman and Fletcher 2017), knowledge uncertainty (So *et al.* 2019) and media consumption (Feldman *et al.* 2014).

The field work was carried out through an online questionnaire, active between 1 October and 31 November 2020. Snowball sampling was used, which allows invitations to circulate (via WhatsApp, Telegram, Twitter, Facebook,

Instagram and LinkedIn), explaining the reasons for the questionnaire and providing the access link.

The Argentine population estimated for 2020 is 45.4 million inhabitants. A representative sample would need a total of 397 surveyees. A total of 945 surveyees started the survey. The database was debugged (Morrow *et al.* 2014) by eliminating incomplete responses or those answered in an improbable timeframe. The final sample for the analysis was based on 466 questionnaires completed by the target population. The data were encoded into operational variables for statistical analysis (Bardin 1996) and once operationalised and re-encoded, they were processed with Statistical Package for the Social Sciences (SPSS) through a multivariable analysis with frequencies, contingency tables, significance levels (Chi-square test) and concordance coefficient (Cohen's Kappa).

In the sample, 56.9% are women, 42.5% are men, and 0.6% do not have binary gender. All age groups were present in the sample. As for their level of education, 47.2% are graduates and 31.1% are postgraduates, 14.8% have no academic qualifications and 6.9% are PhDs.

For this research, an analysis has been made per province. However, the sample was not considered to be large enough to provide statistically significant differences. Data were obtained from the 23 provinces and the Autonomous City of Buenos Aires. Most of the cases (73.8%) correspond to the provinces of Buenos Aires, Córdoba and Autonomous City. These three districts account for more than 40% of the national population. As regards the employment situation (in a context of moonlighting), 48.5% work in the public sector, another 27.9% in the private sector, and 28.3% are self-employed. Of the sample, 4.7% are healthcare workers. Regarding the socioeconomic situation, 75% of the sample are located in the highest monthly household income brackets. According to INDEC 2020 data, during the first semester of that year, the average monthly total household income in poor homes was 25,759 pesos (about US$320 at the official exchange rate), but the basic food basket reached 43,785 pesos (about US$545).

Key findings

The data obtained have allowed us to characterise the ways in which citizens faced the crisis in terms of media consumption, the best-valued sources of information, trust in the government and the information frameworks built. In addition, we analysed them by age and level of education. All this also allows us to interpret and discuss the factors that have influenced the government's action.

Most used and complementary means during the crisis

The five most used channels to obtain information on COVID-19 by the Argentine population were: Online newspapers (68%), Twitter (59.9%), television

Table 12.1 Information channels used during the COVID-19 crisis

Channels	*Percentages*
Online newspapers	68 %
Twitter	59.9%
Television	57.7%
Radio	46.4%
Websites/blogs of public institutions	35.2%
WhatsApp	30%
Scientific websites/blogs	23%
Facebook	22.1%
Instagram	22.1%
Healthwebsites/blogs	21.5%
Print newspapers	18.5%
YouTube	15%
Magazines	8.4%
Alternative therapy websites/blogs	3.4%
Telegram	2.6%

Source: Authors

Note: Q1: Which of the following information channels do you rely on to get COVID-19 information? Scale 1 (Never) – 7 (A great deal). Percentages: Frequency based on scale points 5–7.

(57.7%), radio (46.4%), and websites/blogs of public institutions (35.2%). Following were WhatsApp, with 30%, scientific websites/blogs (23%) and health websites/blogs (21.5%). Print newspapers came in at 18.5%. Instagram and YouTube are the least-consulted channels of the social media group. Alternative therapy websites/blogs (3.4%) are almost negligible. The same is true for Telegram, although this is related to the degree of penetration that the messaging platform has in Argentina. (See Table 12.1.)

During the months of COVID-19, the main online newspapers, most of them with restricted access by subscription, 'released' the consumption of pandemic news to be free. The recognition that the official information channels have had is very important.

When we analyse the most widely chosen information channels according to age groups (Table 12.2), we observe that online newspapers prevail among the youngest, and that television and the websites/blogs of public institutions are also consulted, followed by WhatsApp. In the age group of 30–39 years, online newspapers prevail. In the 40–49 age group, WhatsApp is the second most significant channel, above the rest of the groups. An interesting fact is that nearly 10% of the 50–59 age group use social media (Twitter) for information during the crisis.

Perception of the government's communication strategy and message retention

'Has always been clear and sufficient' and 'Has been the most reliable information' are the two options least chosen by those with a master's degree (Table 12.3).

Table 12.2 Information channel used during the crisis by age group

Channel	*Age*				
	29 or younger	*30–39 years*	*40–49 years*	*50–59 years*	*60 or older*
Television **	18.22%	31.23%	24.16%	21.19%	5.20%
WhatsApp **	14.29%	26.43%	30.0%	22.14%	7.14%
Online newspapers **	34.15%	62.8%	48.78%	38.41%	9.15%
Websites/blogs from public institutions **	16.46%	34.76%	23.17%	20.73%	4.88%
Twitter **	7.17%	8.96%	10.39%	9.32%	1.43%

Source: Authors

Note: Q1: Which of the following information channels do you rely on to get COVID-19 information? Scale 1 (Never) – 7 (A great deal). Percentages: Frequency based on scale points 5–7.

**Highly significant difference (chi-squared $p \leq 0.01$).

Table 12.3 Perception of the government's communication strategy by highest academic/educational level

Perception	*Doctorate*	*Master*	*Graduate (Bachelor, Diploma, etc.)*	*No academic degree*
Has always been clear and sufficient**	6.93%	28.71%	47.52%	16.83%
Has not revealed the whole truth**	3.68%	36.76%	44.85%	14.71%
Has been scheduled at the appropriate times**	5.49%	32.97%	39.56%	21.98%
Has confused the population**	5.53%	33.17%	46.23%	15.08%
Has been the most reliable information**	5.71%	28.0%	48.0%	18.29%
Has generated social alarm**	4.29%	31.43%	48.57%	15.71%

Source: Authors.

Notes: RQ2: To what extent do you agree with the following statements regarding the government's communication on COVID-19? RQ8: Please specify your highest academic/educational level. Scale: 1 (Strongly disagree) – 7 (Strongly agree). Percentages: Frequency based on scale points 5–7.

** Highly significant difference (independent simple T-test $p \leq 0.01$).

The statement 'Has not revealed the whole truth' was the most widely chosen. On the other hand, although the option 'Has confused the population' is among the most widely chosen by PhDs, most do not agree with the following assessment: 'Has generated social alarm'. 'Has been scheduled at the right times' is the strategy most valued by those who have no undergraduate training. University-educated citizens mostly maintain that the government has 'generated social alarm'.

The three main messages withheld by citizens in Argentina issued by the government are: 'COVID-19 is easily spread, and you must stay home to protect the elderly and sick' (36.88%), 'COVID-19 only affects elderly and sick people with previous pathologies' (18.92%) and 'COVID-19 is dangerous and the borders should have been closed to people from countries with a high level of contagion' (17.4%). (See Table 12.4.)

This result is highly significant because the first two options coincide. Firstly, this is because the strategy focused on the greater vulnerability of the elderly and those with previous pathologies. With time, this was globally recognised as an error, and undoubtedly a condition of greater dissemination. Secondly, there is the so-called extreme myth. In Argentina, this has a double implication: one, a feeling of victimisation, that the problem came from abroad; the other, that the upper classes who travel abroad and do not take care of themselves are to blame for 'harming the poor'.

Furthermore, although to a lesser extent, the future economic impact is used as a coercive argument. It is mixed with impressions such as the low danger that the disease has, on one hand, and on the other, the potential state of chaos and food shortages (a very painful memory for Argentines).

Trust in the sources and the knowledge frameworks about COVID-19

Trust is a key dimension in crisis management and the role of communication. In Argentina, trust in sources is shared by 15% of 'prestigious health

Table 12.4 Public perception of government communication according to message retention

Perception	*Frequency*	*Percentages*
COVID-19 spreads easily and you must stay home to protect the elderly and sick	388	36.88%
COVID-19 only affects elderly and sick people with previous pathologies	199	18.92%
COVID-19 is dangerous and borders should have been closed to persons from countries with a high level of contagiousness	183	17.40%
COVID-19 spreads easily and you must stay home so that the economy does not suffer a longer interruption	145	13.78%
You must be calm because COVID-19 is not dangerous for most of the population	111	10.55%
COVID-19 will cause a state of emergency and the most important thing is to have food at home	26	2.47%

Source: Authors

Note: RQ3: In your opinion, what are three main messages that the government has given on COVID-19?

personalities (for example, epidemiologists)', 14% 'Personal information from the health sector', 11% the 'COVID-19 committee' and also the World Health Organization and the government, with 10% (Table 12.5).

The media are valued with just 4%, very close to 'affinity groups', which may be friends or social networks, or influencers on other topics. The low level of trust in local authorities is very significant, especially given the role that they will play in managing proximity.

The complementarity of the communication media, the lack of trust in the different sources and the dispersion and lack of precision in the key messages transmitted end up having an impact on the knowledge reference frameworks citizens have on the subject (Table 12.6). This becomes evident when analysing the main knowledge citizens claim to have about COVID-19. In Argentina, the main topics are: 'Washing your hands and staying away from others are effective ways to protect yourself' (16.6%), 'COVID-19 can be transmitted by touching infected surfaces' (10.1%) and 'Jokes contribute to misinformation' (9%). It is noteworthy that two messages oriented towards action and prevention stand out, along with one that somehow challenges the ethical dimension and individual and collective responsibility. These are aspects we return to in the discussions and conclusions that follow.

Based on the results, the national government had to modify its crisis communication management, considering a better weighting of the strategic factors that determine a crisis; reinforcement of social media strategies without neglecting traditional media; greater precision and coherence in the actions and messages deployed and consequently greater trust as a source of information;

Table 12.5 Trust in the sources of information

Sources	*Percentages*
Prestigious healthcare personalities (e.g., epidemiologists)	15%
Personal information from the health sector	14%
COVID-19 committee	11%
World Health Organization	10%
Government	10%
Associations of health groups (e.g., professional associations of doctors, etc.)	9%
Regional authorities	7%
Unknown health personnel who have spread on social networks	6%
Health influencers	5%
Local authorities	5%
Media	4%
Friends on social networks	3%
Influencers of other topics (not health) on social networks	1%
Influencers on alternative therapies	1%

Source: Authors

Note: Q4. Which sources of information do you have the most trust in? Scale 1 (Strongly disagree) – 7 (Strongly agree). Percentages: Frequency based on scale points 5–7.

Table 12.6 Top five knowledge frameworks on COVID-19

Know about COVID-19	*Frequency*	*Percentages*
Washing your hands and keeping distance from others are effective ways to protect yourself.	456	16.6%
COVID-19 can be transmitted by touching infected surfaces.	276	10.1%
Jokes contribute to misinformation.	246	9.0%
The measures taken by the government have been declared too early.	225	8.2%
COVID-19 is like a bout of flu for most of the population.	154	5.6%

Source: Authors

Note: Q5: What do you know about COVID-19? Top five.

and further empowering experts and middle managers, thus moderating prominence and high-level political overexposure.

Questions and remarks

The data obtained from the analysis provide interesting information from the context described and from the possible theoretical discussions and implications, for both the practice and strategic planning of future crises. The findings contribute to the field of political communication, strategic communication and risk and crisis management.

Basically, the results provide evidence that government communication is responsible for how sources of information and trust influence various sectors of the publics' assessment of public communication.

A first key element presented for discussion is the set of driving factors involved in the strategic complexity (Zerfass *et al.* 2018), mainly motivated by geopolitical, social and economic characteristics. Undoubtedly, this approach is not always easy to apply to specific cases. It makes it possible to discuss and understand what makes a topic strategic according to its complexity, and the margins for manoeuvre, in terms of handling the conversation built on the topic. Indeed, strategic problems (COVID-19 undoubtedly is one) and their complexity (political and communication management) first require recognition of the different drivers, factors that intersect, which are not necessarily self-exclusive. This exercise already vindicates the communication function in crisis management and legitimises its advisory function and the improvement of its performance towards excellence (Tench *et al.* 2017).

In Argentina, different factors have been considered when assessing the crisis at a strategic level. The 'risk' factor is obvious, but in this case it is broadened by the other factors. The shortage of 'resources', the criticality of health policies and infrastructure and the frailness of existing productive and social security systems have all been important and conditioning factors of this complexity. The 'operational' factor has also been important and conditioning since normal operation and exceptionality in management have been constant. As for 'competence', at the provincial and supranational levels, the country has placed a special focus on what Brazil and the United States were doing (to stand out from the rest), and endeavoured to emulate Europe. In the relationship with Russia first and with China later, the 'innovation' factor was the one with the greatest impetus. The 'environment' factor was particularly influential. It is not an agenda topic, although it is true that certain government actions (especially at the local level) were motivated by this dimension: for example, mobility and transport issues and urban space designs, or some controversial measures such as the ban on smoking. Finally, the 'engagement' factor has driven the strategic decision of the management, especially considering that the government had recently come to power (four years ahead of the legislature), with high levels of positive assessment and positioning. In this sense, especially at the beginning of the crisis management, the measures were assertive and enjoyed considerable consensus despite their severity and their comparative regional mismatch.

From the strategic perspective, communication must be intentional and substantial to ensure the survival and the sustained success of those who exercise it, attempting to participate in conversations that are strategically important to their objectives. However, communication must play different roles in formulating, reviewing, presenting, executing, implementing and operationalising strategies (Zerfass *et al.* 2018). At this point, the classic theories of crisis communication generally tend to neglect the role of the media and focus on the interaction between the type of crisis and the crisis communication strategy. The findings of this study offer further evidence of the implications of the 'Complementary Theory of the Channel' in the field of risk, crisis and emergency communication.

Moreover, if we take the COVID-19 Action Plan Guide 'Risk communication and community involvement (RCCE)' (WHO 2020b, 2020c) as a reference, it stresses that a key component of preparedness and response is to guarantee information in real time from reliable sources to people at risk, structuring the communication plan into five aspects: building or maintaining trust, anticipating the information, being transparent, activating listening mechanisms, and planned management. In this regard, the results provide information on how the forms and sources of information influence the information-seeking behaviour of the public and the perception of response strategies during crises. An important fact in this respect is the need to carefully incorporate the social networks into crisis communication plans without neglecting traditional media strategies, which continue to be significantly transcendental.

On the other hand, in times of confinement, the high penetration of fixed and mobile communication devices is a factor that deserves to be addressed in its entire complexity. Ubiquity has a tremendous impact on the news (verified, rumours or fake) that circulates globally in real time and emerges from institutionalised sources, the media and concurrently by individuals on their social and digital networks (Canel 2020).

Lastly, a cross-cutting aspect on the new 'COVID-19 way' proposed by Morin seeks to recover 'lessons', 'challenges' and a 'policy' for the nations, for civilisation, for humanity and for the Earth. The change implies a 'regenerated humanism' (Morin 2020, p. 93), a macro dimension we shall also have to address.

Conclusions

In going through the factors that configure the profile of the national government as the 'strategic manager' of the COVID-19 crisis, and the impact this has had on the population in terms of the selection and use of sources, trust in them, assimilation of key messages and referential frameworks constructed, we are able to point out some lessons learned, at least from the singularity of the case in question, and of course, provide future recommendations on a practical and theoretical level.

The current geopolitical configuration and ideology has undoubtedly conditioned the decisions (alliances, restriction policies, leadership models, etc.) and their effectiveness, especially in comparison with the results analysed in other countries. This provides substantial evidence for the singularities of the context of a left-wing populist government such as the present one in Argentina, and the use of the media, government responses, sources and frameworks of understanding. The particularity of the case analysed here represents a substantial contribution to the study of a global phenomenon that requires the finding of common ground, while also paying attention to extremes and exceptionalities.

The key findings revealed that social media (e.g., Twitter), online newspapers and TV are key sources of information and that media selection has an impact on the direction of the pandemic. The actions and messages deployed have not been precise and there is a wide dispersion in their degree of acceptance and rating. In turn, the study corroborates that media consumption during the health emergency crisis can be better explained through the theory of channel complementarity, such as high consumption and simultaneous search for information in multiple media and channels.

Unlike other contexts and previous research, citizens place more trust in governments than in experts as sources of information. This is also related to the hyper-prominence that the governments and their highest authorities have had.

In addition, and taking other studies that have also explored the communication management of the COVID-19 crisis in Argentina (Cabas 2021) as a reference, we can highlight some recommendations:

- *Strategic and operative function:* Assuming the crisis from a strategic perspective must not involve overestimating the operative factor. It should be

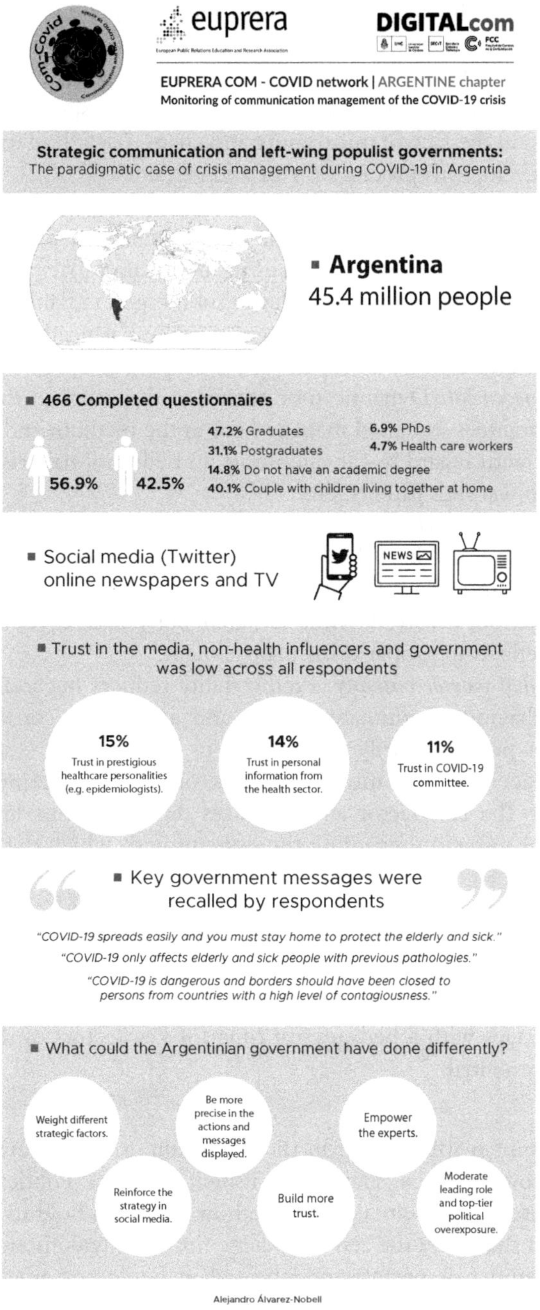

Infographic 12.1 Strategic communication and left-wing populist governments: The paradigmatic case of crisis management during COVID-19 in Argentina

applied in particular to preventive communication and multilevel spokespersons, gradually increasing the pedagogical tone. This type of communication should not be concentrated in the highest authorities.

- *Leadership:* In this type of crisis, the central position of communication must be occupied by the political sector, which is responsible for providing certainties in the face of uncertainty and chaos. Clear leadership is a condition to develop this process of trust and certainty.
- *Reactivity versus proactivity:* In general, communications concentrate on reducing vulnerabilities – especially in preventive actions – while there is communication on interventions in increasing capacities and resources. However, the innovation factor (even submerged in banks of uncertainty) appears randomly as a proactive sign. A more balanced presence in long-term communication contributes to developing trust and credibility.
- *Issues management:* Dynamic monitoring of the issues in their taxonomic range guarantees sustained management in the medium and long term, for example, with regard to the economic and educational crisis, work transformation, vaccine patents, etc.
- *The double way of technological evolution:* The advance of digitalisation entails several changes in the habits of society and its ways of relating. Governments must anticipate these trends in order to manage the impact and the transformations involved, while simultaneously making use of their potentials and effects in proper crisis management.
- *Routines that provide certainty:* Predictability reduces uncertainty and moderates behaviour, legitimates media and actors and consolidates habits. This does not necessarily bring value to management – it is exhausting and bureaucratic. But mismanagement of the information in this sense aggravates the risk factor and produces direct negative impacts, such as doubt and suspicion regarding the honesty with which the information is handled.
- *Tone:* Communication presents strong technicality and/or moralism, wasting the opportunity offered by technical speeches and those focused on values.
- *Segmentation by interests:* Segmentation tactics in communications and specific messages with a pedagogical tone for key sectors of the COVID-19 crisis are essential.

One last point is still missing in the discussion, a new element that should be proposed to define how strategic an issue it is: Ethics. Politics often chooses to test or tighten up the situation to see how far it can hold its own decisions which are not shared by the rest of society, not socially consensual. This trial-and-error dilemma or permanent rehearsal in liquid and uncertain contexts may be an explanation for numerous reversals of decisions. This explains the precariousness of consensus, the volatility of governments where strange things happen and the improvised and apparent lack of professionalism of communication strategies to manage the crisis.

Bibliography

Álvarez-Nobell, A., *et al.* (2021). *Comunicación estratégica en América Latina: ciberseguridad, situación de las mujeres, retos éticos, nuevas competencias y crisis del COVID-19. Resultados de una encuesta en 20 países.* Bruselas: EUPRERA.

Austin, L., Liu, B.F., and Jin, Y. (2012). How audiences seek out crisis information: Exploring the social-mediated crisis communication model. *Journal of Applied Communication Research*, 40(2), pp. 188–207. doi:10.1080/00909882.2012.654498

Bardin, L. (1996). *Análisis de contenido.* Madrid: Akal.

Beck, U.,1998. *La sociedad del riesgo. Hacia una nueva modernidad.* Barcelona: Paidós.

Cabás, P. (2020). Gestión de la Comunicación de crisis del COVID-19 en la isla de Tierra del Fuego, Argentina. *Revista ComHumanitas*, 11(3), pp. 96–125.

Cabas, P.A. (2021). La gestión comunicacional de la crisis del COVID-19 en Tierra del Fuego AIAS. Análisis comparado de las estrategias del gobierno provincial de Tierra del Fuego, AIAS y de las municipalidades de Ushuaia y de Río Grande. *Studia Politicæ*, (53). http://revistas.bibdigital.uccor.edu.ar/index.php/SP/article/view/5185

Canel, M. J (2020). Webinar: El futuro del branding gubernamental post COVID-19. Escuela de Posgrados en Comunicación [online]. *Universidad Austral.* Available from: www.youtube.com/watch?v=dVkqOtX15v8&feature=youtu.be [Accessed 15 May 2021].

Casero-Ripollés, A. (2020). Impact of COVID-19 on the media system. Communicative and democratic consequences of news consumption during the outbreak. *El Profesional de la información*, 29(2), e290223.

Castillo-Esparcia, A., Fernández-Souto, A.B., and Puentes-Rivera, I. (2020). Comunicación política y COVID-19. Estrategias del Gobierno de España. *El Profesional de la información*, 29(4), e290419.

Comisión de Ciencias Sociales de la Unidad Coronavirus COVID-19 (2020). *Comunicación y medios en COVID-19* [online]. *Grupo de trabajo de Comunicación.* Septiembre – diciembre 2020, pp. 96–125. Available from: www.sociales.uba.ar/wpcontent/blogs.dir/219/files/2020/04/Informe_Final_Covid-Cs.Sociales.pdf [Accessed 25 May 2021].

Coombs, W.T. (1995). Choosing the right words: The development of guidelines for the selection of the 'appropriate' crisis-response strategies. *Management Communication Quarterly*, 8(4), pp. 447–476.

Crespo, I. and Garrido, A. (2020). The coronavirus pandemic: Crisis communication strategies. *M as Poder Local*, 41, pp. 12–19.

Dutta-Bergman, M.J. (2004). Interpersonal communication after 9/11 via telephone and Internet: A theory of channel complementarity. *New Media & Society*, 6(5), pp. 659–673. doi:10.1177/1461444804047086

Dutta-Bergman, M.J. (2006). Community participation and Internet use after September 11: Complementarity in channel consumption. *Journal of Computer-Mediated Communication*, 11(2), pp. 469–484. doi:10.1111/j.1083-6101.2006.00022.x

Edelman (2020). *Special report: Trust and the Coronavirus* [online]. Available from: https://bit.ly/2TERtFx [Accessed 10 May 2021].

Feldman, L, Myers, T.A., J Hmielowski, J.D., Leiserowitz, A. (2014). The mutual reinforcement of media selectivity and effects: Testing the reinforcing spirals framework in the context of global warming. *Journal of Communication*, 64(4), pp. 590–611.

Gaspar, R., Gorjão, S., Seibt, B., Lima, L., Barnett, J., Moss, A., and Wills, J. (2014). Tweeting during food crises: A psychosocial analysis of threat coping expressions in Spain, during the 2011 European EHEC outbreak. *International Journal of Human-Computer Studies*, 72(2), pp. 239–254. doi:10.1016/j.ijhcs.2013.10.001

González-Harbour, B. (2020). *Cinco fallos y cuatro aciertos del Gobierno en la comunicación de esta crisis* [online]. El País. Available from: https://elpais.com/sociedad/2020-04-30/cinco-fallos-y-cuatro-aciertos-del-gobierno-en-la-comunicacion-de-esta-crisis.html [1 May 2021].

González-Herrero, A., and Smith, S. (2008). Crisis communications management on the web: How internet-based technologies are changing the way public relations professionals handle business crises. *Journal of Contingencies and Crisis Management*, 16(3), pp. 143–153. doi:10.1111/j.1468-5973.2008.00543.x

Moreno, Á., Fuentes-Lara, C., and Navarro, C. (2020). COVID-19 communication management in Spain: Exploring the effect of information-seeking behavior and message reception in public's evaluation. *El profesional de la información*, 29(4), e290402. doi:10.3145/epi.2020.jul.02

Moreno-Millán, E. (2008). Gestión de la información y la comunicación en emergencias, desastres y crisis sanitarias. Emergencias. *Revista de la Sociedad Española de Medicina de Urgencias y Emergencias*, 20(2), pp. 117–124.

Morin, E. (2020). *Cambiemos de vía. Lecciones de la pandemia*. Barcelona: Paidós.

Morrow, J.A., and Skolits, G.J. (2014). The twelve steps of data cleaning: Strategies for dealing with dirty data [online]. *Workshop conducted at the 28th Annual conference of the American Evaluation Association*, Denver, CO. Available from: www.eval.org/evaluation2014 [Accessed 6 July 2021].

Newman, N., and Fletcher, R. (2017). *Bias, bullshit and lies: Audience perspectives on low trust in the media* [online]. Available from: https://papers.ssrn.com/sol3/papers.cfm?abstract_id=3173579 [Accessed 1 July 2021].

Park, S., Boatwright, B., and Johnson-Avery, E. (2019). Information channel preference in health crisis: Exploring the roles of perceived risk, preparedness, knowledge, and intent to follow directives. *Public Relations Review*, 45(5), p. 101794. doi:10.1016/j.pubrev.2019.05.015

Prado, G.S., Braguinsky, G., and Biagini, G. (2021). Pandemia del COVID-19: estado, comunicación y construcción social en Argentina. In Uzcátegui J.L., Tetelboin Henrion, C., Iturrieta Henríquez, D., and Schor-Landman., C., 2021. *América Latina. Sociedad, política y salud en tiempos de pandemia*. Ciudad Autónoma de Buenos Aires: CLACSO; Xochimilco: Universidad Autónoma Metropolitana; Xalapa: Universidad Veracruzana; Cochabamba: Universidad Mayor de San Simón; Valparaíso: Universidad de Valparaíso.

Reynolds, B. (2002). *Crisis and emergency risk communication*. Atlanta, GA: Centers for Disease Control and Prevention.

Reynolds, B., and Seeger, M. (2005). Crisis and emergency risk communication as an integrative model. *Journal of Health Communication*, 10(1), pp. 43–55. doi:10.1080/10810730590904571

Riorda, M. (2008). 'Gobierno bien pero comunico mal': análisis de las rutinas de la comunicación gubernamental. *Revista del CLAD Reforma y Democracia*, 40,1–15.

Riorda, M. (2020). Antes de comunicar el riesgo o la crisis: hay que diferenciarlos. *Más poder local*, 41, pp. 20–23. Available from: http://maspoderlocal.es/ediciones/comunicacion-politica-COVID-19-no41

Riorda, M., and Bentolila, S. (2020). *Cualquiera tiene un plan hasta que te pegan en la cara. Aprender de las crisis*. Buenos Aires: Paidós.

So, J., Kuang, K., and Cho, H. (2019). Information seeking upon exposure to risk messages: Predictors, outcomes, and mediating roles of health information seeking. *Communication Research*, 46(5), pp. 663–687.

Tench, R., Verčič, D., Zerfass, A., Moreno, A., and Verhoeven, A. (2017). *Communication excellence: How to develop, manage and lead exceptional communications*. London: Springer.

Van-der-Meer and Tony, G.L.A. (2018). Public frame building: The role of source usage in times of crisis. *Communication Research*, 45(6), pp. 956–981. doi:10.1177/0093650216644027

Van der Wurff, R. (2011). Are news media substitutes? Gratifications, contents, and uses. *Journal of Media Economics*, 24(3), pp. 139–157.

WHO (2011). *Report of the review committee on the functioning of the international health regulations (2005) in relation to pandemic (H1N1) 2009* [online]. Geneva, Switzerland: World Health Organization. Available from: https://apps.who.int/gb/ebwha/pdf_files/WHA64/A64_10-en.pdf [Accessed 1 May 2021].

WHO (2020a). COVID-19. *Consejos para informar. Guía para periodistas* [online]. Available from: www.paho.org/es/documentos [Accessed 1 July 2021].

WHO (2020b). *Risk communication and community engagement (RCCE) action plan guidance COVID-19 preparedness and response. COVID-19: Risk communication and community engagement* [online]. Available from: www.who.int/publications/i/item/risk-communication-and-community-engagement-(rcce)-action-plan-guidance [Accessed 15 July 2021].

WHO (2020c). *2019 novel Coronavirus (2019-nCoV): Strategic preparedness and response plan* [online]. Available from: www.who.int/docs/default-source/coronaviruse/srp-04022020.pdf [Accessed 1 July 2021].

Xifra, J. (2020). Comunicación corporativa, relaciones públicas y gestión del riesgo reputacional en tiempos del COVID-19. *El profesional de la información*, 29(2), pp. 1–18. http://eprints.rclis.org/39942/1/xifra.pdf

Yale, R.N., Carcioppolo, N., Jensen, J.D., and Sun, Y. (2015). Examining first-and second-order factor structures for news credibility. *Communication Methods and Measures*, 9(3), pp. 152–169.

Zerfass, A., Verčič, D., Nothhaft, H., and Werder K.P. (2018). Strategic communication: Defining the field and its contribution to research and practice. *International Journal of Strategic Communication*, 12(4), pp. 487–505. doi:10.1080/1553118X.2018.1493485

Zhang, X., and Zhou, S. (2019). Clicking health risk messages on social media: Moderated mediation paths through perceived threat, perceived efficacy, and fear arousal. *Health communication*, 34(11), pp. 1359–1368. doi:10.1080/10410236.2018.1489202

Zhao, X., Zhan, M., and Liu, B.F. (2018). Disentangling social media influence in crises: Testing a four-factor model of social media influence with large data. *Public Relations Review*, 44(4), pp. 549–561. doi:10.1016/j.pubrev.2018.08.00

Zhu, L., Anagondahalli, D., and Zhang, A. (2017). Social media and culture in crisis communication: McDonald's and KFC crises management in China. *Public Relations Review*, *43*(3), pp. 487–492.

13 Brazil and the COVID-19 pandemic

Crisis communication management as opposed to public communication

Andréia Silveira Athaydes, Karen Cristina Kraemer Abreu and Marcus Vinicius de Jesus

Introduction

On 26 February 2020, Brazil was the first country in Latin America and the Caribbean to notify the contagion of its citizens by COVID-19 to the World Health Organization (WHO). In less than a month, on 10 March, it hosted a training workshop for the use of Go.Data software to ensure that Latin government bodies dedicated to health maintained the same standard for entering and analysing data on the disease in Latin America (OPS 2020). These attitudes, initially proactive and showing concern and collaboration with the health situation, did not guarantee that the country would avoid making history in the negative world ranking, becoming the second nation in terms of confirmed cases and deaths by COVID-19; and the first one, by deaths per million inhabitants (Gazeta do Povo 2021). This fact, associated with the negationist behaviour of the Brazilian government and of the society itself about the existence of the pandemic (Veras 2020) and the self-centred, authoritarian and self-truth generator profile of President Bolsonaro (Brum 2019; Frota Torres *et al.* 2021), who disseminated fake news about early coronavirus treatment without medical evidence on his personal Twitter account, calls into question the role of strategic communication in the government sphere.

This chapter, based on data obtained in the COM-COVID survey, promoted by EUPRERA, contributes to the reflection on the risk communication and crisis communication studies existing in Brazil. From the identification of the most consulted channels, the most credible sources and the perception of the main messages issued by the Brazilian government during the first year of the pandemic in the country, the relationship between these variables and their role in risk and crisis communication in the governmental sphere was verified. In this way, empirical studies on the themes addressed here are corroborated and the Brazilian academic production, which is internationally unknown due to language barriers, becomes partly visible.

DOI: 10.4324/9781003184669-20

Experiencing COVID-19: an overview of the pandemic in Brazil

Since 2020, Brazil has been experiencing an almost unimaginable experience regarding contamination by SarS-Cov-2. Thousands of diagnosed patients and countless deaths are the results of contamination by COVID-19, and these statistical data have been daily reported by the press. The media's fulfilling its role of informing and alerting Brazilian society about the seriousness of the situation led the president of the republic to accuse it of overestimating the facts relating to the disease. By 31 March, the Health Departments of the Brazilian states reported 5,812 infected patients and 202 deaths due to severe acute respiratory syndrome (SRAG), the new coronavirus.

The media vehicles sought data that were often hidden by the Ministry of Health, through various practices of censorship, boycott and self-truths (Brum 2019). Government attitudes in 2020 can be summarised in ten major themes:

1. Delaying epidemiological bulletins
2. Changing the time of day for disclosing daily information
3. Implementing new methodology to measure confirmed cases and number of deaths, erasing the consolidated data that were available on the Ministry of Health website
4. Inaccuracies in the information: not counting data from some states in the numbers of deaths and of those infected on certain days
5. Divergences between the information released by the Ministry of Health and the sum of the data reported by the states' health departments
6. Disregarding and denying the disease, even after COVID-19 was declared a pandemic by the WHO, summarised in the president's public declaration calling it 'a little flu'
7. Insisting on disseminating scientifically ineffective medicines for COVID-19
8. Delaying the acquisition of immunising agents to vaccinate the population, which would avert serious cases of SarS-Cov-2 infection
9. Non-disclosure of advertising campaigns in the media informing health protocols, methods of prevention and attitudes to be taken when symptoms of the disease are identified
10. Insistence by the federal government that the national routine should not change – not recommending a lockdown with the justification of preserving jobs and keeping the economy active.

It is also worth noting the rapid turnover of three health ministers in the first year of the pandemic in Brazil: the first one, a physician, was dismissed because, in addition to taking a stand against President Bolsonaro's recommendations, he held constant press conferences to inform the population, gaining media visibility; the second one, also a doctor, was removed after a month in the ministry for disagreeing with the president's position; and the third, a military officer in the logistics area and in line with the president's speech, was the manager who spent the longest time in the position. However, after about nine months of management, he was dismissed by political pressure and public opinion due to the lack of control in the fight against the new coronavirus.

In economic terms, the forecasts for Brazil in 2020 were: inflation around 3.6%, dollar quotation at R$4.09 and expected growth of 2.3% in gross domestic product, according to information disclosed in the *Focus* bulletin of the Central Bank in December 2019 (Fordelone 2020). However, with the COVID-19 pandemic, the health and economic crisis and unemployment were the items that grew, unveiling a more difficult scenario for the structural national socioeconomic inequality. In September 2020, 14 million Brazilians were unemployed (Fordelone 2020). With the quarantine causing the closure of the non-essential trade and services sectors, GDP shrank, showing a decrease of 13.5% in the period (Ibre 2020). Although the recovery of the economy began in the third quarter of 2020 and registered a growth of 7.7%, in the 12-month accumulated period, the Brazilian economy registered a drop of 3.4%.

It should also be noted that during this pandemic period, the federal government has been resuming neoliberal issues, proposing the closure of state-owned companies or negotiating them for the private sector. The rules established in the Consolidation of Labor Laws, created to protect workers from abusive contracts, which have governed private sector employment contracts since 1943, are being breached with the government's approval. The impoverishment of the population, the decline number of people in Class "C" – the educated professional working demographic – (Continuous PNAD 2018), in the past two years caused the return of millions of people to the poverty line. In an attempt to reduce the economic crisis, the Minister of Economy proposed reforms that create emergency and long-term mechanisms to balance public accounts at the federal, state and municipal levels. However, they remain stalled in the National Congress. Flexibility has also been adopted as a palliative emergency step: by Provisional Measure, an exclusive regime was created to reduce working hours and cut payroll taxes so that the slowing economy did not increase unemployment (Brigatti 2020).

Finally, the Brazilian Institute of Geography and Statistics (IBGE) indicates that contamination, recovery rates and death by COVID-19 in Brazil are related to the level of education (Pnad COVID-19 2020). In the group of patients with higher education level, the investigation shows a rate of 77.46% of recovered and 22.54% of deaths. At the other end, among uneducated patients contaminated by COVID-19, 28.69% recover, while 71.31% die. In December 2020, the Press Consortium reported the existence of 7,675,973 confirmed cases and 194,949 lives lost to COVID-19 in the country, showing an increase of 65% in cases of the disease in only the last month of the year, according to data published by the newspaper *Estado de Minas* (Ronan 2020). Brazil reached 2021 as first in the international ranking of the pandemic by deaths per million inhabitants in (Gazeta do Povo 2021). Meanwhile, using Twitter to spread his ideas (Viscardi

2021), President Bolsonaro has resorted to and maintains different narratives of denial of the new virus and of its alleged low lethality (Calil 2020).

The state of play: application of the COM-COVID survey in Brazil

Research method

To find out how Brazilians perceived government communication about the COVID-19 pandemic, an online questionnaire was applied through the Google Forms application during October and November 2020. This data collection instrument followed the basic structure adopted in the other countries participating in the COM-COVID/EUPRERA project: Questions to survey the sociodemographic profile and five closed questions about the habits of participants regarding information about COVID in Brazil. The response options followed a Likert scale from 1 to 7. For this chapter, we are interested in discussing and relating three questions: Q1) the most credible sources about COVID-19; Q2) the main messages issued by the federal government; and Q3) the main channels used to seek information about COVID-19. The analysis of the data was conducted based on the following two hypotheses:

H1: The Brazilian federal government is not a reliable source of information on the pandemic. Therefore, the population seeks various information channels to obtain guidance about the disease.

H2: People with higher socioeconomic status do not consider the government a reliable source; they consume other information channels and identify the main messages of the president, yet people in different age groups and with different levels of education perceive the messages issued by the president differently.

The final sample is composed of 866 Brazilian citizens, whose main characteristics are: women (69%), over 40 years old (57%), with graduation and/or post-graduation education *lato sensu* (64%), white (75%), heterosexuals (83%), with 50% of them claiming monthly salaries equivalent to US$1,401 to US$5,879 or more, representing the upper middle to upper classes of the country.

Even if this profile is not representative of the totality of the Brazilian people, it is a specific and relevant sample, considering the level of education above the national average, whose length of study of 15 years or more corresponds to only 13% of the population (IBGE 2015). It is also important to emphasise that the sample was concentrated in the Brazilian states of Rio Grande do Sul (49.3%), Bahia (18.1%) and São Paulo (11.4%), whose cultural characteristics are different from each other (Stoodi 2020) but will not be covered here.

Results

The sources of credibility for Brazilians and the perception of the government's messages

When consulted about the sources of credibility (Table 13.1) about the COVID-19 pandemic in Brazil, the sample indicated practically twice the level of distrust in the federal government (81.6%) compared to state governments (43%). This data is the result of manifestations contrary to the federal government's conduct in managing the pandemic (Carta Capital 2020). The

Table 13.1 COVID-19 sources of credibility in Brazil, 2020

Sources	*I totally distrust*	*I distrust a lot*	*Distrust*	*I neither trust nor distrust*	*I trust*	*I trust a lot*	*I totally trust*	*Total*
Federal government	55.7%	13.6%	12.4%	8.5%	3.5%	3.1%	3.2%	100.0%
State government	13.3%	13.0%	16.7%	21.7%	24.8%	7.4%	3.0%	100.0%
Municipality government	13.9%	12.0%	19.9%	20.9%	23.1%	6.8%	3.5%	100.0%
Media	6.9%	7.9%	12.4%	21.4%	25.9%	17.7%	8.0%	100.0%
Friends	16.5%	15.8%	21.0%	32.8%	9.7%	3.0%	1.2%	100.0%
Health professionals (anonymous)	34.2%	16.7%	18.7%	17.9%	7.0%	3.5%	2.0%	100.0%
Health professionals (friends)	2.9%	2.9%	6.7%	11.4%	28.9%	22.5%	24.6%	100.0%
Digital influencer – health	20.8%	11.2%	14.2%	25.4%	17.3%	7.4%	3.7%	100.0%
Digital influencer – alternative therapies	35.9%	12.9%	17.0%	23.9%	6.6%	2.5%	1.2%	100.0%
Digital influencer – other areas	43.3%	15.0%	16.5%	19.5%	4.0%	1.2%	0.5%	100.0%
WHO	6.0%	3.6%	5.1%	6.8%	16.2%	22.9%	39.5%	100.0%
Health professional associations	4.8%	3.2%	6.5%	13.9%	29.1%	22.7%	19.7%	100.0%
Prestigious personalities	4.0%	2.2%	6.4%	8.3%	21.4%	25.9%	31.9%	100.0%
Others	40.6%	8.2%	10.2%	30.0%	5.4%	3.0%	2.5%	100.0%

Source: Authors

Note: *N*=866. Seven-point Likert scale with 1= "Totally Distrust" and 7 = "Totally Trust."

government of states where a large part of the sample resides were concerned with creating crisis committees on COVID-19, unlike the federal government, whose installation of the committee took place in 2021 (Rede Brasil 2021).

On the opposite side, the greatest credibility of the sample is for the WHO (78.6%), followed by health professionals known to the respondents (76%) and the media (51.5%). Given the controversial information about the disease, confirming data directly with health professionals and the media becomes a safeguard for the population.

The fact that the federal government has little credibility in relation to the sample is also related to the population's perception of the messages issued by it. The data collected (in bold Table 13.2 below) indicate that the perception of the three main messages issued by the Brazilian federal government is related to controversial phrases uttered by President Bolsonaro that were widely publicised in the national and international media. These are messages that prioritise

Table 13.2 Main messages issued by President Bolsonaro about the COVID-19 pandemic, 2020

Message number	*Samples*	*% total of samples (866)*	*Total of messages' percentage*	*Messages from President Bolsonaro*
2	593	68.5%	22.6%	**Life must go on. Jobs must be maintained. The livelihood of families must be preserved. Normality must be restored.**
1	567	65.5%	21.6%	**The press is inflating the COVID-19 impact.**
7	522	60.3%	19.9%	**COVID-19 panic is not necessary, as it is just an ordinary flu.**
3	349	40.3%	13.3%	COVID-19 affects only elderly and people with pre-existing health conditions.
8	336	38.8%	12.8%	You must be calm because COVID-19 does not affect most people.
6	125	14.4%	4.8%	COVID-19 spreads easily. Stay home to protect seniors and people who are already sick.
4	77	8.9%	2.9%	COVID-19 will lock down the cities, so it's important to hoard food.
5	52	6.0%	2.0%	Countries should close their borders and not allow entrance to people coming from countries with high rates of COVID-19.
Total	**2621**	**302.66%**	**100.00%**	

Source: Authors

Note: Multiple choice.

the economy over public health and that detract from the seriousness of the disease: *Life must go on, jobs must be maintained, families' livelihoods must be preserved, normality must be restored*; and *it is a little flu*. They discredit anyone who says otherwise. The press: *is overstating the pandemic*; health professionals: with the resignation of two medical ministers during the pandemic; and WHO through the press statement *it does not get anything right* (Schuch 2020).

Regarding the respondents' level of education (Table 13.3), the sample points out as the main messages from the federal government those with more alarmist content or measures adopted by other countries, in addition to the relationship between the virus and the elderly: *COVID-19 will cause a state of emergency, and the most important thing is to have food at home*; and *it is dangerous and the borders should have been closed for people from countries with a high level of contagion*. Neither was publicised by the Brazilian government but by the national press, when publicising the closing of the borders of Argentina, Peru and Honduras due to COVID-19 and shortages of food and other products (Cazarré 2020; Grandin *et al.* 2021). Brazilians with postgraduate degrees (master's and doctorates), on the other hand, recognise as the main messages of the federal government the three most controversial statements made by President Bolsonaro that were widely publicised in the press (BBC 2020).

As for the main messages issued by the federal government from the perspective of the various age groups, younger people's perception points to statements that were not issued by the federal government: *COVID-19 is dangerous,*

Table 13.3 Key messages from President Bolsonaro about COVID-19 by level of education, 2020

Education	*Message 1*	*Message 2*	*Message 3*	*Message 4*	*Message 5*	*Message 6*	*Message 7*	*Message 8*
Early years foundation stage	0.2%	0.2%	0.3%	0.0%	0.0%	0.0%	0.4%	0.0%
Primary education	0.7%	1.0%	1.4%	0.0%	2.3%	1.8%	1.5%	1.2%
Secondary education	7.3%	8.5%	8.2%	22.2%	21.2%	32.7%	10.1%	10.4%
Higher education	33.7%	35.4%	35.6%	25.9%	33.3%	41.8%	34.0%	37.0%
Postgraduate education	34.2%	31.4%	34.7%	35.8%	32.6%	16.4%	31.2%	34.1%
Master's degree	14.0%	13.6%	10.5%	8.6%	9.1%	1.8%	13.6%	10.7%
Doctorate	8.2%	8.3%	7.9%	7.4%	0.8%	5.5%	8.0%	5.5%
Postdoctoral degree	1.7%	1.7%	1.4%	0.0%	0.8%	0.0%	1.1%	1.2%
Total	100.0%	100.0%	100.0%	100.0%	100.0%	100.0%	100.0%	100.0%

Source: Authors.

Message number	*Messages from President*
1	The press is inflating the COVID-19 impact.
2	Life must go on. Jobs must be maintained. The livelihood of families must be preserved. Normality must be restored.
3	COVID-19 affects only elderly and people with pre-existing health conditions.
4	COVID-19 will lock down the cities, so it's important to hoard food.
5	Countries should close their national borders and to people coming from countries with high rates of COVID-19.
6	COVID-19 spreads easily. Stay home to protect seniors and people who are already sick.
7	COVID-19 panic is not necessary, as it is just an ordinary flu.
8	You must be calm because COVID-19 does not affect most people.

Source: Authors

Table 13.4 Key messages from President Bolsonaro about COVID-19 by age group, 2020

Key messages	*Age group*				
	18 to 24	*25 to 39*	*40 to 59*	*Over 60*	*Total*
The press is inflating the COVID-19 impact.	12.70%	25.75%	42.15%	19.40%	100.0%
Life must go on. Jobs must be maintained. The livelihood of families must be preserved. Normality must be restored.	19.21%	25.42%	36.35%	19.02%	100.0%
COVID-19 affects only elderly and people with pre-existing health conditions.	18.91%	29.23%	36.68%	15.19%	100.0%
COVID-19 will lock down the cities, so it's important to hoard food.	22.08%	22.08%	32.47%	23.38%	100.0%
Countries should close their borders to people coming from countries with high rates of COVID-19.	28.80%	24.00%	34.40%	12.80%	100.0%
COVID-19 spreads easily. Stay home to protect seniors and people who are already sick.	28.85%	13.46%	38.46%	19.23%	100.0%
COVID-19 panic is not necessary, as it is just an ordinary flu.	17.62%	26.05%	36.97%	19.35%	100.0%
You must be calm because COVID-19 does not affect most people.	18.75%	25.00%	40.48%	15.77%	100.0%
Total	166.92%	190.99%	297.95%	144.14%	

Source: Authors

and borders should have been closed to people from highly contagious countries; and *COVID-19 spreads easily and you should stay home to protect the elderly and sick.* The older ones, 40 to 49 years of age and over 60, identify the messages issued by President Bolsonaro: *The press is overstating the devastating effect of COVID-19.* It should be noted that each age group paid attention to different messages, some being issued, and others not, by President Bolsonaro.

As for the channel consumption preference to search for information about the pandemic, the Brazilian sample prioritising the traditional ones: television, online and printed newspapers, and radio. In contrast, social networks such as Facebook (13.7%), Twitter (10.6%) and Instagram (10%) are the least preferred when it comes to COVID-19, contrary to some international reports that point to a use greater than 70% for such networks and that 81% of Brazilians aged 13 and over are active on social networks (We Are Social 2019). In the case of Twitter and considering the profile of the Brazilian sample, it is inferred that it was not used as much as it might have been because President Bolsonaro used this channel to express himself, including as head of government and state, against measures of protection to COVID-19.

That said, the empirical research triggered by the COM-COVID/EUPRERA project in Brazil enabled to:

1 Prove the hypotheses related to the most credible sources in the country on the subject: the government, especially at the federal level, was the one that aroused the greatest mistrust on the part of the sample. Therefore, they sought information from other sources about the pandemic, such as WHO and health professionals from their personal networks, who ensured clarification of its prevention, and agility in the dissemination of statistical data on the disease (media)

Table 13.5 The most used information channels in the pandemic

Channels	*Always use*
TV	48.5%
Online newspapers	41.5%
Printed newspapers	24.1%
Radio	22.1%
Public websites	18.0%
WhatsApp	17.3%
Health websites	16.4%
Facebook	13.7%
Twitter	10.6%
Instagram	10.0%
YouTube	7.2%
Magazines	6.1%

Source: Authors

Note: Multiple choice question. The percentages presented refer only to the answer option of 'Always'.

2 Prove the hypotheses related to the main messages issued by the Brazilian federal government: the youngest respondents, from 18 to 24 years old, were unable to identify them, while the groups with a higher level of education perceived the messages issued by the president. And, according to the age group, there were variations in the indication of the main messages, some attributed to the government and others not
3 Prove that the Brazilian population made use of different channels of communication, especially the mass media, considering the absence of a government campaign to guide and prevent COVID-19 and the president's controversial statements on social networks. The choice of traditional channels is more recurrent in higher education levels.

Next, some concepts chosen to discuss the data obtained in the empirical research are discussed.

Observations and interrogation

Risk and crisis communication in the government sphere

Risk and crisis communication are developed by both companies and governments concerned with building and maintaining their reputation (Forni 2010, 2019; Cardia 2015; Prado 2020). In the governmental instance, this type of communication follows the guidelines of public communication, which is the communicative process that is established in the public sphere between the state, the government and society, taking information to the public through public debate and the publicisation of actions for general knowledge, such as information campaigns, which move public opinion (Brandão 1998; Zémor 2003). Especially for health-related matters, it is crucial that the government, within the scope of public communication, establishes its risk and crisis communication policies and guidelines, both to maintain its reputation – objective of the politician and their respective party aiming at the next elections – to fulfil its constitutional duty to preserve the physical and mental integrity of the population, and the rights and duties of every citizen (Cruz 2014).

Public communication encompasses state communication (public media system at the service of the state) and government communication (communication policies and guidelines of a specific government management). Since state communication disputes the versions of political facts covered by the media, it will comply with 'the principles of public communication governed by the public interest when informing, explaining, making available, training, enabling, listening and contributing to the exercise of citizenship' (Weber 2011, p. 102). For this, Weber (2011) categorises seven types of strategies that demarcate state communication and expand its bond with citizens: visibility (repercussion and memory), credibility (recognition and legitimacy), autonomy (bureaucratisation and instrumentalisation), direct relationship (interactivity and participation), advertising (information and persuasion) and public image (history and identity).

Within the scope of public communication, Brazil has already faced several health crises: meningococcal meningitis in the 1970s; AIDS in the 1980s; cholera and measles in the 1990s (Barata 2000) and, as of 2010, dengue, zika and chikungunya (Bomfim 2020). In all of these, governmental spheres were mobilised to overcome them, and the Brazilian theoretical framework on risk communication and crisis communication had its contribution, disseminated in events and publications in the areas of communication, administration and health. Villela (2016) synthesises the difference between them, saying that risk communication provides knowledge about something that has already happened and, therefore, contributes to prevention; while crisis communication is designed to explain the position of an organization due to the criticism received for its involvement in a particular crisis. Alves (2007), however, had already warned that risk communication in Brazil, a fundamental element of crisis management, is still restricted to hazard information. Organizations may be alert to the problem, but do not plan alternatives to avoid and/or resolve it quickly. Thus, Brazilian literature still prioritises discussions in the context of crisis communication.

In the crisis management manuals existing in the country, one of the first recommendations is the installation of a permanent crisis committee to reflect on the probabilities of crisis occurrence and the respective preventive and emergency actions. Soon after, there is guidance to define the spokesperson for the media and society, as well as their training to clarify technical issues related to the crisis and coaching to develop their communicative and empathic skills (Forni 2007; Bueno 2013; Neves 2020). Also recommended are attention to the clarity, veracity, and currency of the information to be disseminated, as well as the definition of keywords to be disseminated by the different channels and their reinforcement, with a view to guaranteeing public access and understanding (Forni 2007). Shinyashiki *et al.* (2007), based on a survey of national and international literature, propose a model of crisis management actions, based on nine categories: crisis prevention, contingency procedure planning, attention directed to stakeholders, management commitment to the crisis and its impact, motivational stimuli from leadership to subordinates, maintenance of organizational values, creativity, speed in actions and post-crisis care.

Still, in terms of literature, international researchers collaborate within the scope of strategies for the recovery and restructuring of the image of organizations after the crisis (Coombs 1995, 1998; Benoit 1997). The image repair theory (Benoit 1997) is one of them. It has had its 14 strategies synthesised into four, namely: *denial, diminishment, reconstruction* and *reinforcement*, which are the response strategies used by the situational theory of crisis communication (Coombs 1995, 1998). This study is especially interested in the *denial strategy*, which removes connections between the organization and the crisis, suggesting that the organization is not to blame for it. In this case, such a strategy uses the attack on the accuser, the unrestricted denial of the crisis and the use of a scapegoat, accusing a third party. The second block of crisis response strategies is the *decrease*, based on the excuse which denies the intention to harm and states that, if it did harm, it was because of ignorance; and in justification, which admits the harm but emphasises that it is not as harmful as it seems.

Returning to the Brazilian market, it is worth emphasising the experience of FSB, a public relations agency specialising in crisis communication that occupies first place in the revenue ranking in 2020 (Mega Brasil 2021). To guide its clients, including public organizations, FSB has established a decalogue of key actions for efficient crisis management. The document highlights recommendations for the agile and concise construction of the affected organization's positioning based on real-time monitoring of the impact of the crisis, awareness of the real impact on the organization and its responsibility in the crisis. The agency guides its clients to assume their responsibility, clearly speaking what they will do to minimize the situation created by it. (FSB 2020).

In a pandemic situation, such as the one that started in 2020, the WHO (2009) advises that communication with the public is based on the principles of trust, on the immediacy of announcing news on the subject (preferably from an official source), in transparency regarding crisis management, in the analysis and understanding of the audiences and in the planning of risk communication. In fact, in a pandemic that is affecting hundreds of thousands of people in Brazil, with a growing number of contaminated and with vaccines being distributed slowly, the government's communication should strive for the well-being of the nation, avoiding polarisations and demonstrating confidence in the protocols to be adopted, in addition to taking responsibility and promoting a communication campaign that uses various channels and spokespersons with clear, accurate, truthful and constantly updated information.

Expanding accesses: The theory of channel complementarity and infodemic

In the crisis management contingency planning already presented, attention to channels ensures assertive communication with stakeholders with the speed and reliability necessary to sustain key messages. In this sense, the theory of channel complementarity (Dutta-Bergman 2004) accords with the Brazilian literature to explain how individuals seek information from different sources. Such theory advocates that individuals use multiple sources, in this case media channels, during the information search process to confirm and expand their knowledge on a given topic. Later, other researchers expanded the media conception of the origin of channels to include interpersonal sources such as family, friends and health professionals (Tian and Robinson 2008).

Even though Dutta-Bergman (2004) advocates that channel complementarity occurs between media channels, the study by Nieves-Cuervo *et al.* (2021) where they describe the behaviour of the dissemination of false news on the internet in six Latin American countries – Argentina, Brazil, Chile, Colombia, Mexico and Peru – brings the infodemic scenario as an influencing factor for people's search for complementary and reliable information channels.

About Brazil, Nieves-Cuervo *et al.* (2021, p. 4) point out that 'with the exception of Brazil, where government actions were limited, the remaining five Countries analysed quantified the impact of the pandemic and actions to control the infodemic were implemented in their territories, as they were promoted nationally and internationally'. According to the Dutta-Bergman theory of channel complementarity (2004) the consumption of other media should have positive effects, as public interest in quality information on offer generated greater trust. However, in Brazil, the effect was the opposite: without a correct government reference, the informational dynamic was contaminated by misinformation.

> In Brazil, it is difficult to assess the role played by fake news and mortality behaviour, because the management of the pandemic has been characterized by poor implementation of political and governmental actions, governance problems, changes in health ministers and insufficient response to the pandemic in general, which has led the country to rank among the nations with the highest COVID-19 incidence and mortality in the world.
>
> (Nieves-Cuervo *et al.* 2021, p. 5)

Although Nieves-Cuervo *et al.* (2021) warn that there is no cause-effect relationship between the low capacity to recognize fake news in more than half of the population of the six countries evaluated, the data presented show that the countries with greater confidence in the content of social media generally had high mortality rates, a concrete situation in Brazil during the pandemic.

With this in mind, the collaborations of Dutta-Bergman (2004), Tian and Robinson (2008) and Nieves-Cuervo *et al.* (2021) enable crisis communication managers, especially in the governmental sphere, to comply with the principles of public communication more efficiently, as well as anchor the direct relationship and advertising strategies which demarcate state communication (Weber 2011).

Conclusion

The COM-COVID survey in Brazil, by bringing empirical data on the population's perception of the sources, messages and channels used at the beginning of the pandemic in the country, leads to a brief situational analysis under the theoretical perspective of crisis communication in the government sphere, the complementarity of channels and in the infodemic. The main learning experience is related to the governmental federal and state spheres of the country that used crisis communication strategies during the pandemic, however dissonant from each other. And such opposition is reflected in the sample's perception of the public and private communication process existing in the health crisis.

On one hand, we have the federal government, represented in the figure of President Bolsonaro. His statements, from the onset to the worsening of the

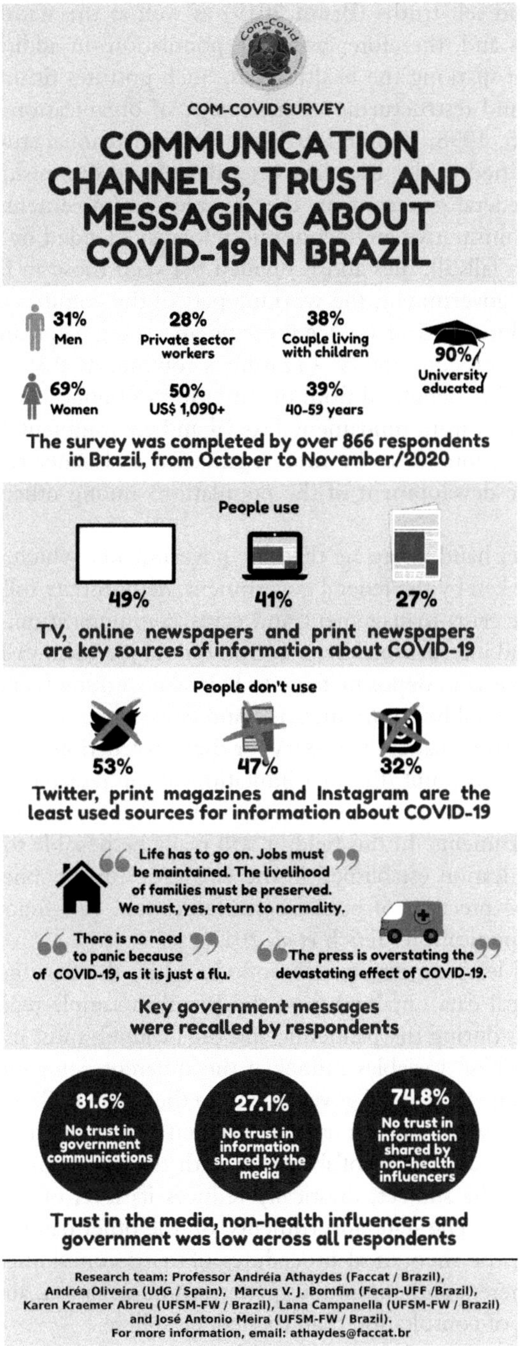

Infographic 13.1 Communication channels, trust and messaging about COVID-19 in Brazil

pandemic in Brazil, indicate the denial of the disease, deliberate dissemination of untruths and self-truths (Brum 2019) as well as the withholding of data from the press and, therefore, from the population, in addition to accusing third parties of sparking the health crisis. Such postures fit into strategies for the recovery and restructuring of the image of organizations after the crisis (Coombs 1995, 1998; Benoit 1997), whose international studies record two of them identified in the Brazilian case: denial and diminishment. By being used by the federal government, they enable the implementation of several neoliberal administrative and economic reforms defended by it. Thus, while the population falls ill, dies and is divided between those in favour or not of the Bolsonaro government, the working part of the country sees their labour rights being eliminated or reduced, giving an even greater unequal favouritism to the business community – a business community that, in different economic sectors, has benefited from privatisation of public companies and laws that exempt them from fundamental social and environmental responsibilities in a society that intends to be more egalitarian and generate sustainably the socioeconomic development of the population, among others not addressed in this study.

On the other hand, there are the state governments, which, contrary to the denial stance taken by the federal government, demonstrate following the basic procedures for crisis management and crisis communication, as indicated in the national and international literature on the subject (Shinyashiki *et al.* 2007). Thus, they serve as an opposing force to federal government practices, asserting the principles of public communication and government communication strategies (Weber 2011) that are necessary for the construction and maintenance of citizenship. At this point, the first limitation of the research is registered: not analysing the communicative structures and strategic planning of the federal and state governments. In this field, it will really be possible to verify whether crisis communication established in the two government spheres, in addition to meeting the precepts of public communication, also follow the scope of strategic communication (Tench *et al.* 2017).

The second learning experience, influenced by the first one, is confirmed by the empirical data obtained from the Brazilian sample regarding the most reliable sources during the pandemic and the channels most used to search for information. These variables influence the different perception of the main messages given by the federal government, in the figure of President Bolsonaro. The Brazilian government, by using denial and crisis reduction strategies in its communication, as well as collaborating with the infodemic (Nieves-Cuervo *et al.* 2021) on the subject, drastically reduces its level of confidence in the sample consulted. The state governments, on the other hand, by following, in part or totally, the theoretical procedures of crisis communication, trying to maintain a coherent and continuous pattern of information, are seen as a more reliable source of consultation than the federal sphere.

The level of trust in the sources is influenced by the channels that the Brazilian sample consumes and is manifested in the different perception that each subgroup of the sample has about the main messages given by the federal government. A sample with a higher educational level seeks more traditional channels and more consistent sources on the subject to understand the pandemic situation. In this case, it is worth remembering the efforts of the national media to obtain information withheld by the federal government through the consortium of communication vehicles created at the beginning of the pandemic and through its recent campaigns against the fake news in the country. The media, then, becomes more trustworthy than the federal and state governments, losing out to health organizations and professionals. These, in turn, assume a greater role due to the position adopted by the Bolsonaro government and for being, in essence, authority on the theme of the existing crisis. Thus, the theory of channel complementarity (Dutta-Bergman 2004; Tian and Robinson 2008) is applicable in the Brazilian COM-COVID study and collaborates with it, adding more information for reflection. In this case, Brazilians with higher education levels seek information through more channels and can better understand the health crisis and, therefore, are able to preserve their own health and lives. Official IBGE data indicate that Brazilians in this condition, if contaminated by COVID-19, are less likely to die and more likely to recover than are illiterate Brazilians.

The conclusions end by understanding that the study presented here satisfies the general objectives of the EUPRERA research, even if another limiting factor was the characteristic of the sample, which is not a full representation of Brazil in socioeconomic terms. Nevertheless, it is pertinent to look at the demands and characteristics of the Brazilian population, whose diversities and inequalities interfere in how they perceive information and how they relate to government communication. Considering the role of EUPRERA in cross-cultural studies, there are some recommendations for the continuation of this international research in 2021 and 2022, collaboratively opening the research framework to: 1) consider factors that reveal the behaviour of citizens compared to their respective nation-states, in order not to be restricted to analysing only the communicative flows of communication systems and strategies; 2) observe the epistemic dispute of communication, one of the factors for the generation of misinformation whose mediation takes place in public, governmental or private media within the public sphere, with the press, social media, digital influencers and controversial public spaces that interfere in the media reception of public interest and key messages for coping with the pandemic; and 3) the adjustments in the research framework may bring other perspectives, comparing the experiences of European countries with countries in the Global South, especially in Latin America, as the European experience in terms of public and governmental communication differs from the Brazilian and Latin American experience. Finally, it is understandable that, due to the historical bias that constitutes the construction of nation-states and the evolution of their democratic systems, the investigation of communication processes and strategies permeates the investigation and construction of critical and structural elements of countries.

Bibliography

Alves, J.E.P. (2007). Comunicação de risco, elemento-chave na gestão de crises corporativas e um desafio para o século XXI: a teoria na prática, situação atual e tendências. [13 June 2007] *Organicom, Revista Brasileira de Comunicação Organizacional e Relações Públicas*, 4(6) [online] São Paulo, pp. 86–99. doi:10.11606/issn.2238-2593.organicom.2007.138927 [Accessed 15 April 2021].

Barata, R.B. (2000). Cem anos de endemias e epidemias. *Ciência & Saúde Coletiva* [online], 5(2) 333–345. doi:10/frw7c4 [Accessed 15 April 2021].

BBC News Brasil (2020). Relembre frases de Bolsonaro sobre a COVID-19 [online]. *British Broadcasting Corporation BBC*. Available from: www.bbc.com/portuguese/brasil-53327880 [Accessed 20 April 2021].

Benoit, W.L. (1997). Image repair discourse and crisis communication. *Public Relations Review*, 23(2), pp. 177–186.

Bomfim, C. (2020). Dengue, Zika ou Chicungúnya: saiba diferenciar essas três doenças. *Universo On Line – UOL, Viva Bem* [online]. Available from: www.uol.com.br/vivabem/noticias/redacao/2020/04/06/e-dengue-zika-ou-chikungunya-saiba-diferenciar-essas-tres-doencas.htm [Accessed 12 April 2021].

Brandão, E.P. (1998). Comunicação pública. In: Sociedade Brasileira de Estudos Interdisciplinares de Comunicação. *XXI Congresso Brasileiro de Ciências da Comunicação – Intercom* [online]. Recife, September 1998. Available from: https://fasam.edu.br/wp-content/uploads/2020/07/Comunica%C3%A7%C3%A3o-P%C3%BAblica-Paper-Intercom.pdf [Accessed 15 April 2021].

Brigatti, F. (2020, April 2). Como as medidas tomadas pelo governo me afetam? Veja seu caso. *Folha de São Paulo* [online]. Available from: www1.folha.uol.com.br/mercado/2020/04/veja-as-medidas-do-governo-para-conter-demissoes-e-ampliar-assistencia-social-duraante-crise-do-coronavirus.shtml [Accessed 15 April 2021].

Brum, E. (2019). *Brasil, Construtor de Ruínas. Um olhar sobre o Brasil, de Lula a Bolsonaro*. Porto Alegre: Arquipélago Editorial.

Bueno, W.C. (2013). Gestão e estratégias de comunicação em situações críticas. *Comunicação e Sociedade*, 34(2) [online]. doi:10.15603/2175-7755/cs.v34n2p41-66 [Accessed 15 April 2021].

Calil, G.C. (2020). A negação da pandemia: reflexões sobre a estratégia bolsonarista. *Serviço Social & Sociedade*, 140 30–47 [online]. doi:10.1590/0101-6628.236 [Accessed 15 April 2021].

Cardia, W. (2015). *Crise de Imagem e Gerenciamento de Crises*. Rio de Janeiro: Mauad.

Cazarré, M. (2020, March 16). Países fecham fronteiras para evitar propagação do coronavírus: medida foi tomada por Argentina, Honduras e Peru. *Agência Brasil EBC* [online]. Available from: https://agenciabrasil.ebs.com.br/geralnotícia/2020-03/paises-fecham-fronteiras-para-evitar-propagacao-do-coronavirus [Accessed 20 July 2021].

Coombs, W.T. (1995). Choosing the right words: The development of guidelines for the selection of the 'appropriate' crisis-response strategies. *Management Communication Quarterly*, 8(4) 447–476.

Coombs, W.T. (1998). An analytic framework for crisis situations, *Journal of Public Relations Research*, 10.

Cruz, M.F.R. (2014). *O dever do Estado na efetivação do direito à saúde: os papéis dos poderes Executivo, Legislativo e Judiciário*. Master's Dissertation. Faculdade de Saúde Pública, Universidade de São Paulo USP, São Paulo. Available from: www.teses.usp.br. doi:10.11606/D.6.2014.tde-17102014-101022 [Accessed 15 April 2021].

Dutta-Bergman, M.J. (2004). Interpersonal communication after 9/11 via telephone and internet: A theory of channel complementarity. *New Media & Society*, 6(5) 659–673. Thousand Oaks, CA: SAGE Publications London. doi:10.1177%2F146144804047086 [Accessed 15 April 2021].

Fordelone, Y. (2020). *Econoweek – retrospectiva 2020.* Universo On Line – UOL [online]. Available from: https://economia.uol.com.br/colunas/econoweek/2020/12/01/retrospectiva-2020-o-que-aconteceu-na-economia.html [Accessed 29 April 2021].

Forni, J.J. (2007). Comunicação em tempos de crise [13 June 2007]. *Organicom, Revista Brasileira de Comunicação Organizacional e Relações Públicas*, 4(6) [online] São Paulo, pp. 196–214. doi:10.11606/issn.2238-2593.organicom.2007.138934

Forni, J.J. (2010). O Papel da Comunicação na Gestão de Crises. *Comunifé Revista de Comunicación Social*, 10(X), pp. 127–140. [online]. doi:10.33539/comunife.2010.n10.2035 [Accessed 15 April 2021].

Forni, J.J. (2019). *Gestão de Crises e Comunicação. O que os gestores e profissionais de comunicação precisam saber para enfrentar crises corporativas*, 3rd. ed. São Paulo: Atlas.

Frota Torres, T.J., de Sousa Júnior, A.R., and Freire Brazil, V.T. (2021). As características e os impactos da narrativa de Jair Messias Bolsonaro. *Boletim de Conjuntura (BOCA)*.5(15) 01–14. doi:10.5281/zenodo.4553171 [Accessed 15 April 2021].

FSB Comunicação (2020). *Gerenciamento de crise na prática: tudo o que você precisa saber* [online]. Available from: www.fsb.com.br/noticias/gerenciamento-de-crise/ [Accessed 15 April 2021].

Fundação Getúlio Vargas, FGV (2020). *Monitor do PIB.* Instituto Brasileiro de Economia – IBRE, FGV. Available from: https://portalibre.fgv.br [Accessed 5 April 2021].

Gazeta do Povo (2021). *Números da COVID-19 hoje no Brasil e no Mundo: mortes e casos, Gazeta do Povo, Especiais* [online]. Available from: https://especiais.gazetadopovo.com.br/coronavirus/numeros/ [Accessed 20 April 2021].

Grandin, F., Sarmento, G., and Tooge, R. (2021). Coronavírus e desabastecimento: veja perguntas e respostas. *G1 Globo* [online]. Available from: htps://g1.globo.com/economia/notícia2020/03/20/coronavirus-e-desabastecimento-veja-perguntas-e-respostassobre-a-questao-dos-alimentos-no-brasil.ghtml [Accessed 15 April 2021].

Instituto Brasileiro de Economia, IBRE (2020). Fundação Getúlio Vargas – FGV, *Monitor do PIB*, Instituto Brasileiro de Economia – IBRE, FGV. Available from: https://portalibre.fgv.br [Accessed 5 April 2021].

Instituto Brasileiro de Geografia e Estatística – IBGE (2015). Available from: https://brasilemsintese.ibge.gov.br/educacao/anos-de-estudo.html [Accessed 15 July 2021].

Mega Brasil Comunicações (2021). *Anuário da Comunicação Corporativa.* Available from: www.virapagina.com.br/megAprilasil/anuario2021/2/ [Accessed 30 April 2021].

Mino Carta (2020). Governadores de 20 estados divulgam carta após discurso de Bolsonaro. *Carta Capital* [online]. Available from: www.cartacapital.com.br/política/governadores-de-20-estados-divulgam-carta-apos-discurso-de-bolsonaro [Accessed 15 April 2021].

Neves, R.C. (2020). *Crises empresariais com a opinião pública: como evitá-las e administrá-las.* Rio de Janeiro: Mauad.

Nieves-Cuervo, G.M., Manrique-Hernández, E.F., Robledo-Colonia, A.F., and Grillo, A.E.K. (2021). Infodemia: noticias falsas y tendencias de mortalidad por COVID-19 em seis países de America Latina. *Panam Salud Publica*, 45(e44). doi:10.26633/RPSP.2021.44. [Accessed 15 April 2021].

Organización Panamericana de La Salud, OPS (2020). *Respuesta de la OPS/OMS. 31 de Marzo del 2020. Informe 1. Pan American Health Organization/World Health Organization.*

Washington. Available from: https://iris.paho.org/bitstream/handle/10665.2/52404/COVID-19SitRep1_spa.pdf

Pesquisa Nacional por Amostra de Domicílios – PNAD Contínua, (2018). *Condições de vida, desigualdade e pobreza, PNAD Contínua.* IBGE. Available from: https://ibge.gov.br/estatisticas/multidominio/condicoes-de-vida-desigualdade-e-pobreza/17270-pnad-continua.html [Accessed 8 April 2021].

Pesquisa Nacional por Amostra de Domicílios – PNAD COVID-19 (2020). Available from: https://covid19.ibge.gov.br/pnad-covid/ [Accessed 15 April 2021].

Prado, E. (org.) (2020). *Gestão de reputação. Riscos, Crise e Imagem Corporativa.* São Paulo: Aberje Editorial.

Redação Brasil Atual, (2021) [online]. Comitê de combate à pandemia: um ano atrasado. *Rede Brasil Atual.* Available from: www.redebrasilatual.com.br/politica/2021/03/bolsonaro-comite-combate-pandemia-um-ano-atrasado/ [Accessed 15 April 2021].

Ronan, G. (2020). Brasil fecha 2020 com 194.949 mortes por COVID-19. *Estado de Minas.* Available at: www.em.com.br/app/noticia/nacional/2020/12/31/interna_nacional,1225164/brasil-fecha-2020-com-194-949-mortes-por-covid-19.shtml [Accessed 10 April 2021].

Schuch, J.B. (2020). Bolsonaro critica OMS e diz que entidade no acerta nada. *Valor Econômico,* [online]. Available from: https://valorinveste.globo.com/mercados/brasil-e-politica/noticia/2020/06/18/bolsonaro-critica-oms-e-diz-que-entidade-no-acerta-nada.ghtm [Accessed 18 June 2021].

Shinyashiki, R.T., Fischer, R.M., and Shinyashiki, G. (2007). A importância de um sistema integrado de ações na gestão de crises. *Organicom, Comunicação de risco e crise: prevenção e gerenciamento,* 4(6), São Paulo, pp. 149–159. [online]. [13 June 2007]. doi:10.11606/issn.2238-2593.organicom.2007.13893 [Accessed 15 April 2021].

Stoodi (2020). *Diversidade cultural: o que é e divisão no Brasil!* Available from: www.stoodi.com.br/blog/geografia/diversidade-cultural/ [Accessed 15 April 2021].

Tench, R., Verčič, D., Zerfass, A., Moreno, A., and Verhoeven, P. (2017). *Communication excellence: How to develop, manage and lead exceptional communications.* London: Publisher Palgrave MacMillan, ISBN: 978-3-319-48860-8. doi:10.1007978-3-319-48860-8.

Tian, Y., and Robinson, J.D. (2008). Media use and health information seeking: An empirical test of complementarity theory. *Health Communication,* 23, pp. 184–190. doi:10.1080/10410230801968260 [Accessed 15 April 2021].

Veras, T. (2020). Negacionismo viral e política exterminista: notas sobre o caso brasileiro da COVID-19. *Voluntas: Revista Internacional de Filosofia,* 11, e45. doi:10.5902/2179378643934 [Accessed 15 April 2021].

Villela, E. (2016). Comunicação de risco versus comunicação de crise na saúde pública: o discurso das autoridades diante de uma epidemia de dengue. *Revista Eletrônica de Comunicação, Informação e Inovação em Saúde,* 10(4). doi:10.29397/reciis.v10i4.1178 [Accessed 15 April 2021].

Viscardi, J.M. (2020, May–August). Fake news, verdade e mentira sob a ótica de Jair Bolsonaro no Twitter. *Trabalhos em Linguística Aplicada.* 59(2), Campinas, pp. 1134–1157. doi: 10.1590/01031813715891620200520 [Accessed 15 April 2021].

We are social (2019). *Resumo e relatório* [online]. Available from: www.amper.ag/post/we-are-social-e-hootsuite-digital-2021-resumo-e-relat%C3%B3rio [Accessed 15 April 2021].

Weber, M.H. (2011). Estratégias da comunicação de estado e a disputa por visibilidade e opinião. In K. M.M.K. (org.). *Comunicação pública, sociedade e cidadania.* São Caetano do Sul: Difusão Editora, pp. 101–119.

World Health Organization, WHO (2009). *Comunicação eficaz com a mídia durante emergências de saúde pública – um manual da OMS* [online]. Título original: Effective Media Communication during Public Health Emergencies: A WHO handbook, 2007. Tradução: Ministério da Saúde, Série A, Normas e Manuais Técnicos. Available from: www.saude.gov.br/bvs [Accessed 3 March 2021].

Zémor, P.A. (2003). Comunicação pública. Tradução: Elisabeth Brandão. In M., L. (org.). *Algumas abordagens em Comunicação Pública.* Brasília: Casa das Musas, pp. 76–103.

America – North

14 Factors influencing Americans' preventive behaviours during the COVID-19 pandemic

Lessons for strategic health and risk communicators

Sung In Choi, Yan Jin and Mark Badham

Introduction

This chapter examines factors influencing Americans' preventive behaviours, including their intentions to take the COVID-19 vaccine, in response to the U.S. government's strategic communication about COVID-19 guidelines for Americans to follow. We understand preventive health behaviour to mean 'any activity undertaken by an individual who believes himself to be healthy for the purpose of preventing or detecting illness in an asymptomatic state' (Kasl and Cobb 1966, p. 246). Given that containment of the pandemic in the USA depends on the majority of Americans following the government's recommended actions, especially taking the vaccine, understanding what affects individuals' preventive behaviours is important to current and future strategic communicators dealing with major public health crises. The infectious disease threat (IDT) appraisal model (Jin *et al.* 2020) advocates that it is critical for strategic health and risk communicators to identify those factors that might boost the public's preventive behaviour in the face of an IDT.

Accordingly, this chapter draws on the theory of planned behaviour (TPB) (Ajzen 1985) to shed light on three factors that shape conscious decision-making and can therefore help strategic health and risk communicators predict future behaviour. These factors are *attitude* toward a recommended vaccine, *social norms* (i.e., the likelihood that individuals will follow others' opinions about recommended behaviour) and *self-efficacy* (i.e., individuals' confidence in their own ability to follow recommended behaviour). Other studies examining how individual behaviours comply with government recommendation (e.g., vaccination) have focused on factors predicting behavioural intention such as communicative action (i.e., information seeking, information attending, information forwarding and information sharing) (Chon and Park 2021) and sociodemographic variables (Papageorge *et al.* 2020). Sociodemographic differences in crisis responses can play a critical role in predicting public health behaviours (Harrington *et al.* 2011). For example, studies demonstrate that age and education levels can shape preventive behaviours (Levy and Myers 2004; Lodi-Smith *et al.* 2010; Uddin *et al.* 2021).

DOI: 10.4324/9781003184669-22

However, very few studies have combined TPB and sociodemographic factors to predict public behavioural responses to health authorities' COVID-19 communications. To address this research gap, this chapter aims to understand, within the U.S. COVID-19 context, 1) whether and how sociodemographic factors of *age* and *education* levels might affect TPB factors of *attitude, social norms* and *self-efficacy*, and 2) how the cause-effect associations between these sociodemographic-TPB factors might influence the public's intention to take the COVID-19 vaccine. Using a dataset from an online survey in October and November 2020 of a representative adult sample (N=500) in the United States, recruited by a professional survey firm, this study examines the relationships between these TPB and sociodemographic factors. Based on regression models, the results reveal that self-efficacy and social norms, together with age and education, are significant positive predictors of participants' intention to follow recommended preventive actions.

This chapter discusses this and other results with a view to advancing strategic health communication theory and practice by identifying essential factors in predicting health behaviours among adults in the United States. Our results provide insights for improving effectiveness of COVID-19 messages and public communications in motivating publics to take recommended preventive actions in current and future public health risk and crisis situations. We conclude the chapter with practical recommendations for strategic health communicators facing these challenges.

Experiencing COVID-19

This study took place during October and November 2020, a turbulent time in the United States as the country continued to set new highs for COVID-19 infections each week. As shown in Figure 14.1, in November 2020, U.S. COVID-19 cases passed 4 million, doubling the record set in October (Centers for Disease Control and Prevention [CDC] 2021). In fact, daily COVID-19 deaths in the U.S. at this time began to reflect the record level set back in April of that year (Stobbe 2020). Political tensions surrounding the pandemic were also rising in the lead-up to the 2020 U.S. presidential elections set for 3 November. In the midst of a political firestorm as well as a global pandemic, the U.S. government, primarily represented by U.S. President Donald Trump, the U.S. Centers for Disease Control and Prevention (CDC), and the White House Coronavirus Task Force, had been trying to manage its COVID-19 messaging via daily press briefings, CDC and White House websites, and social media.

Mixed COVID-19 messages about recommended personal behaviours (e.g., face masks, social distancing and vaccinations) and pandemic severity were emanating from the U.S. Government, particularly from President Trump himself (Balog-Way and McComas 2020). For example, a month after the U.S. Surgeon General tweeted that face masks 'are NOT effective' for the general public (Jingnan 2020), the CDC recommended wearing 'cloth face coverings' in public (CDC 2020). A few days after President Trump had played down the severity of the virus by comparing it to the annual flu (26 February 2020), he later stated: 'This is not the flu. It is vicious' (31 March) (Watson 2020; Bennett and Berenson 2020). Although a COVID-19 vaccine was at the forefront of the CDC's strategy to fight the pandemic, the American public were showing signs of a lack of trust in the vaccine at this time. The first vaccine, produced by Pfizer, was scheduled for release to the American population on 20 November following emergency use authorization approval by the U.S. Food and Drug Administration (FDA). With expectations that influenza cases would begin to increase in October, thus complicating containment of the spread of COVID-19, the CDC began recommending that Americans take a 2020–2021 flu vaccine (FDA 2020). However, according to a Gallup poll in September 2020, only half of Americans indicated they would take the vaccine, increasing slightly to 58% in late October (Reinhart 2020). Despite the U.S. government working closely with pharmaceutical companies to speed up the production of a COVID-19 vaccine, some political leaders (e.g., presidential candidate Joe Biden, vice presidential candidate Kamala Harris, and U.S. House Speaker Nancy Pelosi) publicly conveyed scepticism towards the vaccine, stating that the White House was fast-tracking approval for vaccine production and distribution for political reasons (Osborne 2020; Satter 2020).

Our study, situated in this turbulent period, captures a picture of how individual Americans were responding to the U.S. government's strategic communication aimed at informing them about the most effective ways to avoid contracting the virus and thus to prevent its spread. Grounded in public health theory, our findings shed further light on the associations of sociodemographic factors and individuals' varied responses to COVID-19 messages from the U.S. government. We also offer recommendations for effective strategic communication management during future public health emergencies such as pandemics.

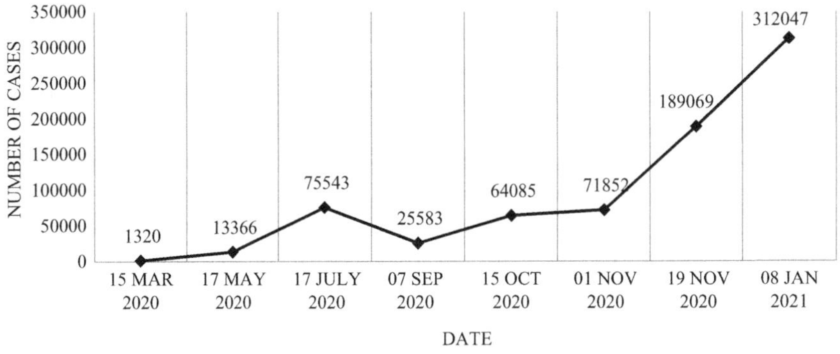

Figure 14.1 Trends in number of COVID-19 cases in the United States reported to CDC

Source: COVID Data Tracker from Centers for Disease Control and Prevention. Available from: https://covid.cdc.gov/covid-data-tracker/

The state of play

This study used the theory of planned behaviour to examine factors influencing Americans' preventive behaviours.

Theory of planned behaviour

One way to model the factors affecting an individual's health-related decision is through the theory of planned behaviour (TPB) (Ajzen 1985). The TPB, an extension of the theory of reasoned action (Ajzen and Fishbein 1980), is a value-expectancy model that presumes an individual is a rational decision maker who considers choices and consequences of a behaviour before engaging in it. The TPB is known as a robust theory to investigate the factors that underlie conscious decision-making across multiple contexts (Chan *et al.* 2020; Chirico *et al.* 2020; Lee *et al.* 2014; Wiemken *et al.* 2015). According to the theory, behavioural intention, which refers to a person's tendency to perform a particular behaviour, is the most crucial predictor of future behaviour. Individuals with a strong behavioural intention to perform a specific behaviour are much more likely to engage in the behaviour than those with a weak behavioural intention.

In TPB, there are three elements – attitude, social norms, and self-efficacy – predicting health-related behaviour. First, there is significant evidence that individuals' attitudes toward a recommended behaviour have an impact on compliance with recommended behaviour. For example, individuals' attitudes toward HIV vaccine influence their vaccine acceptance (Gagnon and Godin 2000), and their beliefs and practices can influence their vaccine hesitancy and future behaviour (Xiao and Wong 2020). Second, social norms function as different types of normative beliefs and are determined by a series of normative beliefs and an individual's motivation to comply with them. Normative beliefs are the individual beliefs that underlie social norms; they involve specific individuals (e.g., a friend, parent or religious leader) or groups (e.g., church, sorority or school) that may influence how individuals perceive a particular behaviour. In one study, for example, parents reported other family members, health associations and health professionals as salient referent groups that would approve of them serving vegetables to their children (Villarrubia 2006). Other evidence indicates that normative approaches can influence young adults' health, specifically related to parents' willingness to take a vaccine. Third, self-efficacy is related to perceived behavioural control and refers to the perception that performance of a specific behaviour is within a person's volitional control (Ajzen 1991). Self-efficacy can be seen as a capacity to execute seemingly easy behaviours at one end and more demanding behaviours (e.g., those behaviours that require more resources, information or specialised skills) at the other (Ajzen 1991). This is an important variable in the current context of the COVID-19 pandemic, as individuals often do not feel entirely in control of whether they can implement healthy behaviour. Therefore, our study poses the question:

RQ1: How do Americans' (a) attitude, (b) social norms and (c) self-efficacy influence their actual preventive behaviours in response to the U.S. government's COVID-19 guidelines?

In a health-related crisis setting, organizations and publics are both regarded as being affected by the crisis (Kim and Jin 2020). Informing people of recommended behaviours and persuading them to follow the instructions are among the top priorities in managing public health crises. Previous studies have focused on how individuals' behavioural compliance with the government's recommendation (e.g., vaccination) is formed by examining which factors are involved with the behaviour (Chon and Park 2021). The identified factors include communicative action and sociodemographic variables. For example, Chon and Park's (2021) study demonstrated that communicative action (i.e., information seeking) predicted behavioural intention to follow CDC recommendations among the U.S. survey participants. Sociodemographic variables such as age and education were also found to be related to public support for government guidelines on how to deal with a public health crisis (Paek 2008). In the COVID-19 communication context, considering that vaccination intention is one of the most important variables in managing a public health crisis, our study further examines U.S. adults' vaccination intention within a wide spectrum of compliance behaviours recommended by the U.S. government. Seeking to understand whether Americans' overall intention to follow the government's recommendations in the context of the COVID-19 pandemic predicts their vaccination intention specifically, we posit the following question:

RQ2: How do Americans' age and education moderate their (a) attitude, (b) social norms and (c) self-efficacy towards preventive behaviours in response to the U.S. government's COVID-19 guidelines?

Sociodemographic differences in crisis responses can play a critical role in predicting health behaviour (Papageorge *et al.* 2020). In fact, existing studies have demonstrated the association between age and self-preventive behaviour (Jones and Salathé 2009; Lau *et al.* 2007). Jones and Salathé (2009) found that older age was associated with more frequent hand washing during the H1N1 swine flu outbreak. Older people showed they would take self-protective behaviours in the outbreak of avian influenza (Lau *et al.* 2007). Despite a revealed association between gender and age difference in risk-related responses, these two factors have not been studied in relation to intention to comply with public health recommendations. In addition, especially in the U.S., individuals with a high education level tend to have higher intention to follow health behaviours such as reducing soft drink consumption (Ahn and Lee 2019) and taking a flu vaccine (Lau *et al.* 2007). Therefore, based on the theory of TPB mentioned previously, age and education levels are expected to moderate between attitude, social norms and self-efficacy on actual behaviour. Hence, the following research question is asked:

> RQ3: How does Americans' intention to take the vaccine influence their actual decision to take the vaccine?

Online survey among U.S. adults

In order to investigate whether and how sociodemographic factors (i.e., age and education, in this study) function as key predictors that help explain the disparities in health behaviour outcomes (Lin *et al.* 2020b) in the context of COVID-19 communication in the U.S., the study we report in this chapter is based on a survey conducted during October and November 2020 in the U.S. by a professional online survey firm. The survey was conducted using computer-assisted web interviewing (CAWI) methodology and the questionnaire was presented online through a web interface. The survey questioned 500 American respondents, a representative sample of the population as stratified by age, gender and ethnicities in the U.S.

Measurements

Vaccine attitude

Vaccine attitude was adapted from measures in Kim *et al.*'s (2020) study. For instance, participants were asked this question: 'Please indicate how you feel about getting a COVID-19 vaccine. If it becomes available, getting a COVID-19 vaccine will be . . .'. The items were averaged together to create an index that ranged from 1 (Bad) to 7 (Good) as a semantic scale.

Social norms

Social norms to follow government recommendations were adapted from measures from Ahn *et al.*'s (2020) study. For instance, one of the items regarding intention to follow recommendations was adapted as 'Most of the people who are important to me think that I should perform preventive COVID-19 behaviours'. The items were averaged together to create an index that ranged from 1 (Totally disagree) to 7 (Totally agree).

Self-efficacy

Intention to follow government recommendations was adapted from measures from So *et al.*'s (2019) study. For instance, one of the items regarding self-efficacy was adapted as 'It is easy for me to prevent COVID-19 infection'. The items were averaged together to create an index that ranged from 1 (Totally disagree) to 7 (Totally agree).

Actual preventive behaviour

Participants were asked this question: 'How often do you perform the following behaviours that the WHO/CDC recommended?' Actual preventive behaviour measures in this study were adapted from measures in Lin *et al.*'s (2020a) study. For instance, one of the items was adapted as 'Maintain distance between yourself and others'. The items were averaged together to create an index that ranged from 1 (Never) to 7 (Always).

Vaccination intention

Vaccination intention was adapted from measures in Gerend and Shepherd's (2007) study. Participants responded to the three questions. For instance, one of the questions was adapted as 'How likely is that you will consider getting a COVID-19 vaccine if it is available?' The items were averaged together to create an index that ranged from 1 (Very unlikely) to 7 (Very likely).

Data analysis

A series of multivariate regression analyses were conducted to examine which factors affect preventive behaviour and vaccination intentions. First, we analysed how vaccine attitude, social norms and self-efficacy affect preventive behaviour. Second, the effect of preventive behaviour on vaccination intention was measured. Then, Macro Process Model 2 was used to examine the moderating effects of age and education levels between the three independent variables and preventive behaviour. Analyses were weighted, and SPSS 26.0 was used for all analyses.

Results

Predictors of preventive behaviour

After controlling age and education level for known predictors of preventive behaviour, attitude, social norms and self-efficacy were found to be significant predictors of preventive behaviour (see Table 14.1).

Mediated effects of age and education levels

To test mediational pathways between TPB-related independent variables (i.e., attitude, social norms and self-efficacy) and preventive behaviour (RQ1), we used a Process Macro model 4 with 5000 bootstrap estimates to construct a 95% bias-corrected confidence interval effect (Preacher *et al.* 2007). This parallel multiple mediation model included attitude, social norms and self-efficacy as the independent variables, age and education level as mediators,

Table 14.1 Results of the hierarchical regression model: Predicting preventive behaviour

	Preventive behaviour		
	β	*SE*	*95% CI*
Step 1: Control variables	(0.40)		
Age	.158**	.007	.96–1.22
Education	.065	.052	.97 – .98
Step 2: Predictors	(0.43)		
Attitude	.141**	.091	.81–1.18
Social norms	.160***	.121	.82–1.10
Self-efficacy	.216***	.478	1.96–2.71

Source: Authors.

and preventive behaviour as the outcome variable (see Figures 14.1, 14.2 and 14.3).

Results indicate no indirect effect of age and education levels on the effect of attitude on preventive behaviour (indirect effect = -.04, *SE* = .02, 95% CI [-.08, -.00]). It shows no significant mediated effect of age and education levels between attitude and preventive behaviour (see Figure 14.1). As Figure 14.2 shows, there is an indirect effect of age level on the effect of social norms on preventive behaviour (indirect effect =.12, *SE* = .02, 95% CI [.08, .12]). As the age level decreased ($b = -.15$, *SE* = .24, $t = -1.50$, $p < .05$), the effect of self-efficacy on preventive behaviour increased ($b = .19$, *SE* = .34, $t = 5.12$, $p < .01$). The indirect effect of education level on the effect of social norms on behavioural intention was not significant ($b = -.22$, *SE* = .13, $t = -1.73$, $p = .48$). In addition, there is a significant moderating effect of both age and education levels on the effect of self-efficacy on preventive behaviour (indirect effect =.32, *SE* = .02, 95% CI [.08, .21]). As the age level decreased ($b = -.21$, *SE* = .11, $t = -1.71$, $p < .05$), the effect of self-efficacy on preventive behaviour increased ($b = .13$, *SE* = .24, $t = 2.60$, $p < .01$). Individuals with a higher education level tend to have higher self-efficacy, which leads to a higher level of preventive behaviour ($b = -32$, *SE* = .17, $t = 2.73$, $p = .08$).

Results of preventive behaviour and vaccine intention

The results show a positively significant relationship between preventive behaviour and vaccination intention (β= .27, SE= .55, p<.001). In other words, people who follow government health recommendations well tend to have higher vaccination intentions.

Observations and interrogation

This chapter, based on data from a recent U.S. adult online survey, examined U.S. adults' actual behaviour of following general COVID-19 health recommendations and their specific intention to receive the COVID-19 vaccine. Our

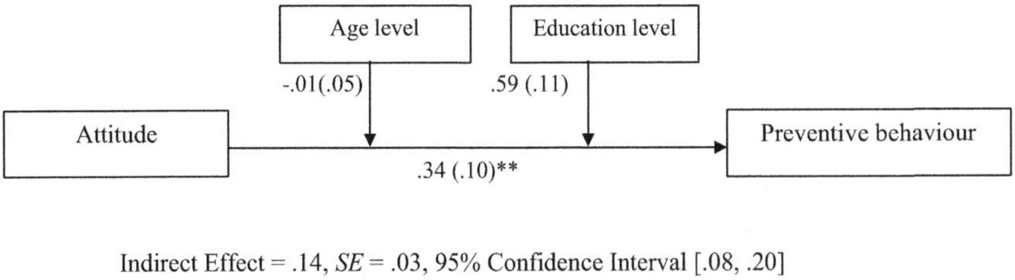

Figure 14.2 Results of moderating effect of age and education levels on the relationship between attitude and preventive behaviour

Source

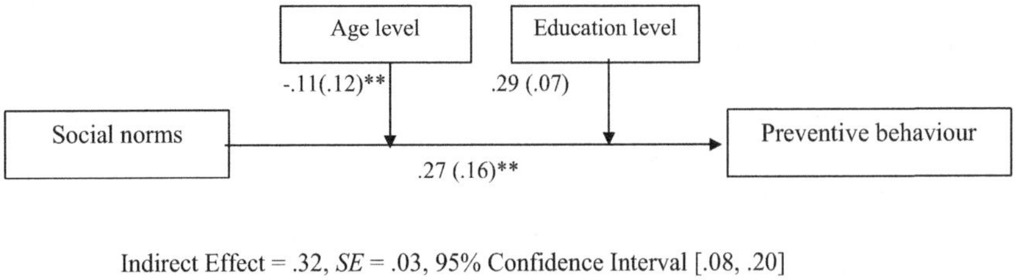

Figure 14.3 Results of moderating effect of age and education levels on the relationship between social norms and preventive behaviour

Source

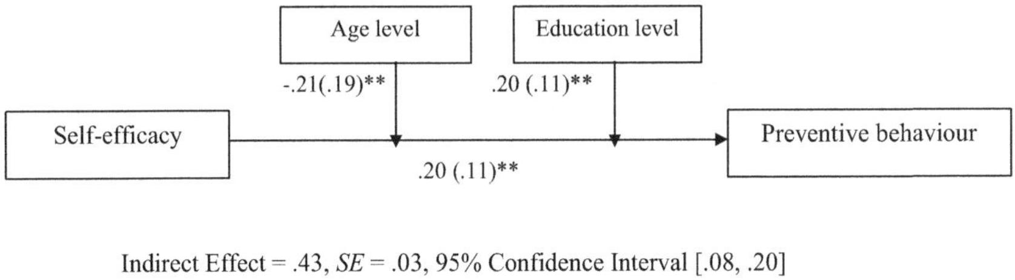

Figure 14.4 Results of moderating effect of age and education levels on the relationship between self-efficacy and preventive behaviour

Source: Authors

study also investigated factors associated with those behaviours. Overall, our survey participants reported high actual behaviour in following U.S. government health recommendations, which leads to higher vaccination intention in particular. Several sociodemographic and TPB-related variables were also found to be associated with higher and lower preventive behaviours. Next, we discuss the implications of these findings and suggest areas for future work, including research and practical application for strategic health risk communication led by governments and government health agencies.

High preventive behaviour and vaccination intention: A reflection on compliance indicators

Significantly, our U.S. survey participants reported relatively high individual preventive behaviour (on a 7-point scale, participants reported an average of 5.70). Though this is not quite a ceiling effect, we believe this suggests strong support for containing the spread of COVID-19, more so because no vaccine had been fully tested and no treatment had been made available to the public at the time of survey data collection. Our findings are consistent with other recent studies examining perceptions of COVID-19, showing high preventive behaviour among U.S. individuals (Clements 2020; Wise *et al.* 2020). Previous research shows that the relationship between behavioural intention and actual behaviour, while usually significantly positive, is not always a perfect correlation and that different predictors (e.g., perceived susceptibility, doctor recommendation) may predict intentions and actual behaviours differently (Krawczyk *et al.* 2012; Webb and Sheeran 2006). Therefore, while participants in this study reported high actual preventive behaviour against COVID-19, these findings should be interpreted cautiously. Actual preventive behaviour in following government agencies' and health authorities' recommendations will likely depend on many factors, including the status of the COVID-19 pandemic at the time (Finset *et al.* 2020). Of note for strategic communication scholars, these findings suggest that social normative messaging could capitalise on the high level of preventive behaviour. Social norms campaigns use descriptive norms (i.e., descriptive statistics) to correct or reinforce the frequency with which others are performing a behaviour, with the assumption that individuals seek to conform to the pressures of societal norms (i.e., subjective norms; see Burchell *et al.* 2013). In previous research, while most social norms campaigns target audiences who easily tend to overrate the frequency of an unhealthy behaviour (e.g., binge drinking; see Campo *et al.* 2004), the same normative principles have been revealed to predict HPV vaccination acceptance among young adults (de Visser *et al.* 2011). In the context of COVID-19, social norms messages can address COVID-19 vaccine hesitancy by highlighting the high intentions to vaccinate expressed by the majority of people in one's social network. This approach will require strategic communication practitioners to engage in more formative research to develop and test messages with different audiences, especially given the differences we observed in preventive behaviour across individuals of different socioeconomic characteristics such as age and education.

Age and education make a difference

In our study, U.S. participants with a lower education level reported a lower behaviour in following recommendations. Education is often related to health literacy (White *et al.* 2007), suggesting the critical importance of educating the public on the role of preventive behaviour in reducing COVID-19 prevalence through herd immunity. These efforts have to be completed in conjunction with messages about how herd immunity works, as previous work has shown that limited knowledge can reduce preventive behaviour (Sobo 2016). The effective implementation of 'flatten the curve' – a phrase previously not commonly used among laypeople when addressing an infectious disease outbreak – via social media is an example of effectively educating the public about complex health recommendations in accessible ways. Interestingly, participants who are younger indicated a higher self-efficacy but lower preventive behaviour. This can imply that younger individuals may have thought that preventing COVID-19 infection is easy and thus that they are not easily infected. This was contrary to what was expected. Previous work has shown that high self-efficacy results in increased healthy behaviour (Lee and Oh 2020). Given that self-efficacy can be related to trust (Alfansuri and Soetjipto 2020) or risk perception toward disease (e.g., severity of vulnerability; see Yıldırım and Güler 2020), some participants who answered this question may have limited perception about the role of self-efficacy in preventing infectious diseases. We believe further work is needed to clarify this finding. Nonetheless, our results clearly indicate that, to younger audiences and high education level audiences, self-efficacy is a strong predictor of their compliance in following government recommendations. Strategic communication practitioners in the U.S. should focus on messages emphasising self-efficacy to induce more preventive behaviours among younger and more educated groups. Also, more research is needed to examine what message strategies will be more effective in motivating older people and audiences with lower education levels to take preventive measures to protect themselves and their loved ones, thus overcoming the challenge associated with health literacy gaps and the digital divide associated with age and education as identified by health communication literature. Because effective strategic health risk communication can save lives (Seeger *et al.* 2020), this becomes more urgent than ever in a pandemic.

Conclusions

Effect of attitudes, social norms and self-efficacy on preventive behaviours

Our study found that a relatively high proportion of Americans during the survey period (October and November 2020) were adopting government-recommended behaviours to prevent infection and spread of the virus. We found that Americans' attitudes, social norms and self-efficacy influenced their preventive behaviours. Accordingly, we recommend that when planning communication to influence public behaviour during a major public health crisis, strategic health communicators should take into account the effect of people's attitudes, social norms and self-efficacy on their preventive behaviours.

Effect of preventive behaviours on vaccination intention

In our study we found that Americans who follow the government's recommended behaviours tend to have higher vaccination intentions. Accordingly, when planning communication to boost public vaccination numbers during a pandemic, strategic health communicators should take into account the effect of individuals' preventive behaviours on their intention to take the recommended vaccine. Therefore, we recommend that strategic health communicators should first try to influence the public's adoption of recommended behaviours. When high levels of behaviour adoption have been achieved, strategic health communicators should then reach out to those following government guidelines to encourage them to take the vaccine.

Effect of age and education on attitude, social norms and self-efficacy affecting preventive behaviours

When planning communication to influence public behaviour during a major public health crisis, strategic health communicators should take into account the effect that sociodemographic factors such as age and education have on people's attitude, social norms and self-efficacy towards preventive behaviours. The following takeaways from our research and the associated recommendations are based on our study's main findings.

Age as an influencer of social norms

To get more Americans adopting preventive behaviours during a pandemic, strategic health communicators should consider age as an influencer of social norms surrounding government recommended actions. For example, our study shows that younger Americans are more likely to be influenced by social norms to adopt recommended behaviours. In other words, younger Americans' preventive behaviours are influenced by other people's opinions about those behaviours. The younger they are, the more social norms will drive their adoption of preventive behaviours. Thus, strategic communicators should try to influence the opinions of those people who influence younger Americans, such as social media influencers, families and close friends.

Age as an influencer of self-efficacy

To get more Americans adopting preventive behaviours during a pandemic, strategic health communicators should consider Americans' age as an influencer of self-efficacy (i.e., confidence in their ability to follow recommended behaviours). Our study shows that younger Americans have higher levels of self-efficacy than older Americans. Accordingly, communication to younger Americans recommending proper actions in response to a pandemic is more likely to result in higher levels of preventive behaviours among this group.

Because we found that older Americans have lower self-efficacy towards adopting recommended behaviours, when communicating with older Americans, strategic health communicators should try to boost their confidence in their own ability to adopt recommended behaviours. This may be achieved through showing them clear, easy-to-follow steps and telling them stories of how other older people have been able to follow the guidelines.

Education as an influencer of self-efficacy

To get more Americans adopting preventive behaviours during a pandemic, strategic health communicators should consider education as an influencer of self-efficacy. Our study found that Americans with higher education levels tend to have higher self-efficacy to follow recommended actions, thus leading to higher levels of preventive behaviour. On the other hand, those with lower education tend to have lower self-efficacy, thus causing lower levels of preventive behaviour. Accordingly, when communicating to Americans with lower education levels, strategic health communicators ought to focus on ways to boost their confidence in their ability to adopt recommended behaviours. Our study indicates that when communicating to Americans with higher education levels, it is more likely that they will adopt preventive behaviours because they tend to have more confidence in their ability to do so.

Factors influencing attitudes towards recommended vaccine

Although our study shows that attitude can influence vaccination intention, it also reveals that age and education do not influence this causal relationship between attitude and vaccination intention. Accordingly, we recommend that strategic health communicators create messages that induce positive attitudes toward the vaccine, regardless of the public's age and education. Indeed, we recommend that strategic health communicators create messages that induce positive attitudes toward vaccines, regardless of age and education.

Future research

Given our study's findings that younger Americans' preventive behaviours are influenced by other people's opinions about those behaviours, future research could investigate factors that influence young people's social norms. For example, parental or peer behaviour can affect social norms of young people. Future research could also look into how to improve older Americans' low level of self-efficacy towards adopting recommended health behaviours. As a recent COVID-19 communication study shows, young people in Brazil and the UK are more vulnerable to pandemic misinformation, whereas older people in these two countries are more alert to misinformation but their efficacy in participating in corrective communication is yet to be addressed due to age-associated digital divide (Vijaykumar *et al.* 2021). Whether the same pattern holds among U.S. younger and older adults is yet to be observed empirically.

Given that the individual factors included in this study did not point to influencers of participants' attitudes towards getting vaccinated, future research could investigate what factors influence Americans' attitudes towards vaccination. One of

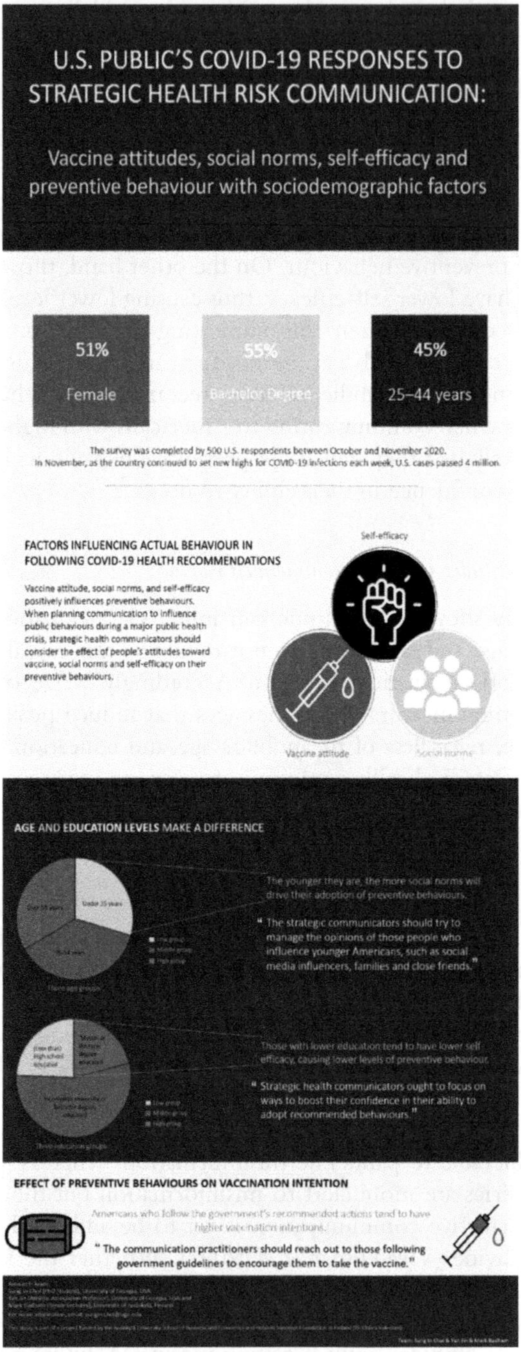

Infographic 14.1 U.S. public's COVID-19 responses to health risk communication

the possible factors influencing their vaccine attitude can be distrust of government sources. The lack of trust in government sources may lead to negative attitudes toward vaccines (Yaqub *et al.* 2014). Additionally, fear of side effects or uncertain information on vaccines could be another influential factor of these attitudes (Yaqub *et al.* 2014), which might have the same impact on COVID-19 vaccines. The uncertainties about vaccines and vaccination information can contribute to distrust toward vaccines (e.g., the recent pausing and then resuming of the Johnson & Johnson COVID-19 vaccine in the U.S. market), which can result in hesitancy toward vaccination. Future studies need to examine what individual and situational factors influence people's attitude and social norms in the U.S. and worldwide.

Bibliography

Ahn, Y., and Lee, J. (2019). The effect of participation effort on CSR participation intention: The moderating role of construal level on consumer perception of warm glow and perceived costs. *Sustainability*, 12(1), p. 83.

Ahn, J., Kahlor, L.A., Noh, G.-Y. (2020). Outbreak! Socio-cognitive motivators of risk information sharing during the 2018 South Korean MERS-CoV epidemic. *Journal of Risk Research*, 23, pp. 945–961.

Ajzen, I. (1985). From intentions to actions: A theory of planned behavior. In J. Kuhl and J. Beckmann, eds. *Action-control: From cognition to behavior.* Heidelberg: Springer, pp. 11–39.

Ajzen, I. (1991). The theory of planned behavior. *Organizational Behavior and Human Decision Processes*, 50(1991), pp. 179–211.

Ajzen, I., and Fishbein, M. (1980). *Understanding attitudes and predicting social behavior.* Englewood Cliffs. NJ: Prentice Hall.

Alfansuri, A.F., and Soetjipto, B. (2020). Integrating dimension of trust into the theory of planned behavior: A case study of electronic wallet amidst the Coronavirus outbreak. *SSRN Electronic Journal* [online]. doi:10.2139/ssrn.3750767 [Accessed 13 April 2021].

Balog-Way, D.H., and McComas, K.A. (2020). COVID-19: Reflections on trust, tradeoffs, and preparedness. *Journal of Risk Research*, 23(7–8), pp. 838–848.

Bennett, B., and Berenson, T. (2020, March 19). 'Our Big War.' as Coronavirus Spreads, Trump Refashions Himself as a Wartime President'[online]. *Time*. Available from: https://time.com/5806657/donald-trump-coronavirus-war-china/ [Accessed 13 April 2021].

Burchell, K., Rettie, R., and Patel, K. (2013). Marketing social norms: Social marketing and the 'social norm approach'. *Journal of Consumer Behaviour*, 12(1), pp. 1–9.

Campo, S., Cameron, K.A., Brossard, D., and Frazer, M.S. (2004). Social norms and expectancy violation theories: Assessing the effectiveness of health communication campaigns. *Communication Monographs*, 71(4), pp. 448–470.

Centers for Disease Control and Prevention (2020). *Recommendation regarding the use of cloth face coverings, especially in areas of significant community-based transmission.* Centers for Disease Control and Prevention [online]. Available from: www.cdc.gov/coronavirus/2019-ncov/prevent-getting-sick/cloth-face-cover.html#studies/ [Accessed 13 April 2021].

Centers for Disease Control and Prevention (2021). *COVID data tracker.* Centers for Disease Control and Prevention [online]. Available from: https://covid.cdc.gov/covid-data-tracker/ [Accessed 19 April 2021].

Chan, D.K., Zhang, C.-Q., and Weman-Josefsson, K. (2020). Why people failed to adhere to COVID-19 preventive behaviors? Perspectives from an integrated behavior change model. *Infection Control & Hospital Epidemiology*, 42(3), pp. 375–376.

Chirico, A., Lucidi, F., Galli F., Giancamilli, F., Vitale, J., Borghi, S., Torre, A.L., and Codella, R. (2020). COVID-19 outbreak and physical activity in the Italian population: A cross-sectional analysis of the underlying psychosocial mechanisms. *Frontiers in Psychology*, 11.

Chon, M.-G., and Park, H. (2021). Predicting public support for government actions in a public health crisis: Testing fear, organization-public relationship, and behavioral intention in the framework of the situational theory of problem solving. *Health Communication*, 36(4), pp. 476–486.

Clements, J.M. (2020). Knowledge and behaviors toward COVID-19 among US residents during the early days of the pandemic: Cross-sectional online questionnaire. *JMIR Public Health and Surveillance*, 6(2). doi:10.2196/19161/

de Visser, R., Waites, L., Parikh, C., and Lawrie, A. (2011). The importance of social norms for uptake of catch-up human papillomavirus vaccination in young women. *Sexual Health*, 8(3), pp. 330–337.

Dubé, E., Gagnon, D., and MacDonald, N.E. (2015). Strategies intended to address vaccine hesitancy: Review of published reviews. *Vaccine*, 33(34), pp. 4191–4203.

Finset, A., Bosworth, H., Butow, P., Gulbrandsen, P., Hulsman, R.L., Pieterse, H.A., Street, R., Tschoetschel, R., Weert, J.V. (2020). Effective health communication: A key factor in fighting the COVID-19 pandemic. *Patient Education and Counseling*, 103(5), pp. 873–876.

Food and Drug Administration (2020). *Emergency use authorization (EUA) for an unapproved product review memorandum*. Food and Drug Administration [online]. Available from: www.fda.gov/media/144416/download/ [Accessed 19 April 2021].

Gagnon, M.-P., and Godin, G. (2000). Young adults and HIV vaccine: Determinants of the intention of getting immunized. *Canadian Journal of Public Health*, 91(6), pp. 432–434.

Gerend, M.A., and Shepherd, J.E. (2007). Using message framing to promote acceptance of the human papillomavirus vaccine. *Health Psychology*, 26(6), p. 745.

Harrington, J., Fitzgerald, A.P., Layte, R., Lutomski, J., Molcho, M., and Perry, I.J. (2011). Sociodemographic, health and lifestyle predictors of poor diets. *Public Health Nutrition*, 14(12), pp. 2166–2175.

Jennings, W., Valgardsson, V., and Stoker, G. (2020). *Political trust and the COVID-19 crisis: Pushing populism to the backburner? A study of public opinion in Australia, Italy, the UK and the USA*. n.p., Democracy 2025 [online]. Available from: www.democracy2025.gov.au/documents/Final%20Pushing%20populism%20to%20the%20backburner.pdf/ [Accessed 13 April 2021].

Jingnan, H. (2020). 'Why there are so many different guidelines for face masks for the public. *NPR*, 10 April 2021 [online]. Available from: www.npr.org/sections/goatsandsoda/2020/04/10/829890635/why-there-so-many-differ-ent-guidelines-for-face-masks-for-the-public [Accessed 13 April 2021].

Jin, Y., Iles, I.A., Austin, L., Liu, B., and Hancock, G.R., (2020). The infectious disease threat (IDT) appraisal model: How perceptions of IDT predictability and controllability predict individuals' responses to risks. *International Journal of Strategic Communication*, 14(4), pp. 246–271.

Jones, J.H., and Salathé, M. (2009). Early assessment of anxiety and behavioral response to novel swine-origin influenza A(H1N1). *PLoS ONE*, 4(12), e8032.

Kasl, S.V., and Cobb, S. (1966). Health behavior, illness behavior, and sick role behavior. *Archives of Environmental Health*, 12, pp. 531–541.

Kim, S., and Jin, Y (2020). Organizational threat appraisal by publics: The effects of perceived temporal distance on health crisis outcomes. *International Journal of Communication*, 14, 21.

Krawczyk, A.L., Perez, S., Lau, E., Holcroft, C.A., Amsel, R., Knäuper, B., and Rosberger, Z. (2012). Human papillomavirus vaccination intentions and uptake in college women. *Health Psychology*, 31(5), pp. 685–693.

Lau, J.T.F., Tsui, H.Y., Kim, J.H., Chan, P.K.S., and Griffiths, S. (2007). Anticipated and current preventive behaviors in response to an anticipated human-to-human H5N1 epidemic in the Hong Kong Chinese general population. *BMC Infectious Diseases*, 7(1). doi:10.1186/1471-2334-7-18/.

Lee, K.-Y., Lan, L.-C., Wang, J.-H., Fang, C.-L., and Shiao, K.-S. (2014). How to reduce the latent social risk of disease: The determinants of vaccination against rabies in Taiwan. *International Journal of Environmental Research and Public Health*, 11(6), pp. 5934–5950.

Lee, M.K., and Oh, J. (2020). Health-related quality of life in older adults: Its association with health literacy, self-efficacy, social support, and health-promoting behavior. *Healthcare*, 8(4), p. 407.

Levy, B.R., and Myers, L.M. (2004). Preventive health behaviors influenced by self-perceptions of aging. *Preventive Medicine*, 39(3), pp. 625–629.

Lin, C.Y., Imani, V., Majd, N.R., Ghasemi, Z., Griffiths, M.D., Hamilton, K., Hagger, M.S., and Pakpour, A.H. (2020a). Using an integrated social cognition model to predict COVID-19 preventive behaviours. *British Journal of Health Psychology*, 25(4), pp. 981–1005. https://doi.org/10.1111/bjhp.12465

Lin, Y., Hu, Z., Alias, H., and Wong, L.P. (2020b). Knowledge, attitudes, impact, and anxiety regarding COVID-19 infection among the public in China. *Frontiers in Public Health*, 8, 236.

Lodi-Smith, J., Jackson, J., Bogg, T., Walton, K., Wood, D., Harms, P., and Roberts, B.W. (2010). Mechanisms of health: Education and health-related behaviours partially mediate the relationship between conscientiousness and self-reported physical health. *Psychology & Health*, 25(3), pp. 305–319.

Osborne, H. (2020, October 6). Anti-vaxxers feed off democrats' skepticism of COVID vaccine. *Newsweek* [online]. Available from: www.newsweek.com/anti-vaccine-covid-trust-skepticism-democrat-politicization-1535559/ [Accessed 3 May 2021].

Papageorge, N., Zahn, M.V., Belot, M., Van den Broek-Altenburg, E., Choi, S., Jamison, J.C., and Tripodi, E. (2020). Socio-demographic factors associated with self-protecting behavior during the Covid-19 pandemic. *Journal of Population Economics*, 34, pp. 691–738.

Paek, J.S. (2008). Management communication strategies of politicians against sexual harassment based on Coombs' theory. *Journal of Safety and Crisis Management*, 4(2), pp. 32–42.

Preacher, K.J., Rucker, D.D., and Hayes, A.F. (2007). Addressing moderated mediation hypotheses: Theory, methods, and prescriptions. *Multivariate Behavioral Research*, 42(1), pp. 185–227.

Reinhart, R.J. (2020, November 17). More Americans now willing to get COVID-19 vaccine. *Gallup* [online]. Available from: https://news.gallup.com/poll/325208/americans-willing-covid-vaccine.aspx/ [Accessed 3 May 2021].

Satter, R. (2020, September 15). *Kamala Harris says Trump not credible on possible COVID-19 vaccine*. Reuters [online]. Available from: www.reuters.com/article/health-coronavirus-usa-politics-idUSKBN25X01L/ [Accessed 3 May 2021].

Seeger, M.W., and Sellnow, T.L. (2019). *Communication in times of trouble*. Hoboken, NJ: Wiley-Blackwell.

Seeger, M.W., Reynolds, B., and Sellnow, T.L. (2020). Crisis and emergency risk communication in health contexts: Applying the CDC model to pandemic influenza. In *Handbook of risk and crisis communication*. Routledge, pp. 493–506.

So, J., Kuang, K., and Cho, H. (2019). Information seeking upon exposure to risk messages: Predictors, outcomes, and mediating roles of health information seeking. *Communication Research,* 46(5), pp. 663–687. https://doi.org/10.1177/0093650216679536

Sobo, E.J. (2016). What is herd immunity, and how does it relate to pediatric vaccination uptake? US parent perspectives. *Social Science & Medicine*, 165, pp. 187–195.

Stobbe, M. (2020, November 11). US hits record COVID-19 hospitalizations amid virus surge. *AP News* [online]. Available from: https://apnews.com/article/doctors-better-equipped-virus-surge-743c0448c3ada001d327d73a6f2ed9d7/ [Accessed 19 April 2021].

Uddin, S., Imam, T., Khushi, M., Khan, A., and Ali Moni, M. (2021). How did socio-demographic status and personal attributes influence compliance to COVID-19 preventive behaviours during the early outbreak in Japan? Lessons for pandemic management. *Personality and Individual Differences*, 175, 110692.

Vijaykumar, S., Jin, Y., Rogerson, D., Lu, X., Sharma, S., Maughan, A., Fadel, B., De Oliveira Costa, M.S., Pagliari, C., and Morris, D. (2021). How shades of truth and age affect responses to COVID-19 (mis)information: Randomized survey experiment among WhatsApp users in UK and Brazil. *Humanities and Social Sciences Communications*, 8(88). doi:10.1057/s41599-021-00752-7/.

Villarrubia, A. (2006). Understanding parents' decisions about serving vegetables to their children. *LSU Master's Theses*. 1735. Available from: https://digitalcommons.lsu.edu/gradschool_theses/1735

Watson, K. (2020). A timeline of what Trump has said on Coronavirus. *CBS News*, April 3 2021 [online]. Available from: www.cbsnews.com/news/timeline-president-donald-trump-changing-statements-on-coronavirus./ [Accessed 13 April 2021].

Webb, T.L., and Sheeran, P. (2006). Does changing behavioral intentions engender behavior change? A meta-analysis of the experimental evidence. *Psychological Bulletin*, 132(2), pp. 249–268.

White, S., Kutner, M., Greenberg, E., Jin, Y., and Paulsen, C. (2007). Health literacy of America's adults: Results from the 2003 National Assessment of Adult Literacy. *PsycEXTRA Dataset* [online]. Available from: https://nces.ed.gov/pubs2006/2006483.pdf/

Wiemken, T.L., Carrico, R.M., Kelley, R.R., Binford, L.E., Peyrani, P., Ford, K.D., Welch, V. and Ramirez, J.A. (2015). Understanding why low-risk patients accept vaccines: A socio-behavioral approach. *BMC Research Notes*, 8(1). doi:10.1186/s13104-015-1816-2/

Wise, T., Zbozinek, T.D., Michelini, G., Hagan, C.C., and Mobbs, D. (2020). *Changes in risk perception and protective behavior during the first week of the COVID-19 pandemic in the United States*. The Royal Society Publishing. Available from: https://royalsocietypublishing.org/doi/10.1098/rsos.200742

Xiao, X., and Wong, R.M. (2020). Vaccine hesitancy and perceived behavioral control: A meta-analysis. *Vaccine*, 38(33), pp. 5131–5138.

Yaqub, O., Castle-Clarke, S., Sevdalis, N., and Chataway, J. (2014). Attitudes to vaccination: A critical review. *Social Science & Medicine*, 112, pp. 1–11.

Yıldırım, M., and Güler, A. (2020). Factor analysis of the COVID-19 Perceived Risk Scale: A preliminary study. *Death Studies*, pp. 1–8.

Europe – East and South East

15 Crisis communication by the government of Georgia during the COVID-19 pandemic

Natia Kaladze, Leli Bibilashvili and Mari Bandzeladze

Introduction

Communication campaigns play a significant role in determining the public's response and behaviour as well as crisis management of the pandemic across the country. Therefore, communication can play a crucial role in tackling the pandemic and ensuring a strategy for timely recovery from the crisis. The goal of the research was to assess the effectiveness of the crisis communication management process during the COVID-19 pandemic by Georgia's governing bodies. As such, this would help to determine effective and credible communication channels/sources and awareness of COVID-19 among the population.

The final sample included 1,200 responses, with 54% of respondents from the capital, Tbilisi, and the rest of the sample from seven different regions of the country.

Experiencing COVID-19

Almost one month after the first confirmed case of coronavirus was reported in Georgia (26 February 2020), the country faced a new challenge. A new threat had emerged in parallel to the intensive cluster spread of the infection, during which it was impossible to trace the source of infection and, correspondingly, to take the necessary preventive measures of isolating individuals, as well as identifying and locating their existing and potential contacts.

Given the nature of the virus, in cases of internal transmission the virus reproduction index varied between 2.5 and 3 on average. By that time, based on the calculations and observation of other countries' experience, Georgia was facing a serious risk. This was indicated by the various scenarios developed by the Ministry of Internally Displaced Persons from the Occupied Territories, National Center for Disease Control (NCDC), and Labor, Health and Social Affairs, as well as partner organizations, which were prepared using the mathematical analysis methods of leading international universities.

Additionally, observation revealed that the degree of compliance with the non-mandatory recommendations was low at the time. According to the epidemiologists' forecasts, in the event of a critical scenario unfolding, the country

DOI: 10.4324/9781003184669-24

was facing the risk of thousands of people becoming infected and the healthcare system collapsing.

It should be noted that given the problems associated with the imposition of restrictions on the country's economy, the government of Georgia initially chose the path of mainly issuing recommendations and conducting information campaigns. Accordingly, almost one month after the first reported case of the novel coronavirus (26 February to 21 March), the government conducted active information campaigns and issued recommendations, which included: the 'stay at home' universal recommendation policy and social distancing; the observance of personal and public sanitary-hygienic norms; the transitioning of employees to working remotely; and avoiding congregating in public spaces, entertainment venues, and so forth. However, detailed observation of the resulting epidemiological situation revealed that the recommendations were not sufficient, as a large part of the public didn't follow the recommendations, which increased the risk of virus transmission and collapse of the country's healthcare system. Consequently, in the second half of March 2020, when the country entered a more active phase of the spread of the virus and faced a high risk of the uncontrolled internal transmission of the virus, it became necessary to implement mandatory measures and to declare a state of emergency. As of 28 April 2021, the situation remained risky (Table 15.1).

Edicts concerning significant restrictions and regulations, as well as the corresponding aims and consequences, were as follows: The Suspension of Air and Land Traffic; The Suspension of the Educational Process and the Transition to a Remote Mode of Operation; The Prohibition of Travel by Car; Strict Quarantine in Individual Municipalities; The Restriction of Public Transport; Restrictions in Penitentiary Facilities; The Curfew; The Restriction of the Gathering of More Than 10/3 People; The Restriction on Entering or Leaving Big Cities; The Restriction of Economic Activity.

State of emergency management was established on 30 March 2020. The Operational Headquarters of the Management of the State of Emergency (hereinafter Operational Headquarters) was put in charge of coordinating the enforcement of emergency restrictions and monitoring the

Table 15.1 Dynamics of the pandemic situation in Georgia as of 28 April 2021

	Total Cases by 28 April 2021	*Number of confirmed cases in the 24 hour period*
	307,401	1551
Number of Recovered	28,816	878
Fatal outcome	4077	17
	Test positivity	*5.26%*
	Under quarantine	*221*
	Under hospital supervision	*3780*
	Persons at clinical hotels	*707*

Source: Authors

implementation of instructions from the Interagency Council. These functions were fulfilled by the Operational Headquarters through local operations headquarters.

The Operational Headquarters was engaged in coordinating divisional agencies and ensuring the efficient resolution of critical problems. With direct engagement with state institutions, the headquarters developed proposals and recommendations for the Interagency Council, vis-à-vis matters such as movement regulation, issues identified through hotlines, support for agriculture, healthcare and the economy, monitoring international cargo transport drivers and coordinating regional command centres.

In terms of ensuring proper epidemiological management and public awareness, an important role was played by several hotline methods introduced in the country. Throughout the state of emergency, the governmental hotline 114 was developed on the basis of the Public Safety Management Center 112 (hereinafter 112).

By November 2020, when daily cases escalated from 5,000 to 7,000, the healthcare system failed to manage the increased number of patients and there was a shortage of hospital beds for those needing healthcare.

The government of Georgia and Interagency Coordination Council declared that provision of detailed information to the public should be a priority and implemented the following steps: daily briefings; development of the dedicated website StopCov.ge; unified hotline; dissemination of informational and educational materials; online consultation provided by infectious disease physicians; development of anti-crisis economic plan, and so forth (*Government of Georgia. Measures Implemented by the Government of Georgia Against COVID 19.* Report).

The COVID-19 outbreak was not readily covered during the Georgian media's prime time. The first glimmers of public interest came through Georgian entertainment webpages that mocked people in other countries for wearing unusual face masks and outfits. Considering the fact that Georgia emerged from the H1N1 swine flu in 2010 and the H1N5 chicken flu in 2014 relatively unscathed, the word 'epidemic' in early 2020 reports was initially considered an exaggeration. However, the increasing numbers of virus-related deaths and global media attention pushed the Georgian media to begin covering the outbreak more actively. As the media began to increase its coverage, it initially focused intermittently on casualty statistics and rare footage from the quarantined city of Wuhan. Even after COVID-19 was declared a global pandemic, TV stations chased sensational exclusives instead of handling the health emergency with the seriousness it deserved. When the first case in the country was confirmed, reporters rushed to the entrance of a Tbilisi hospital to interview a potential virus patient, neglecting their own safety and ignoring the possibility of transmission to get the latest scoop. The NCDC later apologised for 'an impromptu scenario', implying that they allowed journalists to talk to a sick patient before he was dragged back into the hospital by nurses.

In addition to the initial lack of serious attention given to COVID-19, the Georgian media struggled to turn away from political news and focus on the public health emergency (Jangiani 2020).

The Media Development Foundation conducted content analysis of traditional and social media. The aim of the research was to identify main messages and their sources. The monitoring covered the period between 1 January 2020 and 1 January 2021, and the key findings of the research were as follows:

- The coronavirus was presented as something that was introduced for the aim of establishing global control and new world order that was human-made and spread artificially to establish digital dictatorship.
- Closure of borders due to the pandemic was portrayed as a possible means of stopping migration and expansion into foreign countries by ultranationalist groups.
- Closure of borders (with Iran and China) due to the pandemic was demanded by far-right organization Georgian March as well as by the founder of the United National Movement and former president Mikheil Saakashvili (the border with China).
- Besides the xenophobic context, far-right groups perceived the pandemic in an anti-Western context, viewing the coronavirus as a divine retribution for sins which stem from liberalism and the Western lifestyle Kintsurashvili *et al.* (2020).

The state of play

The key findings were analysed according to the research objectives:

- The most frequently used channels for receiving information on COVID-19.
- Trust and credibility towards information sources among the population of Georgia.
- Communication campaign by the government of Georgia.
- Level of awareness vis-à-vis COVID-19 among the population of Georgia.

The period of research spanned October 2020 to January 2021. It is worth mentioning that this period could be described as the peak of the virus transmission and infection circulation.

The research was conducted via an online structured questionnaire. The number of participants surveyed in the quantitative research was 1200, where 54% of respondents came from Tbilisi, the capital of Georgia, and the rest from seven other Georgian cities (see Figure 15.1).

The maximum sampling error for the entire data was 3%. Quantitative research was conducted using quota sampling and the results are representative of the general population.

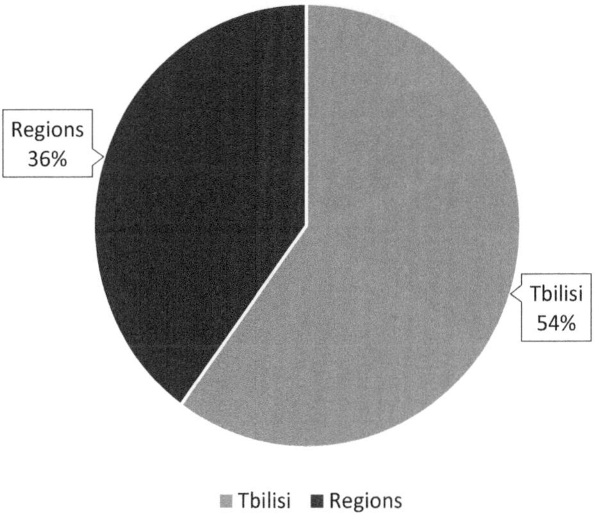

Figure 15.1 Key demographic profile: Geography

Source: Authors

As the research was conducted using online platforms, it determined the age parameters of the participants and limited the number of older members of the population in the surveys to what would be a proportional representation.

Once the data had been analysed, the two main means for receiving information about COVID-19 among the Georgian population were identified. The first and the most popular source of information was found to be online media, where Facebook leads (avg. 6.23), followed by Instagram and YouTube. It's worth mentioning that websites specialising in health issues are also among the trusted and frequently used media. Among them are StopCov.ge and WHO, with avg. 4.65. (See Figure 15.2.)

However, traditional media channels, mainly television, are still an active source of information. Television is an effective means to reach a wider audience and benefits from credibility among viewers, especially in the municipal regions of the country outside the captial. According to the data, an avg. 5.54 of participants named television as their main source of information.

In summarising the collected data, it could be concluded that for effective communication to the target audience, it is important to use the two main channels, online and television.

One of the important research criteria referred to the credibility and trust towards communication sources. The highest points were given to WHO (avg. 5.55 out of 7) and well-known medical personnel within the communities (avg. 5.13 out of 7). Findings show that participants have a high level of trust towards sources of information on healthcare issues, in terms of process management and public awareness about COVID-19, on both a global and local level.

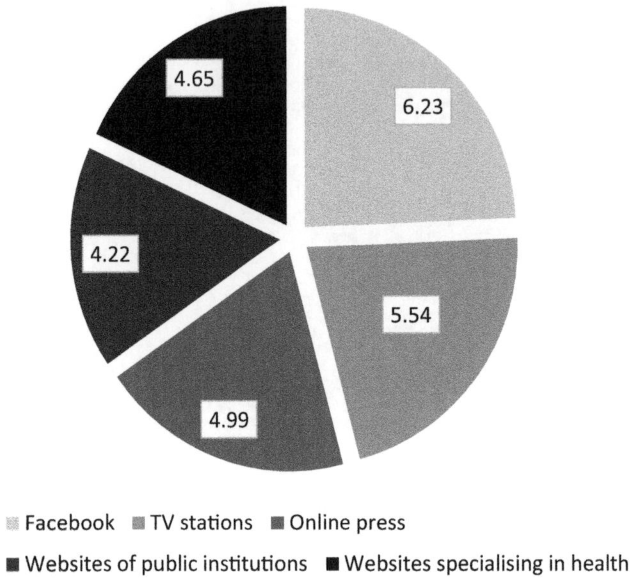

Figure 15.2 Key communication channels: Most popular info channel about COVID-19 among the Georgian population

Source: Authors

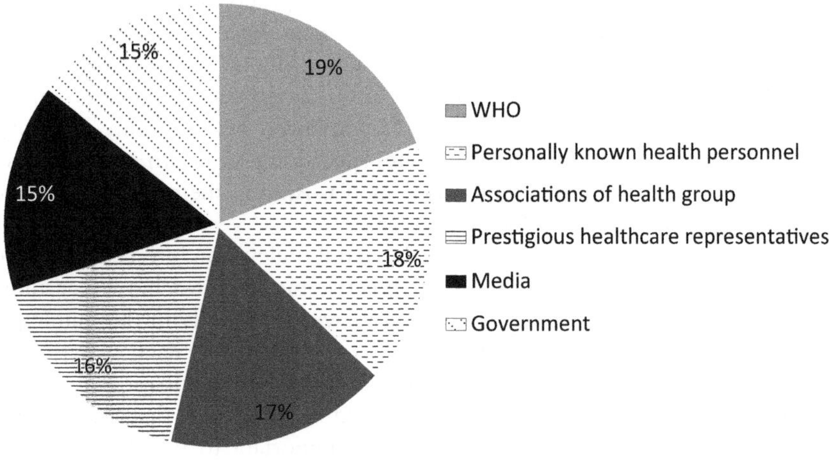

Figure 15.3 Population's agreement with sources of trusted communication on COVID-19

Source: Authors

The responses indicate rational judgement from a population that believes in the competency of professionals within the field. Findings revealed six main trustworthy sources, and, of these sources, government agencies had the lowest credibility. This is a negative finding vis-à-vis the process of crisis management, especially when it comes to the pandemic, because effective crisis management and communication is ensured by the citizens' trust toward government as the main communicator.

Despite the low rate of credibility vis-à-vis government information sources, participants positively rated the clarity/sufficiency of the information policy and the timeline for its dissemination. They described information received as appropriate, transparent and relevant for healthcare management.

However, participants had low trust vis-à-vis the COVID-19 communication campaign in terms of information reliability (avg. 3.98 out of 7) and revealing the truth (avg. 3.33 out of 7). Although the highest rate was given to the criteria 'scheduled and appropriate time of providing information' (avg. 4.87 out of 7) and 'clear and sufficient message content' (avg. 4.64 out of 7) for the virus prevention campaign, the overall results indicate mistrust, a critical attitude toward the strategic message and a failure to influence public opinion.

An effective and influential communication campaign by government agencies is key for raising public awareness in its management strategy to contain the pandemic in the short and long term.

The main message that participants (64.7%) recalled from the government campaign related to prevention measures against virus transmission was to maintain hygiene by following the guidelines (wearing a face mask, social distancing, etc.). A comparably high percentage (10.9%) could recall the campaign message about the particular risks that the virus posed for the elderly and sick people with previous pathologies; and 17.9% were of the opinion that COVID-19 spreads easily and that staying home is important to protect at-risk groups. (See Figure 15.4.)

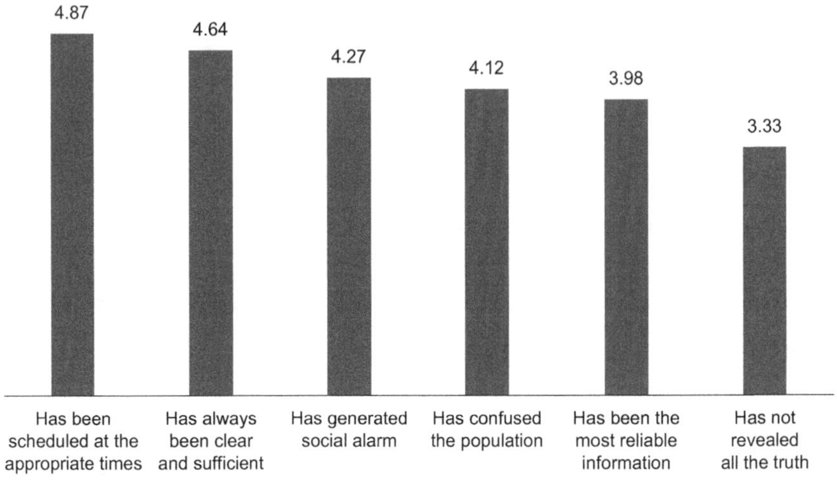

Figure 15.4 Message retention: Main message(s) from government communication for the population in Georgia

Source: Authors

On the one hand, the communication campaign's message might be received correctly, but on the other hand it results in irregular perceptions, because almost 11% of the target audience perceives COVID-19 as dangerous only for at-risk groups. These unfounded perceptions might become a hindering factor in the following of guidelines and mobilising the population for action.

Public knowledge and general beliefs about COVID-19 were affected by the active circulation of propaganda and disinformation by different interest groups: that COVID-19 affects only the elderly and patients with chronic diseases (85.52%); COVID-19 is the same as ordinary flu (42.26%); COVID-19 was created in a laboratory for commercial reasons (19.11%); asymptomatic patients do not transmit infection (18.11%). It is noteworthy that 22.3% of participants believe that government measures for preventing COVID-19 have been instituted too late. (See Figure 15.5.)

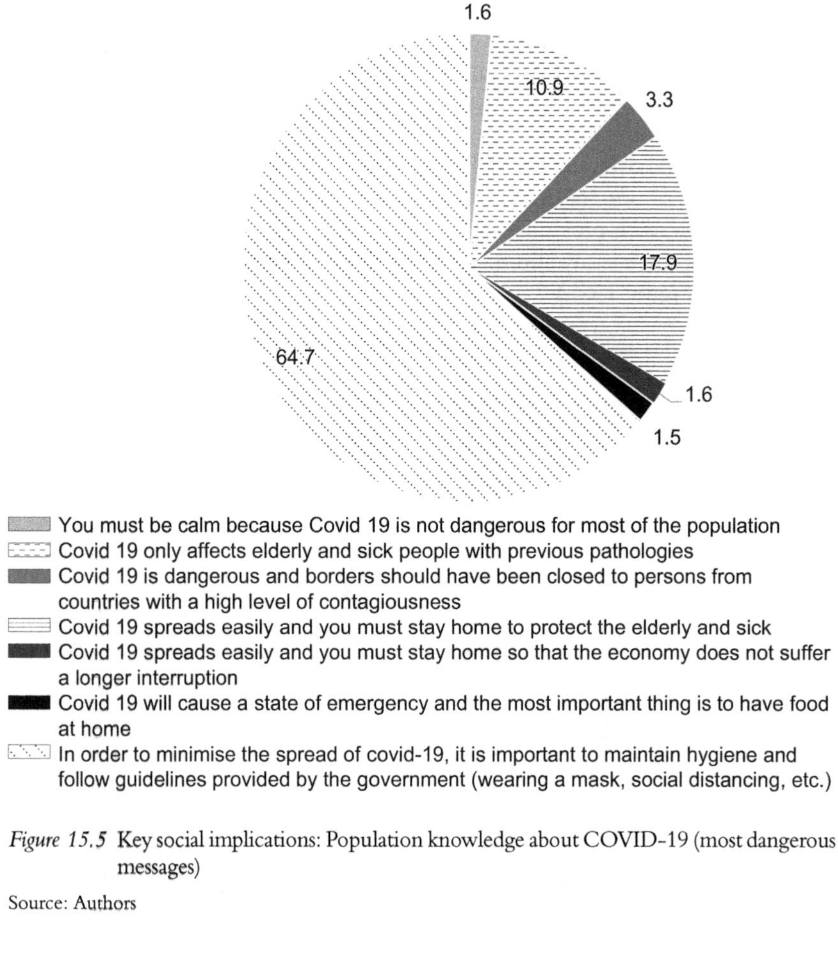

Figure 15.5 Key social implications: Population knowledge about COVID-19 (most dangerous messages)

Source: Authors

The following perceptions are noteworthy:

- If one does not have symptoms, the virus can't be spread; and visiting the doctor is recommended only in urgent cases (7.1%).
- The COVID-19 virus has been created in labs and disseminated for commercial reasons – namely, to sink Western economies and to lessen the number of dependents in the pension system (5.4%).

All of these perceptions are dangerous during crisis management; they should not be ignored as they can hinder the pandemic management process.

Among alarming perceptions is the belief (among 50% of respondents) that the need to visit doctors is not pertinent. It indicates that the majority of the population still do not acknowledge the potential for fatality from the virus. (See Figure 15.6.)

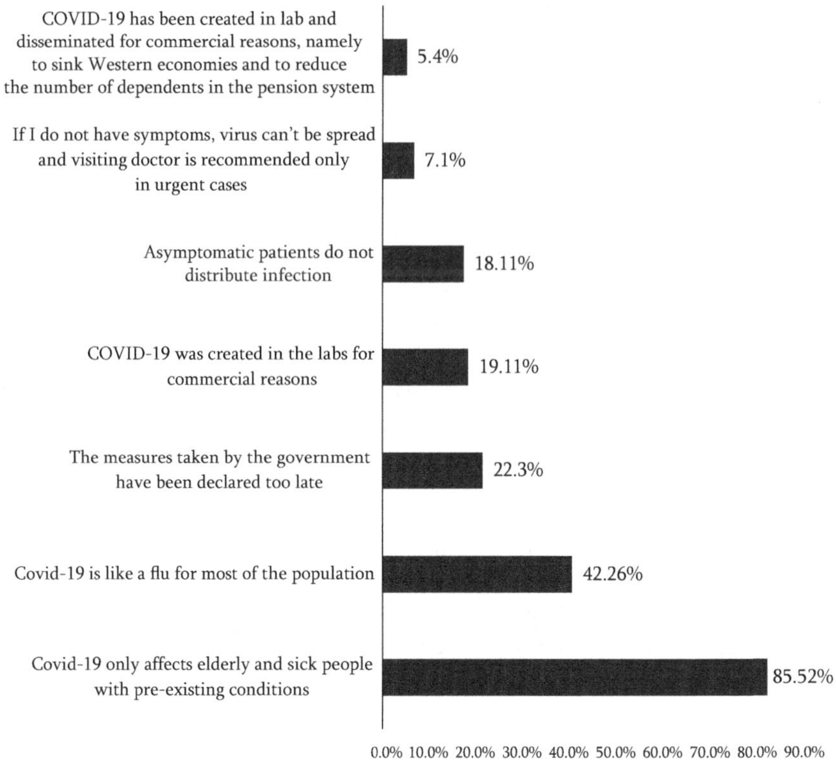

Figure 15.6 Key social implications: Population knowledge about COVID-19 (less dangerous messages)

Source: Authors

Zealous circulation of false and dangerous information is caused by inconsistent and incorrect crisis communication, which results in failure of delivering the right messages to the target audience through the right channels. Controlling the plethora of information disseminated to the population is important to manage the risks associated with pandemic management and crisis communication, as there are high levels of irrational and inaccurate information appearing in large parts of society, increasing the risk of infection. Similarly, the circulation of accurate and rational information in society is a prerequisite for the proper management of the pandemic, and the goal of both the government and the media should be to increase public awareness, to shape attitudes and thus help overcome the crisis. Therefore, it is necessary to focus on the dissemination of clear and accurate messages (as highlighted by the results of the Georgian population survey).

The following messages contribute to effective pandemic management:

- Frequent hand washing and social distancing are an effective way to protect yourself against COVID-19.
- Even in the case of mild symptoms, one should consult a doctor and stay at home; this will protect the country's economy from collapse, as well as protect oneself and others from the virus.

It is also important to consider the messages that will help the public to lessen risk. The data from the survey indicated that it is possible to leverage existing awareness. For example, almost 40% of participants knew how to inform official healthcare agencies in case of symptoms; 36.4% were aware that COVID-19 can be transmitted by touching infected surfaces; 35.3% believed that jokes about COVID-19 spread throughout social media might contribute to misinformation. (See Figure 15.7.)

The data showed that the public has a correct perception and belief in the main messages that are consistent with those of WHO and the country's authorities:

- To reduce the risk of spreading COVID-19, it is important to follow personal hygiene and the rules recommended by world health authorities and local governments.
- COVID-19 is spreading fast; we need to stay home in order to protect the country's economy, health and education systems, and, most importantly, the elderly and people at risk.

An important point is that these messages in the government's communication campaign relate to effective ways to protect oneself and others from the pandemic; the messages avoid intimidating the population, triggering panic and/or arousing false optimism.

Among the most important findings vis-à-vis the Georgian population's perceptions of the effectiveness of preventive actions are the following: Government

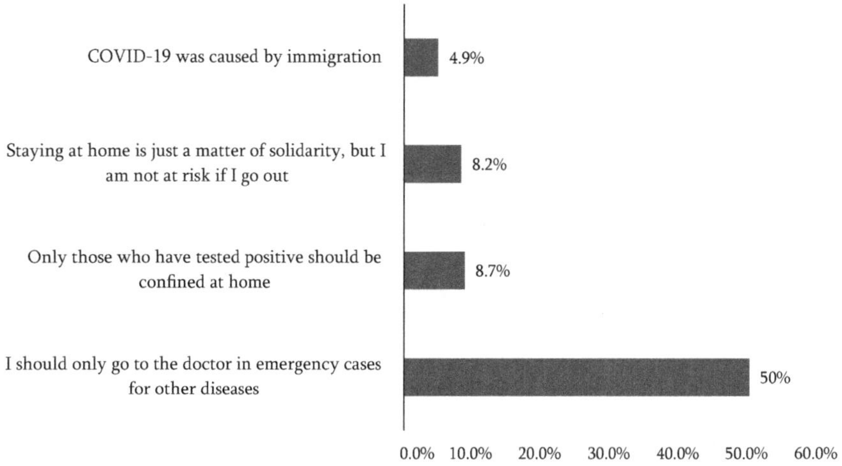

Figure 15.7 Key social implications: Population knowledge about COVID-19 (positive messages)

Source: Authors

actions destroy and limit access to the educational system (41.40%); due to less effective management of the process, public schools and higher education institutes in particular – as well as their beneficiaries – were at risk of being left without education because of both technical and cognitive problems with online learning opportunities; preventive actions lead to economic collapse, business failure and poverty (33.32%) – due to the transition to an online system of business services, an almost total ban of the opening of physical workplaces has left tens of thousands unemployed in the country and increased the number of families below the poverty line, and government subsidies were not enough to meet even their basic needs; the actions taken by the government are generally evaluated as illogical and the measures taken were ineffective and inconsistent, which led to the problems we have listed (25.25%); COVID-19 does not exist and governments fabricated the story to intimidate the population (3.3%); the existence of this position clearly indicates the failures of crisis communication and the problems vis-à-vis formation of relevant perceptions and beliefs among the general public (see Figures 15.8 and 15.9).

The rather serious accusations that the Georgian population had about their government's management of the pandemic crisis are significant and noteworthy.

Observations and interrogation

The recognition that a crisis has occurred is often accompanied by extreme emotional reaction, stress, fear, anger, shock, general disbelief and sometimes

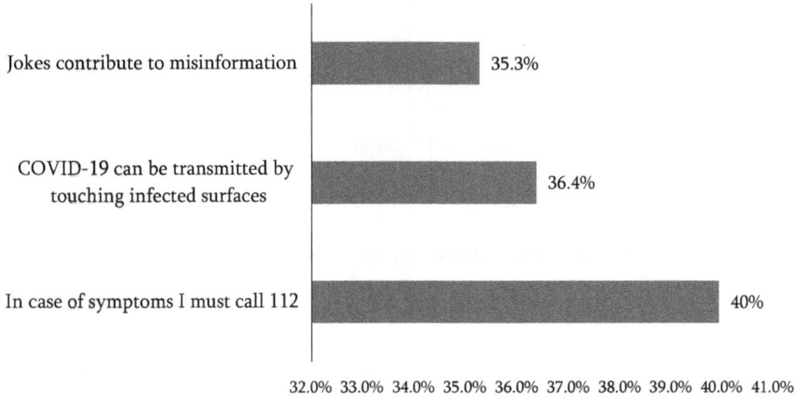

Figure 15.8 Key social implications: Georgian population knowledge about COVID-19
Source: Authors

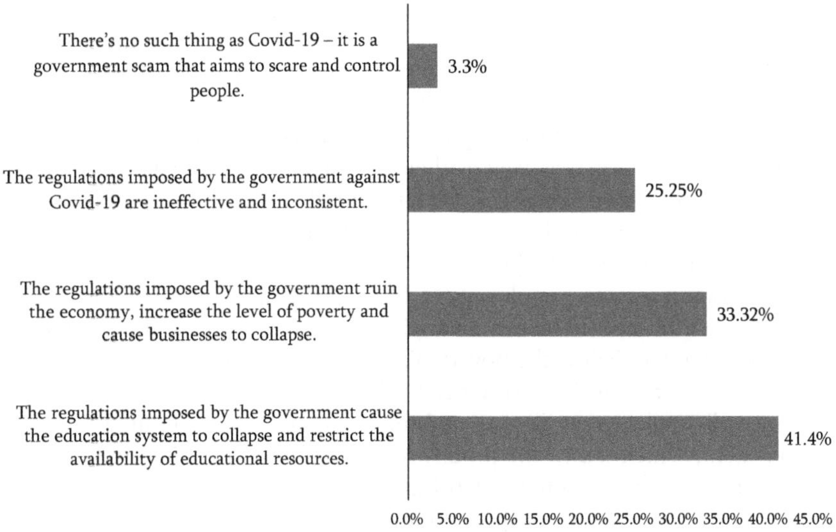

Figure 15.9 Key social implications: Georgian population knowledge about COVID-19 – negative messages and misinformation

denial. Panic in the form of extreme maladaptive responses, although a feature of some situations, is relatively rare (Tierney 2003). More often, it is the overwhelming confusion about what is happening that disrupts the basic capacity to understand. The crisis stage is where harm is initiated and where a majority of the direct damage occurs. Harm may take many forms and may extend beyond the boundaries of the immediate scene.

The three-stage model has been very influential as a basic conceptual framework for crisis analysis. The pre-crisis/crisis/post-crisis framework has also been adopted by the professional community in public relations as a basic conceptual framework for understanding crises and developing strategies for management (Coombs 2007). Others have suggested that these three phases can be understood simply as prevention, response and recovery (Hale *et al.* 2005). This representation is a natural way to describe the development of a crisis. One of the useful features of this model is that it tracks how those experiencing the crisis characterise its evolution.

This study in Georgia fits with the 'mental model' approach to message crafting. Morgan tackles the idea of the need for goals for risk and crisis messages early on in his discussion of the mental models approach to message crafting (Morgan 2002). One of his key points is that much risk and crisis communication is often done ad hoc, with limited planning and forethought. He raises the flag that this type of message development is risky at best, as the impact on the lives of the audience can often be significant. It also leads to message delivery that is more likely to fail, leaving the communicator confused and frustrated. Morgan believes that message development rarely involves any audience needs analysis, is rarely analysed before delivery and is just as rarely evaluated after the fact to determine whether or not the messages have succeeded. He argues that it is not a difficult process to undertake the process of message development from beginning to end. Risk communications are not simply opportunities to speak to an audience but to engage the audience in meaningful dialogue and consensus building: 'The goal of risk communication is to promote public involvement that is informed, reasonable, thoughtful, solution-oriented, and collaborative' (U.S. Environmental Protection Agency 2007, p. 10). And: 'The goal of the risk communication strategy is to increase the understanding and involvement of interested parties in the process rather than reach unanimity' (U.S. Environmental Protection Agency 2007, p. 9). "The significance of the establishment of trust and credibility prior to the message delivery" (U.S. Environmental Protection Agency 2007).

One of the simplest tools available to help develop goals and objectives in nearly every setting is the acronym SMART: Specific, Measurable, Achieveable, Realistic, Time. This technique has been effectively used in a multitude of goal setting activities, such as risk and crisis messages. If we evaluate crisis communication campaign messages according to the SMART model, we can make assumptions about the effectiveness of the campaign as well as right message delivery and internalisation.

- **Specific**. The goal was to provide information about the pandemic, its symptoms and preventative measures, helping the public to be prepared for virus outbreak and understand the difference between the ordinary flu and COVID-19.
- **Measurable**. Messages provided by the authorities described measurable tendencies of restrictions and regulations, so evaluation of the success of

the strategic message was demonstrated by getting the public to practise effective social distancing techniques during the pandemic by a number of restrictions (for example: gathering more than 10 people, distance learning, shut down big malls and centres, etc.).

- **Achievable/Realistic**. Imposed restrictions were not challenging enough to make them successful because, if they were sufficiently challenging, they would not cause economic collapse, business failure and poverty. Furthermore, the goal was unrealistic, due to the fact that the end point was so unreasonable that the audience would not try at all.
- **Time**. Imposed restrictions including curfews were perceived as unreasonable and effort by the public was compromised. It put forward a long and undefined period of time without any justification from the authorities, which caused mistrust toward decisions made by the government agencies.

For successful crisis management, communication goal setting and strategic message development are the essential criteria for creating an overall message plan and then identifying the concrete objectives that will need to occur in order to achieve the target. The subsequent planning process that follows the setting of objectives was an important step for achieving the SMART goal. The cited criteria clarify that failure in strategic messaging and crisis communication – in terms of achievability, realism and timeliness – led to the unsuccessful implementation and the lack of persuasive communication.

From the very beginning of the campaign, there was no targeted communication with the public. As an overarching means of segmenting audiences, the categories of the public created by Fearn-Banks (2016) are helpful because they create a framework for identifying both the internal/external public and recognise that different messages must be crafted for each group.

Audience emotions such as anger, mistrust, fear, panic and apathy should be taken into consideration during the crisis campaigns. If the audience's exposure to and danger from the hazard is perceived to be under the control of the organization, or predominantly so, the level of anger can be expected to increase dramatically. To rectify this situation, the organization needs to effectively communicate that the audience's perception of the organization's control over the hazard was off the mark, or at least that the organization is doing all it can to reduce the risk. Additional factors that strongly influence audience anger levels include whether or not other members of the audience are equally at risk, particularly if the subgroup to which the audience member belongs is at greater risk, and the perceived morality of the risk.

Lundgren and McMakin (2004) add additional depth to the assessment of an audience's anger level by noting that organizational credibility also affects the anger level. They also note that audiences who feel they are being placated by the communicator are more prone to anger, once again demonstrating the importance of empathy. Finally, they noted that audiences who feel as though their concerns are being ignored, who feel that they are being asked to make significant life changes and who are having difficulties understanding the risk or the data being presented are more likely to be angrier (Lundgren and McMakin 2004). Effectively dealing with an audience's anger involves addressing multiple concerns and trigger points, usually at the same time. According to research data, the high level of mistrust might be interpreted by the public as signifying that their concerns are being ignored; they have been asked to make significant life changes, resulting in worsening economic conditions; this would result in a conclusion that all of these factors were not considered by the government and that they failed to deal with audience anger effectively.

While anger is perhaps the most common emotion displayed by an audience during risk and crisis communication events, mistrust is also one that surfaces quite readily. Although both emotions are related and often occur together, they can also exist separately.

In 1988 Covello and Allen provided a summary of five strategies for building trust and credibility (Covello and Allen 1988):

1 Accepting and involving the public as a partner helps to allay fears, dispel misinformation and build consensus on the best methods to mitigate risks.
2 Appreciating the public's specific concerns to convey a sensitivity to normal human fears and worries. Empathy and shared emotions provide needed answers and information, and are respectful.
3 Being honest and open helps the public understand the risk and learn how to protect themselves. Misleading information later discovered makes regaining trust and credibility nearly impossible.
4 Working with other credible sources reduces confusion and mistrust and increases the chance that the audience will both accept the information and take appropriate actions.
5 Meeting the needs of the media not only helps them to inform the public but will be done with or without the communicator's assistance. Help the media ensure the information they provide is accurate and enlightening.

Lundgren and McMakin (2004) and Sandman (2003, 2004) both deal with the emotions of fear, panic and apathy. These related emotions are often aroused when factors such as dread and lack of control are in place. Other factors of importance include risks that are alien and unknown or unknowable and, to a lesser degree, those for which the audience's memory of a past similar risk is recent or strong. Both Lundgren and Sandman agree that true panic is a rare occurrence in an audience.

Sandman also raises another variation of a risk communicator's concern about audience panic: panicking an audience more than you want to with the risk communication message. In other words, he is talking about messages designed to move the outrage level that succeed more than expected, thereby moving the outrage level of the audience into panic. While Sandman agrees this possibility exists, he reminds again that it is rare. Using it as a reason for not providing honest and meaningful information to an audience is not only foolish but unethical. Determining whether to withhold information from an audience, how much and when is nearly impossible to determine in any specific moral context.

More often what communicators refer to as panic is a variation of this emotion – denial, which can be a true obstacle for risk and crisis communicators. Denial refers to the shutdown of coping behaviours and the suspension of active listening. Audience members in true denial may appear to be listening and may even agree to behave in a certain way but are not actually capable of either. More often than not, an audience in this emotional state will be quiet and, as Lundgren and McMakin (2004, p. 63) suggest, 'deceptively calm'. They also suggest an intensive audience profile as the best means to better understand the audience's true emotional state in order to craft messages designed to achieve understanding of the message content and behaviour change. Sandman suggests that denial occurs when audiences simply cannot bear their emotions because they are too frightening and even, on occasion, hurtful and guilt producing. People who ignore obvious signs of health problems but refuse to seek medical attention are classic examples of this type of behaviour.

Finally, apathy can also occur when an audience hears the risk assessment and understands it, but simply disagrees. While many risk assessments are quantifiable, some are less so, and individual audience members can come to different conclusions about the data, even when they understand it. In these situations, simply repeating the data won't necessarily change the audience's understanding and perception of it, but finding commonalties in the risk perception of the communicator and audience may be effective.

Research results showed that the crisis communication campaign was not effective in considering audience profiling and emotional dimensions. Communication was oriented toward the general public, but not to the specific target groups, which caused anger, panic and mistrust.

The insights revealed in the study provide important information for monitoring the management of pandemic-induced processes as well as for the preparation of the next stage, which is increasing the volume and effectiveness of vaccination.

It is important that the government be aware of the main, effective and credible communication channels, employment of which leads to the desired results faster and creates or enhances credibility during crisis communication and beyond, not only in relation to episodes of COVID-19 pandemic but also in times of crisis generally.

Identifying effective communication channels for different demographic groups of the population and identifying the disruptive/facilitating information that accompanied the pandemic crisis is an important step forward for the next stage of proper communication management, whether in terms of messages or strategy and tactics.

Conclusions

As of today, Georgian public opinion is imbued with both true, false and disruptive information about COVID-19 and its management.

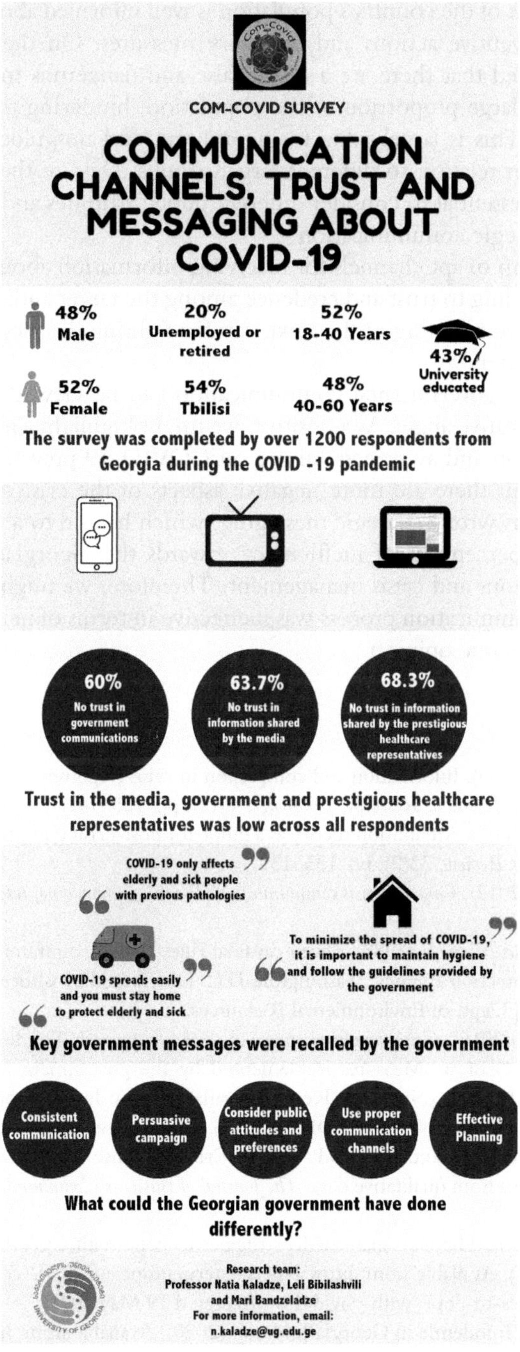

Infographic 15.1 Key government messages were recalled by the population

In favour of the information campaign led by the government, it must be said that a large part of the country's population is well informed about COVID-19, including preventive actions and necessary measures. On the other hand, it should be noted that there are a lot of false and dangerous messages that are believed by a large proportion of the population, hindering the management of the crisis. This is largely due to inconsistent and misguided communication policies in relation to different target groups. Despite the general public problem, it is essential to consider different public attitudes and preferences for successful strategic communication.

Identification of apt channels for receiving information about the pandemic and factors leading to trust and credence among the target audience are important for effective planning of the next step for fighting the pandemic and vaccination campaign.

In summary, governmental communication can be viewed from a positive angle and a negative angle. As a positive, we might highlight the huge information distribution and awareness-raising on COVID-19 prevention among the population. But there are more negative aspects of the crisis communication process, such as wrong strategic messaging, which has led to a critical attitude, mistrust and perception of inefficiency towards the Georgian government's preventive actions and crisis management. Therefore, we might conclude that the crisis communication process was ineffective in terms of persuasion and the formation of public opinion.

Bibliography

Coombs, W.T. (1999). Information and compassion in crisis responses: A test of their effects. *Journal of Public Relations Research. Routledge*, 11(2), pp. 125–142.

Coombs, W.T. (2007). Attribution theory as a guide for post-crisis communication research. *Public Relations Review*, 33(2), pp. 135–139.

Coombs, W.T. (2012). *Ongoing crisis communication: Planning, managing, responding*. Thousand Oaks, CA: Sage.

Covello, V.T., and Allen, F. (1988). Seven cardinal rules of risk communication. U.S. Environmental Protection Agency, Washington, D.C. Distributed by Office of Public Liaison [Pennsylvania] Dept. of Environmental Resources.

Fearn-Banks, K. (2016). *Crisis communications: A casebook approach*. London: Routledge.

Government of Georgia. Measures implemented by the government of Georgia against COVID 19.) [online] (No date), Report. Available from: https://stopcov.ge/Content/files/COVID_RESPONSE_REPORT__ENG.pdf [Accessed 19 May 2021].

Hale, J.E., Dulek, R.E., and Hale, D.P. (2005). Crisis response communication challenges: Building theory from qualitative data. *The Journal of Business Communication (1973)*, 42(2), pp. 112–134.

Jangiani, G. (2020). The Georgian media struggles to cope with COVID-19. *New Eastern Europe* [online]. Available from: https://neweasterneurope.eu/2020/05/07/the-georgian-media-struggles-to-cope-with-covid-19/ [Accessed 19 May 2021].

Kintsurashvili T. Infodemic in Georgia [online]. (2020). Available from: http://mdfgeorgia.ge/uploads//Publication-ENG-with%20hyperlink-web.pdf?fbclid=IwAR2cLue9wmsGlXzJlY-IlBmJFAU6VWhMbTNJSdlnfiFI8J-reZKs4s8ZR6M [Accessed 19 May 2021].

Lundgren, R.E., and McMakin, A.H. (2004). *Risk communication: A handbook for communicating environmental, safety, and health risks*, 3rd ed. Columbus, OH: Battelle Press.

Morgan, M.G. (2002). *Risk communication: A mental models approach*. Cambridge, MA: Cambridge University Press.

Morgan, M.G., Fishhoff, B., Bostrom, A., and Atman, C.J. (2002). *Risk communication: A mental models approach*. New York: Cambridge University Press.

Ray, S.J. (1999). *Strategic communication in crisis management: Lessons from the airline industry*. Westport, CT: Quorum Books.

Sandman, P. (2003). Four kinds of risk communication. *Issue of The Synergist*, pp. 26–27.

Sandman, P., 2004 . *Worst Case Scenarios* [online]. Available from: www.psandman.com/col/birdflu.htm [Accessed 19 May 2021].

Tierney, K. (2003). Disaster beliefs and institutional interests: Recycling disaster myths in the aftermath of 9–11. In L. Clarke, and W.R. Freudenburg, eds. *Terrorism and disaster: New threats, new ideas* (Vol. 11). Elsevier. Vol. 11, pp. 33–51.

Timothy, L. Sellnow, and Seeger, M.W. (2013). *Theorizing crisis communication*. John Wiley & Sons, Inc.

U.S. Environmental Protection Agency (2007). *Effective risk and crisis communication during water security emergencies*. EPA 600 -R07–027.

16 Information-seeking behaviour and governmental communication assessment during the COVID-19 pandemic in Romania

Camelia Cmeciu, Anca Anton and Anamaria Nicola

Introduction

The social disruption associated with the COVID-19 pandemic (Teti *et al.* 2020) has brought a new normality in which 'a mix of facts, fears, rumours and speculations' (Lovari 2020, p. 458) still prevails. The recontextualisation of social practices during the pandemic could bring a change in personality traits, especially for neuroticism (e.g., anxiety, depression) that is the most reactive to stress (Sutin *et al.* 2020, p. 9). Informing channel selection plays an important role during a global public health crisis (Park *et al.* 2019). Because citizens act as information seekers during a crisis, the urgency of sense-making and sense-giving in the interaction with citizens (Palttala and Vos 2012) should be essential for authorities. The official sense-giving is important because a chaotic flow of information or lack of information may trigger public distrust. We conducted a national survey seven months after the COVID-19 outbreak in Romania. We intend to understand what information seeking activities Romanian respondents used in order to get informed and how they assessed the government communication during the COVID-19 pandemic. Using the health-information-seeking behaviour (HISB) concept (Lambert and Loiselle 2007; Zimmerman and Shaw 2020), we investigate the HISB method and information dimensions. The first research purpose was to explore what information sources the Romanian respondents used and what type of information they know about COVID-19.

The COVID-19 pandemic has been a challenge for authorities because the excessive amount of information makes it difficult for people to 'distinguish between evidence-based information and a broad range of unreliable misinformation' (Naeem and Bhatti 2020, p. 233). Therefore, adequate message tailoring plays a significant role in public health crisis and governmental communicators should acknowledge people's fears during a health crisis (Guidry *et al.* 2017). Hence, the second research purpose is to investigate Romanians' assessment of the governmental communication during the pandemic.

DOI: 10.4324/9781003184669-25

Experiencing COVID-19 in Romania

In mid-January 2020, shortly after the World Health Organization (WHO) gave a global warning concerning the perils of the new COVID-19, the Romanian government issued several legislative initiatives and general warnings for the population, preparing the health system and the population for the moment the first cases would be confirmed. The government implemented travel restrictions and quarantine for people coming to Romania from countries where Romanian immigrants live and work.

The first case of COVID-19 in Romania was confirmed on 26 February. Restrictions and quarantine measures were taken immediately, and the complete lockdown was declared on 24 March two days after the Ministry of Health announced the first deaths due to COVID-19 of Romanian citizens. The national lockdown and the state of emergency were in place for two months, the government regulating how and when people were allowed to leave their houses. They were replaced in mid-May with a state of alert that remained active throughout the year.

The government's decision-making process was coordinated by the National Committee for Emergency Situations, and the entire communication on COVID-related topics was managed by a Strategic Communication Group, whose structure the government refused to disclose for almost a year despite journalists and NGOs repeatedly demanding transparency in the government's strategic communication. Most of the official communication was undertaken by the Romanian president and different representatives of the government in the first eight months of the pandemic. Although throughout the first year of the pandemic spokespersons changed (in part due to having three different Ministers of Health in one year), the constant communicators remained the president, Klaus Iohannis, and the secretary of state, Raed Arafat, the two most trusted public figures on a national level according to a national survey (IRES April 2020).

In the second half of 2020, studies showed that 60% of Romanians were satisfied with the decisions taken by European authorities and institutions to fight the pandemic, compared to the 45% European average (European Commission October 2020). Of Romanians, 48% were satisfied or very satisfied with the measures taken by the Romanian government, and 81% of Romanians said they primarily got their official information by watching TV, while social media, radio and online media were the other go-to channels for acquiring information (IRES July 2020).

Literature review: (online) health-information-seeking behaviour during the COVID-19 pandemic

Bridging the knowledge gap related to COVID-19 health issues was essential worldwide. The World Health Organization (2020) urged the population to get information only from the official WHO website and local health authority platforms and to follow preventive practices from trusted sources. These WHO messages show the importance of information sources and types and the dangers related to an abundance of misinformation that maximises fear.

Health-information-seeking behaviour (HISB) is defined as 'active or purposeful behaviour undertaken by an individual with the objective of finding information about health' (Zimmerman and Shaw 2020, p. 4) It was operationalised in two dimensions: the method dimension and the information dimension. The method dimension focusses on 'the discretionary actions employed by people to obtain health information' (Zimmerman and Shaw 2020, p. 10). Lambert and Loiselle (2007) mention that individuals use both personal (e.g., family, friends) and impersonal sources (e.g., books, internet). The information dimension focusses on the features of the information sought: type, amount and preference (Lambert and Loiselle 2007).

Several studies related to the COVID-19 pandemic were carried out taking into account the HISB dimensions. Trust in authorities (social media accounts of health organizations or the Ministry of Health website) as the main information sources was reported among parents from Bahrain (Ebrahim *et al.* 2020) and among Egyptian students (Shehata 2020). On the contrary, the young participants from Indonesia ranked social media (Instagram) as the most used source of information, but only half of the respondents believed in social media's reliability (Roselina *et al.* 2021). Trust in online communication with friends and family was ranked as a valuable source of information in China (Liu 2020), in German-speaking countries (Dreisiebner *et al.* 2020) and in Spain (Moreno *et al.* 2020). The HISB information dimension related to the COVID-19 pandemic was also discussed. Two information types could be identified: information needs (varying from preventive measures to updates on the pandemic; see Dreisiebner *et al.* 2020; Ebrahim *et al.* 2020; Liu 2020) and criteria for choosing certain sources. These criteria were dependent on the respondents' selection of sources. The ranking of official authorities and traditional channels as the most used information sources was associated with credible information or journalist quality as criteria for choosing a source (Dreisiebner *et al.* 2020) whereas the ranking of social media as a main source of acquiring information was linked to reasons related to easy and frequent accessibility and better understandability (Roselina *et al.* 2021).

To better understand Romanians' information-seeking behaviour during the pandemic, this chapter addresses the following research questions:

RQ1: What differences could be observed in the actions employed by the respondents to obtain COVID-19 information?

RQ2: How does the respondents' opinion of reliability differ among the sources of information?

RQ3: What type of information do the Romanian respondents know about the pandemic?

Governmental communication during health crises

Official sense-making and sense-giving during health crises are essential since publics show a greater urgency on information needs. The studies on governmental communication during various epidemics (Avery 2017; Guidry *et al.* 2017; Liu and Kim 2011; Park *et al.* 2019) showed there is a need for a synergy of channels in the communication of the authorities. This co-action of traditional media and social media in official message tailoring and dissemination has several advantages: active information flow, an official limitation of confusion through uncertainty acceptance (Liu and Kim 2011), message penetration across various risk perception groups (Park *et al.* 2019), misinformation debunking through addressing people's concerns and fears and combating negativities using positive messages (Guidry *et al.* 2017). Since participants with different levels of risk perception acquire information from different sources, public information officers (PIOs) should consider the interpersonal networks (medical professionals, friends and family) since they imply a more active and convincing process (Park *et al.* 2019).

Channel preference is only one aspect of the governmental communication during a health crisis. Compliance with public health recommendations depends on the level of trust in authorities. Therefore, persuading the public to follow the governmental measures depends on sociocultural contexts. The message content, the shared cultural or historical knowledge about past events and the value system are important factors which influence the level of trust (Vaughan and Tinker 2009).

The same behavioural measures for fighting the COVID-19 pandemic were perceived differently in various countries (Margraf *et al.* 2020). The findings showed that a high level of perceived usefulness and adherence depends on the citizens' feeling of being well informed and on a communication strategy in the interests of the people. Vardavas *et al.*'s (2020) study showed that the respondents who reported doctors/healthcare providers as the most credible sources were more likely to report disapproval with and reliance toward the official actions. Adherence to and approval of the governmental actions were reported by those participants who ranked governments/politicians and family/friends as the most trusted sources.

The studies on the efficacy of the Romanian governmental strategies during the COVID-19 pandemic revealed the following: sociocultural factors such as corruption or religious convictions influence the management of the pandemic (Dascălu 2020), as do confusing and timid initial communicative responses (Cernicova-Buca and Palea 2021) and the lack of a real-time online dialogue between authorities and citizens (Cmeciu 2021). Romanians (54.5%) consider that there is abundant corruption in the country (World Values Survey 2020). The army (84%) and the Romanian Orthodox Church (61%) were among the most trusted institutions during the pandemic (IRES April 2020). Dascălu (2020) emphasises that these sociocultural elements should be taken into account by authorities in the context of a health crisis and an efficient channel of communication should be established to reach all layers of society.

Drawing on the previous studies on communication management during health crises, two additional research questions are proposed:

> RQ4: How did the respondents assess the Romanian governmental communication during the pandemic?
> RQ5: What types of messages did the respondents consider to be information provided by the Romanian government?

Methodology

An online questionnaire in Romanian was distributed during the period 1–31 October 2020. Before accessing the questionnaire, the potential participants were informed about the purpose of the research, data confidentiality and voluntary participation in the survey. The questionnaire included socio-demographic items, neuroticism facets, HISB factors, and assessment of governmental communication. Six socio-demographic items were taken into account: age, gender, education, occupational status, income and place of residence. The neuroticism facets included a six-item self-assessment which allowed us to identify two groups: low anxiety level group versus high anxiety level group.

We selected three main factors from the HISB concept analysis and included them in the questionnaire: information sources (14 items, 7-point rating scale), level of trust in information sources (14 items, 7-point rating scale), and type of information about COVID-19 considered to be true (19 statements). The assessment of the Romanian government's communication management included two aspects: evaluation of governmental messages (6 items, 7-point rating scale) and the retention degree of the official communication of the Romanian government (6 statements). For each research question, we correlated the socio-demographic items and the anxiety levels with the respondents' information-seeking behaviour and their perception towards governmental communication in Romania. Out of the 1,003 responses received, 989 responses were considered valid and were included in the final research. This sample runs the minimum probabilistic sample for Romania (approx. 19 million inhabitants), error margin (0.03) and confidence interval (95%).

Statistical data analysis

The dataset was checked for integrity, missing data and outliers and was analysed with SPSS. The database was not weighted. Descriptive statistics were calculated from raw data (measured values). Certain variables were transformed from continuous to ordinal in order to perform significance tests. We used statistical tests such as *t*-test, Chi-square, Cramer's V or Eta and correlation coefficients (Pearson and Kendall's tau-b) to discover and interpret the causal relationships between variables. The significance level was set at $p<0.05$. Throughout the chapter we mentioned how and when the variables were recoded and what statistical tests were applied. Opinion variables were used as dependent or correlated, while socio-demographic variables were used as independent.

Findings

Characteristics of respondents and anxiety level findings

The data in Table 16.1 show that the majority of respondents belong to the 15–24 and 35–44 age groups. Women formed the largest group (74%). Most of the respondents were high school and BA graduates (32%), followed by MA graduates (25%). When taking into consideration the occupational status, 34% worked in the private sector and 24% in the public sector. 40% of the respondents declared that their income exceeds €12,000 per year. The participants living in urban areas formed the largest group, with 83%. The results of the correlation between the socio-demographic items and the anxiety level show that 60% of the Romanian respondents had a low anxiety level. The age, education level and income variables were negatively associated with the anxiety level. The older the respondents were, the lower the anxiety level was reported (r=-0.245, p=0.000). This was different from our expectations since older persons were considered one of the risk groups for COVID-19. Lower education level respondents registered a higher anxiety level (τ_b=-0.079, $p<0.01$). The greater the income was, the lower the anxiety level was (τ_b=-0.092, $p<0.01$). A positive correlation was observed with the gender variable.

Media usage behaviour during the COVID-19 crisis in Romania

In October 2020, after the end of summer holidays and the beginning of the school year, Romanians were looking for news regarding the evolution of the COVID-19 pandemic. RQ1 explored the HISB method dimension, focussing on what sources the Romanian respondents used to acquire information about the pandemic. As shown in Table 16.2, they turned to online press (53%), television (49%), the websites/blogs of public institutions (39%) and Facebook (33%).

The top two information sources exhibited opposing correlations with the age variable: while television registered a positive correlation value (τ_b= 0.064, $p<0.01$), online press registered a negative one (τ_b=-0.073, $p<0.01$). Therefore, the older someone is, the more likely they are to use television more frequently when looking for information. However, the correlations values indicated only a slight, not a categorical distribution, as percentages were also high and the variation between the lowest and the highest age groups was no higher than 16% (for television) and 8% for online press. We also found a negative

Table 16.1 Characteristics of respondents (n = 989)

Variable/categories	*No./% of respondents*	*Anxiety level*	
		Low anxiety	*High anxiety*
	989/100%	*60%*	*40%*
		r/τb/η, p-value, % from row category	
Age		r=-0.245**, $p=0.000$	
15–24	272/28%	43%	57%
25–34	181/18%	55%	45%
35–44	209/21%	67%	33%
45–54	190/19%	73%	27%
55–64	88/9%	68%	32%
65+	49/5%	82%	18%
Gender		r=0.070*, $p<0.05$	
Female	727/74%	58%	42%
Male	259/26%	66%	34%
Other	3/0.3%	33%	67%
Education level		τ_b=-0.079**, $p<0.01$	
HS	317/32%	52%	48%
BA	321/32%	68%	32%
MA	247/25%	63%	37%
PhD/Post-doc	66/7%	62%	38%
Other	47/5%	57%	43%
Occupational status		η=0.191**, $p=0.000$	
Not currently working	153/15%	63%	37%
Self-employed	56/6%	63%	38%
Public sector work	240/24%	68%	32%
Private sector work	336/34%	64%	36%
Student	204/21%	42%	58%
Income (EUR/year)		τ_b=-0.092**, $p<0.01$	
0–3600	77/8%	51%	49%
3601–6000	166/17%	53%	47%
6001–12000	347/35%	60%	40%
>12000	399/40%	65%	35%
Place of residence		*Not statistically significant*	
Rural	164/17%		
Urban	825/83%		

Source: Authors

Notes: Correlation coefficient calculated with Pearson (r) – age, gender, place of residence, Kendall's tau_b (τ_b) – education level, income, and Eta (η) – anxiety dependent (occupational status).

** Correlation is significant at the 0.01 level (2-tailed).

* Correlation is significant at the 0.05 level (2-tailed).

correlation between age and websites/blogs of public institutions as information sources (τ_b=-0.057, $p<0.05$): the younger someone is (<55 years), the more likely they are to seek information on official governmental communication channels. While all age groups indicated online press and television as the

Table 16.2 Information source usage during the COVID-19 pandemic

Information source	*Overall %*
Online press	53%
TV	49%
Public institutions – websites/blogs	39%
Facebook	33%
Health – websites/blogs	28%
Radio	26%
Scientists – websites/blogs	24%
Scientific journals	20%
YouTube	13%
WhatsApp	9%
Printed press	8%
Alternative therapies – websites/blogs	8%
Instagram	5%
Twitter	4%

Source: Authors

Note: Percentages: Frequency based on the 5–7 scale points (scale 1 = Never, 7 = Very frequently)

primary information sources, the 15–24 age group turned to Instagram (14%) as a stand-out communication behaviour (as does the student group when compared to other occupational categories), while the 65+ age group were the heaviest Facebook users (45%), even if Facebook was their third information source.

The education level (Table 16.3) had strong statistical significance and correlated relatively well particularly with online sources of information. The respondents who held a higher education degree selected more frequently institutional and science-based information sources – scientific journals, health websites/blogs, and websites/blogs of scientists, while high-school graduates used Instagram (14%) and YouTube (16%) the most. Scientific journals were preferred by individuals holding a PhD or a post-doc. While all categories used online media (overall 53%), categories holding less than a university degree appeared not necessarily to favour a set of information sources compared to the higher education group, but rather to seek less information and use any information source less frequently.

The occupational status was statistically significant in correlation to a selection of information sources similar to the selection by education level: online press and the websites/blogs of public institutions were the top two information sources regardless of education or occupation. In addition, there is an information source selection pattern observed in self-employed individuals, private sector employees and students: they added websites/blogs of scientists as their third most frequently used source of information. By contrast, public sector employees had a slight preference for scientific journals as a third source rather than for websites/blogs of scientists, while those not currently

Table 16.3 Information source usage during the COVID-19 pandemic by education level

Information source	*Overall %*	τ_b, *p-value*	*Education level*				
			HS	*BA*	*MA*	*PhD/ Post-doc*	*Other*
Instagram	5%	-0.180**, 0.000	11%	4%	2%	0%	9%
YouTube	13%	-0.074**, 0.006	16%	11%	12%	9%	13%
Online press	53%	0.117**, 0.000	46%	56%	60%	56%	30%
Scientific journals	20%	0.227**, 0.000	10%	24%	26%	32%	13%
Public institutions – websites/blogs	39%	0.122**, 0.000	33%	43%	44%	42%	21%
Health – websites/ blogs	28%	0.103**, 0.000	21%	35%	29%	32%	19%
Scientists – websites/blogs	24%	0.106**, 0.000	17%	30%	25%	24%	19%

Source: Authors

Notes: Percentages: Frequency based on the 5–7 scale points (scale 1 = Never, 7 = Very frequently)
Correlation coefficient calculated with Kendall's tau_b (τ_b).

** Correlation is significant at the 0.01 level (2-tailed).

* Correlation is significant at the 0.05 level (2-tailed).

working (retired, unemployed) used all information sources less frequently by up to 20%.

Evaluation of information source reliability

The HISB method dimension focusses on the actions that individuals employ to obtain health information, but media usage should be combined with source reliability. RQ2 focused on the assessment of the Romanian respondents' level of trust in various sources. The Romanian respondents exhibited a general lack of trust in their information sources, with low values across the board (Table 16.4). In this context, the highest scoring sources were prestigious healthcare personalities (55%), WHO (48%) and, tied for third place (34%), the Romanian presidency and people from inside the health system transmitting personal information. The least trusted sources of information were influencers on alternative therapies (5%) and non-health-related social media influencers (3%). They were joined, somewhat surprisingly, by friends on social media (11%) and unknown health personnel who spread information on social networks (11%), pointing to the fact that the presence or absence of a personal connection was not necessarily a predictor of trust.

A high anxiety level pointed to an increased level of trust (24%) in NGOs as information sources compared to a low anxiety level (17%), while the education level was statistically significant for information sources that represent authority – the Romanian presidency (τ_b=0.117, p=0.000) or expertise – prestigious healthcare personalities (τ_b=0.134, p=0.000). Across the board, a higher education level was correlated with a stronger degree of trust, particularly

Table 16.4 Trust in information sources during the COVID-19 pandemic

Information source	*Overall %*
Prestigious healthcare personalities (e.g., epidemiologists)	55%
World Health Organization	48%
Medical professional associations	37%
Romanian presidency	34%
Personal information transmitted by people from inside the health system	34%
Romanian government	31%
Local authorities	22%
Media	22%
NGOs	20%
Health influencers	12%
Friends on social networks	11%
Unknown health personnel who have spread information on social networks	11%
Others	7%
Influencers on alternative therapies	5%
Influencers of other topics (not health) on social networks	3%

Source: Authors

Note: Percentages: Frequency based on the 5–7 scale points (1 = Never, 7 = Very frequently)

in institutionally, professionally or academically validated information sources. The income variable performed in a similar fashion, but without conditioning trust. However, neither income nor education were statistically significant for WHO as a trusted information source. WHO was negatively correlated with the age variable (τ_b=0.086, p=0.000), with the 15–24 age group registering a trust level of 57%, while all the other groups registered between 41% and 47%. In opposition, prestigious healthcare professionals exhibited a positive correlation with the age variable (τ_b=0.116, p=0.000): the trust in this information source progressively increased from 46% to 67% across the age groups (Table 16.5). Media were not considered a trustworthy information source, peaking within the 35–44 and 55–64 age groups with 30% and 32%, respectively.

Personal knowledge about the pandemic

RQ3 focused on the HISB information dimension. Seven months after the COVID-19 outbreak in Romania, we wanted to assess what types of information the Romanian respondents know about the pandemic. A standard frequency test revealed that almost all respondents (92%) considered the 'washing your hands, wearing a mask and keeping distance from others are effective ways to protect yourself' statement to be true. The other statements that were more frequently considered to be true (Table 16.6) addressed aspects such as symptoms (54%), border measures (45%), risk factors (42%) and untimely governmental response (37%).

No statistically significant difference was observed by anxiety level. Both high and low anxiety level groups (23%) believed in the conspiracy

Table 16.5 Trust in information sources during the COVID-19 pandemic by age

Information source	*Overall %*	τ_b*, p-value*	*Age*					
			15–24	*25–34*	*35–44*	*45–54*	*55–64*	*65+*
Media	22%	0.119**, 0.000	17%	17%	30%	21%	32%	18%
Friends on social networks	11%	0.069**, 0.004	9%	9%	12%	11%	11%	18%
Personal information transmitted by people from inside the health system	34%	0.058*, 0.012	29%	32%	34%	35%	43%	43%
World Health Organization	48%	-0.086**, 0.000	57%	43%	47%	44%	41%	43%
NGOs	20%	-0.091**, 0.000	27%	20%	19%	16%	13%	10%
Medical professional associations	37%	0.052*, 0.023	35%	31%	42%	39%	39%	37%
Prestigious healthcare personalities (e.g., epidemiologists)	55%	0.116**, 0.000	46%	52%	58%	61%	65%	67%

Source: Authors

Notes: Percentages: Frequency based on the 5–7 scale points (1 = Never, 7 = Very frequently).

Correlation coefficient calculated with Kendall's tau_b (τ_b).

** Correlation is significant at the 0.01 level (2-tailed).

* Correlation is significant at the 0.05 level (2-tailed).

theories claiming that COVID-19 was fabricated to ruin the global economy. These socio-demographic variables presented statistical significance when cross-tabulated with COVID-19 statements considered to be true: residence, education, income, occupation and age (p=0.000 for all five variables). A chi-square test of independence pointed to statistically significant associations based on proportions comparisons. Therefore, a series of polarisations became apparent: the highest-income earners were more likely to consider to be true the statements referring to prevention/protection measures (8), to smoking as a risk factor (6) and to office COVID-19 transmission (5) while being less likely to choose conspiratorial statements (18). This evaluation perfectly opposed that of the low-income earners. The rural group was more likely to choose as true statements regarding the vulnerability of the elderly/ill (2), statements critical of the government measures (14) or those related to conspiracy theories (18, 19). High-school graduates made somewhat similar choices to the rural sample (likely to choose statements 1, 2, 14, 18, 19), while BA graduates were less likely to consider conspiracy statements (18, 19) as true. Most of the categories correctly identified governmental preventive and protection messages as true statements, but their statement

Table 16.6 Statements about the COVID-19 pandemic considered to be true

No.	*Statements*	*Overall %*
8	Washing your hands, wearing a mask and keeping distance from others are effective ways to protect yourself	92%
1	COVID-19 is like a flu for most of the population	54%
3	COVID-19 spread can be reduced by closing the borders of affected countries	45%
6	Smoking is a risk factor for COVID-19	42%
15	The measures taken by the government have been declared too late	37%
5	COVID-19 is transmitted through the ventilation system	25%
18	COVID-19 has been created in the laboratory and disseminated to sink the global economy	23%
14	The measures taken are exaggerated	22%
11	You must stay home so that the economy does not suffer a longer interruption	20%
12	The most important thing is to have food and basic necessity products at home	17%
19	COVID-19 has been created in the laboratory and disseminated to lighten the number of dependents in the pension system	16%
16	Only those who have tested positive should be confined at home	14%
2	COVID-19 only affects elderly and sick people with pre-existing conditions	13%
10	Staying at home is just a matter of solidarity, but I am not at risk if I go out	12%
13	I must go to the doctor/hospital if I have mild symptoms	9%
4	You can travel within the country without incurring risks	8%
7	Eating lemon prevents becoming infected with COVID-19	6%
17	If I don't have symptoms, I can't spread it	5%
9	Homeopathy prevents or cures COVID-19	4%

Source: Authors

Note: Percentages: Standard frequency test

selection appeared to be conditioned by the type of information or source they accessed (official, conspiracy, etc.).

Assessment of the Romanian government's communication

RQ4 focused on the evaluation of the government's crisis communication management during the pandemic. The results (Table 16.7) showed that 43% of the respondents considered that the government acted as a social alarm amplifier. At the same time, the Romanian public authority was considered to have confused the population (35%) and not to have revealed all the truth (38%). The most critical aspects were the clarity, the timing of communication and the reliability of the government as an information provider. Less than 25% of the respondents considered that the Romanian authority offered clear, sufficient and timely information. Only 27% appreciated the government as the most reliable source.

Table 16.7 Assessment of governmental communication about the COVID-19 pandemic

Statement	*Overall %*
Has generated social alarm	43%
Has not revealed all the truth	38%
Has confused the population	35%
Has been the most reliable information	27%
Has been scheduled at the appropriate times	22%
Has always been clear and sufficient	21%

Source: Authors

Note: Percentages: Frequency based on the 5–7 scale points (scale 1 = Never, 7 = Very frequently)

There were no statistically significant differences by anxiety level, gender or income. The three negative statements related to the governmental communication exhibited negative correlation values with the age variable (Table 16.8): the older the respondents are, the less negative assessment perception of the government they have. The same negative statements had high correlation values with occupational status: 'The government has confused the population' (φ_c=0.119, p=0.000), 'The government has generated social alarm' (φ_c=0.119, p=0.000) and 'The government has not revealed all the truth' (φ_c=0.107, p<0.01). The respondents who were self-employed or students provided a more negative assessment of the governmental communication than the other occupational categories. Although the positive statements related to the Romanian governmental communication had low scores, a positive correlation could be observed between the education level and the three statements regarding the information clarity (τ_b=0.075, p<0.01), timing (τ_b=0.061, p<0.05) and reliability (τ_b=0.095, p=0.000). The higher the respondents' education level is, the more they consider that the Romanian government provided clear, timely and reliable information.

Governmental message retention

Most respondents correctly retained the governmentally tailored messages, and three messages stood out after conducting a standard frequency test (Table 16.9): 'Inform yourselves only from official sources. Respect the recommendations of the competent authorities.' (80%), 'COVID-19 spreads easily and you must stay home to protect the elderly and sick' (79%) and 'COVID-19 is dangerous and additional measures should be imposed on those persons coming from countries with a high level of contagiousness' (69%). When cross-tabulated with the government messages, only education (p=0.000), income (p<0.05), occupation (p=0.000), age (p=0.000) and gender (p<0.05) presented statistical significance. The messages related to protection measures and to compliance with official recommendations were primarily chosen by respondents holding

Table 16.8 Assessment of governmental communication about the COVID-19 pandemic by age

Statement	*Overall %*	*τb, p-value*	*Age*					
			15–24	*25–34*	*35–44*	*45–54*	*55–64*	*65+*
Has not revealed all the truth	38%	-0.125**, 0.000	47%	34%	39%	37%	26%	18%
Has confused the population	35%	-0.168**, 0.000	49%	36%	31%	30%	22%	12%
Has generated social alarm	43%	-0.168**, 0.000	56%	45%	39%	42%	27%	14%

Source: Authors

Notes: Percentages: Frequency based on the 5–7 scale points (1 = Never, 7 = Very frequently). Correlation coefficient calculated with Kendall's tau_b (τ_b).

** Correlation is significant at the 0.01 level (2-tailed).

* Correlation is significant at the 0.05 level (2-tailed).

Table 16.9 Government messages during the COVID-19 pandemic

Messages		*Overall %*
A	You must be calm because COVID-19 is not dangerous for most of the population	12%
B	COVID-19 only affects elderly and sick people with previous pathologies	29%
C	COVID-19 is dangerous and additional measures should be imposed on those persons coming from countries with a high level of contagiousness	69%
D	COVID-19 spreads easily and you must stay home to protect the elderly and sick	79%
E	COVID-19 spreads easily and you must stay home so that the economy does not suffer a longer interruption	25%
F	Inform yourselves only from official sources. Respect the recommendations of the competent authorities.	80%

Source: Authors

Note: Percentages: Standard frequency test

a BA or MA degree, by employees in the public sector and, to some extent, by the 25–34 age group and women.

Table 16.10 shows the likely associations and the unlikely message association(s) a group may enter. Some polarisations can be observed. Unlike the BA and MA graduates, high school graduates were likely to retain messages that were not issued by the Romanian government: 'You must be calm because COVID-19 is

Table 16.10 Cross-tabulation of government messages during the COVID-19 pandemic and statistically significant socio-demographic variables

Variable	*Categories*	*Messages (see Table 16.9 for message-letter correspondence)*					
		A	*B*	*C*	*D*	*E*	*F*
	HS	D(0.041) E(0.048)	D(0.000) E(0.018) F(0.002)	D(0.003)			
	BA				A(0.046)		A(0.028)
	MA				B(0.006)	B(0.015)	B(0.013)
	PhD/ Post-doc						
	Other						
Income (EUR/ year)	0–3600						
	3601–6000		D(0.043)				
	6001–12000						
	>12000						
Occupational status	Not currently working						
	Self-employed						
	Public sector work						B(0.042)
	Private sector work						
	Student		A(0.002) C(0.008) D(0.000) E(0.000) F(0.000)				
Age	15–24		C(0.038) D(0.002) E(0.001) F(0.000)				
	25–34		A(0.043)	A(0.013)	A(0.004)	A(0.005)	A(0.007)
	35–44						
	45–54						
	55–64						
	65+						
Gender	Female		A(0.007)		A(0.016)	A(0.047)	A(0.019)
	Male	B(0.007) D(0.016) E(0.047) F(0.019)					

Source: Authors

Notes: Table generated through a chi-square test of independence. Results are based on two-sided tests. For each significant pair, the key of the category with the smaller column proportion appears in the category with the larger column proportion.

Significance level for uppercase letters (A, B, C) = 0.05

Tests are adjusted for all pairwise comparisons within a row of each innermost subtable using the Bonferroni correction.

not dangerous for most of the population' and 'COVID-19 only affects elderly and sick people with previous pathologies'. Another polarisation was observed in the case of the gender variable: men were more likely to choose the message focussing on calm behaviour since COVID-19 was not dangerous (message A) and not to select the protection messages, while women were more likely to perform the opposite selection. Low-income individuals, students and the 15–24 age group were more likely to incorrectly attribute the message on selective infection distribution among population groups (message B) to the government and they were less likely to select the other options as the main governmental messages.

Discussion

During public health emergencies characterised as urgent and unexpected crises (Freimuth *et al.* 2008), citizens try to make sense of the new normality by seeking and sharing information while public authorities try to give sense by tailoring messages adapted to the sociocultural contexts. The uncertainty and fear related to health crises determined us to take into account the neuroticism facets, distinguishing between low and high anxiety level groups. The findings related to the anxiety level are consistent with Sutin *et al.*'s (2020) study on personality traits during the acute phase of COVID-19 pandemic, suggesting the neuroticism trait did not increase during the pandemic; on the contrary, a decrease of anxiety could be observed among the Romanian respondents. In the same line with Ebrahim *et al.*'s (2020) results, a higher anxiety level was observed among the Romanian female participants and the level of anxiety significantly decreased across the age group. The public information officers (PIOs) should consider this psychological assessment alongside the respondents' socio-demographic profiles as similar messages have a lower impact than messages tailored to age, gender or anxiety level groups.

Despite the global proliferation of social media, Eriksson (2018) suggests that there should be a continuation of traditional media usage in crisis situations alongside social media. The analysis of the Romanian respondents' HISB during the COVID-19 pandemic shows that mainstream media channels (online press and television) were highly used, followed by specific new media (websites/blogs of public institutions) and social media (Facebook). These findings are in line with previous studies on health crises (Avery 2017; Dreisiebner *et al.* 2020; Guidry *et al.* 2017; Liu and Kim 2011; Park *et al.* 2019), highlighting the importance of a synergy of media channels in the public authorities' communication. But unlike previous studies on information-seeking behaviour during the pandemic (Dreisiebner *et al.* 2020; Ebrahim *et al.* 2020; Shehata 2020; Roselina *et al.* 2021), the Romanian respondents across all age groups considered online press and television as their main information sources although they were not evaluated as the most trustworthy sources.

Although the level of risk perception played an important role in channel selection and usage for information seeking during other epidemics (Park *et al.* 2019), no significant difference was observed when considering the relationship between media usage and the anxiety level among the Romanian respondents. Despite the pervasive usage of online press and television, which was also observed among the Spanish respondents (Moreno *et al.* 2020), some differences could be noticed in Romania. Official governmental communication channels ranked as the third source of information among participants aged under 55 years. Whereas Instagram was mostly used by young respondents (<24 years old) who had the highest anxiety level, the heaviest Facebook users were the individuals belonging to the 65+ age group, who had the lowest anxiety level. Therefore, social media were the third information source for younger and older participants regardless of their anxiety level.

Channel preference should be associated with source reliability. The results are consistent with previous studies (Ebrahim *et al.* 2020; Shehata 2020), suggesting a high level of trust in science during the COVID-19 pandemic. But unlike the respondents from Bahrain and Egypt, the Romanian participants ranked the Romanian government as the fifth reliable source, placing prestigious healthcare personalities and WHO as the most reliable sources. Unlike German-speaking respondents (Dreisiebner *et al.* 2020), the Romanians did not consider the personal connection with family and friends as a trust indicator. The correlation analysis showed that participants with high and low anxiety levels display the same trust in science, the only difference being in the evaluation of NGOs as reliable sources, the participants with high anxiety level ranking NGOs as more reliable than those with low anxiety levels. Therefore, following Park *et al.*'s (2019) suggestion that PIOs should consider interpersonal networks (medical professionals, friends and family) in their communication and taking into account the sociocultural context, a practical implication emerges: Romanian PIOs should emphasise the role of prestigious healthcare professionals and of NGOs when tailoring their messages during health crises.

Unlike previous studies which focused on information needs during the pandemic (Dreisiebner *et al.* 2020; Ebrahim *et al.* 2020), we related the HISB information dimension to the respondents' knowledge about COVID-19. The findings showed four aspects: 1) a consistency with other studies (Ebrahim *et al.* 2020; Liu 2020; Moreno *et al.* 2020) which revealed the salience of prevention and protective measures among the most important subjects that respondents know about the pandemic; 2) the emphasis on a local narrative related to the closing of borders for the Romanian diaspora which brought a state of hysteria at the Romanian borders (Bărgăoanu and Durach 2020, p. 127); 3) dissatisfaction with the Romanian government's actions; and 4) fringe rather than mainstream conspiratorial thinking related to the pandemic. This last aspect presents a challenge for the Romanian government seeking to encourage citizens to debunk the fake news related to the COVID-19 pandemic.

The reluctance towards Romanian public authorities was also emphasised in the respondents' assessment of governmental communication. Framed as a social alarm amplifier, the Romanian government received low rankings on information clarity, timing, and reliability. Despite this low credibility associated with the public authorities, most respondents had a correct retention of the messages focused on prevention measures, compliance to official information, or protection from foreign contamination. The negative public assessment of the Romanian governmental communication goes in line with previous research (Dascălu 2020; Margraf *et al.* 2020; Vardavas *et al.* 2020) suggesting that the levels of approval and trust depend on sociocultural aspects. Within a context where more than half of the Romanians consider that corruption prevails in society (World Values Survey 2020) and where three successive Ministers of Health were appointed in one year, the Romanian respondents were aware of the importance of informing themselves from official sources and of following the prevention measures, but preferred to get their information more from prestigious healthcare personalities or WHO.

The findings revealed that the government assessment is dependent on age and occupational status: the older participants had a more positive perception of public authority, whereas the self-employed or students had a more negative evaluation of governmental communication. A clear discrepancy could be observed between anxiety level and governmental message retention. Although the 15–24 and 25–34 age groups displayed the highest anxiety level, they incorrectly attributed messages to the government. One explanation for this inconsistency could be the infodemic that all governments had to deal with. More than 20 websites and Facebook groups were reported in Romania to have spread misinformation about COVID-19's origin, or about treatments, most of them belonging to nationalist, extremist or religious groups (Eurocommunication Association 2020). The Romanian Ministry of Health started to debunk the fake news related to COVID-19 one week after the European Commission urged the countries to combat the infodemic. There is a clear need for the public authorities to provide a timely communication and to more convincingly combat the mis/disinformation on health issues.

Conclusions

This chapter brings the Romanian insights into the HISB dimensions and into the Romanian governmental assessment. The sociocultural context alongside the small differences across the socio-demographic categories and the anxiety level groups associated with the dissatisfaction regarding the government and with the conspiratorial thinking show that there is a general distrust in public authorities in Romania which may be amplified by fringe (but loud) voices. Therefore, this chapter brings three recommendations: 1) an increase of trust in Romanian governmental communication is conditioned by a decrease of corruption, a stable political environment and timely and clear communication; 2) governmental messages should be tailored and delivered on those media that various age or anxiety level groups use; 3) the source credibility could be obtained through an empowerment of interpersonal networks (healthcare professionals and well-known health organizations). This chapter has two limitations. First, a generalisation of the results should be carefully considered since the online survey limits the access to a part of the population. Second, some respondents' reluctance towards the issues related to the pandemic and their strong belief that the virus does not exist could have potentially affected some of the responses.

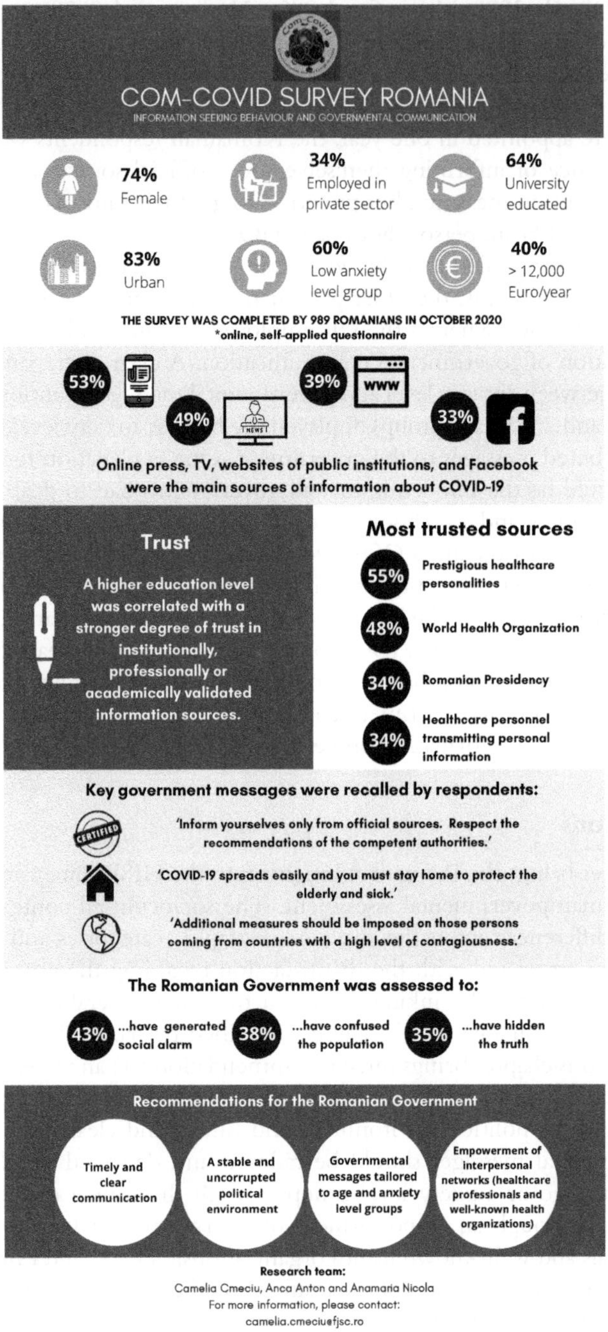

Infographic 16.1 COM-COVID survey Romania: Information-seeking behaviour and governmental communication

Bibliography

Avery, E.J. (2017). Public information officers' social media monitoring during the Zika virus crisis, a global health threat surrounded by public uncertainty. *Public Relations Review*, 43(3), pp. 468–476.

Bărgăoanu, A., and Durach, F. (2020). The COVID-19 infodemic: An accelerated version of the new digital ecosystem. *Romanian Journal of Communication and Public Relations*, 22(2), pp. 125–129.

Cernicova-Buca, M., and Palea, A. (2021). An appraisal of communication practices demonstrated by Romanian district public health authorities at the outbreak of the COVID-19 pandemic. *Sustainability*, 13(5), p. 2500.

Cmeciu, C. (2021). Keep calm and get informed: Risk communication and engagement during the COVID-19 pandemic in Romania. In L. Oliveira, F. Tajariol, and L.B. Gonçalves, eds. *Digital services in crisis, disaster, and emergency situations*. Hershey: IGI Global, pp. 246–267.

Dascălu, S. (2020). The successes and failures of the initial COVID-19 pandemic response in Romania. *Frontiers in Public Health*, 8(344).

Dreisiebner, S., März, S., and Mandl, T. (2020). Information behavior during the Covid-19 crisis in German-speaking countries. To be published in *arXiv* [Preprint]. Available from: https://arxiv.org/abs/2007.13833 [Accessed 20 March 2021].

Ebrahim, A.H., Saif, Z.Q., Buheji, M., ALBasri, N., Al-Husaini, F.A., and Jahrami, H. (2020). COVID-19 information-seeking behaviour and anxiety symptoms among parents. *OSP Journal of Health Care and Medicine*, 1(1). Available from: www.ospublishers.com/COVID-19-Information-Seeking-Behavior-and-Anxiety-Symptoms-among-Parents.html#Article [Accessed 11 March 2021].

Eriksson, M. (2018). Lessons for crisis communication on social media: A systematic review of what research tells the practice. *International Journal of Strategic Communication*, 12(5), pp. 526–551.

Eurocommunication Association (2020). *Infodemia COVID-19 in Romania*. Available from: www.antifake.ro/wp-content/uploads/2020/10/Eurocomunicare_Raport-Infodemia-COVID-19-in-Romania_octombrie-2020-1.pdf [Accessed 23 October 2020].

European Commission, (October 2020). *Standard Eurobarometer 93*. Available from: https://europa.eu/eurobarometer/surveys/detail/2262 [Accessed 10 March 2021].

Freimuth, V.S., Hilyard, K.M., Barge, J.K., and Sokler, L.A. (2008). Action, not talk: A simulation of risk communication during the first hours of a pandemic. *Health Promotion Practice*, 9(4), 35S–44S.

Guidry, J.P.D., Jin, Y., Orr, C., Messner, M., and Meganck, S., (2017). Ebola on Instagram and Twitter: How health organizations address the health crisis in their social media engagement. *Public Relations Review*, 43(3), pp. 477–486.

IRES/Romanian Institute for Evaluation and Strategy, (April 2020). *State and authority. The trust in public figures and institutions. An evaluation of measures*. Available from: https://ires.ro/articol/386/romania-in-pandemie-partea-i [Accessed 12 May 2020].

IRES/Romanian Institute for Evaluation and Strategy, (July 2020). *Romania. State of mind and social climate after 5 months of COVID-19*. Available from: https://ires.ro/articol/407/romania-stare-de-spirit-i-climat-social-dupa-5-luni-de-covid-19 [Accessed 12 March 2021].

Lambert, S.D., and Loiselle, C.G. (2007). Health information seeking behaviour. *Qualitative Health Research*, 17(8), pp. 1006–1019.

Liu, B.F., and Kim, S. (2011). How organizations framed the 2009 H1N1 pandemic via social and traditional media: Implications for U.S. health communicators. *Public Relations Review*, 37(3), pp. 233–244.

Liu, P.L. (2020). COVID-19 information seeking on digital media and preventive behaviours: The mediation role of worry. *Cyberpsychology, Behavior, and Social Networking*, 23(10), pp. 677–682.

Lovari, A. (2020). Spreading (dis)trust: Covid-19 misinformation and government intervention in Italy. *Media and Communication*, 8(2), pp. 458–461.

Margraf, J., Brailovskaia, J., and Schneider, S. (2020). Behavioral measures to fight COVID-19: An 8-country study of perceived usefulness, adherence and their predictors. *PLoS One*, 15(12), e0243523.

Moreno, Á., Fuentes-Lara, C., and Navarro, C. (2020). Covid-19 communication management in Spain: Exploring the effect of information-seeking behavior and message reception in public's evaluation. *El profesional de la información*, 29(4), e290402.

Naeem, S.B., and Bhatti, R. (2020). The Covid-19 'infodemic': A new front for information professionals. *Health Information and Libraries Journal*, 37(3), pp. 233–239.

Palttala, P., and Vos, M. (2012). Quality indicators for crisis communication to support emergency management by public authorities. *Journal of Contingencies and Crisis Management*, 20(1), pp. 39–51.

Park, S., Boatwright, B., and Avery, E.J. (2019). Information channel preference in health crisis: Exploring the roles of perceived risk, preparedness, knowledge, and intent to follow directives. *Public Relations Review*, 45(5), p. 101794.

Roselina, E., Asmiyanto, T., and Andriany, M. (2021). Health information-seeking behavior on the COVID-19 pandemic: Social media usage by Gen Z in Jakarta, Indonesia. *Library Philosophy and Practice (e-journal)*, 1(7). Available from: https://digitalcommons.unl.edu/libphilprac/4920/ [Accessed 15 March 2021].

Shehata, A. (2020). Health Information behaviour during COVID-19 outbreak among Egyptian library and information science undergraduate students. *Information Development.* doi:10.1177/0266666920976181 [Accessed 20 March 2021].

Sutin, A.R., Luchetti, M., Aschwanden, D., Lee, J.H., Sesker, A.A., Strickhouser, J.E., Stephan, Y., and Terracciano, A. (2020). Change in five-factor model personality traits during the acute phase of the Coronavirus pandemic. *PLoS ONE*, 15(8), e0237056.

Teti, M., Schatz, E., and Liebenberg, L. (2020). Methods in the time of COVID-19: The vital role of qualitative inquiries. *International Journal of Qualitative Methods*, 19, doi:10.1177/1609406920920962 [Accessed 11 January 2021].

Vardavas, C., Odani, S., Nikitara, K., El Banhawi, H., Kyriakos, C., Taylor, L., and Becuwe, N. (2020). Public perspective on the governmental response, communication and trust in the governmental decisions in mitigating COVID-19 early in the pandemic across the G7 countries. *Preventive Medicine Reports*, 21, 101252.

Vaughan, E., and Tinker, T. (2009). Effective health risk communication about pandemic influenza for vulnerable populations. *American Journal of Public Health*, 99(2), pp. 324–332.

World Health Organisation (2020). *Mental health and psychosocial considerations during the COVID-19 outbreak*. Available from: www.who.int/docs/default-source/coronaviruse/mental-health-considerations.pdf [Accessed 12 March 2021].

World Values Survey (2020). *World values survey wave* 7. Available from: www.worldvaluessurvey.org/WVSContents.jsp [Accessed 20 March 2021].

Zimmerman, M.S., and Shaw, Jr. G. (2020). Health information seeking behaviour: A concept analysis. *Health Information and Libraries Journal*, 37(3), pp. 173–191.

17 COVID-19 communication in Turkey

Exploring the public's information-seeking behaviour

Özlem Alikılıç, Ebru Gökaliler and İnanç Alikılıç

Introduction

In the process of gathering information, getting to know the current developments regarding the pandemic, and having individuals understand the decisions made by the government, means of communication around the world became important. In trying to understand the demands of both health and social life, many individuals turned to all channels of access to information, with the Internet at the forefront. In the pandemic period, individuals who feel desperate and helpless, especially in the face of the unknown, make efforts to access information. However, they are negatively affected psychologically and physically for reasons such as imperfect information, misinformation, conflicting information and the 'infodemic'.

The Turkish people were involved in the communication process regarding COVID-19 only by following the developments in the world until 11 March 2020. But when the first case in Turkey was registered, they adapted to the new order of life to learn the means of protection, economically and socially. In Turkey, the number of people who got COVID-19 was 4,750,026 until 29 April 2021; 39,398 people died. As for the process of vaccination, 21,130,936 doses of vaccines were administered (WHO 2021). In Turkey, the government started the communication on the pandemic through open and daily press meetings without interrupting the daily information flow. Although the language used by the government in communication was clear and understandable, and successful crisis communication was initiated based on trust and confidence, in retrospect, the increase of questions in the minds of the Turkish population, the uncertainty process and the complexity of the messages during the restrictions stood out as factors that reduced trust.

In this study, the importance of government communication during the pandemic crisis was investigated. Results indicated that government communication is the strongest source of information during the COVID-19 period. It influences the public's information-seeking behaviour. To determine how government communication was perceived by the public during the pandemic crisis, a survey was conducted with Turkish individuals between 1 October and 1 November 2020, the initial period of the second wave in Turkey. A total

DOI: 10.4324/9781003184669-26

of 513 individuals participated in the study. It was found that the respondents of the study mainly preferred online channels as sources of information. The research revealed that individuals acted with distrust towards government news compared to other channels and that individuals' need for trust in the flow of information was paramount. It was found that Turkish people have more confidence in health professionals they know than in health institutions or in respected health specialists compared to the government. It was found that the state's call to stay at home, to protect especially medical patients and the elderly, has stuck in the minds the most.

Information seeking and government communication in the COVID-19 pandemic in Turkey

Although people's motivations for seeking information do not change in the face of crises such as a pandemic, the channels to which they turn to differ depending on the period. In emergencies that affect public health worldwide, government agencies develop communication strategies to protect the public from current and potential threats. At the onset of a pandemic, states that propose behaviours that clarify and prevent risk have the power to reduce the spread of disease and deaths (Lin *et al.* 2014). Information is a precious resource for today's information society. In information-seeking behaviour, the information sought, the means of seeking and the sources of information needed cover the individual's personal reasons for seeking information (Kumar 2013).

Information behaviour refers to the activities of individuals in determining their own information needs, seeking such information in any form, and using and communicating that information. In this context, information-seeking behaviour expresses how people locate and use information (Wilson 1997; Cheuk Wai-Yi 1998; Ellis *et al.* 2002; Kundu 2017). Health information-seeking behaviour plays an influential role, and it is framed as self-control and self-care (Roselina *et al.* 2021). In health crises, trust is as vital as providing accurate information. The terms 'trust' and 'confidence' in this study are based on trust efforts in crisis management. While trust refers to the establishment of a social and relational bond, confidence is based on experience and evidence and is the belief that certain incidents are likely to continue in the future (*Understanding Social Trust*, no date).

Slovic (1993) found that confidence-destroying incidents have a much stronger effect than positive incidents. Being perceived as trustworthy by the public is one of the most important components of crisis communication. Low public trust in politicians weakens the trust relationship between communicators and the public. To build trust in risk and pandemic communication, it is important to empathise with the public and be clear and transparent. The environment of mistrust arises from various circumstances, such as the public's lack of trust in officials' knowledge and skills, lack of trust in their fairness and lack of trust in their honesty (Abraham 2011). In order to build trust in crisis communication, the insights of the society are supported in many aspects, such as the right of access to information, transparency and empathy. However, today's communication technologies have facilitated disinformation and manipulation as much as access to information (Chew and Eysenbach 2010). Additionally, people around the world who have not faced such a deadly pandemic in many years first went in search of information about the disease to understand it (Kırık *et al.* 2020). And then, the countries that quickly resorted to restrictions tried to get information about the causes and the extent of the restrictions. But such an intense flow of information has also brought the infodemic to the forefront in Turkey – as in the whole world – in the period of COVID-19 when so many concepts are brand new and uncertainty is at the forefront. Ghebreyesus, the Director-General of WHO, specified that the world is not only facing a pandemic but also an infodemic caused by false information circulating (WHO 2020). The incorrect news content regarding pandemics that promotes fear and panic in individuals, and especially fake and unrealistic content shared on social media, are spreading so fast that followers are having difficulty in distinguishing between correct and incorrect information.

While the rapid nature of change increases the need for information for societies entering a whole new era in economic and social terms, the status for Turkish society is no different (Turan and Çelikyay 2020). In Turkey, there were some mistakes but also positive practices in government communication during the pandemic. Some decisions led to more significant discomfort and sometimes anger among the public, who wanted to be informed. In the first weeks of the COVID-19 pandemic, when there was little information about the disease, the decisions made and the daily news feeds worried the Turkish population. During this period, information and infodemic combined to create confusion.

Turkey followed the news about the COVID-19 pandemic in other parts of the world until 11 March 2020, when it became a reality in the country, with the first declared case being announced. On 10 January 2020, the state officials of Turkey established the Scientific Advisory Board, which consists of medical specialists. Its mandate was to issue measures that would slow the spread of the disease in the country (Turan and Çelikyay 2020). To prevent the spread of the disease by airline passengers, thermal imaging cameras were installed at airports in the first phase, and entry into Turkey was allowed only after conducting health checks on passengers coming from countries where cases had been observed (Narlı 2021). But along with declaring the first official case in Turkey on 11 March 2020, the board acted swiftly to provide information and put in place the restrictions. Starting on 11 March, Fahrettin Koca, the Minister of Health, issued press statements every evening, and clarified the disease and development in the process of seeking information to share with the public. Both the Ministry of Health and the Minister of Health shared the daily number of cases via their personal social media accounts. Furthermore, well-known personalities in Turkey participated in public service announcements telling the public what to do to protect themselves from the pandemic. Since not everyone in Turkey has Internet access, the information was also communicated via telephone (Directorate of Communications of the Presidency of Republic of Turkey 2021).

The Turkish government's communication management used exemplary methods, such as notifying the public via statements based on data; sharing sustainable and up-to-date information; claiming of responsibility by relevant institutions and organizations; and regularly informing the public through various channels. These included multiple crisis spokespersons (including celebrities), infographics, public service announcements, a mobile application called *Hayat Eve Sığar* (Life Fits into the House), a COVID-19 phone line, informative posters and brochures, and SMS text messaging (Directorate of Communications of the Presidency of Republic of Turkey 2021).

In evaluating government communication and public information seeking during the COVID-19 pandemic in Turkey, it is necessary to examine Turkey's administrative structure and the country's infrastructure facilities. In Turkey, on 21 January 2017, the governmental system was changed by the Constitutional Amendment Law and moved to the presidential system by changing the parliamentary governmental system (Küçük and Aydoğdu 2018). Effective governmental communication meant delivering pandemic-related information to the public quickly, and ensured fast decision-making, especially in public institutions. As well, practicing appropriate strategies through all channels facilitated transparency, trust and control. The healthcare reform that the government has implemented in recent years has increased trust in the state in the effective communication process. And they included this status in communication processes to reassure the public.

The COVID-19 pandemic, which caused weakening of social relations and health and economic risks all over the world (Antwi-Boasiako and Nyarkoh 2021), also caused the imposition of significant restrictions in Turkey in the social, economic and political spheres as well as in the religious and cultural spheres. It changed the usual lifestyle and way of working. The first restriction decision in Turkey was taken on 12 March 2020, the day following the determination of the first official case.

Temporary cancellations of social events and official permits were among the first restrictions, but by no means the last.On 23 March2020, school classes were suspended (to be continued online), sports competitions were postponed, citizens returning from Umrah were quarantined, a curfew was imposed on those older than 65 and younger than 20, some businesses were closed, travel restrictions were set within the country, collective worship was suspended, and many more in the fields of education, culture, social life, religion, and business. They have continued until today (Narlı 2021). The supply chain was disrupted, and public health institutions repeatedly urged the people to keep social distance and stay at home as was happening in the whole world. In Turkey, they repeated the slogans of "mask, distance, and cleanliness," and they continuously informed the public.

In this pandemic, two major communication mistakes were made in managing the crisis, which led to a crisis within a crisis. One was increasing the number of crisis spokespersons. In the COVID-19 crisis, multiple spokespersons informed the public about government communications. For example, while it was a correct choice to appoint the Minister of Health as the spokesperson for the pandemic crisis, the ministry's last-minute statement from Internal Affairs regarding the curfew, caused the public to panic and not comply. And the second communication failure caused the public to panic because the statements of the two spokespersons were independent of each other. At 7:00 p.m., the Ministry of Health's stated that lockdown was not an issue, but then at 8:00 p.m., the minister of Internal Affairs said that lockdown would be applied. This caused actions that would increase the risk of infection (Ministry of Internal Affairs 2020). As time passed, distrust began among the Turkish public regarding the government's communication on the pandemic. Both the communication of risk requiring structural change and the messages to be sent through media communication, behavioural communication and mass media on the centreline of social skills and social access are interesting. In this context, the common language of many institutions and clarity and adequate implementation capacity of the same must be considered in terms of government communication during the pandemic period (Gamhewage 2014).

The Turkish Medical Association stated that the number of cases reported each evening was not coded according to the principles established by WHO, and therefore the numbers reported were lower than the actual numbers (Evrensel 2020). There was an inconsistency between the weekly death reports provided by metropolitan communities and the number of COVID-19-based deaths reported by the Department of Health. Meanwhile, it was understood that the numbers were kept low by the health minister's statement that the number of patients was not the daily number of positive cases but only those with symptoms. WHO warned Turkey to report the number of cases (Mediascope 2020) correctly. All these negative circumstances undermined the Turkish public's trust in government communication. The breakdown of effective government communication caused confusion and misunderstanding among the public.

In Turkey, the extended restrictions in the summer were reinstated with the second COVID-19 wave in November 2020. Due to the increase in cases in November, face-to-face teaching, which had partially started, was paused again, cafes were closed, and lockdowns were again practiced at night and on weekends. While provincial restrictions were reassessed by 1 March 2021, restaurant closures and lockdowns were again practiced for the third wave due to the drop in caseloads in April. Between 29 April 2021 and 17 May 2021, full closures were ordered due to an increase in case numbers in Turkey.

EUPRERA issued a call for COVID-19 communication management in Europe to its members to investigate the information-seeking behaviour of societies in different countries when communicating a pandemic crisis. Many countries in different regions of the world responded, and use of the same methodology ensured that the information-seeking behaviour of different countries could be compared accurately. Turkey took part in the study, launched simultaneously, to determine the information-seeking behaviour of the Turkish public during the COVID-19 pandemic. The following are the study's research questions.

RQ1: Which channels did the Turkish public prefer when seeking information during the COVID-19 pandemic?
RQ2: What is the Turkish public's opinion of the Turkish government's communication management?
RQ3: In which sources of information did the population show the most confidence?
RQ4: What messages were sent by the government to the Turkish public that remained before the state of alert was declared?
RQ5: How accurate is the COVID-19 information available to the Turkish people?

Methodology

An online survey was used. In adapting the questions of the scale (Moreno *et al.* 2020) to Turkey, preliminary research was conducted in the form of focus group studies, expert opinions and pilot research. As a result, it was clearly identified what needed to be done to address the cultural and contextual differences and communication barriers that arose from translation, and the necessary interventions were made. After the completion of the questionnaire, the random sampling method was used. The survey was conducted on Google Forms through social media channels (WhatsApp, Twitter, Facebook, etc.) between 1 October and 1 November 2020, when the second COVID-19 wave began.

The online questionnaire included questions about information-seeking behaviour, trust in various sources and channels, perceptions of government communication management, retention of news, and demographic characteristics. Five hundred thirteen respondents completed the questionnaire. The data were analysed using SPSS version 22. Reliability Statistics Cronbach's alpha was .806.

Findings

The socio-demographic information of the respondents in the study is given in Table 17.1.

RQ1: What are the channels that the Turkish public prefers in their information-seeking behaviours during the COVID-19 pandemic?

In the COVID-19 period, the process of intensive information seeking continued. It was noted that in this period, there was a distinct tendency to use non-traditional channels. According to the data in the first section of the questionnaire, the information received from WhatsApp groups ($\bar{x}$ =5.11), information from the online press ($\bar{x}$ =5.09) and Instagram ($\bar{x}$ =4.64) ranked the first three places, respectively, and traditional media ($\bar{x}$ =4.45) and TV ranked in fourth place. Newspapers ($\bar{x}$ =2.13), websites/blogs specialised in alternative

Table 17.1 Socio-demographic information of the respondents

Variables	*N = 513* *n – (%)*
Gender distribution	
Female	329 (64.1%)
Male	184 (35.9%)
Education distribution	
High school or below	85 (16.6%)
Bachelor's Degree	317 (61.8%)
Master's Degree or above	111 (21.6%)
Age distribution	
0–20	91 (17.7%)
21–40	183 (35.7%)
41–60	219 (42.7%)
61–80	20 (3.9%)
Income distribution	
Low	15 (2.9%)
Low-medium	66 (12.9%)
Medium	229 (44.6%)
Medium-high	172 (33.5%)
High	31 (6.0%)
Working status	
I am not currently working	87 (17.0%)
I am self-employed	72 (14.0%)
Public sector work	75 (14.6%)
Private sector work	120 (23.4%)
I am student	144 (28.1%)
I work in healthcare	15 (2.9%)

Source: Authors

therapies ($\bar{x}$ = 2.37), and radio ($\bar{x}$ = 2.45) were the least preferred sources of information (Table 17.2).

As shown in table 17.2, preference for traditional media was low during the COVID-19 period. When examining the channels for accessing information in Turkey during COVID-19, it was found that, as with accessing the information on topics related to health in certain periods around the world (Zhao *et al.* 2020; Majid and Rahmat 2013; Zimmerman and Jr 2020), the Internet was again a preferred channel.

RQ2: What is the Turkish public's opinion of the Turkish government's communication management?

The results for RQ2, the Turkish public's reflections on government communication in the COVID-19 period, were 'Did not reveal the whole truth' ($\bar{x}$ = 5.40) and 'Created confusion among the public' ($\bar{x}$ = 5.31). The Turkish public turned to many different channels for clear information about the number of cases. However, disinformation and infodemic were high. In the context of the study, the lowest mean scores in assessing government communication went to 'was the most reliable information' ($\bar{x}$ = 2.55) and 'was always clear and sufficient' ($\bar{x}$ = 2.70) (Table 17.3). Therefore, individuals in Turkey had a

Table 17.2 Preferred information sources on COVID-19

Information source	*Mean*
WhatsApp	5.15
Online press	5.09
Instagram	4.64
Television	4.45
YouTube	3.99
Twitter	3.83
Websites/blogs by scientists	3.46
Websites/blogs from public institutions	3.34
Websites/blogs specialised in health	3.30
Print press	2.89
Facebook	2.84
Radio	2.45
Websites/blogs specialised in alternative therapies	2.37
Journal	2.13

Source: Authors

Table 17.3 Perception of government communication on COVID-19

	N	*Minimum*	*Maximum*	*Mean*	*Standard deviation*
Has not revealed all the truth	513	1	7	5.40	2.044
Has confused the population	513	1	7	5.31	1.868
Has generated social alarm	513	1	7	3.50	1.860
Has been scheduled at the appropriate times	513	1	7	3.12	1.721
Has always been clear and sufficient	513	1	7	2.70	1.703
Has been the most reliable information	513	1	7	2.55	1.748

Source: Authors

negative perception of the Turkish government's communication management during COVID-19.

RQ3: In which sources of information did the population show the most confidence?

In the results for question RQ3, when asked about respondents' trust in institutions and individuals, it was found that trust in government was very low ($\bar{x}$ =2.89), trust in known health professionals was highest ($\bar{x}$ =5.65), followed by respected health professionals ($\bar{x}$ =5.37), and trust in associations of health professionals was highest ($\bar{x}$ =5.06). Similar to the government, trust in local authorities ($\bar{x}$ =3.81) and trust in regional authorities ($\bar{x}$ =3.21) were also found to be relatively low (Table 17.4).

Some management decisions, also previously mentioned, caused greater discomfort and sometimes anger among the public who wanted access to

Table 17.4 Trust level of sources of information on COVID-19

	N	*Minimum*	*Maximum*	*Mean*	*Standard deviation*
Health personnel that I personally know	513	1	7	5.65	1.397
Prestigious healthcare personalities	513	1	7	5.37	1.513
Associations of health groups	513	1	7	5.06	1.700
World Health Organization	513	1	7	4.82	1.708
Local authorities	513	1	7	3.81	1.720
Friends on social networks	513	1	7	3.59	1.649
Health influencers	513	1	7	3.37	1.753
Media	513	1	7	3.26	1.582
Regional authorities	513	1	7	3.21	1.663
Unknown health personnel who have spread on social networks	513	1	7	3.18	1.757
Government	513	1	7	2.89	1.818
Other	462	1	7	2.68	1.514
Influencers on alternative therapies	513	1	7	2.54	1.626
Influencers of other topics (not health) on social networks	513	1	7	1.90	1.359

Source: Authors

information. As a result, Turkish society shifted to the information they received from health professionals they knew and respected rather than government agencies.

RQ4: What messages were sent by the government to the Turkish public that remained before the state of alert was declared?

According to the results, the message 'COVID-19 spreads easily, and you must stay at home to protect the elderly and sick' stuck in the public's mind with a rate of 30.80%, and the message 'COVID-19 spreads easily, and you must stay at home so that the economy does not suffer a long interruption' at a rate of 23.60% (Table 17.5). Although the message 'COVID-19 will cause a state of emergency and the most important thing is to have food at home' was not given by the Turkish government (3.70%), Turkish society turned to online shopping during this period, and there was an increase in the tendency to hoard food. And there was an increase in the tendency to buy and stockpile mainly tea, coffee, detergent, pasta and dried vegetables (İnce and Kadıoğlu 2020). Therefore, it was observed that there was a correspondence between the messages given by the government and the messages in people's minds.

RQ5: How accurate is the COVID-19 information available to the Turkish people?

Table 17.5 The key messages based on government communication retained in the COVID-19 pandemic

	%
COVID-19 spreads easily and you must stay home to protect the elderly and sick	30.80%
COVID-19 spreads easily and you must stay home so that the economy does not suffer a longer interruption	23.40%
COVID -9 only affects elderly and sick people with previous pathologies	20.00%
COVID-19 is dangerous and borders should have been closed to persons from countries with a high level of contagiousness	14.80%
You must be calm because COVID-19 is not dangerous for most of the population	7.30%
COVID-19 will cause a state of emergency and the most important thing is to have food at home	3.70%

Source: Authors

The messages issued by the government were correctly perceived by the public. The respondents had to choose from 24 statements regarding risks, treatment or prevention of COVID-19 which they believed to be correct. In the analysis conducted, it was found that most respondents (13.6%) believed that the information 'Washing hands and keeping your distance are effective ways to protect yourself' (Table 17.6) was correct. These results are consistent with the Ministry of Health's message that has been continuously communicated about the pandemic.

Discussion of the results

Even though there are pandemic communication tools and guidelines, the scope and difficulty of the pandemic caused both a change in the use and style of communication tools, as well as issues in practice (Abraham 2011). While the Turkish public made efforts to find information from many channels during the COVID-19 pandemic, they also resorted to forming their information network by generating and sharing content. The speed of dissemination of photos, videos, voice recordings and written messages circulated through these information networks can sometimes be much faster and more effective than other mass media. Also, according to the research results, WhatsApp was the first choice of the public in receiving information during the second wave in Turkey. It is specified that the content spread among individuals and groups functioned as a 'factory' in notifying, educating, persuading and directing the public (Chew and Eysenbach 2010).

According to the results of the research, print media (newspapers and magazines) and radio became the least preferred sources of information. To explain this fact, it is necessary to look at the traditional media landscape in Turkey. Today, the majority of Turkey's mainstream media organs are in the hands of major capital groups or state capital funds. (Şimşek 2009). In Turkey, social

Table 17.6 COVID-19 Information considered to be true

	Responses	
	N	*Percentage*
Washing your hands and keeping distance from others are effective ways to protect yourself	468	13.60%
The measures taken by the government have been declared too late	280	8.10%
I should only go to the doctor in emergency cases for other diseases	274	7.90%
COVID-19 can be transmitted by touching infected surfaces	256	7.40%
Jokes contribute to misinformation	257	7.40%
The state of emergency should be implemented equally for the entire country	248	7.20%
COVID-19 spread can be reduced by closing the borders of affected countries	239	6.90%
You must stay home so that the economy does not suffer a longer interruption	181	5.20%
COVID-19 is like a flu for most of the population	167	4.80%
I must stay home if I have severe symptoms	157	4.50%
I must go to the doctor if I have mild symptoms	124	3.60%
To get tested I must call 184	96	2.80%
The most important thing is to have food and basic necessity products at home	96	2.80%
COVID-19 only affects elderly and sick people with pre-existing conditions	89	2.60%
COVID-19 has been created in the laboratory and disseminated to sink Western economies	89	2.60%
COVID-19 has been created in the laboratory and disseminated to lighten the number of dependents in the pension system	83	2.40%
COVID-19 has been created in the laboratory and spread to sink the Chinese economy	64	1.90%
You can travel within the country without incurring risks	59	1.70%
Only those who have tested positive should be confined at home	59	1.70%
The measures taken are too alarmist	42	1.20%
COVID-19 was caused by immigration	39	1.10%
If you are not old or sick you can lead a normal life	37	1.10%
Staying at home is just a matter of solidarity, but I am not at risk if I go out	34	1.00%
If I don't have symptoms, I can't spread it	13	0.40%

Source: Authors

media platforms expose evidence that the ruling government resorts to various methods to make journalists put the news or issues in their interest on the agenda. While this created a multifaceted communication model where social media users generated content and created interactions, it also had an impact on the concept of news. In this sense, professional journalism also faced a change, and mainstream media institutions also benefited from the possibilities of interactive and multimedia attributes, the possibility of reaching a wider audience and giving a quick response to the agenda. (Newman 2009). This circumstance facilitated the spread and democratisation of news and the public's access to information. During this time access to information accelerated for countries like Turkey, where the Internet is used extensively and where the agenda is changing.

According to the findings, 56% of the Turkish public consider social media a 'free source for getting news'. Even though there is a tendency for news to spread on social media, it was found that one-third of the society has confidence in the news they get from social media if it matches their own thoughts. In this process, people use social media to get and confirm information (Nalçaoğlu 2020). Turkey is the country where politics and news are most frequently addressed in WhatsApp and Facebook groups, with a rate of 29%. In the research, Turkey was revealed as a country where the use of Instagram to access news is increasing year by year and where news is most read on Instagram (33%) compared to other countries (Newman *et al.* 2019). And this coincides with the finding that the Turkish public is more likely to be online during the period of COVID -19.

Major social media platforms and national online news portals are the most visited websites in Turkey (WeAreSocial 2020). Newspaper websites are also actively preferred to reach the news in Turkey. And these data are consistent with the findings on the Turkish public's tendency towards online press in the research on the COVID-19 pandemic.

Another significant finding of this study was the negativity of perceptions regarding messages received from the government. For example, the Turkish public's thoughts regarding the government's communication during the COVID-19 period were 'Has not revealed all the truth', and 'Has confused the public'. The research indicated that the lowest-ranking results regarding government communication were 'Has been the most reliable information' and 'Has always been clear and sufficient'. It can be said that these results are related to the political climate in Turkey and the perceived trust of the public in the ruling party. Another reason that can be given is the inability of the government to effectively use the clarity strategy regarding the number of cases during the communication about the COVID-19 crisis.

Since the first case was detected in Turkey, many cases have been announced to the public every day. But on 30 September 2020, the Minister of Health stated that these case numbers are only people who have symptoms. And this fact created the perception of deliberate manipulation of some cases among the Turkish public. This also attracted the World Health Organization's (WHO) attention, and it demanded the Ministry of Health share correct data. Although government communications were clearer and stronger at the beginning of the pandemic, the conflicting data in the content of the messages, the contradictory statements of several crisis spokespersons, and the increase in unrest during the widening pandemic period also increased political tensions. They caused the public to be suspicious of government communications.

Another finding that attracted attention was the key message of the government's communication that stuck in people's minds, namely, 'COVID-19 is easily spread, so you need to stay at home to protect the elderly and the sick'. One of the first restrictions of the pandemic in Turkey applied to those over 65.

The Ministry of Internal Affairs imposed closures for people over 65 and the chronically ill starting on 22 March 2020. In the months that followed, citizens over 65 could go out only at certain times. Staying away from the elderly, not visiting them, is far from the norm in Turkish society, so this was not an easy measure to implement in Turkey. For this reason, the Turkish government issued a message that the public, in particular, should be careful to protect those who are 65 and older.

Another finding of the research that attracted attention related to the economy and the second key government communication. Of course, the pandemic affected economic life as well as daily life (Adıgüzel 2021). Therefore, the opinion that the economy would recover if the pandemic lasted for only a short time spread beyond government communication as the Turkish public launched a help campaign for the economically weak under the slogan 'We can get along together'.

According to the findings, Turkish society turns more to the information they receive from public health professionals whom they know and respect rather than from government agencies. A contributing factor was the complexity of government-issued news during the restrictions, which decreased trust and increased questions from the Turkish public, worsening uncertainty in the following period.

Since day one, the Turkish government has prioritised the message of mask, distance, and cleanliness in their communications. In repeated these messages through press statements and posters, brochures, public announcements, and so on. In addition, the government imposed fines so the restrictions would be taken seriously. And as a result, the Turkish public most believed this discourse to be 'true'. 'Washing hands and keeping your distance are effective ways to protect yourself' ranked first. While the top issue that the Turkish public considers 'true' is protection from COVID-19, the second issue that the Turkish public considers 'true' is the opinion that the government has taken action and imposed restrictions too late.

Conclusion

The role of government communication policies and practices is critical during pandemic crises. It is necessary to have accurate information to guide the public's action, and governments need to take proactive measures to prevent such public health crises. This research was conducted to determine the Turkish public communication and discover the Turkish public's information-seeking tendencies in response to the COVID-19 pandemic. To date, both the world and Turkey have paid and continue to pay a high price for the COVID-19 pandemic. If countries and their governments had more secure and proactive health, fiduciary and proactive health communication systems against pandemic crises, this pandemic could have been managed much more effectively. When the COVID-19 crisis is over, the world must recall what governments learned about crisis communication from this global pandemic.

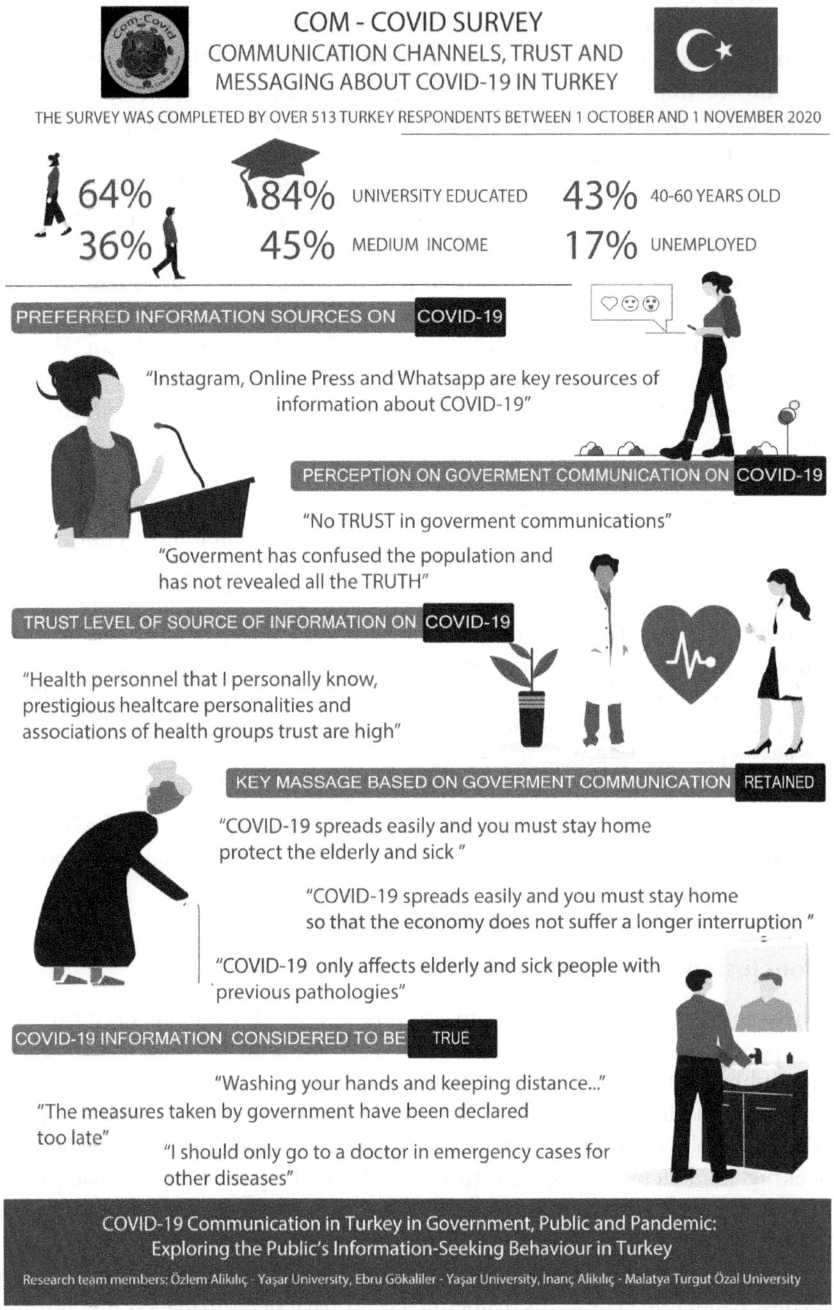

Infographic 17.1 COM-COVID survey: Communication channels, trust and messaging about COVID-19 in Turkey

Countries should use these lessons to prepare for potential health crises effectively. In short, the history of pandemics teaches us that an informed and involved society is critical to maintaining public health. To make this a reality, society needs strategically coordinated health communications and informed and active public policy leadership that uses the right information. The public wants to believe in and be able to follow leadership based on evidence from reliable sources. Robust and effective crisis communications will guide the national response against COVID-19 for both the public and governments and strengthen the health knowledge infrastructure for future potential pandemic crises.

Bibliography

Abraham, T. (2011). Lessons from the pandemic: The need for new tools for risk and outbreak communication. *Emerging Health Threats Journal*, 4(1), p. 7160.

Adıgüzel, M. (2021). Covid – 19 pandemisinin Türkiye ekonomisine etkilerinin makroekonomik analizi. *İstanbul Commerce University Journal of Social Science*, 19 Special(37), pp. 191–221.

Antwi-Boasiako, J., and Nyarkoh, E. (2021). Government communication during the Covid-19 pandemic; the case of Ghana. *International Journal of Public Administration*, 44(11–12), pp. 1039–1040.

Bruns, A. (2018). *Gatewatching and news curation: Journalism, social media, and the public sphere.* New York: Peter Lang.

Cheuk Wai-Yi, B. (1998). An information seeking and using process model in the workplace: A constructivist approach. *Asian Libraries*, 7(12), pp. 375–390.

Chew, C., and Eysenbach, G. (2010). Pandemics in the age of Twitter: Content analysis of tweets during the 2009 H1N1 outbreak. *PLoS ONE*, 5(11), pp. 1–13. doi:10.1371/journal.pone.0014118

Diker, E. (2020). Kovid-19 salgını döneminde sosyal medya kullanımı. *TRT Akademi*. Available from: https://trtakademi.net/koronavirus-kategori/kovid-19-salgini-doneminde-sosyal-medya-kullanimi/ [Accessed 4 May 2021].

Directorate of Communications of the Presidency of Republic of Turkey (2021). *Asrın küresel salgını, Türkiye'nin koronavirüsle başarılı mücadelesi*. İstanbul: Turkey.

Ellis, D., and Wilson, T.D. (2002). Information seeking and mediated searching. Part 5. User-intermediary interaction. *Journal of the American Society for Information Science and Technology*, 53(11), pp. 83–893. doi:10.1002/asi.10133

EuroNews (2020). *Türkiye'de salgın tedbirlerinin gevşetileceği 1 Haziranda neler değişecek?*Available form: https://tr.euronews.com/2020/05/28/erdogan-sehirler-aras-seyahat-k-s-tlamas-1-haziran-dan-itibaren-kald-r-lacak [Accessed 3 May 2021].

Evrensel (2020). *WHO: It was contacted with the Ministry of Health of Turkey, we are waiting for explanation.* Available from: www.evrensel.net/haber/415528/dso-turkiye-saglik-bakanligi-ile-iletisime-gecildi-aciklama-bekliyoruz [Accessed 30 April 2020].

Gamhewage, G.M. (2014). Complex, confused, and challenging: Communicating risk in the modern world. *Journal of Communication in Healthcare*, 7(4), pp. 252–254. doi:10.1179/1753806814Z.00000000094

İnce, M., and Kadıoğlu, C.T. (2020). Effect of consumers increasing stocking request with the Covid19 (Corona) virus on online purchasing behavior. *International Journal of Society Research*, 16(29). doi:10.26466/opus.716041

Kırık, A.M., Altınbaş, V.S.S., Özkoçak, V., and Darıcı, S. (2020). Pandemi dönemlerinde iletişim ve algı yönetimi yeni Koronavirüs hastalığı (COVID-19) örneği. *The Journal of Academic Social Science*, 8(104), pp. 36–57.

Kırık, A.M., and Özkoçak, V. (2020). Social media and new Coronavirus (COVID-19) Pandemia in the context of the new world order. *The Journal of social Science*, 7(April, 45), pp. 133–154.

Kızıl, Ç. (2020). *Türkiye'nin COVID-19 sürecinin karşılaştırmalı satır başları, Türk Tabipleri Birliği, COVID-19 pandemisi altıncı ay değerlendirme raporu.* Available from https://www.ttb.org.tr/kutuphane/covid19-rapor_6/covid19-rapor_6_Part80.pdf

Küçük, A., and Aydoğdu, Y. (2018). Cumhurbaşkanlığı hükümet sisteminde milletvekili seçim sistemi önerileri. *Liberal Düşünce Dergisi*, 23(90), pp. 7–33.

Kumar, A. (2013). Assessing the information need and information seeking behavior of research scholars of MBPG College: A case study. *International Journal of Digital Library Services*, 3(3), pp. 1–12.

Kundu, D.K. (2017). Models of information seeking behaviour: A comparative study. *International Journal of Library and Information Studies*, 7(4), pp. 393–405. Available from: www.ijlis.org [Accessed 27 April 2021].

Li, J., and Zheng, H. (2020). Online information seeking and disease prevention intent during covid-19 outbreak. *Journalism and Mass Communication Quarterly*, pp. 5–10. doi:10.1177/1077699020961518

Lin, L., Savoia, E., Agboola, F., and Viswanath, K. (2014). What have we learned about communication inequalities during the H1N1 pandemic: A systematic review of the literature. *BMC Public Health*, 14(1), pp. 1–13. doi:10.1186/1471-2458-14-484

Majid, S., and Rahmat, N.A. (2013). Information needs and seeking behavior during the H1N1 virus outbreak. *Journal of Information Science Theory and Practice*, 1(1), pp. 42–53. doi:10.1633/jistap.2013.1.1.3

Mediascope (2020). *DSÖ, Türkiye'yi hem övdü hem uyardı, Sağlık Bakanı Koca sadece Türkiye'nin övüldüğü kısmı öne çıkardı.* Available from: https://medyascope.tv/2020/10/03/dso-turkiyeyi-hem-ovdu-hem-uyardi-saglik-bakani-koca-sadece-turkiyenin-ovuldugu-kismi-one-cikardi/ [Accessed 1 May 2021].

Ministry of the Internal Affairs (2020). *Koronavirüs salgını ile mücadele kapsamında toplantılarla ilgili ek genelge.* Available from: www.icisleri.gov.tr/koronavirus-salgini-ile-mucadele-kapsaminda-toplantilarla-ilgili-ek-genelg [Accessed 3 May 2021].

Moreno, Á., Fuentes-Lara, C., and Navarro, C. (2020). COVID-19 communication management in Spain: Exploring the effect of information-seeking behaviour and message reception in public's evaluation. *Profesional de la Informacion*, 29(4), pp. 1–16. doi:10.3145/epi.2020.jul.02

Nalçaoğlu, H. (2020). *Attitudes towards social media.* Available from: https://ingev.org/raporlar/Attitudes_Towards_Social_Media_23042020.pdf [Accessed 20 April 2021].

Narlı, D.B. (2021). *Türkiye'de pandemi: Bir yılda neler yaşandı?* Available from: www.dw.com/tr/türkiyede-pandemi-bir-yılda-neler-yaşandı/a-56822009 [Accessed 2 May 2021].

Newman, N. (2009). *The rise of social media and its impact on mainstream journalism.* Oxford University Research Archive. Available from https://ora.ox.ac.uk/objects/uuid:a980df14-1b49-401b-a136-78d47ab76cdc

Newman, N., Fletcher, R., Kalogeropoulos, A., and Nielsen, R.K. (2019). Reuters institute digital news report 2019. *Reuters Institute for the Study of Journalism.* Available from https://reutersinstitute.politics.ox.ac.uk/sites/default/files/2019-06/DNR_2019_FINAL_1.pdf

Roselina, E., Asmiyanto, T., and Andriany, M. (2021). Health information-seeking behaviour on the COVID-19 pandemic: Social media usage by Gen Z in Jakarta, Indonesia. *Library Philosophy and Practice*, pp. 1–7.

Şimşek, S. (2009). Medya-siyaset-iktidar üçgeninde medya gerçeği. *Selçuk Communication Journal*, 6(1), pp. 124–143.

Slovic, P. (1993). Perceived risk, trust, and democracy. *Risk Analysis*, 13(6), pp. 675–682.

Turan, A., and Çelikyay, H. (2020). Türkiye'de KOVİD – 19 ile mücadele : Politikalar ve aktörler. *Uluslararası Yönetim Akademisi Dergisi*, 3(1), pp. 1–25.

Turkish Statistical Institute (2020). Hanehalkı bilişim teknolojileri (BT) kullanım araştırması, 2020. *Turkish Statistical Institute*. Available from: https://tuikweb.tuik.gov.tr/PreHaberBultenleri.do?id=33679 [Accessed 25 April 2021].

Understanding social trust, no date. Available from: https://understandingsocialtrust.wordpress.com/trust-topics/topic-1/ [Accessed 1 May 2021].

WeAreSocial (2020). *Digital 2020 Turkey*. Available from: www.slideshare.net/DataReportal/digital-2020-turkey-january-2020-v01?from_action=save [Accessed 2 May 2021].

WHO (2020). *Immunizing the public against misinformation*. Available from: www.who.int/news-room/feature-stories/detail/immunizing-the-public-against-misinformation [Accessed 30 April 2020].

WHO (2021). Turkey situation. *WHO*. Available from: https://COVID19.who.int/region/euro/country/tr [Accessed 22 April 2020].

Wilson, T.D. (1997). Information behaviour: An interdisciplinary perspective. *Information Processing and Management*, 33(4), pp. 551–572.

Zhao, X., Fan, J., Basnyat, I., and Baijing, H. (2020). Online health information seeking using '#COVID-19 patient seeking help' on Weibo in Wuhan, China: Descriptive Study. *Journal of Medical Internet Research*, 22(10). doi:10.2196/22910

Zimmerman, M.S., and Jr, G.S. (2020, February). Health information seeking behaviour: A concept analysis Review Article Health information seeking behaviour: A concept analysis. *Health Information and Libraries Journal*, 37(3), pp. 173–191. doi:10.1111/hir.12287

Africa

18 An African perspective of COVID-19 communication

Citizens' perspectives and sense-making of the pandemic in Nigeria

Chinedu Jude Nwasum, Ezinne Chioma Abaneme and Aloysius Chukwuebuka Ifeanyichukwu

Introduction

Communication management has been identified as one of the most important weapons to tackle a pandemic. Lee and Basnyat (2013) argued that effective government communication management during a pandemic is essential in curtailing the spread of such disease to communities and individuals. With adequate and correct information available to the public, the rapid spread of the virus, which has been linked to unclear and sometimes conflicting information about its spread and what individuals need to know and do about it, will reduce drastically (Ratzan *et al.* 2020). This is because effective communication from governments will assist the public to adopt crucial actions and safety measures to restrain the spread of the epidemic, reduce exposure and contain fatality associated with the outbreak (Lee and Basnyat 2013). This is what communication does.

According to Barry (2009), 'In the next influenza pandemic, be it now or in the future, be the virus mild or virulent, the single most important weapon against the disease will be a vaccine. The second most important will be communication' (p. 1039). This implies that the way the government manages communication around the epidemic is crucial in spreading or reducing the tension caused by the pandemic.

The outbreak of COVID-19 in 2020 and subsequent declaration of the virus as a global pandemic by the World Health Organization (Cucinotta and Vanelli 2020) took the entire world by surprise and threw almost all countries into chaos. Since the first case was reported in Wuhan, China, the virus has spread rapidly, with lethal force, to over 224 countries, causing total lockdown at times and strangulating the world economy (BBC 2021). As the disease spread across the globe and now in its second wave, as of this writing there were more than 174 million confirmed cases and 3,762,570 deaths globally (WHO 2020).

In Nigeria, the confirmed cases risen to 256, 958 and 3144 deaths since the index case was recorded in the country (NCDC 2021). In reaction to the first case, and other confirmed cases internationally, on 29 March 2020, the president of Nigeria, Muhammadu Buhari, announced a national lockdown,

DOI: 10.4324/9781003184669-28

closing economic activities and movement across the nation to flatten the curve and contain the pandemic. The unexpected surge and rapid spread of the coronavirus virus across Nigeria after its first case prompted government officials to provide citizens with relevant and necessary information about the virus, such as: how it is being transmitted, preventive measures and necessary measures to undertake when one exhibits some of the major or minor symptoms associated with the virus.

The high fatality incidents have been attributed to the failure of governments around the globe to effectively and efficiently rouse citizens to action through adequate communication. Hoffman and Silverberg (2021) observed that despite many warnings from the scientific community and the lessons that previous health emergencies, including Ebola, the 2002 SARS-CoV, Zika virus outbreaks, 2009 H1N1 influenza and MERS-CoV, governments around the globe have demonstrated low capacities to respond effectively and efficiently to infectious disease outbreaks.

Communication scholars have conducted studies in the field of communication management during health crises and pandemics recently and in the past. Available empirical studies in this area have focused on audience perception of government communication management and information sources during a pandemic (Moreno *et al.* 2020; Reifegerste *et al.* 2017; Zhang and Zhou 2019), public motivations for seeking information during health crisis (Austin *et al.* 2012; Lu and Jin 2020) and the role of trust in government communication during health crises (Siegrist and Zingg 2013). For instance, in Spain, in a study exploring the effect of information-seeking behaviour and message reception in public evaluation, Moreno *et al.* (2020) revealed synchronous adoption of multiple media and platforms for information seeking on COVID-19 by Spanish citizens, that people who relied on traditional news media were most likely to have positive opinions on the government's communication strategy, and that trust in public officials decreased as the health crisis evolved. In terms of seeking information on behalf of others, a study of surrogate health information seeking behaviour in Europe showed that in the past years, 61.0% of the online health information seekers and 61.1% of the offline health information seekers had searched on behalf of someone else (Reifegerste *et al.* 2017). In the U.S., a study by Zhang and Zhou 2019 examined how fear appeal and individuals' image promotion consideration drive users' intention to share fear appeal messages on social networking sites. It revealed that fear heightened the intention of people to seek information on health issues on social media during health crisis.

Further empirical studies have examined trust in government communication during a pandemic (Podlesek *et al.* 2011; Prati *et al.* 2011b; Siegrist and Zingg 2013). Trust in health and government agencies has a positive influence on people's compliance with recommended behaviour (Siegrist and Zingg 2013). For example, a study by Moreno *et al.* (2020) on the effect of information-seeking behaviour and message reception in the public's evaluation in Spain revealed reduction in public trust of government authorities and officials as the health crisis evolved, and this affected public consumption of and reaction to information on COVID-19 emanating from the government.

While literature on crisis communication and government communication during the COVID-19 pandemic is still growing (Austin and Jin 2016) in developed and a few developing countries, less is known about audience perception of government communication during a pandemic in Nigeria. A lot of questions need to be answered about how people receive, internalise, retain and assess information during a pandemic (Austin and Jin 2016; Kim and Liu 2012).

Therefore, the aim of the study is to ascertain public perception of Nigerian government communication management of COVID-19 in autumn 2020. Specifically, the study interrogated the main messages by the government over the period, the opinion of the people on the government messages, the media used by the public during the period and the level of trust in information sources.

Experiencing COVID-19

Interrogating crisis and risk communication during the pandemic

Coombs and Holladay (2010) conceptualised crisis communication as the collection, processing and dissemination of information required to address a crisis. By its nature it comprises not just legitimating strategies but also indicates how government institutions themselves make sense of crises by mobilising pre-existing social representations; they make their present actions coherent for the general public (Brandt and Wörlein 2020). On the other hand, risk communication is seen as raising awareness of the nature, magnitude and significance of risks in the hope of reducing the likelihood of a crisis in the long run (Hampel 2006; Moreno *et al.* 2020; Sheppard and Liu 2012).

Therefore, the main aims are to control harm, give specific and correct information to stakeholders, initiate and improve recovery, build and manage image and perceptions of blame and responsibility, restore trust, garner support and help, clarify and justify action, apologise, and ensure healing and change (Seeger *et al.* 1998). These forms of communication strive to contain harm for the involved people through different but credible communication channels (Reynolds and Seeger 2005).

Previous studies have recognised that communication and public relations play an essential role in managing a health crisis (Lee and Basnyat 2013; Coombs and Holladay 2008; Barry 2009). This is because a gap in communication between authorities and publics has been identified as one of the biggest barriers for successful risk and crisis communication (Barry 2009). Hence, risk and crisis communication play a central role in developing responses to mitigate infectious diseases (Burton-Jeangros 2019). Vaughan and Tinker (2009) affirmed that the consequences of pandemic influenza for vulnerable populations will depend partly on the effectiveness of health risk communication.

In situations of pandemic, such as the COVID-19 pandemic, correct utilisation of effective and efficient communication strategies helps the people to maximise opportunities for prevention, containment, resilience and recovery (Holmes 2008). Equally, Holmes (2008), Blumenshine *et al.* (2008), Cutter (2003) agree that with an expanded role in pandemic planning and response, communication processes can prepare the public to adapt to changing circumstances or uncertainty during an emerging pandemic, educate public health planners about existing vulnerabilities and resources that affect influenza risk for specific populations, facilitate anticipation of surprising events, create dialogue between potentially affected populations and risk managers and foster an environment of mutual trust.

Information seeking, media and sources

During the outbreak of infectious diseases, such as COVID-19, the media play a crucial role in raising public awareness of risks that are mostly unknown by the population (Roslyng and Eskjær 2017). The enormous influence of the media in the society makes a powerful agent of public information and awareness during a pandemic. Studies on public motivations for seeking information during a health crisis (Austin *et al.* 2012; Lu and Jin 2020) showed the need for extra information, the need for timely and reliable information, knowledge about the enormity of the crisis, looking out for family/friends, mobilising and connecting with a community and promoting emotional support (Fraustino *et al.* 2017) as triggers.

Once a pandemic outbreak is announced to the public, they begin to seek and process information from diverse sources, such as newspapers, magazines, television, radio and different social media platforms (Masipet *et al.* 2020). This has caused a global spike in consumption of information from social networks. For example, consumption of information from social networks grew by 55% in Spain, 30% in Italy, 11% in Germany, 18% in the United Kingdom, and 14% in France (Edelman 2020). In the context of seeking information on COVID-19, 70% of the population followed COVID-19 news at least once a day or many times a day, with 52% of 25,000 consumers in more than 30 countries claiming to believe in traditional media (broadcast and newspaper) as a trustworthy source rather than social media (Edelman 2020; WHO 2020).

Recent studies have found that the medium has a greater effect on stakeholders than the content of the message (Schultz *et al.* 2011). For example, in relation to COVID-19, a study by Williams *et al.* (2020) in Spain showed that government communication on COVID-19 influenced the public's adoption and acceptance of the pandemic messages disseminated through different media channels.

Researchers have identified the importance of social media during a pandemic. This is because social media provides unfiltered, current lines of communication and information (Johnson and Kaye 2010) and emotional support during crises (Choi and Lin 2009). Thus, adequately using social media in crisis responses has tangible benefits for organizations (Liu and Kim 2011) and government. For instance, blog readers are likely to perceive a lower level of crisis for an organization than those not exposed to blogs (Sweester and Metzgar 2007). This lays credence to the increase in social media use during crisis events (Fraustino *et al.* 2017). According to J. P Morgan (2020), during the ban on social gatherings, the use of Messenger, WhatsApp, and voice and video calling increased exponentially.

Despite the overwhelming potential of social media for use in crisis response, traditional media in crisis situations has not been entirely displaced . Studies have shown that citizens still perceive traditional media as more credible than social media, hence they use traditional media for information seeking during pandemic or health crises (Austin *et al.* 2012). For example, recent research conducted by Edelman (2020) on COVID-19 in 12 countries during March 2020 revealed that traditional mass media played a vital role during the pandemic. Also, in Spain, Masipet *et al.* (2020) revealed that online newspapers and television were the main sources of information for Spanish people during the crisis.

This shows that the choice of medium is vital in helping the individual make sense of a pandemic (Utz *et al.* 2013). Therefore, additional research is needed to evaluate the effectiveness of information and crisis communication across different platforms (Moreno *et al.* 2020). Also, communication experts need to figure out how pandemic information forms and sources affect the public's acceptance of crisis response strategies (Moreno *et al.* 2020). This study tries to understand this from the Nigerian perspective.

Government communication and COVID-19 strategy

During health crises such as the COVID-19 pandemic, the roles of governments, public agencies and health experts in providing vital information and key messages is crucial to how the people receive, internalise and respond to such emergency (Moreno *et al.* 2020). Yet public governance systems have been observed to be flawed, incompetent and chaotic during health crises (Gu and Li 2020). Studies on communication management during previous health crises such as Ebola, 2009 Influenza A (H1N1), SARS, and others have identified numerous loopholes in coordination of communication across institutions. For instance, a survey conducted by the Swiss national public health agency revealed that a majority of the participants (medical doctors) identified poor communication as the biggest threat they faced, due to the fact that information was limited and inconsistent (WHO 2011). Other studies reported untimely information, absence of transparency, lack of coordinated and coherent strategy and one-way information dissemination strategy as constraints to effective communication during previous global health crises (Quinn *et al.* 2013; Holmes 2008).

Government communication during a pandemic is critical not just to increase awareness and provide direction, it is equally necessary to dispel fake news, rumours and other irrelevant communications. This is because government institutions make sense of crises by mobilising social representations and make their present actions coherent and familiar to the general public (Brandt and Wörlein 2020). An effective government crisis/health communication system is even more crucial for countries like Nigeria with a vulnerable population. Vaughan and Tinker (2009) affirmed that the consequences of pandemic influenza for vulnerable populations will depend partly on the effectiveness of health risk communication.

In Nigeria, the government at various levels and National Centre for Disease Control have been consistent in reaching out to the public regarding the best health practices during the current COVID-19 pandemic through various media platforms including the mainstream media, social media, indigenous language media and mobile phones. There were daily briefings and updates by the members of the Presidential Task Force Against COVID-19. However, a major setback in the Nigerian government communication strategy was the inability of President Muhammadu Buhari to address Nigerians adequately, as other nations' leaders addressed their citizens. According to Fasan (2020), the president was 'AWOL' – 'absent without leave' – when Nigerians needed him most. She said that, at a time when Nigeria is at war against the rapidly escalating Coronavirus pandemic and an increasingly distressed, deteriorating and declining economy, the Commander-in-Chief of the Armed Forces, President Buhari, has not inspired confidence.

However, many commentators view the excuses tendered by President Buhari's media handlers in defence of his continued failure to address the nation as a far cry from sound public relations strategy and positive optics. At all times in democratic governance, the interests of the people are paramount and must be adequately represented. At the start of the pandemic in Nigeria, when the electorate became vocal against the president's continued silence, Adesina *et al.* (2020) said that not addressing Nigerians is a matter of the president's style of communication and never a show of insensitivity. The conclusion that can easily be drawn from this statement is that the president does not consider himself to be an employee of the electorate who must be held accountable; rather, he seems to think voters work for him.

Trust has been identified as an important factor in crisis communication and government communication during a pandemic as it plays a key role in public compliance (Siegrist and Zingg 2013). Studies suggest that trust in health and government agencies has a positive influence on people's compliance with recommended behaviour (Siegrist and Zingg 2013). Researchers have, however, suggested that risk management and health experts' communications to the public during previous pandemics may have reduced public trust (Feufel *et al.* 2010). Many studies have examined the place of trust on risk perception and behaviour during a pandemic, as well as its implications to crisis communication (Siegrist and Zingg 2013; Earle 2010; Earle *et al.* 2007). But these studies are theoretical and the lack of a common construct for trust and its antecedents has hindered progress in the field (Siegrist and Zingg 2013).

Some studies have examined the issue of information channels during a pandemic (Moreno *et al.* 2020; Reifegerste *et al.* 2017; Zhang and Zhou 2019); however, limited studies have evaluated how information channels and sources influence the citizens' assessment of government communication, trust and response during a pandemic. Also, there is no known published quantitative research on public perceptions of Nigerian government communication management on COVID-19 because coronavirus is novel – a gap that the present study addresses.

It is against this backdrop that this study explores the Nigerian public's perception of government communication and management of COVID-19.

This chapter focuses on three research questions: 1) What medium or source did Nigerians prefer for government communication on COVID-19 during the later stage of the COVID-19 outbreak?; 2) What were the main messages by the government and what is the public opinion on government communication?; 3) What sources of information do Nigerians trust most when seeking information on COVID-19?

Insights from this research will enable development of recommendations that will improve the effectiveness of government communication and enhance public trust on government messages in future crises.

The state of play

Questionnaire

This study quantitatively evaluated the public perception of government communication during the COVID-19 pandemic in autumn 2020 in Nigeria. An online questionnaire was designed using Qualtrics and was active between 1 September and 31October 2020. Convenience and snowball sampling techniques were used to deliver invitations explaining the reason for the questionnaire, and links generated from Qualtrics were shared through WhatsApp, Facebook, Instagram and Linkedln. Invited participants were encouraged to share the questionnaire to their contacts. The invitation to participate in the online survey was disseminated among the respondents, who willingly participated without any form of compensation. The online questionnaire contained questions on the channels of preference for seeking information, trust and confidence in different sources and channels, and the main messages by the government and the opinion of Nigerians on the government messages.

To answer research question 1 (RQ1), participants were asked to identify the channels they used for information during the crisis situation (e.g., 'Through what media do you keep yourself updated about COVID-19?'). Fourteen channels were listed: WhatsApp, Facebook, Twitter, Instagram, YouTube, television, radio, print press, online press, journal, website/blog from public institutions, website/blog from private institutions, blog from an alternative health organization, website/blog from scientists.

To ascertain the three main messages of the government and the opinion of Nigerians on government messages (RQ2), participants were asked to indicate the top three messages from the government about COVID-19 based on the list of messages provided:

1 You must stay indoors to stay safe from COVID-19
2 You must wear a face mask or nose mask to avoid getting the virus

3 COVID-19 is dangerous and borders should be closed to countries with a high number of cases
4 COVID-19 spreads easily and you must wash your hands regularly and apply hand sanitisers
5 COVID-19 is dangerous and you must go for a test if you have symptoms
6 You must maintain social/physical distance when outside.

In addition, the participants were asked to indicate their opinion about the government communication by rating the following statements on the seven-point Likert scale with 1 = 'totally disagree' and 7 = 'totally agree'. The statements include: The government communication:

1 Has been clear and adequate;
2 Has not revealed the whole truth;
3 Has been scheduled at the appropriate times;
4 Has been confused;
5 Has been the most reliable information;
6 Has created social alarm.

To answer RQ3, participants were asked to choose one of the sources of information they most trust. and 14 sources were listed for them to rate (1 = no trust and 7 = total trust). The list of sources was:

1 Government (federal government);
2 Regional authorities (state government);
3 Local authorities (local government, traditional institutions, etc.);
4 Media;
5 Friends on social networks;
6 Unknown health personnel who have spread on social networks;
7 Health personnel that I personally know;
8 Health influencers;
9 Influencers on alternative therapies;
10 Influencers of other topics (not health) on social networks;
11 World Health Organization;
12 Associations of health groups;
13 Prestigious healthcare personalities;
14 Others.

Sample

According to the reference website Worldometer, the Nigerian adult population (15 years age bracket and above) is 55.2 million. Using the margin of error and confidence level formula, the representative sample would be a total of 384 participants. In all, a total of 520 participants started the survey. To ensure data quality, Morrow and Skolits' (2014), protocols for cleaning data were observed for the study data. For instance, we removed participants with incomplete answers. In all, the final sample for analysis was based on 458 completed questionnaires by the target population. The questionnaire was divided into two sections: the main questions and demographic data. In terms of gender, 53% are male, 46% female, and 1% are transgender.

Data gathered were analysed using Statistical Package for the Social Sciences (SPSS) 22 after being operationalised and presented using frequencies and percentages. Results from these statistical tests are included in notes in the tables.

Findings

Media use and sources of information during the COVID-19 outbreak

Studies on crisis communication and health communication show there are surges in information seeking and media consumption during crises such as health emergencies. Research question 1 (RQ1) explored the choice of media and channels of information on COVID-19 during autumn in Nigeria. As shown in Table 18.1, WhatsApp (16%), Facebook (13%), online press (11%), Television (10%) Twitter (8%), and Radio (8%) were the most used information channels for information, with WhatsApp emerging as the most used platform for information seeking on COVID-19 in Nigeria, while Instagram (6%), print press (6%), websites/blogs from public institutions (5%), blogs from alternative health organizations (5%), websites/blogs from scientists (4%), online video channels (4%), Journal (4%), YouTube (3%), websites/blogs from private institutions (3%), and others were least used.

Table 18.1 Preferred media and channels for information

S/N	*Information source*	*Percentage*
1	WhatsApp	16%
2	Facebook	13%
3	Twitter	8%
4	Instagram	6%
5	YouTube	3%
6	Television	10%
7	Radio	8%
8	Print press	6%
9	Online press	11%
10	Journal	4%
11	Website/blog from public institutions	5%
12	Website/blog from private institutions	3%
13	Blog from alternative health organizations	5%
14	Website/blog from scientists	4%
	Total	100%

Source: Authors

Note: The percentages indicate the answers to Q1 (Through what media have you read or heard information about COVID-19?).

Government key messages and public perception of government communication

The results of the three key messages from the government showed that messages like 'You must maintain social/physical distance when outside' (23.68%), 'You must stay indoors to stay safe from COVID-19' (19.37%) and 'You must wear a face mask or nose mask to avoid getting the virus' (19.18%) were the dominant messages passed by the government.

The results of the public perception of government communication showed that the majority felt the government communication has not revealed all the truth (46%), has confused the population (46%), has not been the most reliable (43%) and has generated social alarm (41%).

Table 18.2 Government messages on COVID-19

S/N	*Message*	*Percentage*
1	You must stay indoors to stay safe from COVID-19	19.37%
2	You must wear a face mask or nose mask to avoid getting the virus	19.18%
3	COVID-19 is dangerous and borders should be closed to countries with a high number of cases	7.63%
4	COVID-19 spreads easily and you must wash your hands regularly and apply hand sanitisers	16.83%
5	COVID-19 is dangerous and you must go for a test if you have symptoms	13.31%
6	You must maintain social/physical distance when outside	23.68%
	Total	100%

Source: Authors

Note: The percentages indicate the answers to Q3 (In your opinion, what are three main messages that the government has given on COVID-19?).

Table 18.3 Public perception of government communication messages on COVID-19

Government communication on COVID-19	*1*	*2*	*3*	*4*	*5*	*6*	*7*
Has always been clear and sufficient	34.67%	10.00%	11.33%	9.33%	8.67%	5.33%	20.67%
Has not revealed all the truth	18.54%	9.27%	6.62%	5.30%	5.30%	8.61%	46.36%
Has been scheduled at the appropriate times	33.10%	11.72%	12.41%	14.48%	8.97%	2.76%	16.55%
Has confused the population	20.13%	12.08%	4.70%	9.40%	5.37%	2.01%	46.31%
Has been the most reliable	43.24%	10.14%	6.08%	13.51%	7.43%	4.73%	14.86%
Has generated social alarm	20.26%	7.84%	7.19%	8.50%	9.15%	5.88%	41.18%

Source: Authors

Note: The percentages indicated the answers to Q2 (To what extent do you agree with the following statements regarding the government communication [including the Presidential Task Force] on COVID-19?). Answers ranged from 1 = totally disagree, 2 = disagree, 3 = slightly disagree, 4 = don't know, 5 = slightly agree, 6 = agree, 7= totally agree.

Level of trust in information sources on COVID-19 messages

The results for the level of trust in information sources on COVID-19 messages revealed that most participants trust World Health Organization (59%) as a credible source of information on COVID-19, followed by associations of health groups (58%) and prestigious healthcare personalities, respectively, as shown in Table 18.4. The results also showed overwhelming distrust in the government at all levels and public officials as sources of information on COVID-19.

Observations and interrogation

Government communication management during a pandemic is crucial in arresting the spread of infections to individuals and communities (Lee and Basnyat 2013). This is because the availability of correct and factual information to the public affects the decisions, actions and inactions of the people during an outbreak of disease or pandemic like COVID-19.

The results of this exploratory study reveal that citizens depend on different information channels during an outbreak of disease or pandemic to source information and seek correct messages on the right actions to be taken, which is in line with the channel complementarity theory (Moreno *et al.* 2020).

Table 18.4 Level of trust in information sources on COVID-19 by Nigerians

S/N		*No trust (%) 1*	*Trust (%) 7*
1	Government (federal government)	52.11%	14.08%
2	Regional authorities (state government)	50.74%	10.29%
3	Local authorities (local government, traditional institutions, etc.)	47.45%	13.87%
4	Media	21.58%	23.74%
5	Friends on social networks	43.70%	8.15%
6	Unknown health personnel who have spread on social networks	54.01%	8.76%
7	Health personnel that I personally know	6.43%	8.76%
8	Health influencers	13.77%	38.41%
9	Influencers on alternative therapies	26.72%	30.53%
10	Influencers of other topics (not health) on social networks	36.03%	25.74%
11	World Health Organization	7.14%	59.29%
12	Associations of health groups	5.63%	58.45%
13	Prestigious healthcare personalities	7.35%	58.09%
14	Others	37.90%	25.00%

Source: Authors

Note: The percentages indicate the answers to Q4 (Which sources of information do you have the most trust in?). Answers ranged from 1 = No trust to 7 = Total trust.

First, the finding from RQ1 reveals the high use of social media platforms, with WhatsApp reported as the social media platform Nigerians used most for information seeking on COVID-19 during autumn 2020, followed by Facebook and Twitter. This corresponds with the outcome of a study in Spain by Moreno *et al.* (2020). The reliance on social media platforms for information seeking is connected to the fact that social media can provide an unfiltered, current line of communication and information (Johnson and Kaye 2010) and emotional support during crises (Choi and Lin 2009; Macias *et al.* 2009). Adopting social media for crisis responses has tangible benefits for organizations (Liu and Kim 2011), citizens and government. Furthermore, there is also a substantial use of television and radio by Nigerians in sourcing information on COVID-19 during the later stage of the outbreak in Nigeria. Television's wide reach and rapid dissemination of news has meant it remains relevant as a critical medium for instructional messages during crises (Frisby *et al.* 2014). This points to the fact that despite the advantages of social media platforms, traditional media platforms are still potent and relevant in communicating health crisis to the people, so instead of doing away with them, communication professionals need to strategically integrate these media platforms into their crisis communication plans. These results are consistent with previous research (Austin *et al.* 2012; Casero-Ripollés 2020; Masipet *et al.* 2020; Rodero 2020).

This outcome suggests that in planning the release of information during a pandemic, communication experts or government authorities in Nigeria must be strategic and develop messages suitable for different media platforms because to be effective in managing communication, fast and clear dissemination of information via different media platforms is vital (Park *et al.* 2019). Therefore, authorities must not disregard any channel or platform, especially during the later stages of the outbreak of a pandemic.

Although the people agreed that the Nigerian government developed and sent out information to the public, most of the participants felt that the government communication on COVID-19 did not reveal the whole truth about the virus, confused the population, was not reliable and generated social alarm. This could be a result of distrust in the government, as citizens now perceive government-sourced communication with a degree of scepticism (Ogbodo *et al.* 2020). This also can be a result of the misconception at the initial stage that the virus cannot survive in Nigeria. The consequence of a lack of trust in government during health crises is that a majority of citizens are likely to jettison compliance with preventive measures. According to Reynolds and Quinn (2008), open and transparent styles of communication during health crises remain the most effective in galvanising the population to take positive actions.

Findings also show lack of trust in government authorities as the crisis evolved, with Nigerians having more trust in information from health practitioners and the World Health Organization. The great decline in trust could be a result of decades of the political class ignoring the needs of Nigeria's citizens (Donnelly and Hassan 2020). This poses a great danger to the country, as earning trust is essential not only in the fight against COVID-19 but also for future health crises and the longer-term progress of Nigeria. Since trust cannot be suddenly built during a crisis, it becomes crucial that governments of different nations, especially the Nigerian government, employ the services of known health practitioners and communication experts to manage information dissemination and communication as citizens have trust in them. This finding is in conformity with previous research (Omaka-Amari *et al.* 2020).

In all, communication has been described as the most important weapon against a pandemic (Barry 2009) and also the biggest challenge identified by health authorities in the fight against a pandemic (WHO 2020). Studies have shown the effectiveness of communication in assisting the government to supply needed knowledge for informed decision making about risks, trust building and rebuilding, and engagement of stakeholders in dialogue (Covello *et al.* 2001). However, governments can be successful only if they invest in reflective relations and comprehensive management of communication systems before an outbreak of a crisis (Tench *et al.* 2017).

Limitations

Although this study has explored the government communication management of COVID-19 in Nigeria specifically looking at the channels of information, government main messages and opinion of the people on the government communication and the level of trust in information sources, there are limitations to the study. First, the study did not explore the causal relationships between the variables. So, future research should investigate the causal relationship between the variables used in the present study.

Second, this study is in the Nigerian context. We cannot draw conclusions on government communication of COVID-19 in other countries as there may be differences in their approaches. Also, the opinion of government officials needs to be sought to understand how the government's communication was planned and implemented. Despite these limitations, the results of the study are noteworthy.

Conclusion

This chapter adds an important contribution and new knowledge in the field of public relations and crisis communication specifically on the effectiveness of health information gleaned via various media. The findings of the study make an important contribution to the literature in the sense that it examines the effectiveness of government communication management on COVID-19 in the later stage of the pandemic in Nigeria. It was obvious that the social media platforms emerged as the dominant medium for information seeking by the public, yet the mainstream media still played a vital role in informing the public during the later stage of the outbreak. So, in the future, public officials should integrate social media and mainstream media in reaching the public. Results also corroborated previous studies' findings that trust in government has declined: the public believed that the government communication did not

AN AFRICAN PERSPECTIVE ONCOVID-19 COMMUNICATION: CITIZENS' PERSPECTIVES AND SENSE MAKING OF THE PANDEMIC IN NIGERIA

A total of

458

people participated in the survey

The survey lasted for

Two Months

(1 September - 31 October, 2020

PREFERRED CHANNELS OF INFORMATION

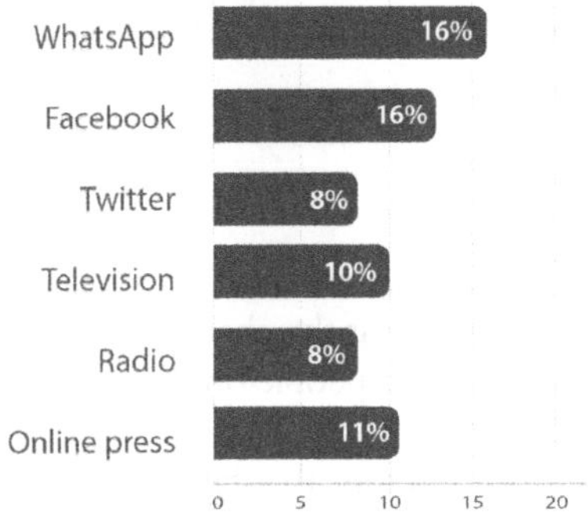

THREE KEY MESSAGES OF NIGERIAN GOVERNMENT ON COVID-19

19.37%
You must stay indoors to stay safe from COVID 19

19.18%
You must wear a face mask to avoid getting the virus

23.68%
You must maintain social/ physical distance when outside

PUBLIC PERCEPTION OF GOVERNMENT COMMUNICATION MESSAGES ON COVID-19

Questions	has always been clear and sufficient	has not revealed all the truth	has been scheduled at the appropriate times	has confused the population	has been the most reliable	has generated social alarm
Totally disagree	34.67%	18.54%	33.10%	20.13%	43.24%	20.26%
Disagree	10.00%	9.27%	11.72%	12.08%	10.14%	7.84%
Slightly disagree	11.33%	6.62%	12.41%	4.70%	6.08%	7.19%
Don't know	9.33%	5.30%	14.48%	9.40%	13.51%	8.50%
Slightly Agree	8.67%	5.30%	8.97%	5.37%	7.43%	9.15%
Agree	5.33%	8.61%	2.76%	2.01%	4.73%	5.88%
Totally agree	20.67%	46.36%	16.55%	46.31%	14.86%	41.18%

LEVEL OF TRUST IN INFORMATION SOURCES ON COVID-19 BY NIGERIANS

S/N		No trust (%)	Trust (%)
1	Government (FG)	52.11%	14.08%
2	Regional authorities (State government)	50.74%	10.29%
3	Local authorities (L.G, traditional institutions, etc.)	47.45%	13.87%
4	Media	21.58%	23.74%
5	Unknown health personnel who have spread on social networks	54.01%	8.76%
6	Health influencers	13.77%	38.41%
7	World Health Organization	7.14%	59.29%
8	Associations of health groups	5.63%	58.45%
9	Prestigious healthcare personalities	7.35%	58.09%

Research team
Chinedu Jude Nwasum, Ezinne Chioma Abaneme, Aloysius Chukwuebuka Ifeanyichukwu

Infographic 18.1 An African perspective on COVID-19 communication: Citizens' perspectives and sense-making of the pandemic in Nigeria reveal the truth, confused a lot of people and generated social alarm. This ineffectiveness can be corrected only if public officials improve their messaging by allowing communication experts to manage the information dissemination during a health crisis to restore public trust in government and ensure that its information strategy remains open and transparent.

Although the sample was limited solely to the Nigerian perspective, other countries may have different experiences with regard to their government communication management during the early stage of the COVID-19 outbreak. Through our study, we have raised more questions than we have answered, and we hope that future research will provide answers to the questions raised in this chapter. Specifically, the role of trust in public adoption of government communication during an outbreak needs to be researched.

Finally, it remains to be seen if the Nigerian government officials can engage communication experts and be consistent in their information to improve the effectiveness of its communication to Nigerians during an outbreak of a pandemic.

Bibliography

Adesina, E., Adeloye, D., Falola, H., Adeyeye, B., Yartey, D., and Kayode-Adedeji, T. (2020). Health communication and behavioural practice towards ending Hepatitis B Virus in Southwest Nigeria. *The Scientific World Journal,* 2020: 4969687. doi: 10.1155/2020/4969687. PMID: 33424487; PMCID: PMC7773454.

Austin, L., and Jin, Y. (2016). Social media and crisis communication: Explicating the social-mediated crisis communication model. In A. Dudo, and L. Kahlor, eds., *Strategic communication: New agendas in communication.*New York: Routledge, Routledge, pp. 175–198.

Austin, L., Liu, B., and Jin, Y. (2012). How audiences seek out crisis information: Exploring the social-mediated crisis communication model. *Journal of Applied Communication Research*, 40(2) 188–207.

Barry, J.M. (2009). Pandemics: Avoiding the mistakes of 1918. *Nature*, 459, pp. 324–325.

BBC (2021). Coronavirus: How the pandemic has changed the world economy by Lora Jones, Daniele Palumbo & David Brown. *BBC News*. Available from https://www.bbc.co.uk/news/business-51706225 [Accessed 24 January 2021].

Beck, U. (1992). *Risk society. Towards a new modernity*. London: Sage Publications.

Blumenshine, P., Reingold, A., Egerter, S., Mockenhaupt, R., Braveman, P., and Marks, J. (2008). Pandemic influenza planning in the United States from a health disparities perspective. *Emerging Infectious Diseases*, 14(5) 709–15.

Brandt, P., and Wörlein, J. (2020). Government crisis communication during the Coronavirus crisis: Comparing France, Germany, and the United Kingdom. *Science Po* (online). Available from: www.sciencespo.fr/cso/fr/content/government-crisis-communication-during-coronavirus-crisis-comparing-france-germany-and-unite.html [Accessed 10 October 2020].

Burke, T.J., Ruppel, E.K., and Dinsmore, D.R. (2016). Moving away and reaching out: Young adults' relational maintenance and psychosocial well-being during the transition to college. *Journal of Family Communication*, 16, pp. 180–187.

Burton-Jeangros, C. (2019). Epidemics and risk communication: Why are lessons not learned? In *Managing the global health response to epidemics*. New York, NY: Routledge.

Casero-Ripollés, A. (2020). Impact of Covid-19 on the media system. Communicative and democratic consequences of news consumption during the outbreak. *El profesional de la información*, 29(2), e290223. doi:10.3145/epi.2020.mar.23

Choi, Y., and Lin, Y.-H. (2009). Consumer responses to Mattel product recalls posted on online bulletin boards: Exploring two types of emotion. *Journal of Public Relations Research*, 21(2), pp. 198–207.

Coombs, W.T., and Holladay, S.J. (2008). Comparing apology to equivalent crisis response strategies: Clarifying apology's role and value in crisis communication. *Public Relations Review*, 34(3), pp. 252–257.

Costa-Sánchez, C., and López-García, X. (2020). Comunicación y crisis del coronavirus en España. Primeras lecciones. *El profesional de la información*, 29(3) 290–304.

Condon, B.J., and Sinha, T. (2010). Who is that masked person: The use of face masks on Mexico city public transportation during the Influenza A (H1N1) outbreak. *Health Policy*, 95, pp. 50–56.

Coombs, T.W., and Holladay, S.J. (2010). *The handbook of crisis communication*. Hoboken, Blackwell Publishing.

Creswell, J.W. (2009). *Research design: Qualitative, quantitative, and mixed methods approaches*, 2nd ed. Thousand Oaks, CA: Sage.

Creswell, J.W., and Clark, V.L.P. (2007). *Designing and conducting mixed method research*. Thousand Oaks, CA: Sage.

Covello, V., Peters, R., Wojtecki, J., and Hyde, R. (2001). Risk communication, the West Nile virus epidemic, and bioterrorism: Responding to the communication challenges posed by the intentional or unintentional release of a pathogen in an urban setting. *Journal of Urban Health*, 78(2) 382–391.

Cutter, S.L. (2003). The vulnerability of science and the science of vulnerability. *Annals of the Association of American Geographers*, 93, pp. 1–12.

Cucinotta, D., and Vanelli, M. (2020). WHO declares COVID-19 a pandemic. *Acta Biomedica*, 91(1) 157–160.

Donnelly, E., and Hassan, I. (2020). Nigeria's political leaders need to win trust to tackle COVID-19. *Chatham House*. https://www.chathamhouse.org/2020/04/nigerias-political-leaders-need-win-trust-tackle-covid-19

Dutta-Bergman, Mohan J. (2004). Interpersonal communication after 9/11 via telephone and Internet: A theory of channel complementarity. *New Media & Society*, 6(5) 659–673.

Dutta-Bergman, Mohan J. (2006). Community participation and internet use after September 11: Complementarity in channel consumption. *Journal of Computer-Mediated Communication*, 11(2) 469–484.

Earle, T.C. (2010). Trust in risk management: A model-based review of empirical research. *Risk Analysis*, 30, pp. 541–574.

Earle, T.C., Siegrist, M., and Gutscher, H. (2007). Trust, *risk perception and the TCC model of cooperation*. In M. Siegrist, T.C. Earle, and H. Gutscher, eds. *Trust in cooperative risk management. Uncertainty and skepticism in the public mind*. London: Earthscan, pp. 1–49.

Edelman (2020). *Special report: Trust and the Coronavirus*. Available from: https://bit.ly/2TERtFx [Accessed 10 October 2020].

Eyrich, N., Padman, M.L., and Sweetser, K.D. (2008). PR practitioners' use of social media tools and communication technology. *Public Relations Review*, 34(4), pp. 412–414.

Fasan, O. (2020, April 6). Buhari goes AWOL from Nigeria's Coronavirus battlefield. *Business Day*. Available from: www.businessday.ng [Accessed 16 October 2020].

Feufel, M.A., Antes, G., and Gigerenzer, G. (2010). Competence in dealing with uncertainty: Lessons to learn from the influenza pandemic (H1N1) 2009. *Bundesgesund heits blatt Gesundheits forschung-Gesundheitsschutz*, (53) 1283–1289. doi:10.1007/S00103-010-1165-1

Fraustino, J.D., Liu, B.F., and Jin, Y. (2017). Social media during disasters: A research synthesis and roadmap. In Lucinda Austin, and Yan Jin, eds. *Social media and crisis communication*. New York, NY: Routledge, pp. 283–295.

Frewer, L.J. (2003). Trust, transparency, and social context: Implications for social amplification of risk. In N.F. Pidgeon, R.E. Kasperson, and P. Slovic, Eds. *The social amplification of risk*. Cambridge, UK: Cambridge University Press, pp. 123–137.

Frisby, Brandi, Veil, Shari, and Sellnow, Timothy (2014). Instructional messages during health-related crises: Essential content for self-protection. *Health Communication*, 29(4), 347–354. doi:10.1080/10410236.2012.755604

Gu, E., and Li, L. (2020). Crippled community governance and suppressed scientific/professional communities: A critical assessment of failed early warning for the Covid-19 outbreak in China. *Journal of Chinese governance*, 5(2). 160–177.

Hampel, J. (2006). Different concepts of risk: A challenge for risk communication. *International Journal of Medical Microbiology*, 296 5–10. doi:10.1016/j.ijmm.2005.12.002 [Accessed 10 October 2020].

Hassan, I. (2020). *The other COVID-19 pandemic: Fake news. 26 March African Arguments*. Available from: https://africanarguments.org/2020/03/26/the-other-covid-19-pandemic-fake-news/ [Accessed 10 October 2020].

Hoffman, S.J., and Silverberg, L.S. (2021). Delays in global disease outbreak responses: Lessons from H1N1, Ebola, and Zika. *American Journal of Public Health*, 108, pp. 329–333. doi:10.2105/AJPH.2017.304245

Holmes, B.J. (2008). Communicating about emerging infectious disease: The importance of research. *Health Risk Soc*, 10, pp. 349–360.

Johnson, T., and Kaye, B. (2010). Choosing is believing? How web gratifications and reliance affect Internet credibility among politically interested users. *Atlantic Journal of Communication*, 18, pp. 1–21.

Jones, K.E., Patel, N.G., Levy, M.A., Storeygard, A., and Balk, D. (2008). Global trends in emerging infectious diseases. *Nature*, 451(7181), pp. 990–93.

Kampf, G., Todt, D., Pfaender, S., and Steinmann, E. (2020). Persistence of corona viruses on inanimate surfaces and their inactivation with biocidal agents. *Journal Hospital Infections*, 104, pp. 246–251. doi:10.1016/j.jhin.2020.01.022 [Accessed 10 October 2020].

Kim, S., and Liu, B.F. (2012). Are all crises opportunities? A comparison of how corporate and government organizations responded to the 2009 flu pandemic. *Journal of Public Relations Research*, 24(1), pp. 69–85.

Kreps, G.L., Bonaguro, G.E., and Query, J.L. (1998). The history and development of field of health communication. In L. Jackson and B. Duffy, eds. *Health communication research*. Westport, CT: Greenwood Press, pp. 1–15.

Lee, S.T., and Basnyat, I. (2013). From press release to news: Mapping the framing of the 2009 H1N1 Avian influenza pandemic, *Health Communication*, 28(2), pp. 119–132.

Liu, B.F., and Kim, S. (2011). How organizations framed the 2009 H1N1 pandemic via social and traditional media: Implications for US health communicators. *Public Relations Review*, 37(3), pp. 233–244.

Lu, X., and Jin, Y. (2020). Information vetting as a key component in social-mediated crisis communication: An exploratory study to examine the initial conceptualization. *Public relations Review*, 46(2).

Macias, W., Hilyard, K., and Freimuth, V. (2009). Blog functions as risk and crisis communication during Hurricane Katrina. *Journal of Computer-Mediated Communication*, 15(1), pp. 1–31.

Masipet, P., Aran-Ramspott, S., Ruiz-Caballero, C., Suau, J., Almenar, E., and Puertas-Graell, D. (2020). Consumo informativo y cobertura mediática durante el confinamiento por el Covid-19: sobreinformación, sesgo ideológico y sensacionalismo. *El Profesional de la Información*, 29(3).

Meredith, L.S., Eisenman, D.P., Rhodes, H., Ryan, G., and Long, A. (2007). Trust influences response to public health messages during a bioterrorist event, *Journal of Health Communication: International Perspectives*, 12(3), pp. 217–232.

Morgan, J.P. (2020). *Media consumption in the age of Covid-19. Against the backdrop of the Coronavirus pandemic, increased media consumption is helping to fill the time.* Available from: www.jpmorgan.com/global/research/media-consumption [Accessed 10 October 2020].

Moreno, Á, Fuentes-Lara, C., and Navarro, C. (2020). Covid-19 communication management in Spain: Exploring the effect of information-seeking behavior and message reception in public's evaluation. *El Profesional de la Información*, 29(4).

Morrow, J.A., and Skolits, G.J. (2014). *The twelve steps of data cleaning: Strategies for dealing with dirty data.* Workshop conducted at the 28th Annual conference of the American Evaluation Association, Denver, CO. Available from: www.eval.org/evaluation2014 [Accessed 10 October 2020].

Mrig, P., Jafferany, M., Lotti, T., Sadoughifar, R., and Goldust, M. (*2020*). Learning from history: Coronavirus outbreaks in the past. *Dermatol Ther*, 28. doi:10.1111/dth.13343 [Accessed 10 October 2020].

NCDC (2021). *Nigerian Centre for disease control.* Available from: https://covid19.ncdc.gov.ng/ [Accessed 24 June 2022].

Ogbodo, J.N., Onwe, E.C., Chukwu, J., Nwasum, C.J., Nwakpu, E.S., Nwankwo, S.U., Nwamini, S., Elem, S., and Ogbaeja, N.I. (2020). Communicating health crisis: A content analysis of global media framing of COVID-19. *Health Promotion Perspectives*, 10(3), pp. 257–269. doi:10.34172/hpp.2020.40

Oleribe, O., Ezechi, O., Osita-Oleribe, P., Musa, A., Omoluabi, A., Fertleman, M., Salako, B., and Taylor-Robinson, S. (2020). Public perception of COVID-19 management and response in Nigeria: A cross-sectional survey *BMJ Open*, 10(04), pp. 19–36.

Omaka-Amari, L.N., Aleke, C.O., Obande-Ogbuinya, N.E., Ngwakwe, P.C., Nwankwo, O., and Afoke, E.N. (2020). Coronavirus (COVID-19) pandemic in Nigeria: Preventive and control challenges within the first two months of outbreak. *African Journal of Reproductive Health*, 24(2), pp. 87–97.

Park, S., Boatwright, B., and Johnson-Avery, E. (2019). Information channel preference in health crisis:Exploring the roles of perceived risk, preparedness, knowledge, and intent to follow directives. *Public Relations Review*, 45(5) 101794. doi:10.1016/j.pubrev.2019.05.015 [Accessed 10 October 2020].

Pieri, E. (2019). Media framing and the threat of global pandemics: The Ebola crisis in UK media and policy response. *Sociological Research Online*, 24(1) 73–9.

Podlesek, A., Roskar, S., and Komidar, L. (2011). Some factors affecting the decision on non-mandatory vaccination in an influenza pandemic: Comparison of pandemic (H1n1) and seasonal influenza vaccination. *Zdravstveno Varstvo*, 50, pp. 227–238.

Prati, G., Pietrantoni, L., and Zani, B. (2011b), A Social-Cognitive model of pandemic influenza H1N1 risk perception and recommended behaviors in Italy. *Risk Analysis*, 31, pp. 645–656.

Quinn, S.C., Kumar, S., Freimuth, V.S., Kidwell, K., and Musa, D. (2009). Public willingness to take a vaccine or drug under emergency use authorization during the 2009 H1N1 pandemic. *Biosecurity and Bioterrorism-Biodefense Strategy Practice and Science*, 7, pp. 275–290.

Quinn, S.C., Parmer, J., Freimuth, V.S., Hilyard, K.M., Musa, D., and Kim, K.H. (2013). Exploring communication, trust in government, and vaccination intention later in the

2009 H1N1 pandemic: Results of a national survey. *Biosecurity and Bioterrorism: Biodefense Strategy, Practice, and Science*, 11(2), pp. 96–106.

Raoult, D., Zumla, A., Locatelli, F., Ippolito, G., and Kroemer, G. (2020). Coronavirus infections: Epidemiological, clinical and immunological features and hypotheses. *Cell Stress*, 40, pp. 66–74. doi:10.15698/cst2020.04.216 [Accessed 10 October 2020].

Ratzan, S., Gostin, L., Meshkati, N., Rabin, K., and Parker, R. (2020). *COVID-19: An urgent call for coordinated, trusted sources to tell everyone what they need to know and do.* NAM Perspectives. Commentary, National Academy of Medicine, Washington, DC. doi:10.31478/202003a [Accessed 10 October 2020].

Reifegerste, D., Bachl, M., and Baumann, E. (2017). Surrogate health information seeking in Europe: Influence of source type and social network variables. *International Journal of Medical Informatics*, 103, pp. 7–14. doi:10.1016/j.ijmedinf.2017.04.006 [Accessed 10 October 2020].

Reynolds, B., and Seeger, M. (2005). Crisis and emergency risk communication as an integrative model. *Journal of Health Communication*, 10(1) 43–55. doi:10.1080/10810730590904571 [Accessed 10 October 2020].

Reynolds, B., and Quinn, S.C. (2008). Effective communication during an influenza pandemic: The value of using a crisis and emergency risk communication framework. *Health Promotion Practice*, 9(4_suppl), 13S–17S.

Rodero, E. (2020). Radio: The medium that best copes in crises. Listening habits, consumption, and perception of radio listeners during the lockdown by the Covid-19. *El profesional de la información*, 29(3), e290306. doi:10.3145/epi.2020.may.06

Roslyng, M., and Eskjær, M. (2017). Mediatised risk culture: News coverage of risk technologies. *Health, Risk & Society*, 19(3) 112–129.

Schultz, F., Utz, S., and Göritz, A. (2011). Is the medium the message? Perceptions of and reactions to crisis communication via Twitter, blogs and traditional media. *Public Relations Review*, 37(1), pp. 20–27.

Scoones, I. (2010). *Avian influenza: Science, policy and politics.* London: Earthscan.

Seeger, M., Sellnow, T., and Ulmer, R. (1998). Communication, organization, and crisis. *Annals of the International Communication Association*, 21(1), pp. 231–276.

Sheppard, J.M., and Liu, B. (2012). *Understanding risk communication theory: A guide for emergency managers and communicators.* Report to Human Factors/Behavioral Sciences Division, Science and Technology Directorate, U.S. Department of Homeland Security. Available from: www.start.umd.edu/sites/default/files/files/publications/UnderstandingRiskCommunicationTheory.pdf [Accessed 10 October 2020].

Siegrist, M., and Zingg, A. (2013). *The role of public trust during pandemics implications for crisis communication. European Psychologist*, 19(1), pp. 23–32.

Slovic, P. (1999). Trust, emotion, sex, politics, and science: Surveying the risk-assessment battlefield. *Risk Analysis*, 19, pp. 689–701.

Sweester, K.D., and Metzgar, E. (2007). Communicating during crisis: Use of blogs as a relationship management tool. *Public Relations Review*, 33(3), pp. 340–342.

Tench, R., Verčič, D., Zerfass, A., Moreno, Á., and Verhoeven, P. (2017). *Communication excellence: How to develop, manage and lead exceptional communications.* Springer.

Tyrrel, D.A., Almedia, D.M., Berry, C.H., Cunningham, D., Hamre, M.S., Hofstad, L., Malluci, L., and McIntosh, K. (1968). Coronavirus. *Nature*, 220, 650.

US Office of Disease Prevention and Promotion (2004). *Health communication, healthy people 2010.* Available from: http://healthypeople.gov/Document/HTML/volume1/11HealthCom.htm# edn4 [Accessed 10 October 2020].

Utz, S., Schultz, F., and Glocka, S. (2013). Crisis communication online: How medium, crisis type and emotions affected public reactions in the Fukushima Daiichi nuclear disaster. *Public Relations Review*, 39(1), pp. 40–46.

Van-der-Meer, T.G.L.A. (2018). Public frame building: The role of source usage in times of crisis. *Communication Research*, 45(6), pp. 956–981.

Vaughan, E., and Tinker, T. (2009). Influenza preparedness and response for vulnerable populations. *American Journal of Public Health*, 99(2).

World Health Organisation (2011). *Report of the review committee on the functioning of the international health regulations 2005, in relation to pandemic (H1N1) 2009*. Geneva, Switzerland: World Health Organization. Available from: https://apps.who.int/gb/ebwha/pdf_files/WHA64/A64_10-en.pdf

World Health Organisation (WHO). Coronavirus Disease (COVID-19). WHO; 2020. outbreak situation (2020a). Available from: www.who.int/emergencies/diseases/novel-coronavirus-2019 [Accessed 10 October 2020].

World Health Organisation (WHO) (2020). World Health Report 2010. Available from: https://www.who.int/publications/i/item/9789241564021

Williams, R., Jenkins, D.A., Ashcroft, D.M., Brown, B., Campbell, S., Carr, M.J., . . . Peek, N. (2020). Diagnosis of physical and mental health conditions in primary care during the COVID-19 pandemic: A retrospective cohort study. *The Lancet Public Health*, 5(10), e543–e550.

Zhang, X., and Zhou, S. (2019). Clicking health risk messages on social media: Moderated mediation paths through perceived threat, perceived efficacy, and fear arousal. *Health Communication*, 34(11), pp. 1359–1368.

Zhou, P., Yang, X.L., and Wang, X.G. (2020). A pneumonia outbreak associated with a new corona virus of probable bat origin. *Nature*, 579, pp. 270–273. doi:10.1038/s41586-020-2012-7

Part IV

Conclusion

19 Implications for the future of strategic communications from the COVID-19 pandemic

Ralph Tench, Juan Meng and Ángeles Moreno

This book has captured international experiences and observations of strategic communication during one of the most impactful health crises of the modern era. The contributors have innovated with scholarship and observations from activities and outputs of strategic communication from diverse regions and countries to provide unique insights into how we, as a global community of citizens, have experienced the COVID pandemic. So, what can be learnt from these critical observations that will inform and guide scholars and practitioners of strategic communication during future health crises?

Trust and communication transparency

Importantly, the book acknowledges the views of diverse actors in the process of communication during the COVID-19 health crisis. It captures a global perspective of how citizens accessed, interpreted and evaluated information during the pandemic. The discussions in the book elicit a number of common starting points. The international overview shows us that across the world the public have consumed news about the pandemic through multiple platforms simultaneously, but at the same time there are local media preferences that reinforce the importance of traditional journalist-driven media which is strongly affected by trust. Trust is found to be given or placed in organizations, individuals and institutions, and it may therefore be placed in a person (micro level), an organization/institution (meso level) or in the broader structures that affect roles, organizations and the like (macro level), such as codes of conduct, industry bodies, relevant law and broader societal norms. Thus, different national cultures are represented by diverse levels of social trust. Trust emerges as a key factor in discussions about the pandemic and in all forms of communication on COVID-19. The first chapter of the book frames trust in the micro, meso and macro levels. Through the different chapters of the book trust is evident as a clear driver for citizens' perceptions and behaviours during a pandemic scenario, and trust in the media and social and public institutions is essential if they are to be viewed as sources of information and as vehicles for dissemination and public retention of up-to-date and accurate evidence.

DOI: 10.4324/9781003184669-30

The importance of trust building during and beyond the pandemic tends to induce and favour communication transparency at all levels. This is because fewer people act as power-holders, monopolising information, and more people serve as active agents, processing and sharing timely and accurate information. When strategic communicators and leaders position themselves in the context of societal purpose, communication transparency is a natural initiative to ease societal uncertainty. Across the chapters, we found several critical contributing factors to explain the general low trust in governmental communication during the pandemic. Lack of transparency in communication is one of those.

Recommendation

It's clear from the studies throughout the book that the role of communicators as trust-builders is reinforced. A practical implication for these findings in the context of health crises is that maintaining citizen trust is key and trust-building through strategic communication should be at the core of corporate, organizational and institutional objectives before health crises emerge. When a crisis scenario does develop, starting from a neutral or negative trust base is almost impossible to reverse. However, previous positive trust sentiments are crucial to convince citizens to adopt recommendations for social and health behavioural changes. Evidence from the discussions also points to the on-going value of experts and scientific sources as reliable reinforcers of trust, and a common approach taken in the international studies reviewed in the book is to build and preserve trust and to negate anti-system groups and voices intent on discrediting evidence-based information.

Adaptation and change

Discussions emerging from chapters in the book demonstrate that strategic communication professionals have adapted during the COVID-19 pandemic and have proven themselves resilient and flexible enough to navigate through the rapid changes that we experienced, as the crisis evolved and placed multiple demands on the systems of communication. Specific chapters explore and highlight the views and perspectives of communication practitioners working in the public and private sectors and how they needed to adapt their professional practice to the evolving pandemic scenarios. Chapters 2 and 3 present an overview of the responses of the industry in North America and Latin America, while chapter 6 goes deeper into the impact of responsible strategic communication during COVID-19 among millennials in Italy.

In a highly connected digital communication environment, social issues and interruptions emerge as a result of the evolving and collective agenda to assert new public values, form new social norms, initiate hopeful responses and mobilise the political, economic and cultural power to translate the changes into action. The social rules are redefined, based on renewed responsibility and effective adaptation, to create conditions that enable individuals, organizations and societies to achieve a shared purpose in the face of uncertainty during the COVID-19 pandemic. It is documented in several of our contributing chapters that the role of governmental leadership in pandemic communication must go beyond the traditional bureaucratic functions and authoritative personae with which they are often presented and identified. The need for adaptation and change at the level of governmental leadership is more urgent and necessary to mobilise its resources and policies. Alongside the deep roots of strategic communication research in sociology, especially within radically different political and social systems in a global setting, swift adaptation in public health policies and effective change in governmental communication will become a primary source of governmental power to foster trust.

Recommendation

What emerges from the shared discussions is a need to give communication functions a central role in developing the strategic responses to health crises. When companies, institutions and all kinds of organizations are focussing efforts to develop required or guided behaviours amongst their stakeholders, then branded educational communication strategies should be deployed which also integrate creativity as a key ingredient. Grabbing the attention of different generations in a single health crisis requires imagination and flexibility to engage, and this is especially true for younger generations.

Utilise the full media landscape

Another focus in the book is understanding the communication approaches applied in diverse regions of the world by utilising shared methodological instruments with nuanced customisation for each locale. This approach permitted researchers to capture cultural idiosyncrasies from different countries in the public's responses to the pandemic, which gives the reader the opportunity to compare and understand the common factors that emerge through the responses to a global issue. Exploring the country-by-country responses in this consistent way gives the reader an appreciation of the diversity and dynamism that each system faced. These range from tightly controlled media systems in China to fake news and disinformation groups in the U.S., or from high cultural trust levels that maintained the support of controversial government decisions in Sweden to low trust in institutions in Nigeria.

As outlined previously, the public in different countries and regions of the world have consumed news about the pandemic through multiple platforms simultaneously, but at the same time there are local media preferences that reinforce the importance of traditional journalist-driven media. News media recovered their importance at the beginning of the pandemic but their positions in different countries show that the agenda is set by whether an approach is taken to rally around the collective national flag or to follow an approach engendering greater political polarisation in the country.

An interesting insight was that there were clear gaps between the use of or access to information and the trust of those channels. As an example, the higher level of social media use does not necessarily imply for many citizens that they are using these platforms to gather credible and accurate information in a critical situation, such as a pandemic. They may indeed be using the tools to enact other roles, such as social interaction and relationship building.

Another important insight we learned from all contributing chapters was that macro-trends related to the pandemic set the context for topic popularity across different media platforms, from traditional to social media, at the global level. At the same time, the media narrative in telling the story in each unique cultural setting builds the values, emotion and action with the sense of efficacy, solidarity and hopefulness required to reach its diverse audience at the local level, which further supports the agenda-setting function of the mass media in communicating an urgent challenge such as the COVID-19 pandemic.

Recommendation

This leads to a suggestion for strategic communicators to guide organizations and institutions during a health crisis to use a comprehensive media mix and to ensure the approach adequately considers and addresses the diversity of the population based on their media consumption preferences and habits. When communicating with older citizens, strategic health communicators should try to boost their confidence in their own ability to adopt recommended behaviours. On the other hand, the younger the citizens, the more that social norms may drive their adoption of preventive behaviours. Thus, strategic communicators should consider the diverse steps and flows of communication and try to align the opinions of those people who impact different age profiles, such as social media influencers, family members and close friends, educators or doctors. It is critical for strategic communicators to build a public narrative and tell a story of self, a story of us and a story of future. A story of self communicates the attention, values and change behaviours that call one to action. A story of us communicates the values and changes shared by those groups in action. Finally, a story of future communicates an urgent responsibility to restore the norm and hope that demands collective action now. Communication professionals carry an enormous responsibility in leading strategic communication in a world of uncertainty, misinformation and disinformation.

Evolving message transmission and consumption

The book also presents some longitudinal interpretations that allow the reader to understand how and why the evaluations about government and institutional communications evolve during the course of the pandemic. We can see how media consumption evolved in the UK during 2020, how low trust in government in Nigeria during the pandemic was an impediment to rejecting resistant voices and how an evaluation of the Spanish authorities' communication detected rapid changes over a critical two-week period.

The era of post-globalisation is characterised by frequent, unexpected and rapid changes. Over the course of the COVID-19 pandemic, the level of uncertainty deepened as the accumulative number of confirmed cases and deaths rose on a daily basis at the global level. When the pandemic brings more moving parts in the media discourse, it also presents more variables in play simultaneously and more dimensions of interest to the audience to shift their media consumption. For example, corporate social responsibility initiatives during the pandemic resonate well with millennials in Italy and prove to be effective in promoting appropriate social behaviours. Vaccination information in the public narrative helps build U.S. citizens' vaccination intention, even though the discussion of vaccination itself has been responded to in a bipartisan way, which leads to a number of trust issues reflected in the U.S.

When individuals have more options with a variety of topics in media consumption and sources of information, open access to transparent communication is a natural call, even in countries with more authoritarian structures and traditions. Information technology facilitates direct access and builds new leadership patterns for those who seek and spread information through influencer communication. This new information consumption pattern, which is more informal, self-organising, self-changing, and flexible, enables individuals to make connections and expand networks of resources more quickly and personally. It further demands that the message transmission be rapid and through the right channel, if the goal is to foster relationships with the target audience.

Recommendation

Governments and corporate and institutional bodies must deliver timely and accurate information during health crises and place themselves as both reliable and responsive go-to sources. By doing so they make themselves a trustable source which ensures they are in an influential position to guide the conversations as they evolve about the issue. The three aspects associated with the quality of communication are timeliness, adequacy and accuracy. These are the key measures strategic communicators should focus on when developing health-crisis-related preventive and control measures, which will ensure consistency of messaging across all communication channels.

As we conclude the book we must pay a compliment to the collective efforts of scientists and governments from around the world who put all their public and private resources into finding medical and science-based solutions to the COVID disease as well as effective preventative behaviours that make a difference. During the dark days at the start of the crisis the challenges looked insurmountable. Who would have believed so much could be achieved in less than 12 months? And yet it was. Although an incredible achievement, it would have counted for nothing if the citizens of our countries had not trusted or believed in the solutions proposed. Strategic health communication was the key to constructing meaning and interpreting the complexity of the science and the treatments so they were believed and taken up by the vast majority.

These chapters reflect diverse perspectives, explain and help us understand the role of strategic communication in one extraordinary case – the COVID-19 pandemic – and cast a light on the new reality we face with health emergencies and pandemics. The findings and discussions provide clearer understanding for the need to not only understand but also to improve the use and application of strategic communication as an essential tool in supporting institutions and society more generally if and/or when we are faced with the next societal health challenge.

As stated in the introduction, this edited volume of collected empirical research serves one primary purpose – to investigate the role of strategic communication in a global pandemic. At a time when individuals, organizations and societies all face the challenge and uncertainty caused by COVID-19, we looked for timely, accurate and effective communication as part of coping solutions, especially in government and other spheres of the public sector. Our view, as editors of this book, is that the current state of scholarly research on strategic communication and the pandemic allow us to confirm the critical role of communication practitioners in information distribution and message development. Despite the fact that the impact of the pandemic in modern history will be multifarious and long lasting from a range of perspectives, strategic communication and effective leadership remain central to the mission and purpose of most public health crises and campaigns. If communication practitioners are expected to develop better and more transparent communication in order to help the public understand the knowledge around the virus and the pandemic, it is important to encourage research with greater rigour across a wide variety of political and cultural systems while being relevant and useful in practice.

Although we recognise that the chapters included in this book already represent diverse societal contexts, we must acknowledge that with the pandemic being at the scale of a global setting, there are many unexplored and uncovered regions, countries, populations and needs. We hope the organisation of this book provides a useful lens on this continuously evolving public health crisis that will be evaluated and discussed form many years to come. Despite the scale and scope of this book, we hope the topics and issues we presented could stimulate future research interests and commitment by providing a much broader range of conversations and writing on related topics. We also believe this edited book offers a useful starting point for scholars, communication practitioners, public health experts and governmental officials seeking to integrate strategic communication into their own research and practice. We hope that research presented in this book helps create a new research agenda in strategic communication and public health that allows us to form better practice which might additional bring improvements to the world.

Index

9781032026961